O N E

I felt the anesthetic take hold.

—ONE

Manga creator ONE began *One-Punch Man* as a webcomic, which quickly went viral, garnering over 10 million hits. In addition to *One-Punch Man*, ONE writes and draws the series *Mob Psycho 100* and *Makai no Ossan*.

Y U S U K E M U R A T A

I draw like the wind.

—Yusuke Murata

A highly decorated and skilled artist best known for his work on *Eyeshield 21*, Yusuke Murata won the 122nd Hop Step Award (1995) for *Partner* and placed second in the 51st Akatsuka Award (1998) for *Samui Hanashi*.

ONE-PUNCH MAN 16

ONE + YUSUKE MURATA

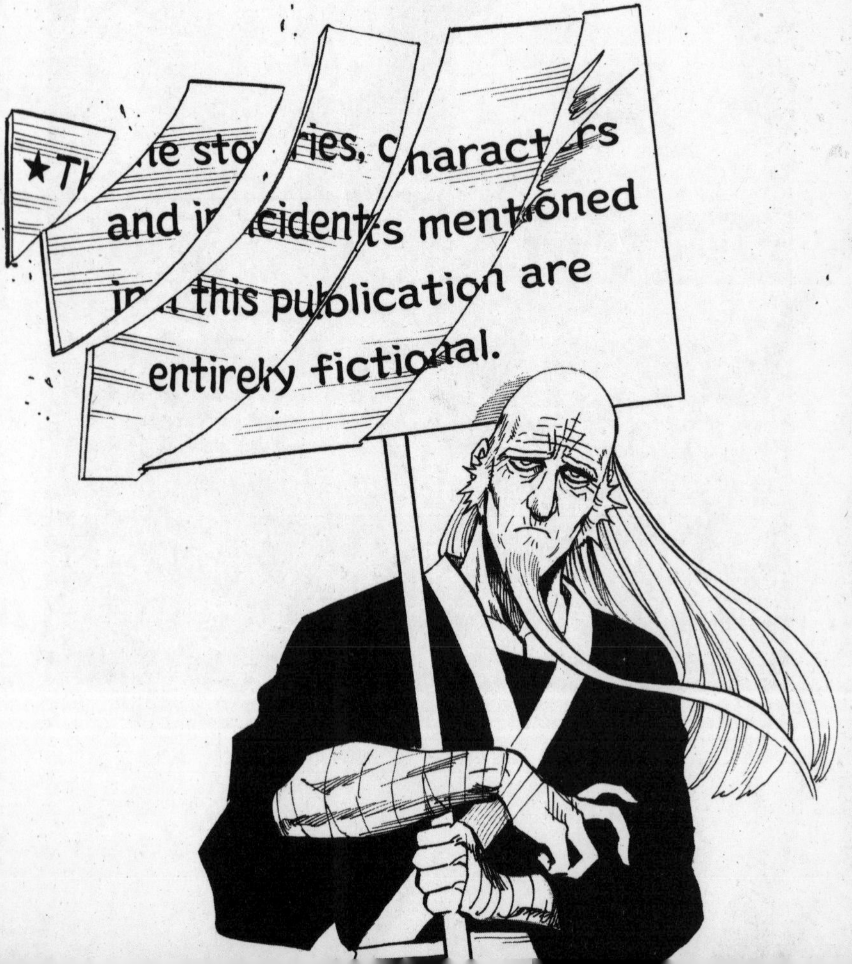
★The stories, characters
and incidents mentioned
in this publication are
entirely fictional.

16 ONE-PUNCH MAN

DEPLETED

STORY BY
ONE
ART BY
YUSUKE MURATA

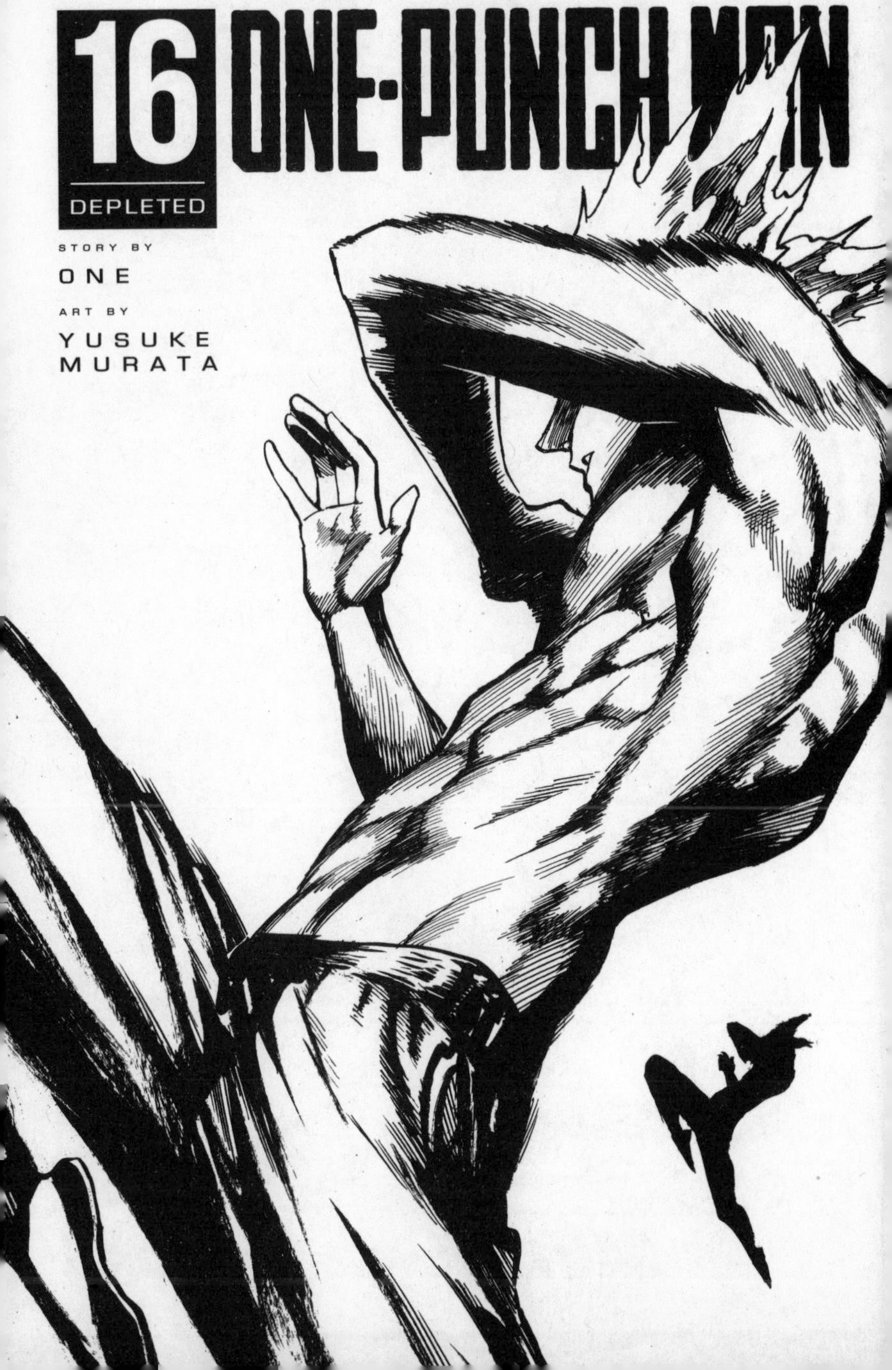

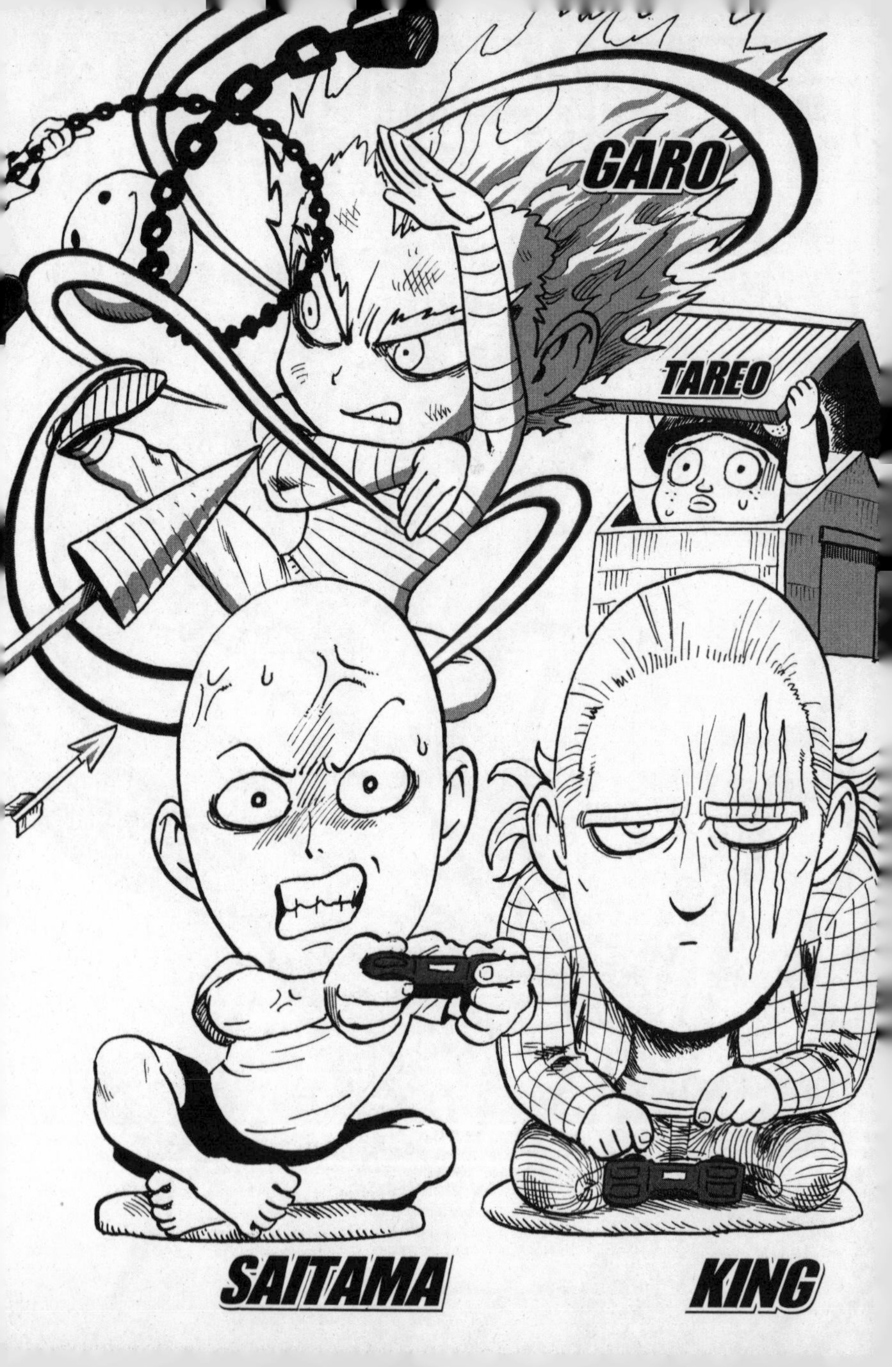
GARO
TAREO
SAITAMA
KING

CHARACTERS

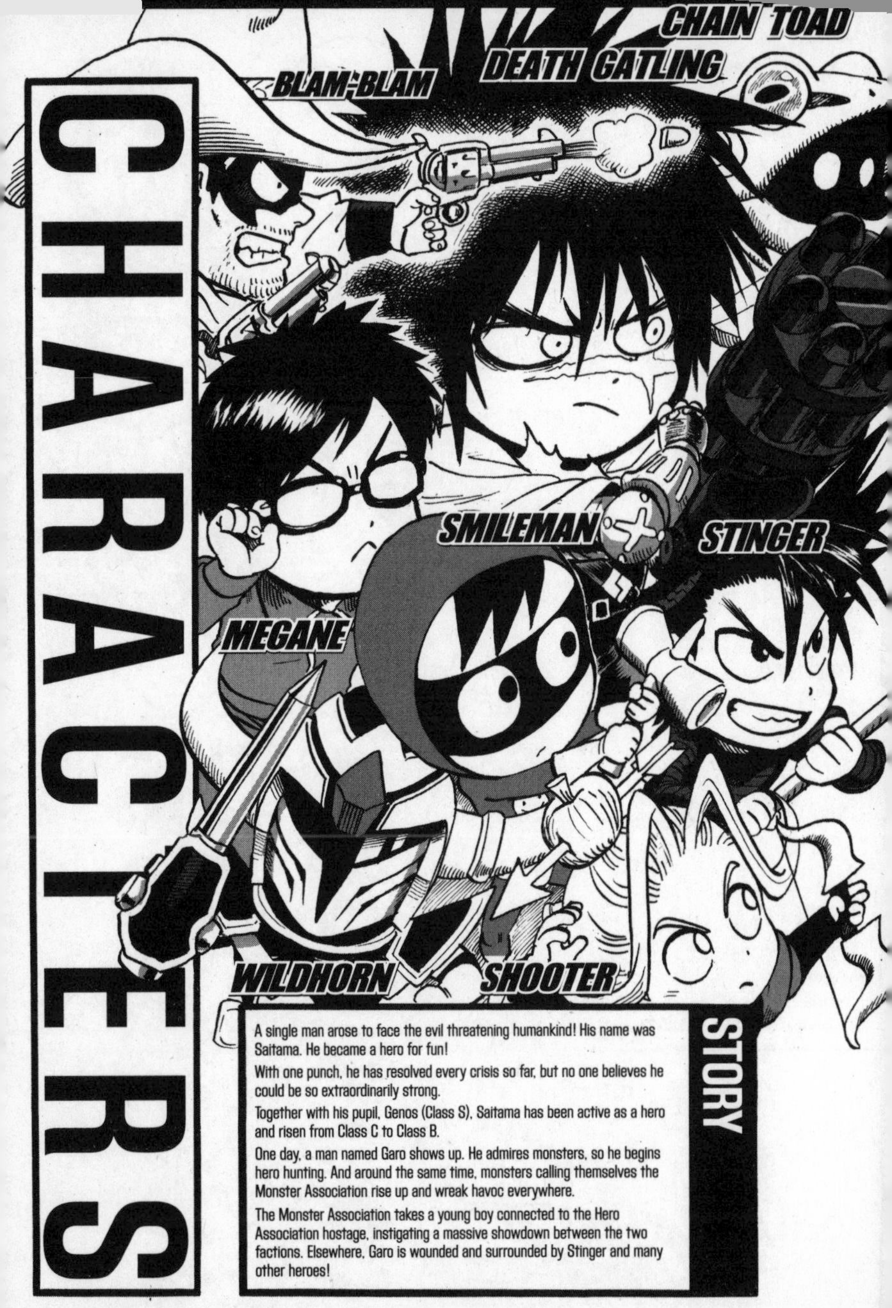
CHAIN TOAD
DEATH GATLING
BLAM-BLAM
SMILEMAN
STINGER
MEGANE
WILDHORN
SHOOTER

STORY

A single man arose to face the evil threatening humankind! His name was Saitama. He became a hero for fun!

With one punch, he has resolved every crisis so far, but no one believes he could be so extraordinarily strong.

Together with his pupil, Genos (Class S), Saitama has been active as a hero and risen from Class C to Class B.

One day, a man named Garo shows up. He admires monsters, so he begins hero hunting. And around the same time, monsters calling themselves the Monster Association rise up and wreak havoc everywhere.

The Monster Association takes a young boy connected to the Hero Association hostage, instigating a massive showdown between the two factions. Elsewhere, Garo is wounded and surrounded by Stinger and many other heroes!

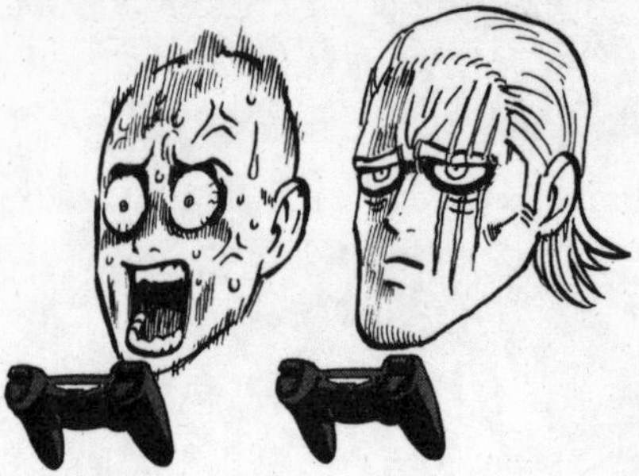

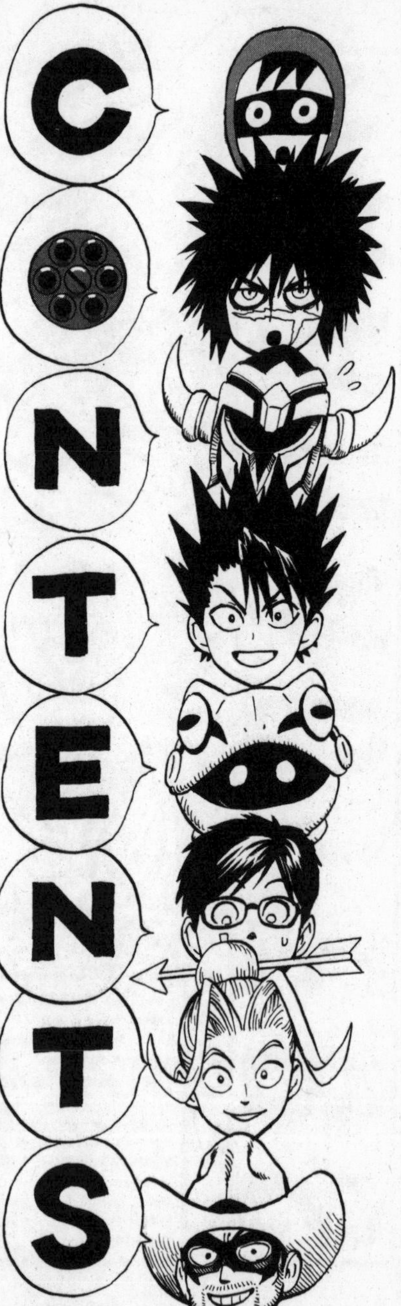

CONTENTS

ONE-PUNCH MAN VOL.16
[DEPLETED]

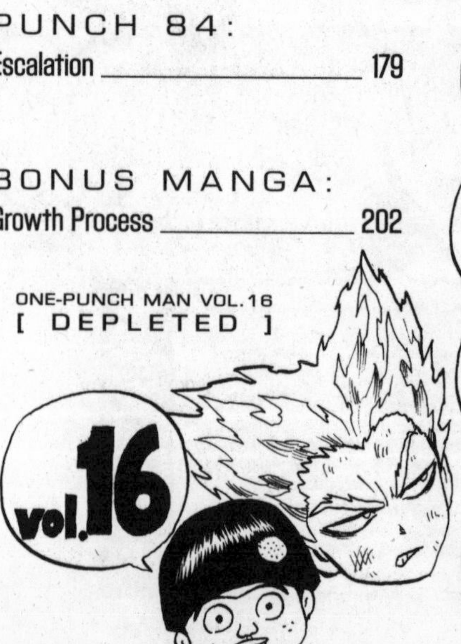

vol.16

PUNCH 81: TENACITY

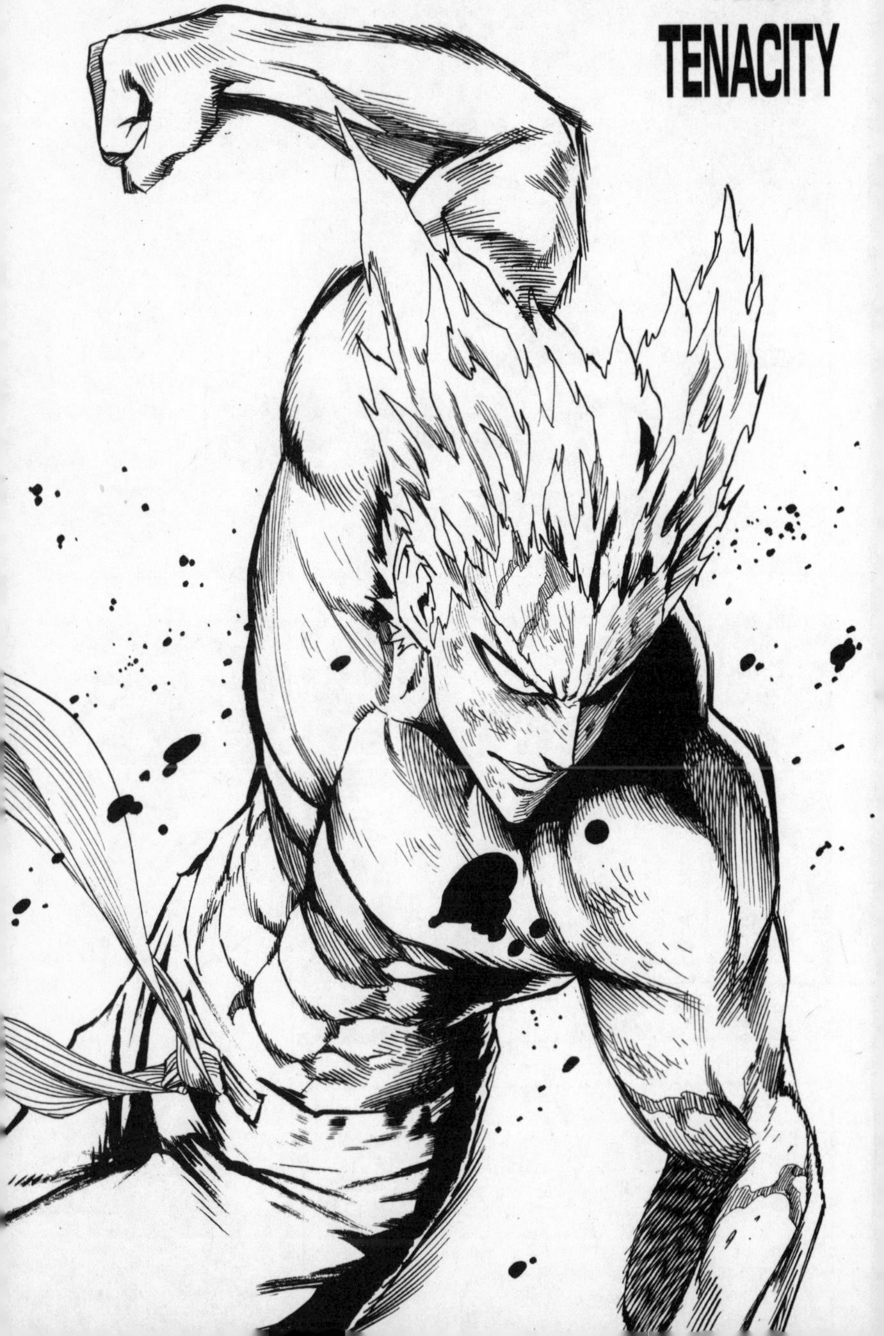

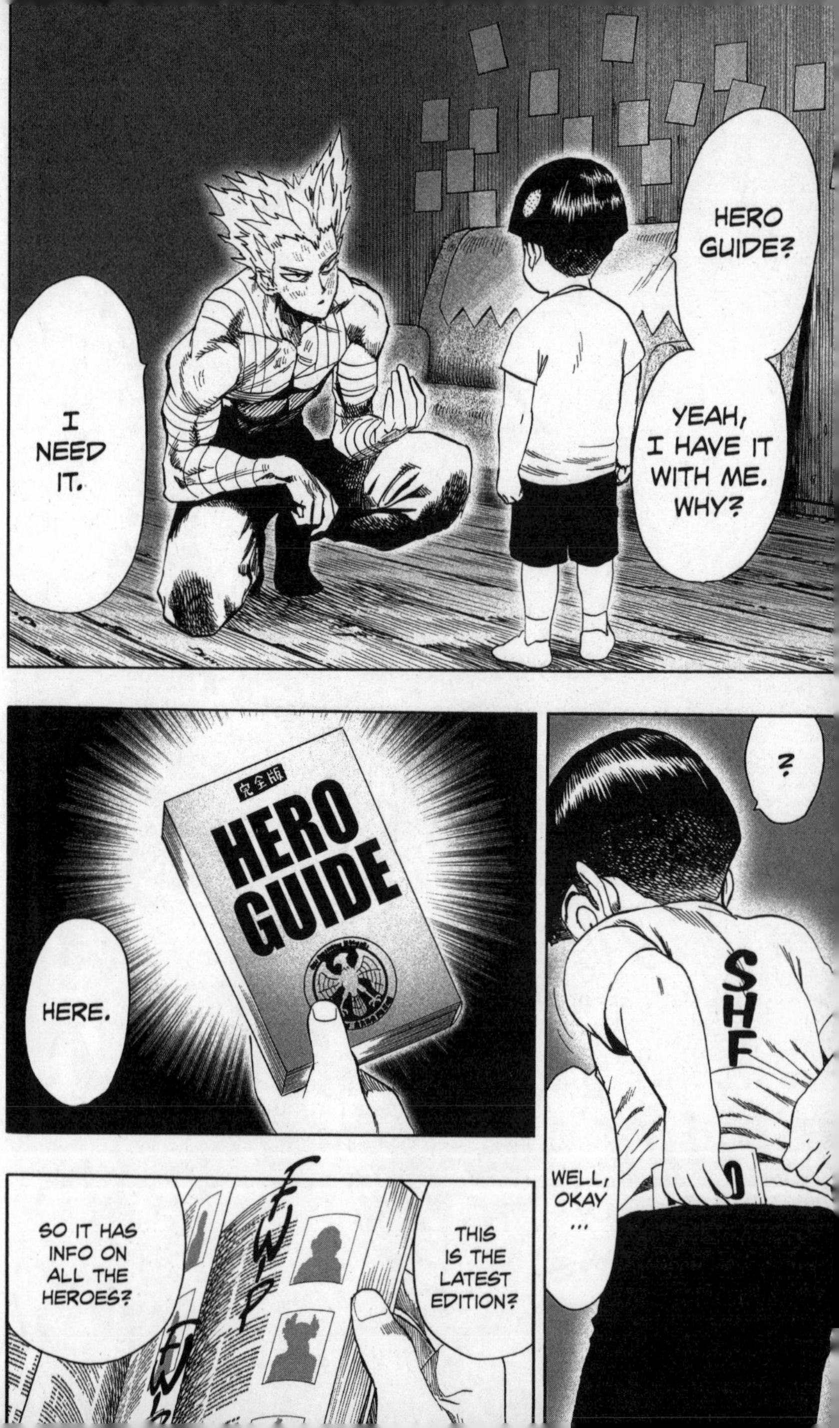
HERO GUIDE?
YEAH, I HAVE IT WITH ME. WHY?
I NEED IT.
?
SHF
WELL, OKAY ...
完全版
HERO GUIDE
HERE.
THIS IS THE LATEST EDITION?
SO IT HAS INFO ON ALL THE HEROES?
FWIP

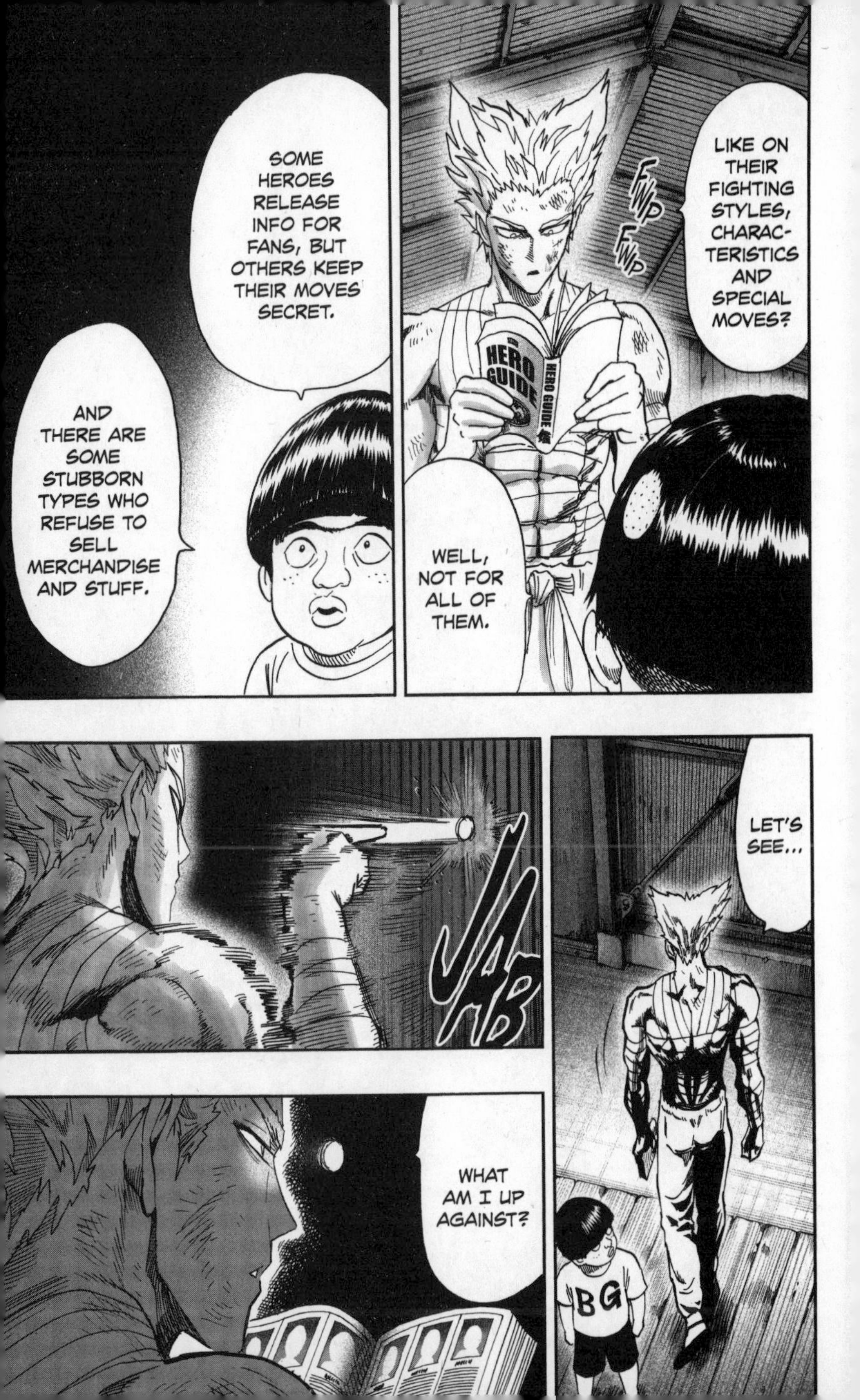
LIKE ON THEIR FIGHTING STYLES, CHARAC-TERISTICS AND SPECIAL MOVES?
FWP FWP
HERO GUIDE
WELL, NOT FOR ALL OF THEM.
SOME HEROES RELEASE INFO FOR FANS, BUT OTHERS KEEP THEIR MOVES SECRET.
AND THERE ARE SOME STUBBORN TYPES WHO REFUSE TO SELL MERCHANDISE AND STUFF.
LET'S SEE...
BG
JAB
WHAT AM I UP AGAINST?

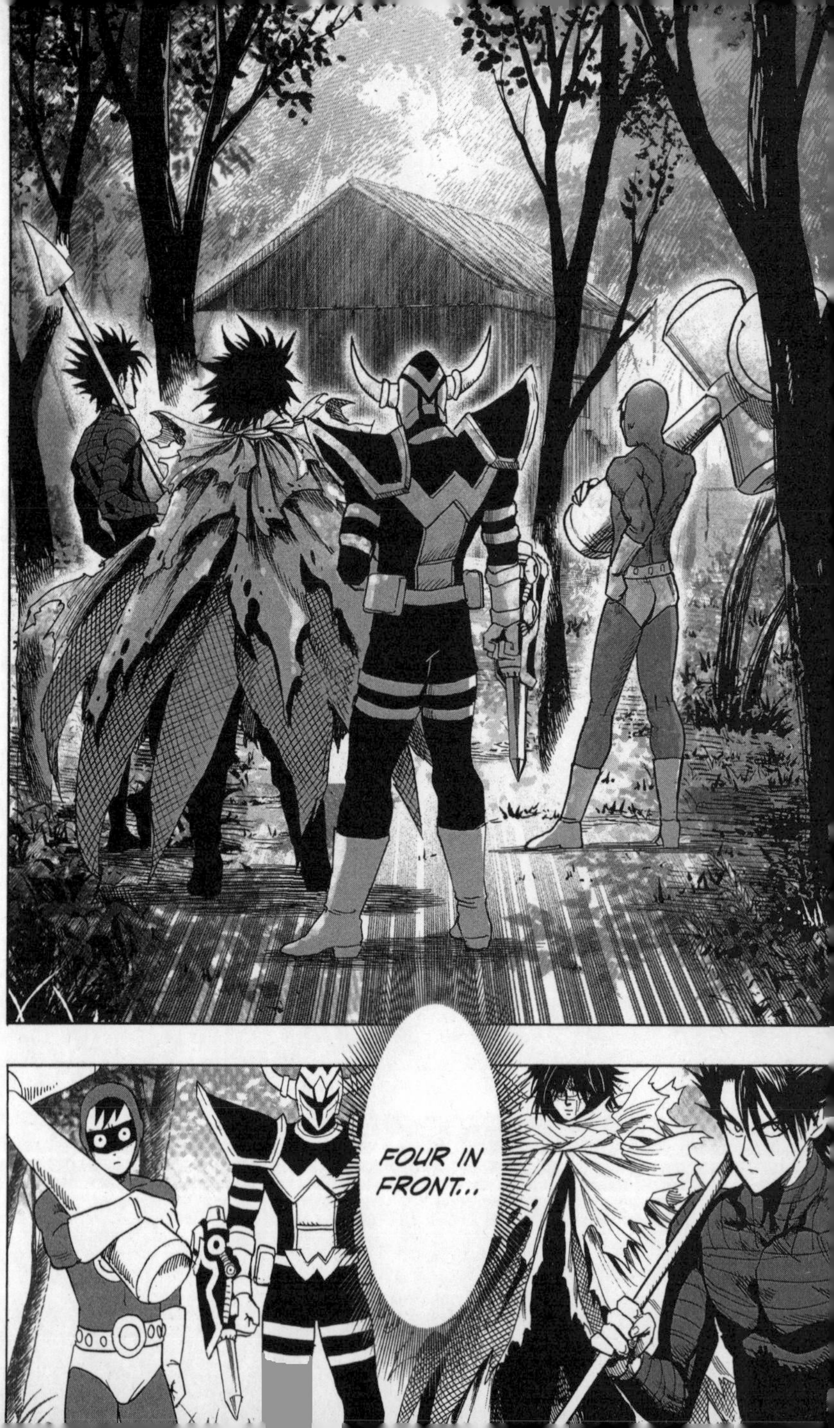
FOUR IN FRONT...

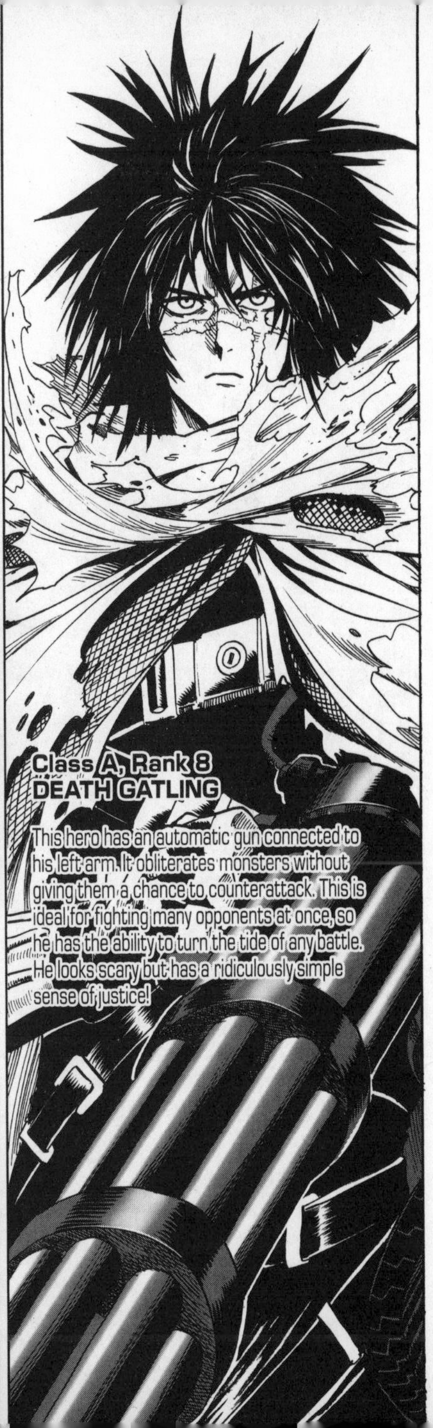
Class A, Rank 8
DEATH GATLING
This hero has an automatic gun connected to his left arm. It obliterates monsters without giving them a chance to counterattack. This is ideal for fighting many opponents at once, so he has the ability to turn the tide of any battle. He looks scary but has a ridiculously simple sense of justice!
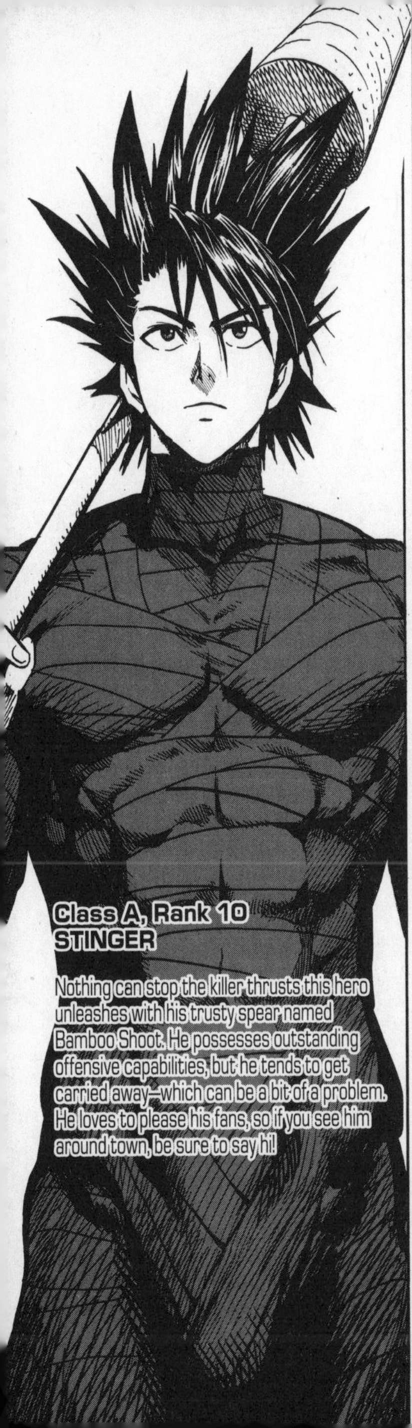
Class A, Rank 10
STINGER
Nothing can stop the killer thrusts this hero unleashes with his trusty spear named Bamboo Shoot. He possesses outstanding offensive capabilities, but he tends to get carried away—which can be a bit of a problem. He loves to please his fans, so if you see him around town, be sure to say hi!

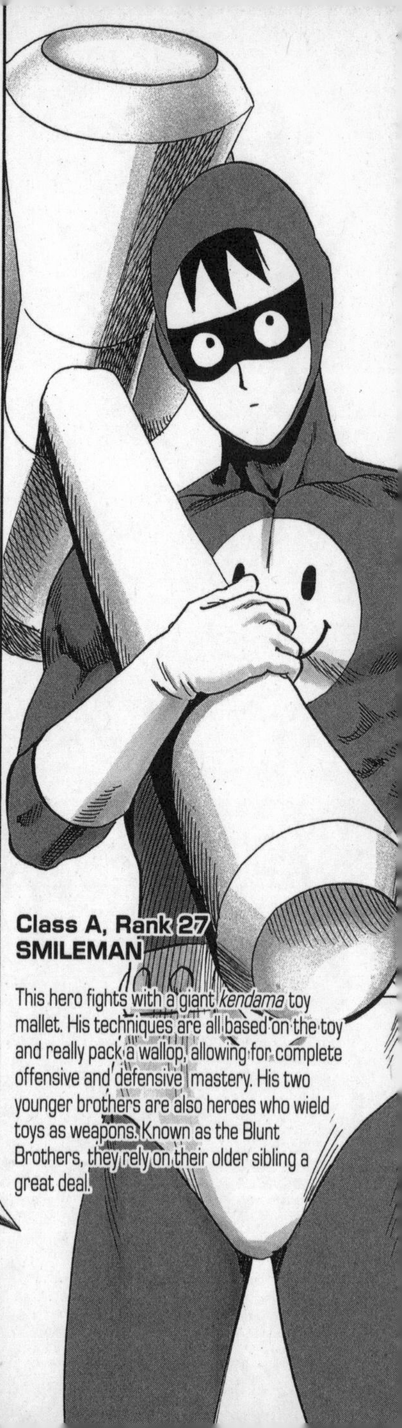
Class A, Rank 27
SMILEMAN
This hero fights with a giant *kendama* toy mallet. His techniques are all based on the toy and really pack a wallop, allowing for complete offensive and defensive mastery. His two younger brothers are also heroes who wield toys as weapons. Known as the Blunt Brothers, they rely on their older sibling a great deal.
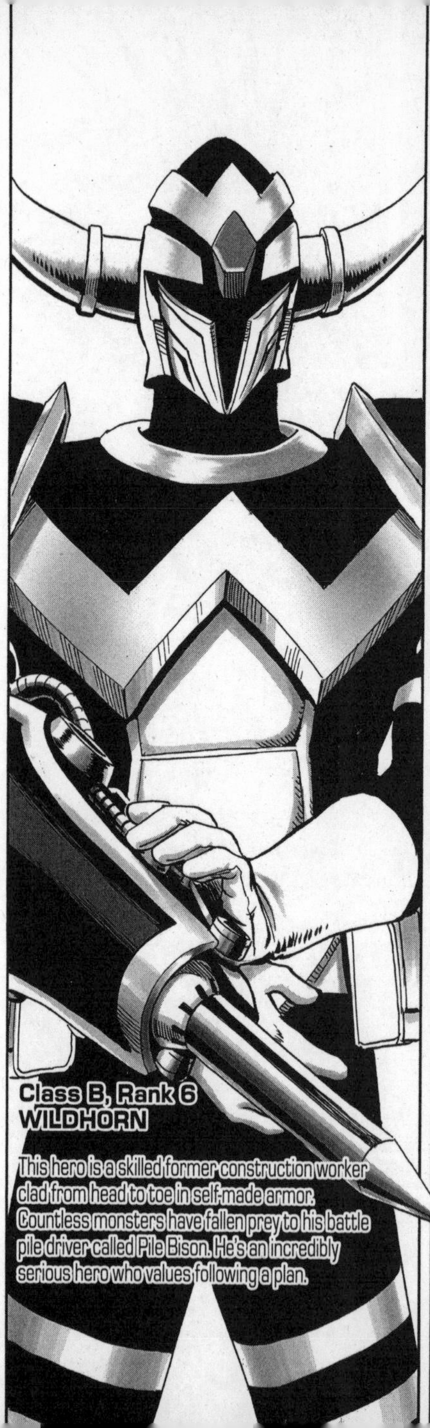
Class B, Rank 6
WILDHORN
This hero is a skilled former construction worker clad from head to toe in self-made armor. Countless monsters have fallen prey to his battle pile driver called Pile Bison. He's an incredibly serious hero who values following a plan.

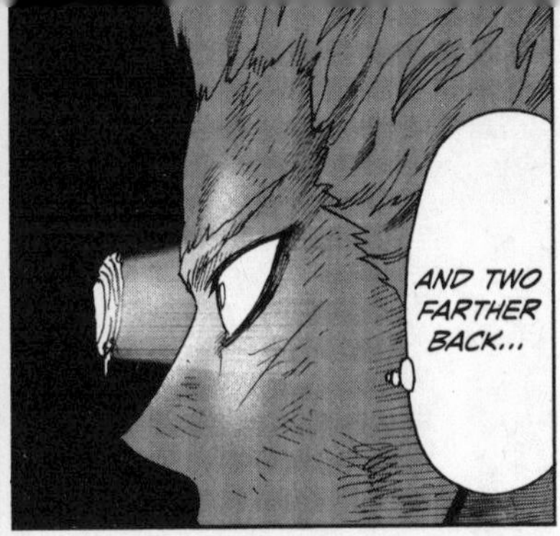
AND TWO FARTHER BACK...

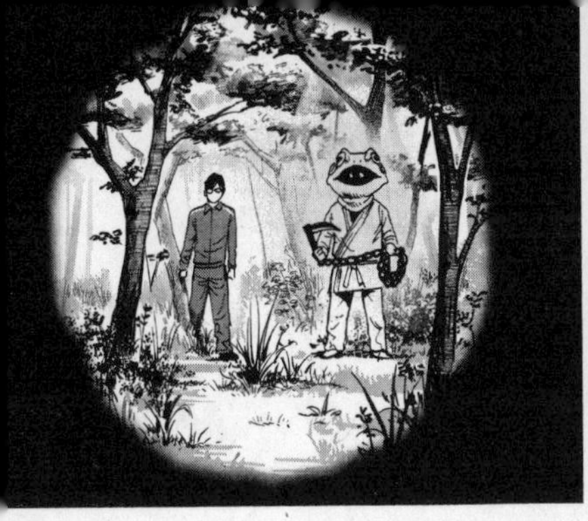

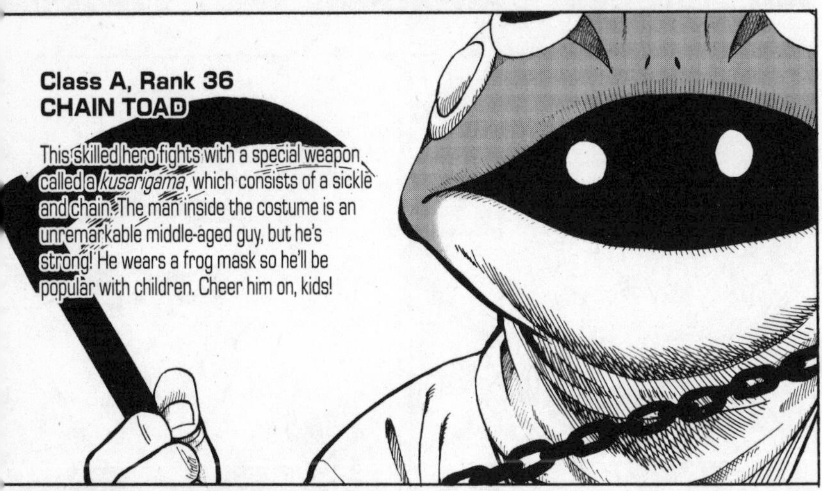
Class A, Rank 36
CHAIN TOAD
This skilled hero fights with a special weapon called a *kusarigama*, which consists of a sickle and chain. The man inside the costume is an unremarkable middle-aged guy, but he's strong! He wears a frog mask so he'll be popular with children. Cheer him on, kids!

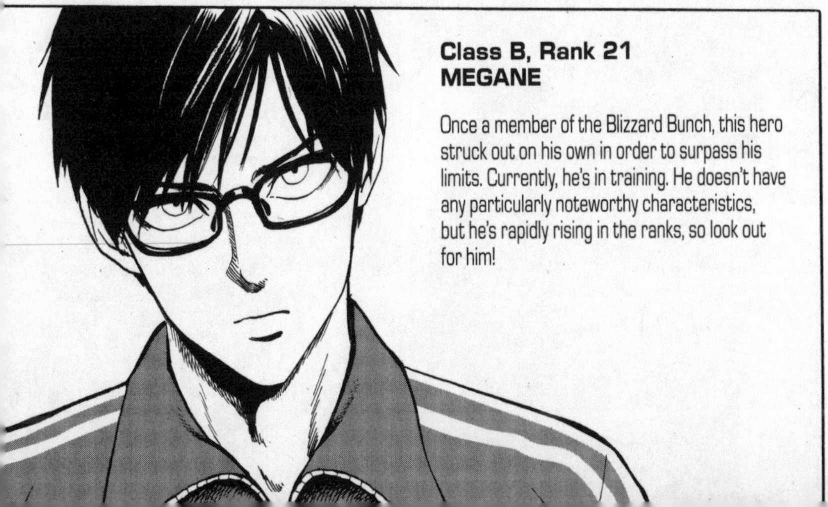
Class B, Rank 21
MEGANE
Once a member of the Blizzard Bunch, this hero struck out on his own in order to surpass his limits. Currently, he's in training. He doesn't have any particularly noteworthy characteristics, but he's rapidly rising in the ranks, so look out for him!

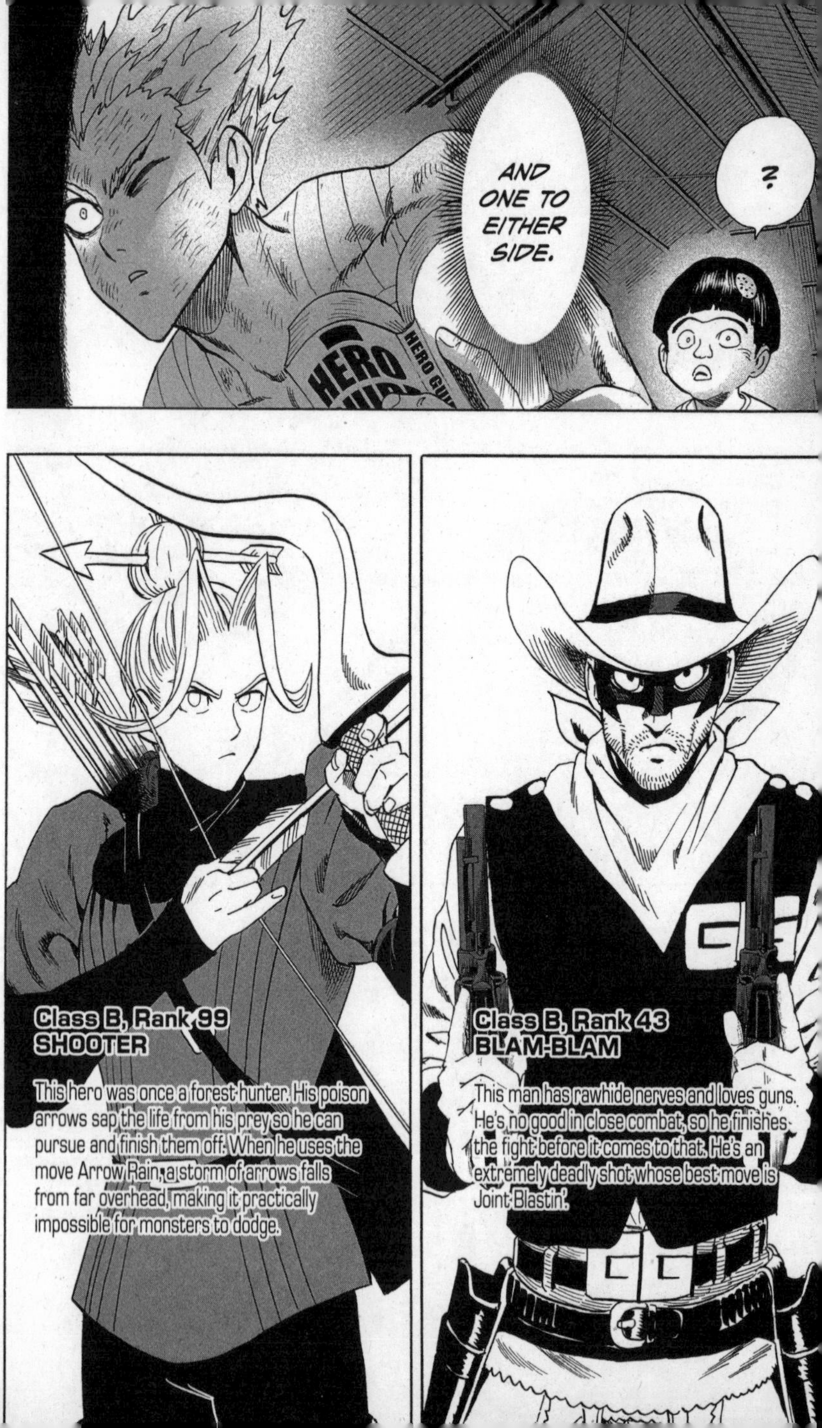
?
AND ONE TO EITHER SIDE.
Class B, Rank 43
BLAM-BLAM
This man has rawhide nerves and loves guns. He's no good in close combat, so he finishes the fight before it comes to that. He's an extremely deadly shot whose best move is Joint Blastin'.
Class B, Rank 99
SHOOTER
This hero was once a forest hunter. His poison arrows sap the life from his prey so he can pursue and finish them off. When he uses the move Arrow Rain, a storm of arrows falls from far overhead, making it practically impossible for monsters to dodge.

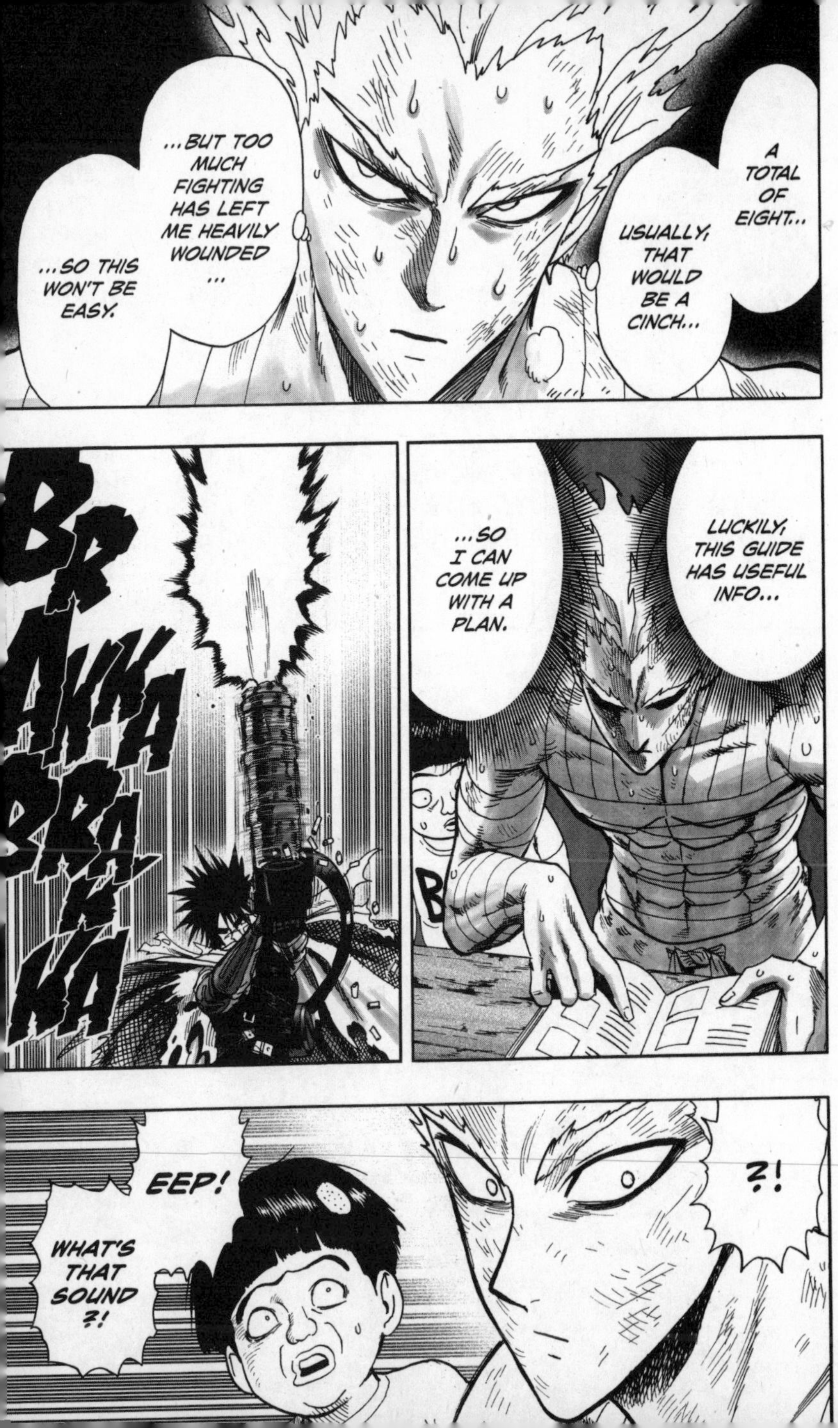
A TOTAL OF EIGHT...
USUALLY, THAT WOULD BE A CINCH...
...BUT TOO MUCH FIGHTING HAS LEFT ME HEAVILY WOUNDED...
...SO THIS WON'T BE EASY.
LUCKILY, THIS GUIDE HAS USEFUL INFO...
...SO I CAN COME UP WITH A PLAN.
BRAKKA BRAKKA
?!
EEP!
WHAT'S THAT SOUND ?!

TCH!

THERE'S NO TIME!

DEATH GATLING

Class A, Rank 8
This hero has an automatic gun con
on his left a... accelerates moon
in his left h...
giving the...
ideal for th...
he has the...
He looks s...
sense of jus...

GET OUT HERE, HERO HUNTER!

YOU MUST BE PANICKED TO HIDE IN THAT HUT!

I'M SURE YOU'VE NOTICED US!

I'M CONCEN- TRATING, SO SHUT YER HOLE!

SOMEONE'S OUTSIDE, OLD DUDE!

RMMMMM

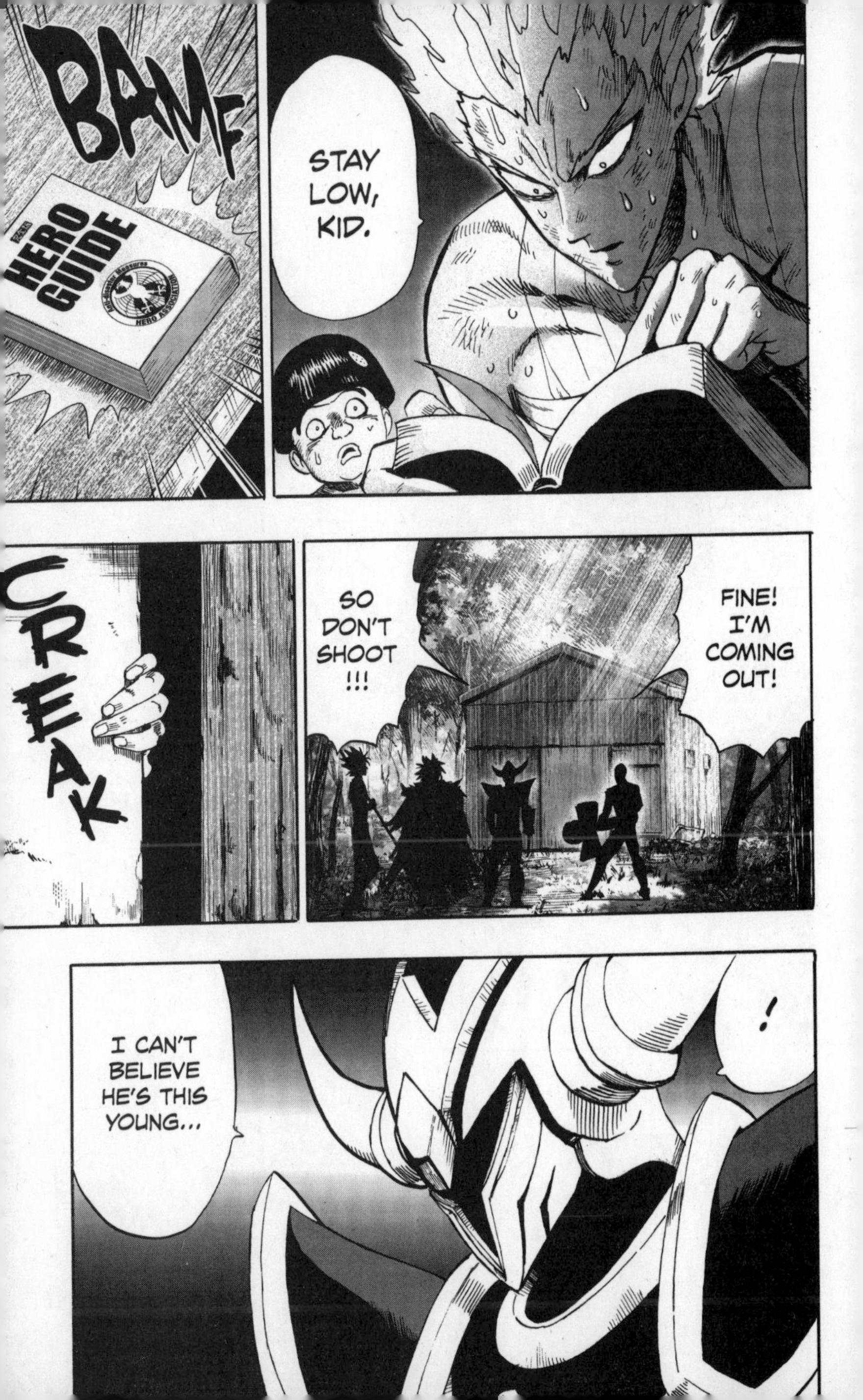
STAY LOW, KID.
BAMF
HERO GUIDE
Anti-disaster Measures
HERO ASSOCIATION
FINE! I'M COMING OUT!
SO DON'T SHOOT!!!
CREAK
!
I CAN'T BELIEVE HE'S THIS YOUNG...

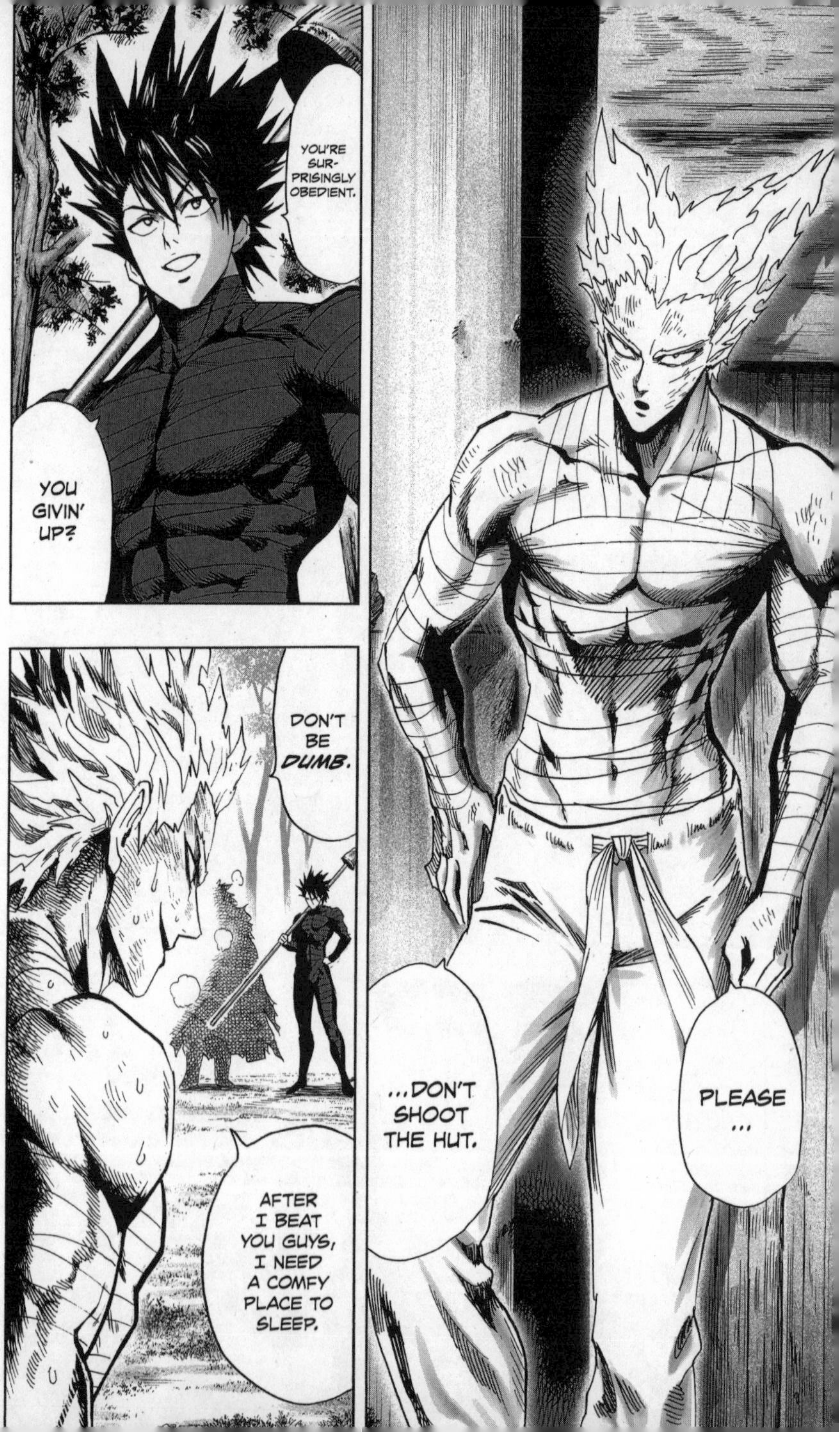
PLEASE...
...DON'T SHOOT THE HUT.
YOU'RE SURPRISINGLY OBEDIENT.
YOU GIVIN' UP?
DON'T BE *DUMB*.
AFTER I BEAT YOU GUYS, I NEED A COMFY PLACE TO SLEEP.

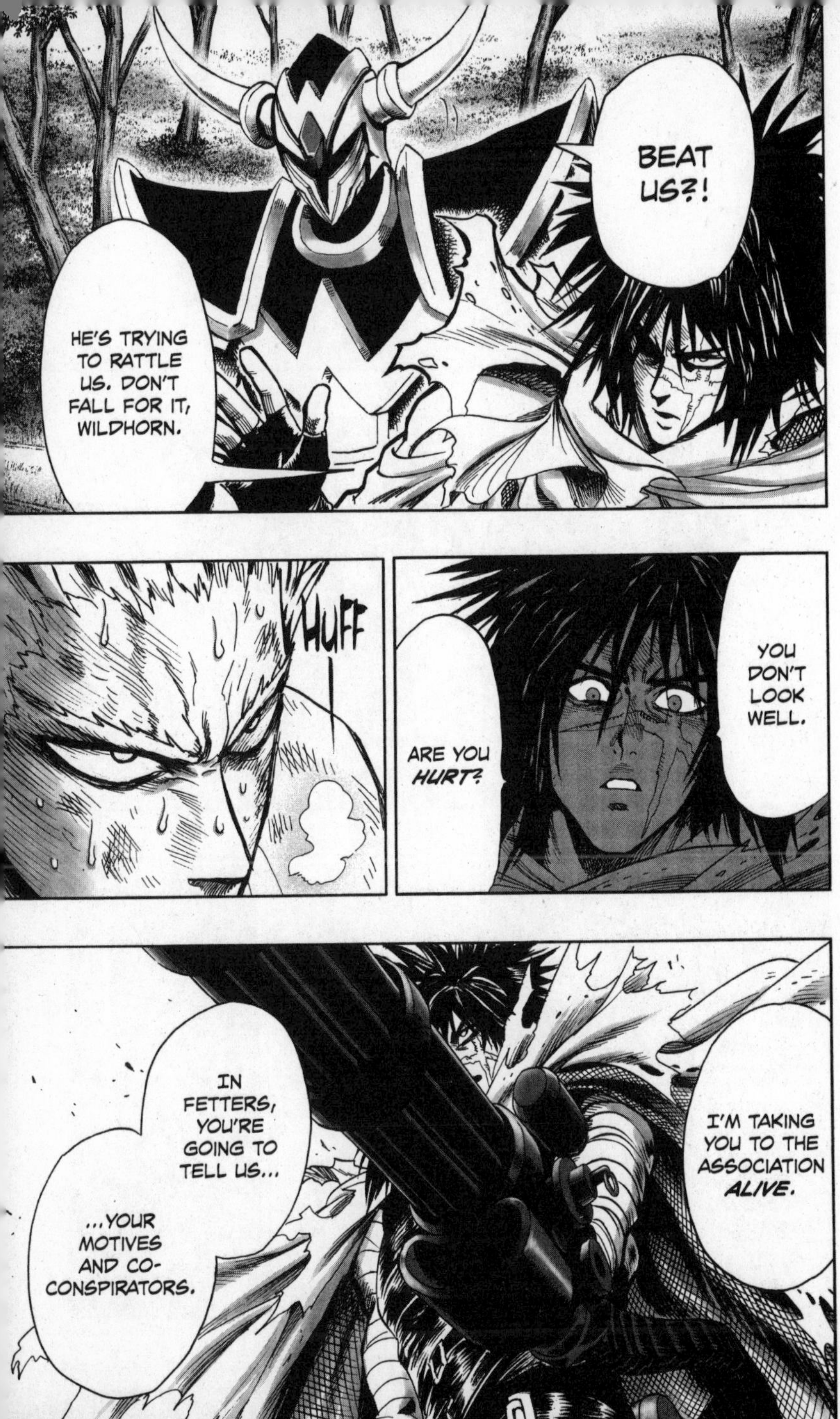
BEAT US?!
HE'S TRYING TO RATTLE US. DON'T FALL FOR IT, WILDHORN.
YOU DON'T LOOK WELL.
ARE YOU *HURT?*
HUFF
I'M TAKING YOU TO THE ASSOCIATION *ALIVE.*
IN FETTERS, YOU'RE GOING TO TELL US...
...YOUR MOTIVES AND CO-CONSPIRATORS.

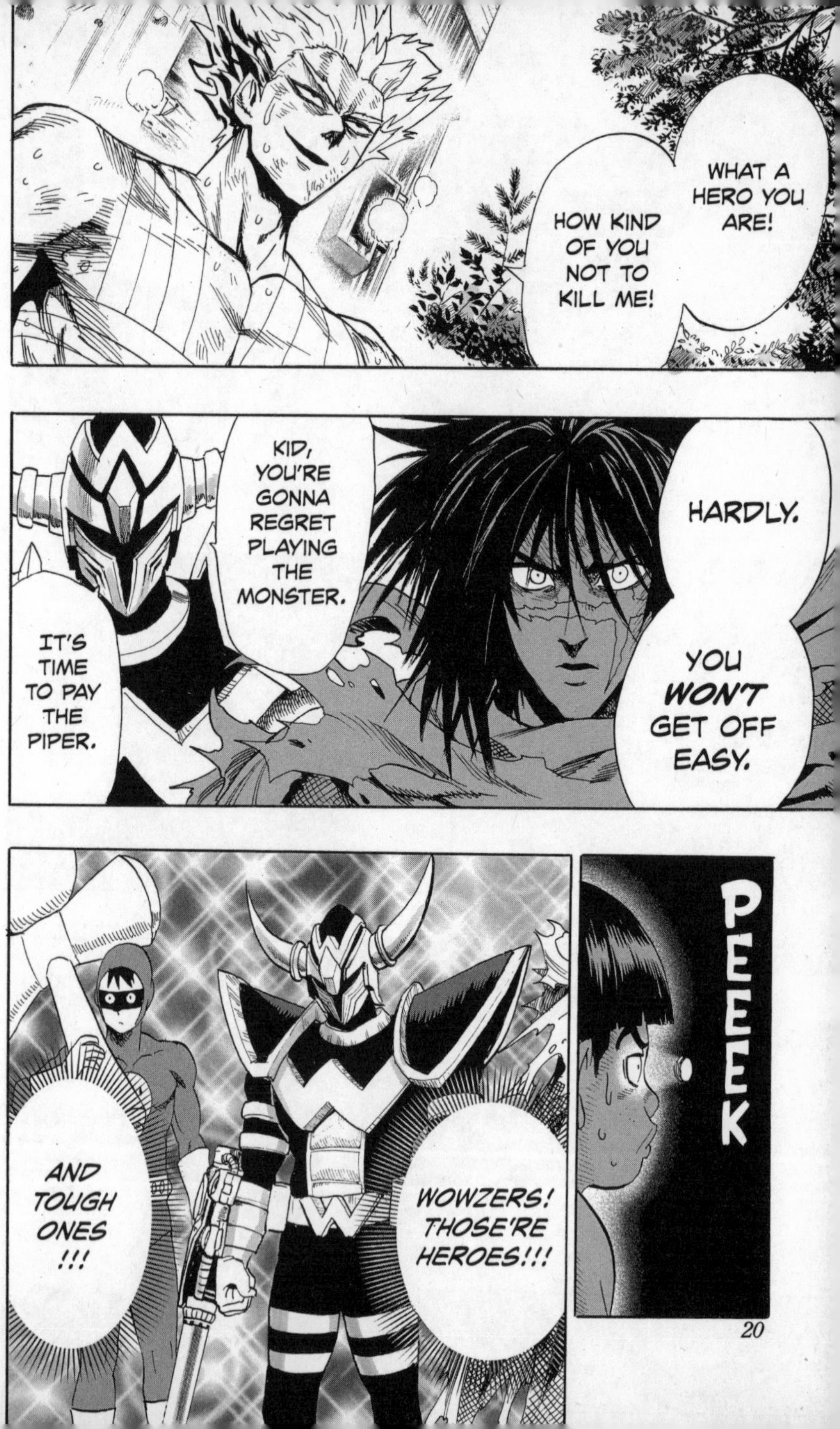
WHAT A HERO YOU ARE!
HOW KIND OF YOU NOT TO KILL ME!
HARDLY.
YOU *WON'T* GET OFF EASY.
KID, YOU'RE GONNA REGRET PLAYING THE MONSTER.
IT'S TIME TO PAY THE PIPER.
PEEEK
WOWZERS! THOSE'RE HEROES!!!
AND TOUGH ONES!!!

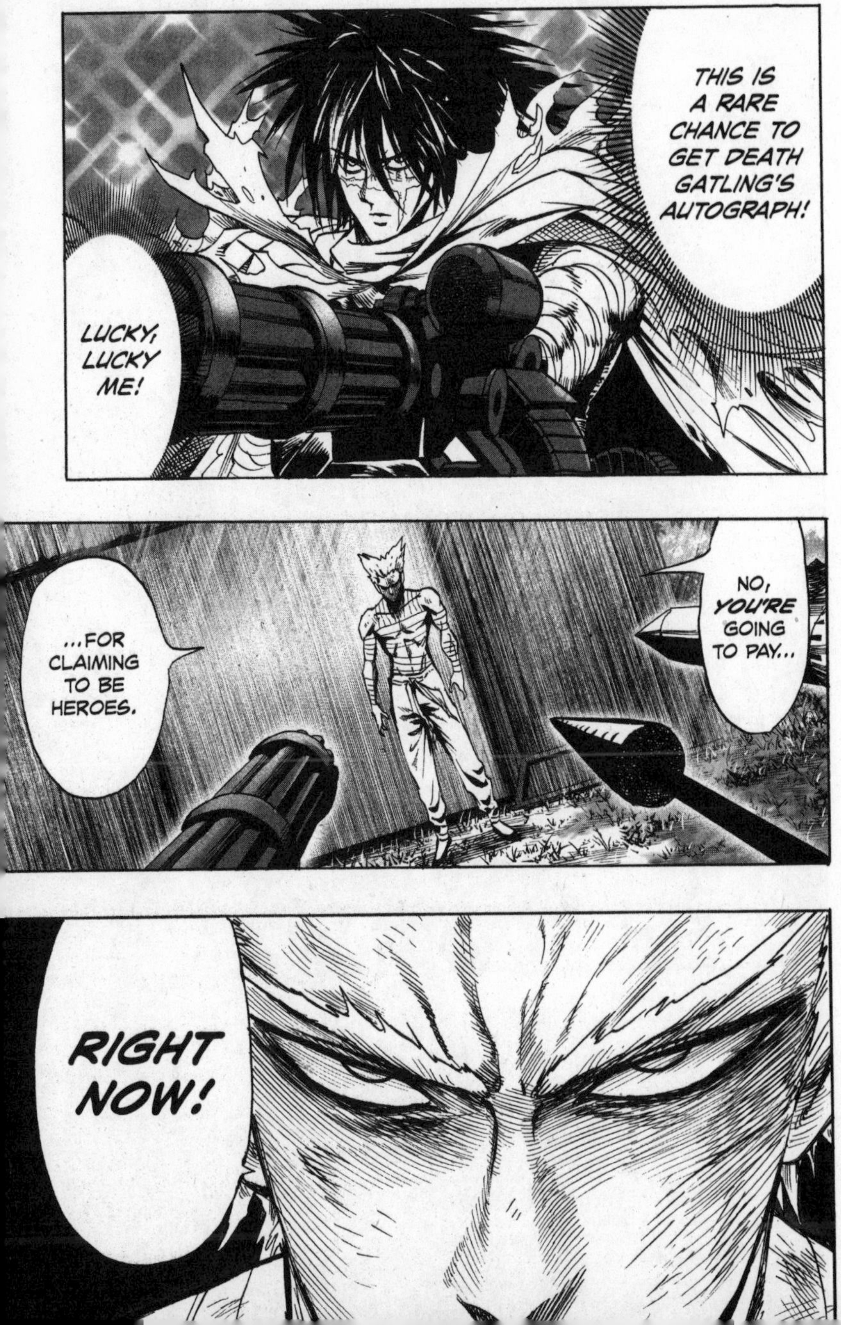
THIS IS A RARE CHANCE TO GET DEATH GATLING'S AUTOGRAPH!
LUCKY, LUCKY ME!
NO, *YOU'RE* GOING TO PAY...
...FOR CLAIMING TO BE HEROES.
RIGHT NOW!

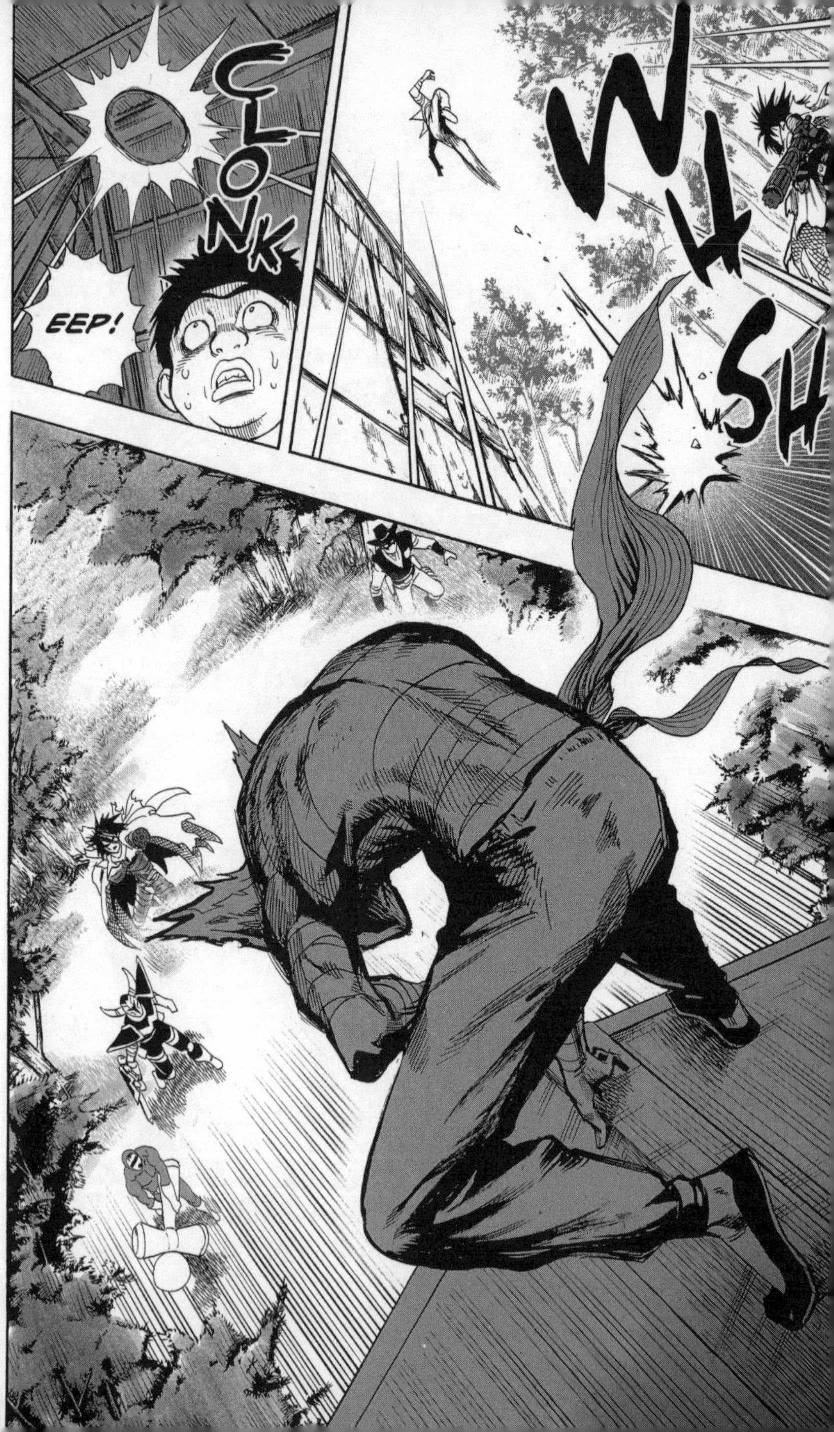
WHSH
CLONK
EEP!

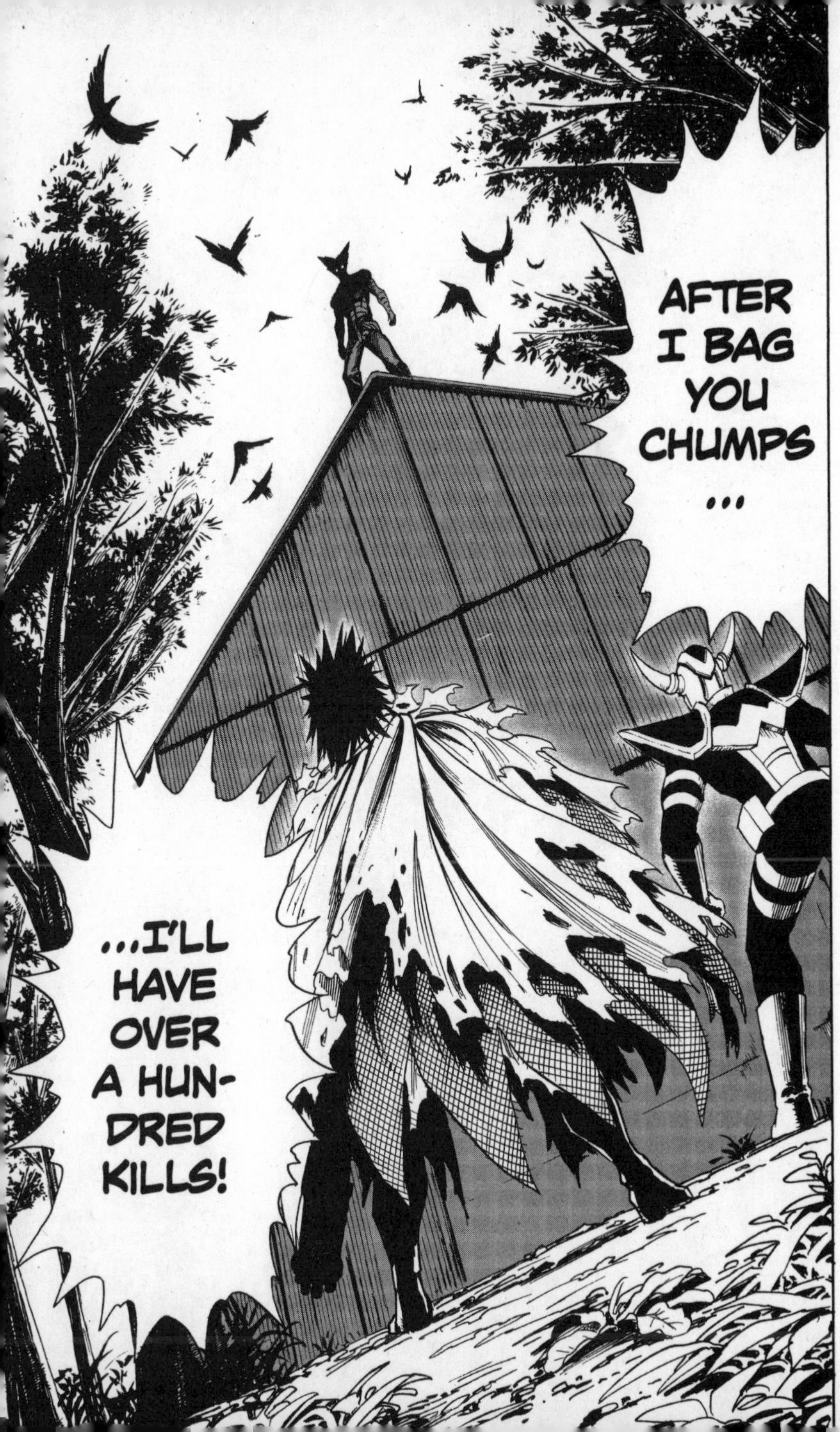
AFTER I BAG YOU CHUMPS ...
...I'LL HAVE OVER A HUN-DRED KILLS!

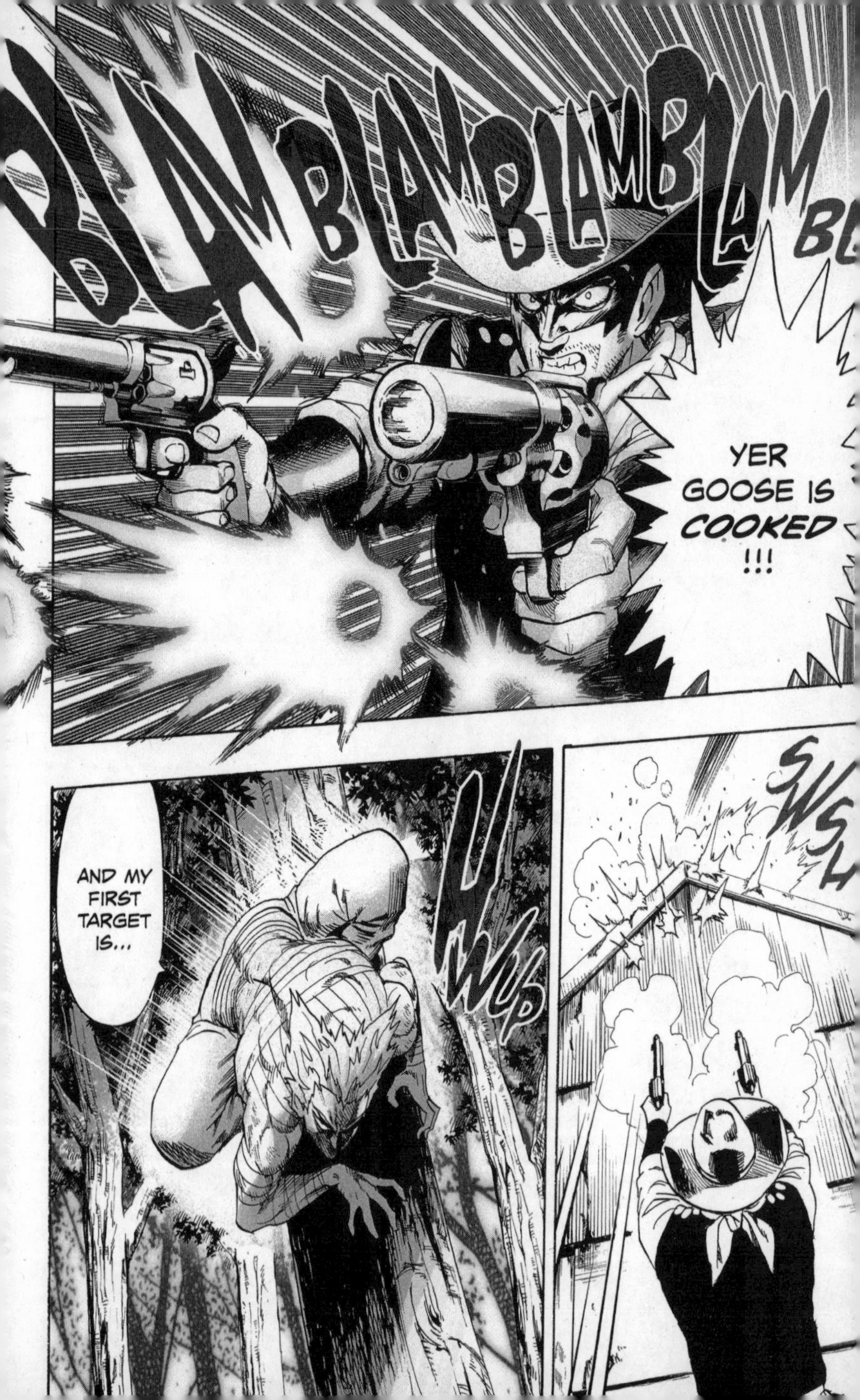
BLAM BLAM BLAM BLAM BLAM BL
YER GOOSE IS COOKED !!!
SWSH
WUP
AND MY FIRST TARGET IS...

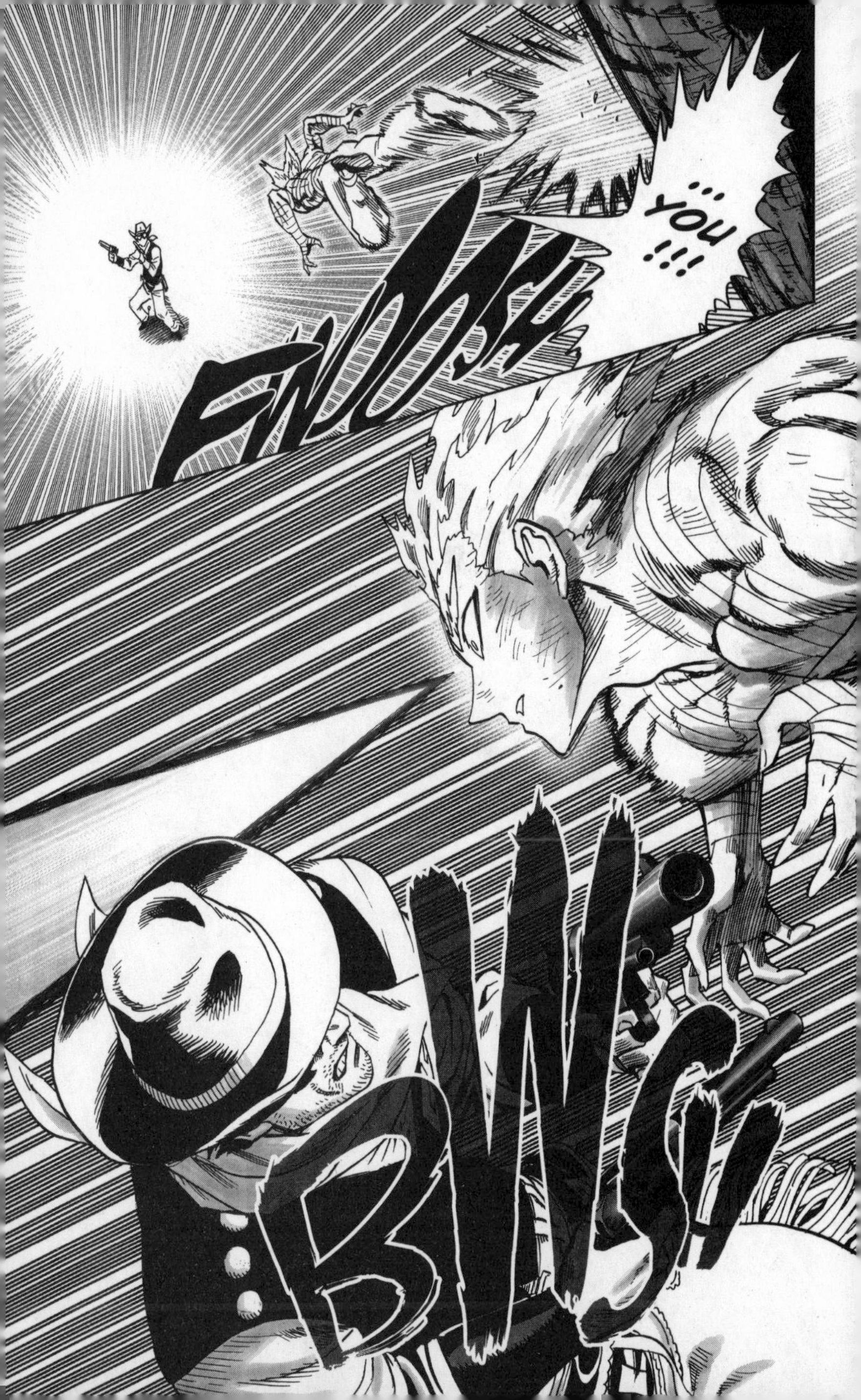
...YOU!!!
FWOOSH

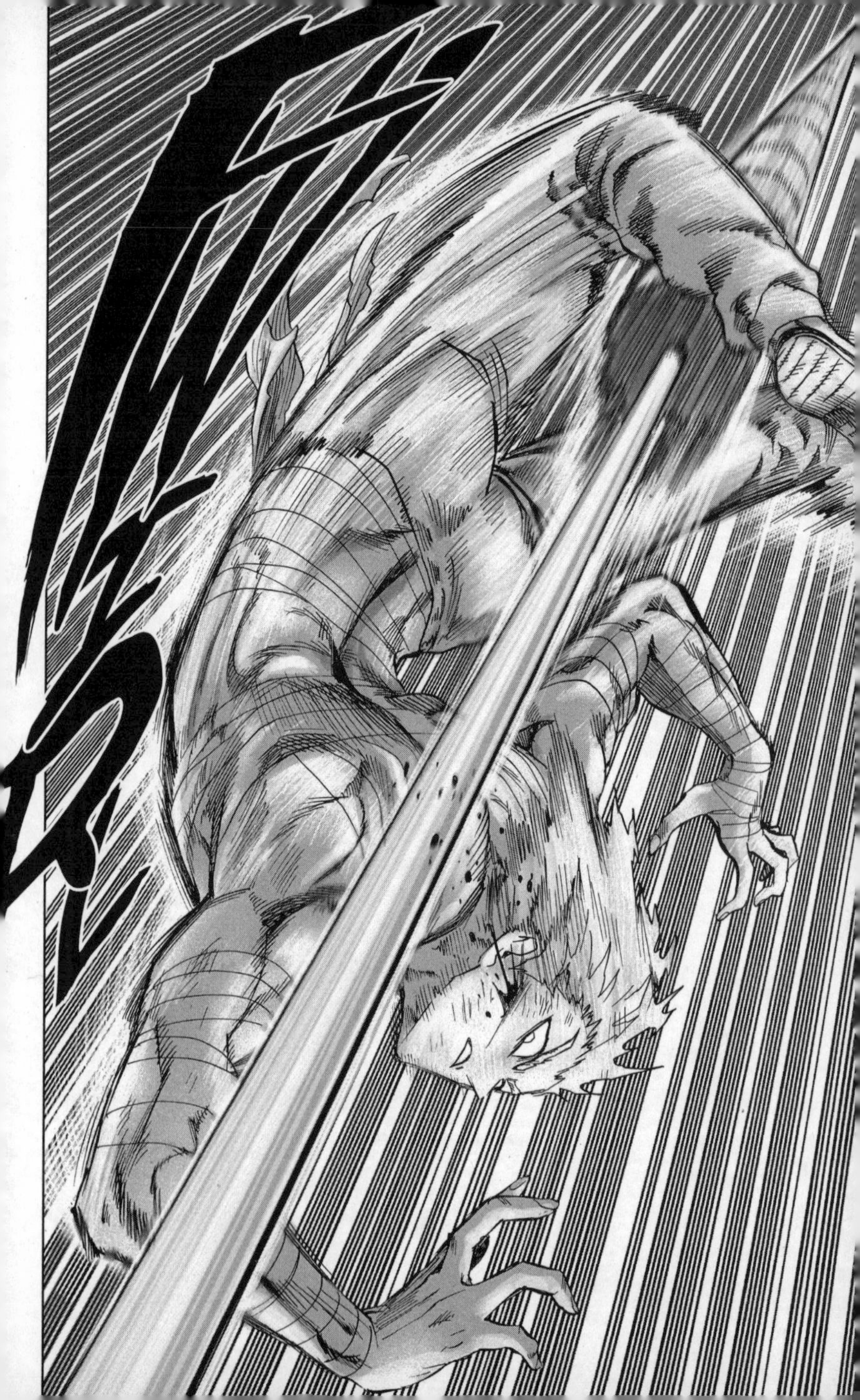

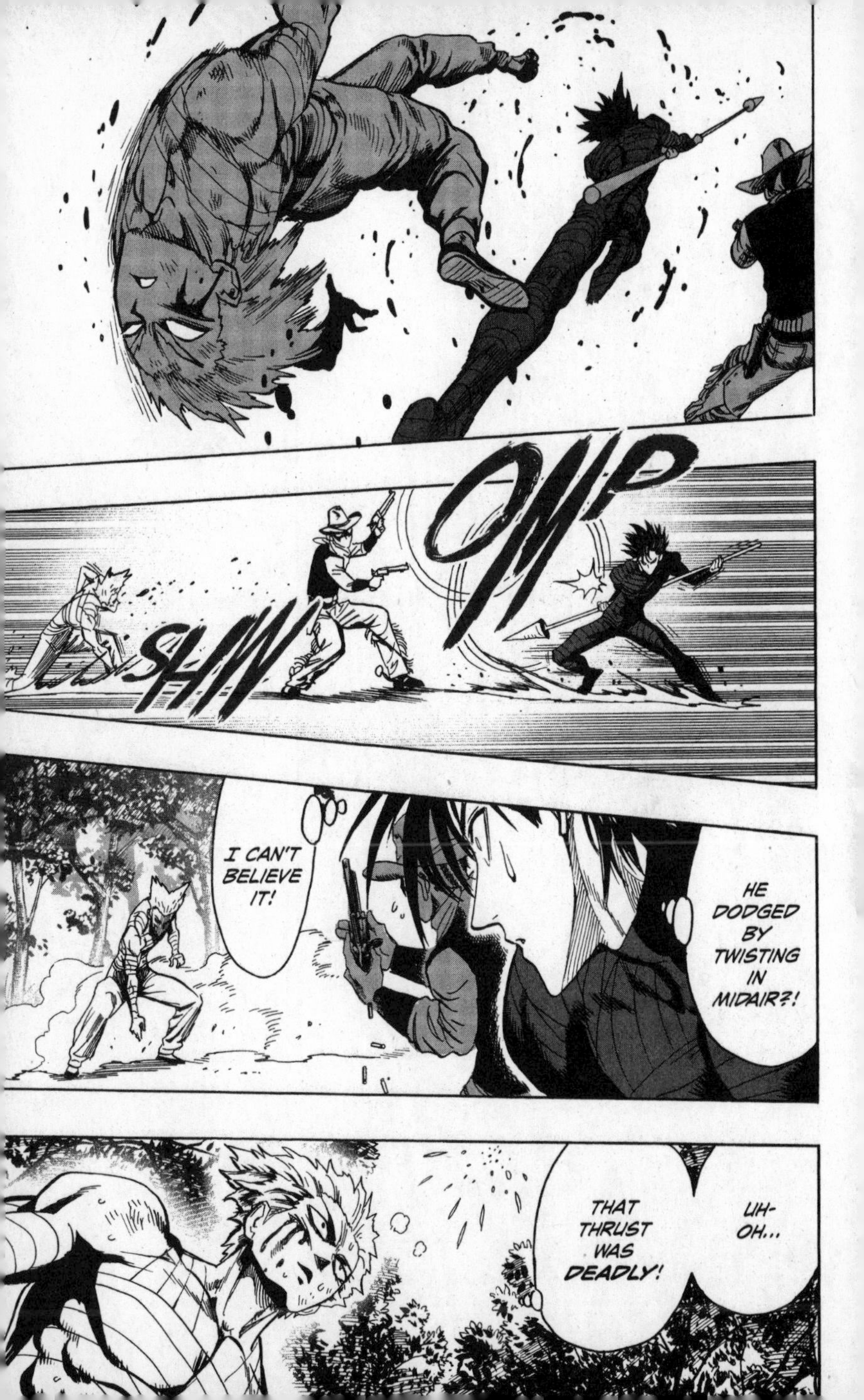

SHW
OMP
HE DODGED BY TWISTING IN MIDAIR?!
I CAN'T BELIEVE IT!
UH-OH...
THAT THRUST WAS DEADLY!

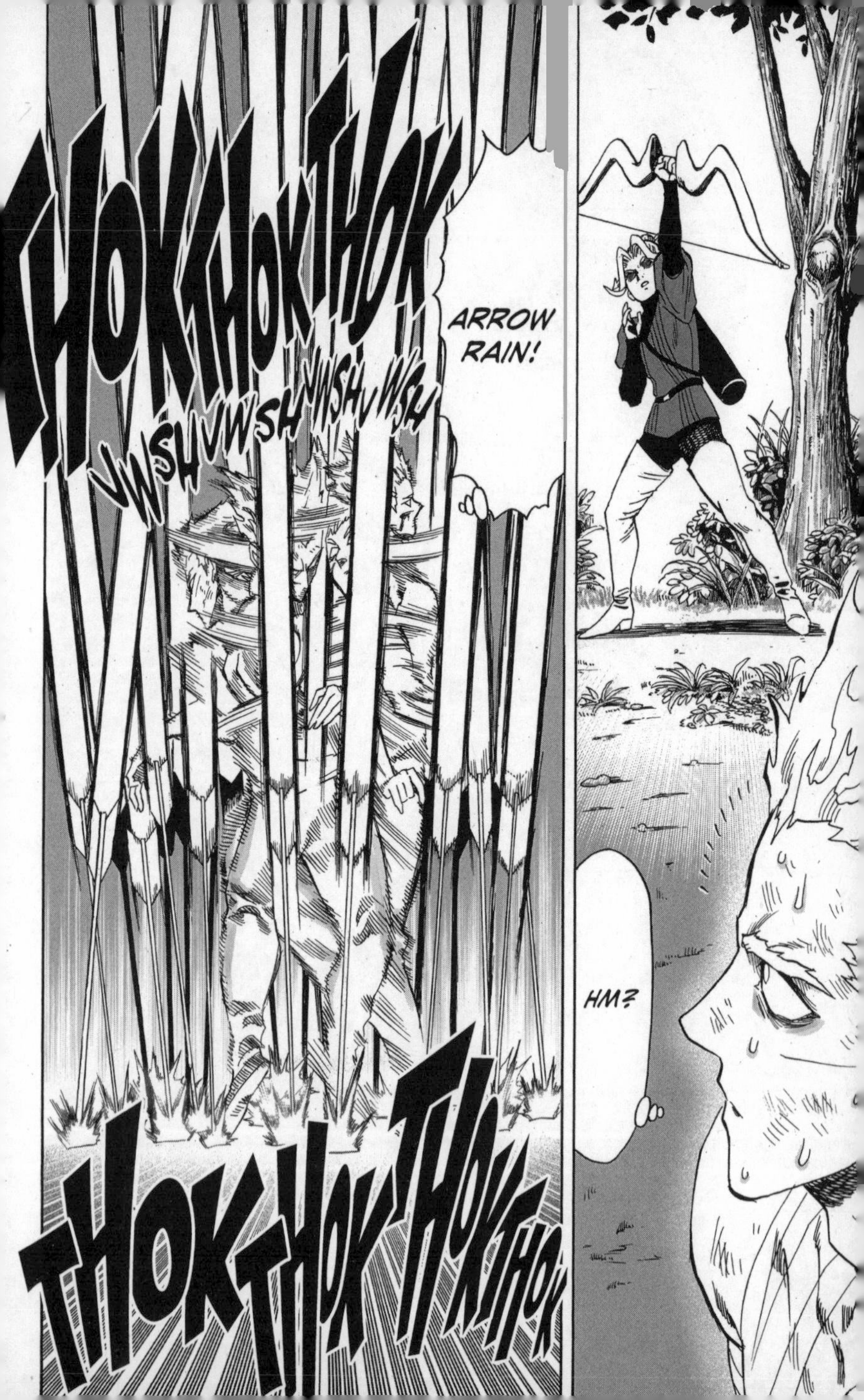
HM?
ARROW RAIN!
THOKTHOKTHOK
VWSHVWSHVWSHVWSH
THOKTHOKTHOKTHOK

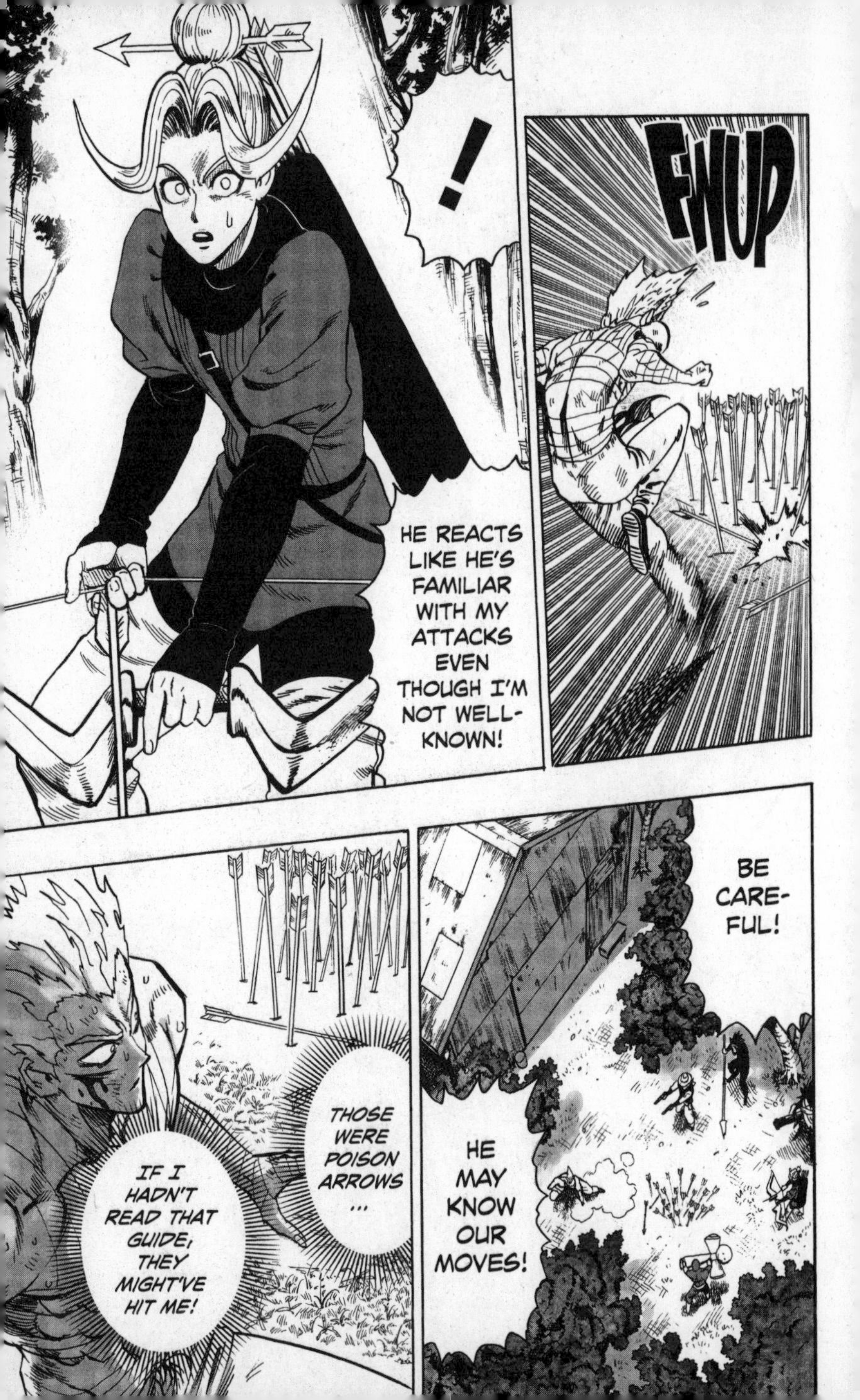
FWUP
!
HE REACTS LIKE HE'S FAMILIAR WITH MY ATTACKS EVEN THOUGH I'M NOT WELL-KNOWN!
BE CARE-FUL!
HE MAY KNOW OUR MOVES!
THOSE WERE POISON ARROWS ...
IF I HADN'T READ THAT GUIDE, THEY MIGHT'VE HIT ME!

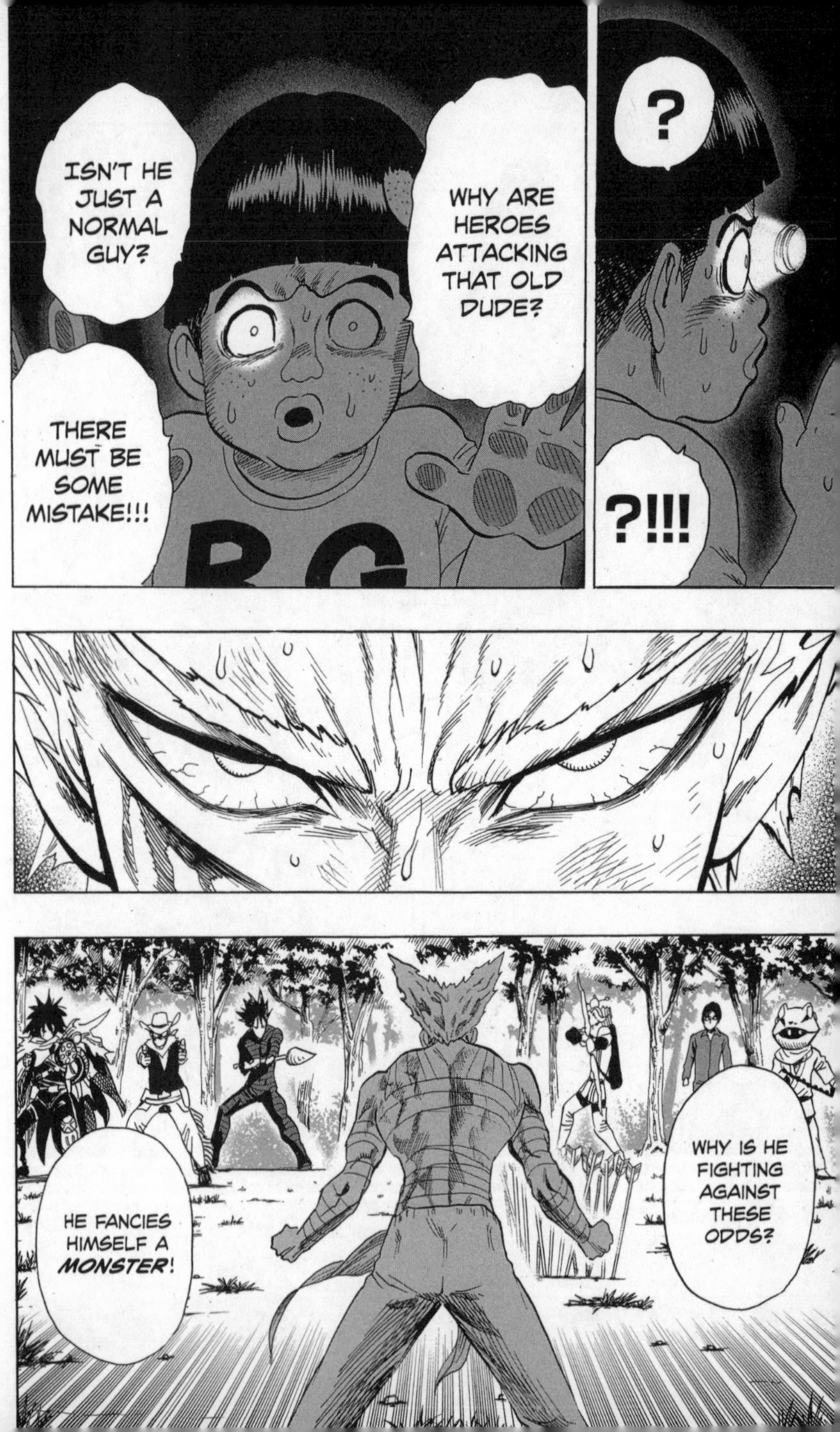
?
?!!!
WHY ARE HEROES ATTACKING THAT OLD DUDE?
ISN'T HE JUST A NORMAL GUY?
THERE MUST BE SOME MISTAKE!!!
WHY IS HE FIGHTING AGAINST THESE ODDS?
HE FANCIES HIMSELF A *MONSTER*!

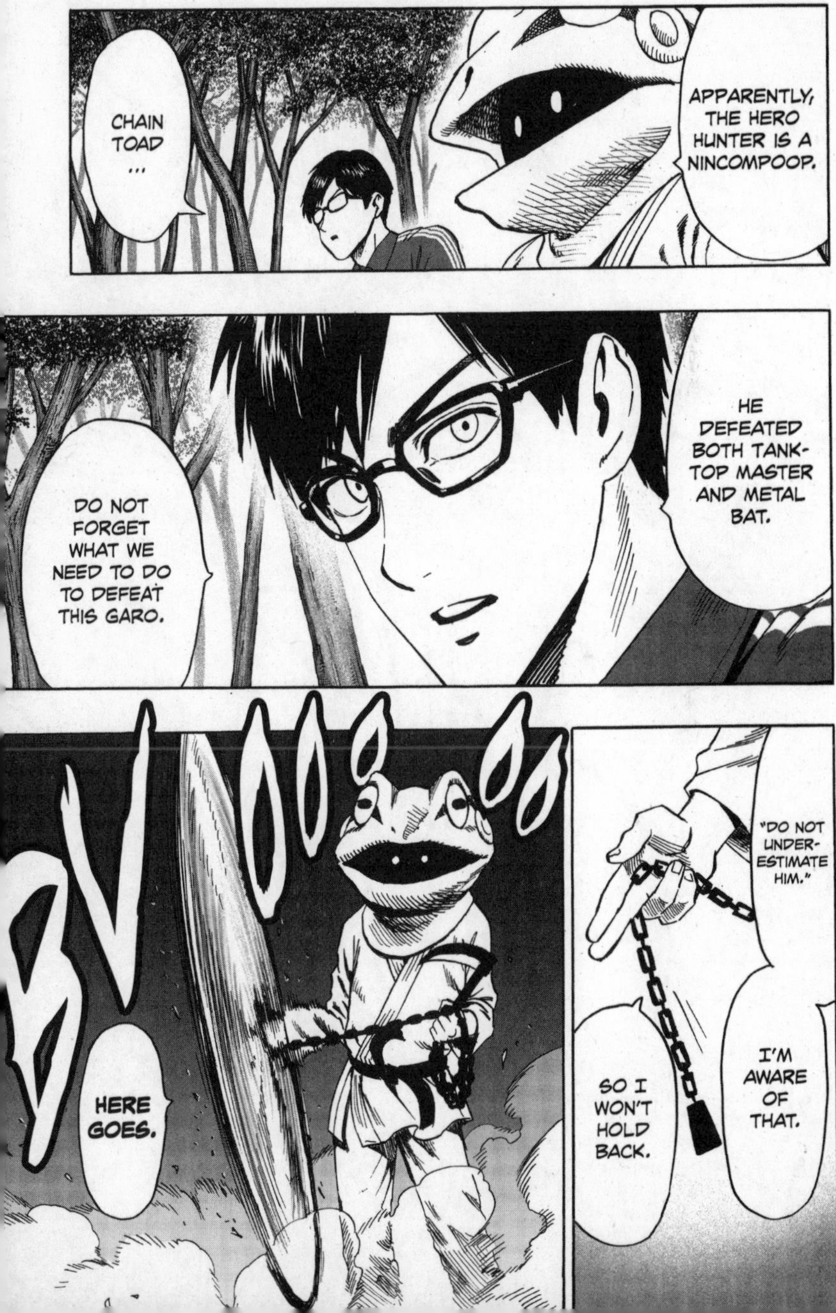
APPARENTLY, THE HERO HUNTER IS A NINCOMPOOP.
CHAIN TOAD ...
HE DEFEATED BOTH TANK-TOP MASTER AND METAL BAT.
DO NOT FORGET WHAT WE NEED TO DO TO DEFEAT THIS GARO.
"DO NOT UNDER-ESTIMATE HIM."
I'M AWARE OF THAT.
SO I WON'T HOLD BACK.
HERE GOES.

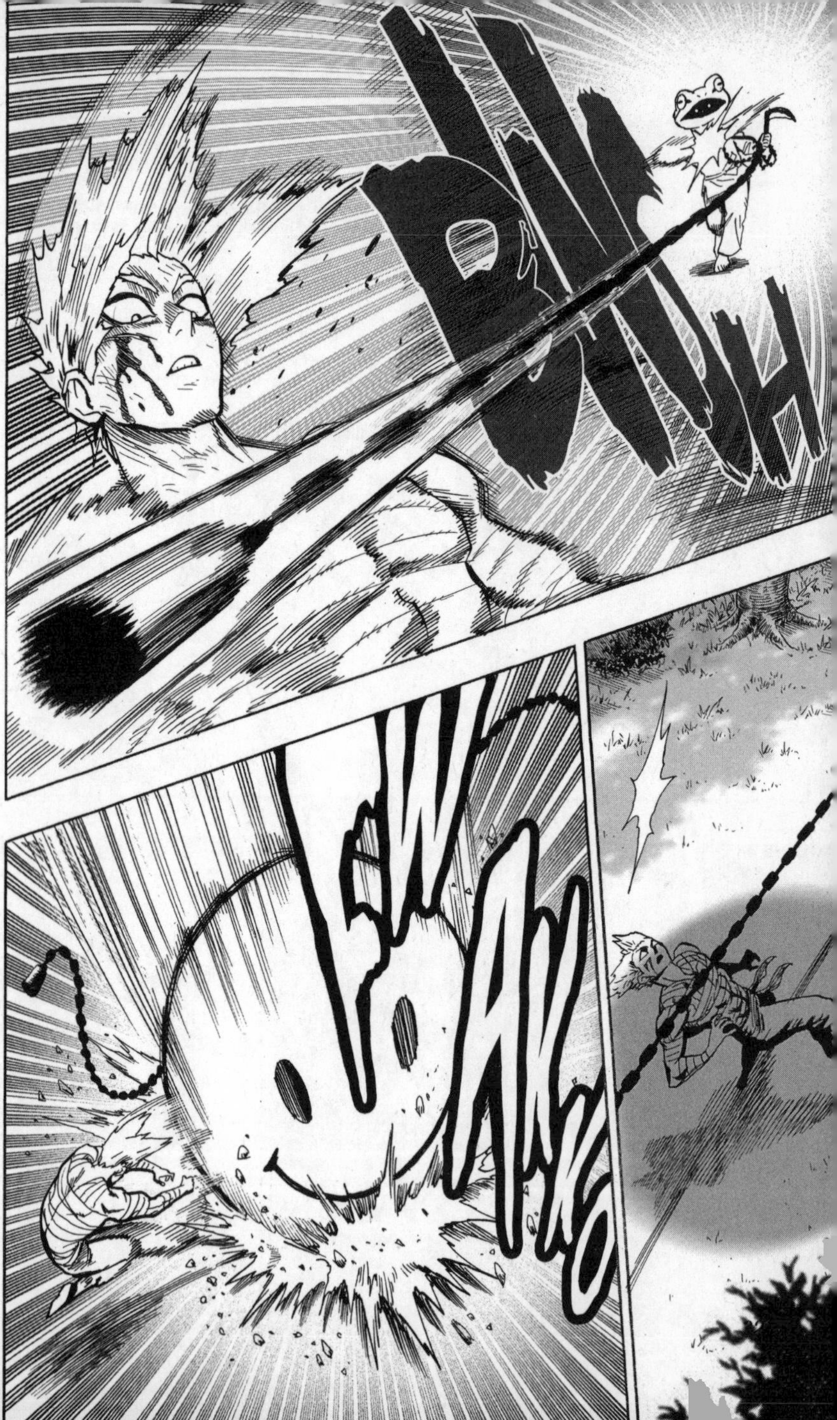

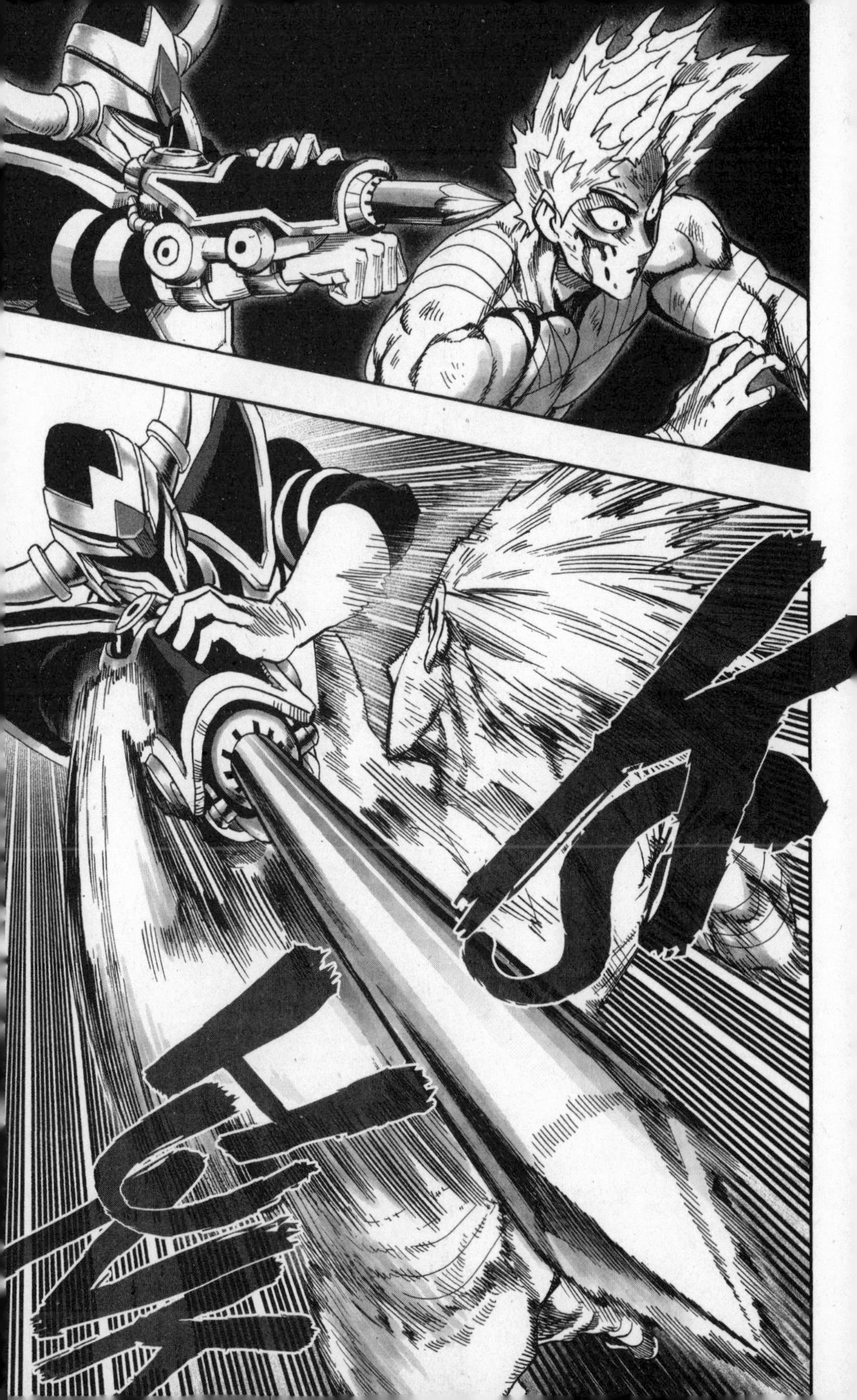

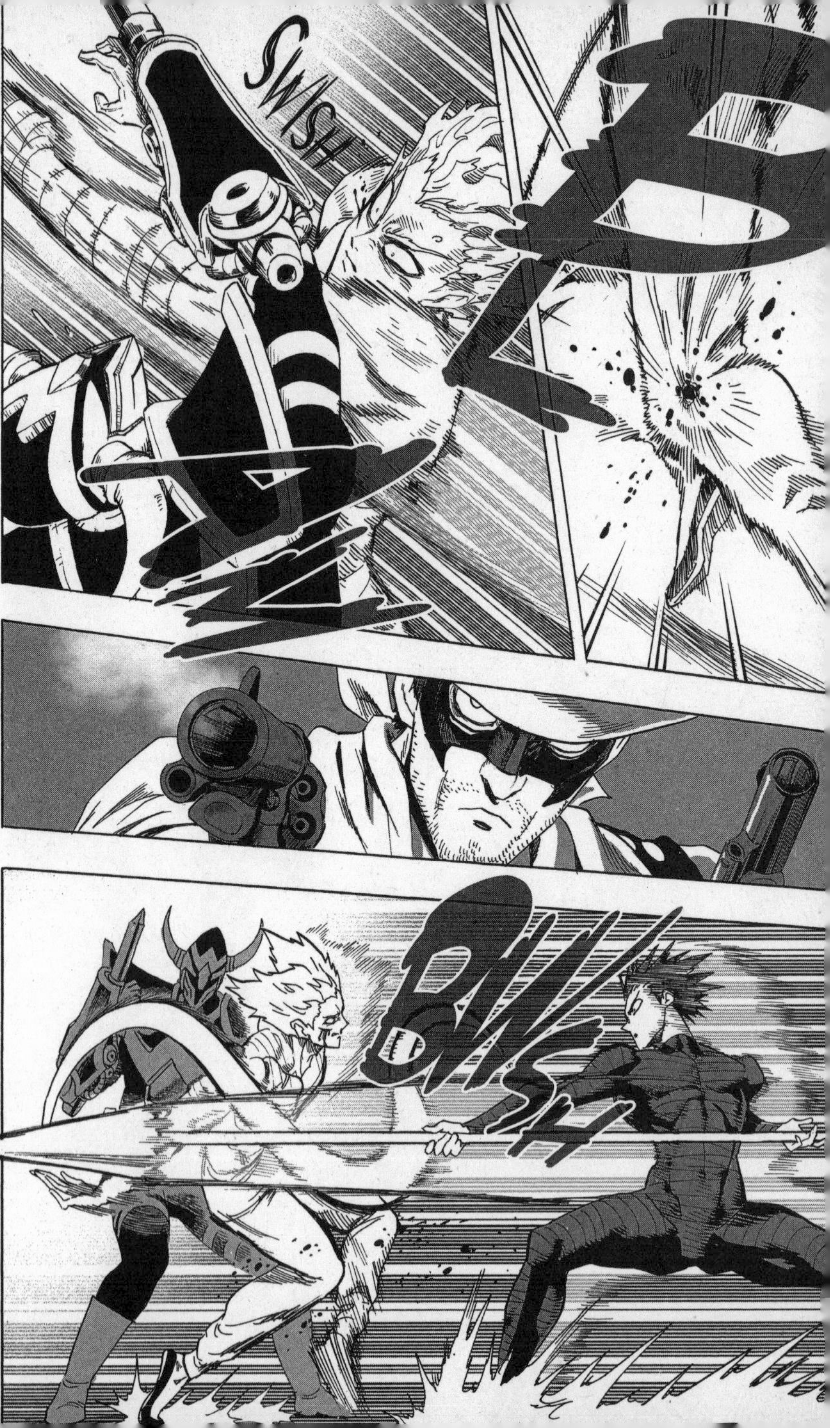
SWISH
BANG
SWISH

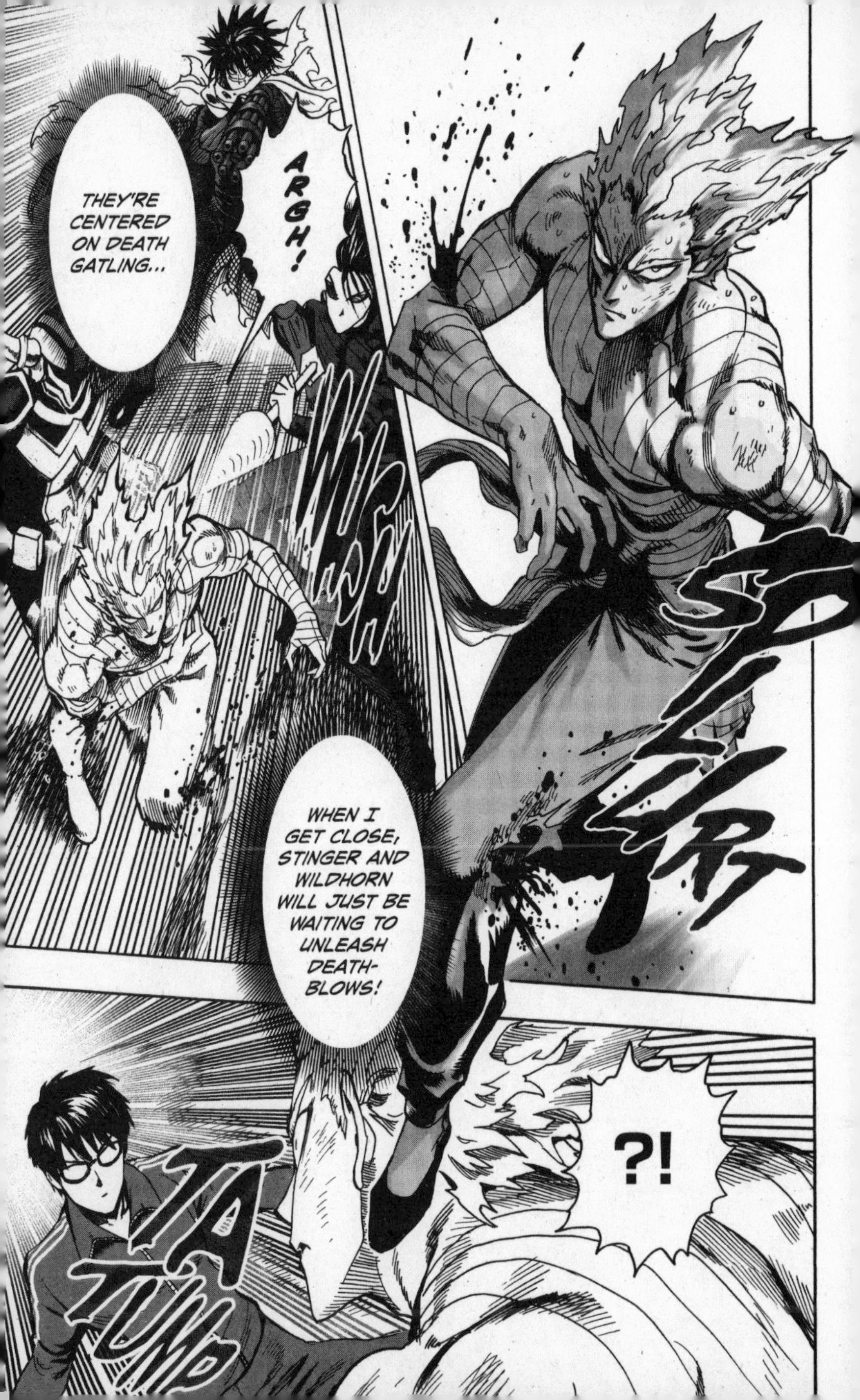

WHEN I GET CLOSE, STINGER AND WILDHORN WILL JUST BE WAITING TO UNLEASH DEATH-BLOWS!
THEY'RE CENTERED ON DEATH GATLING...
ARGH!
?!

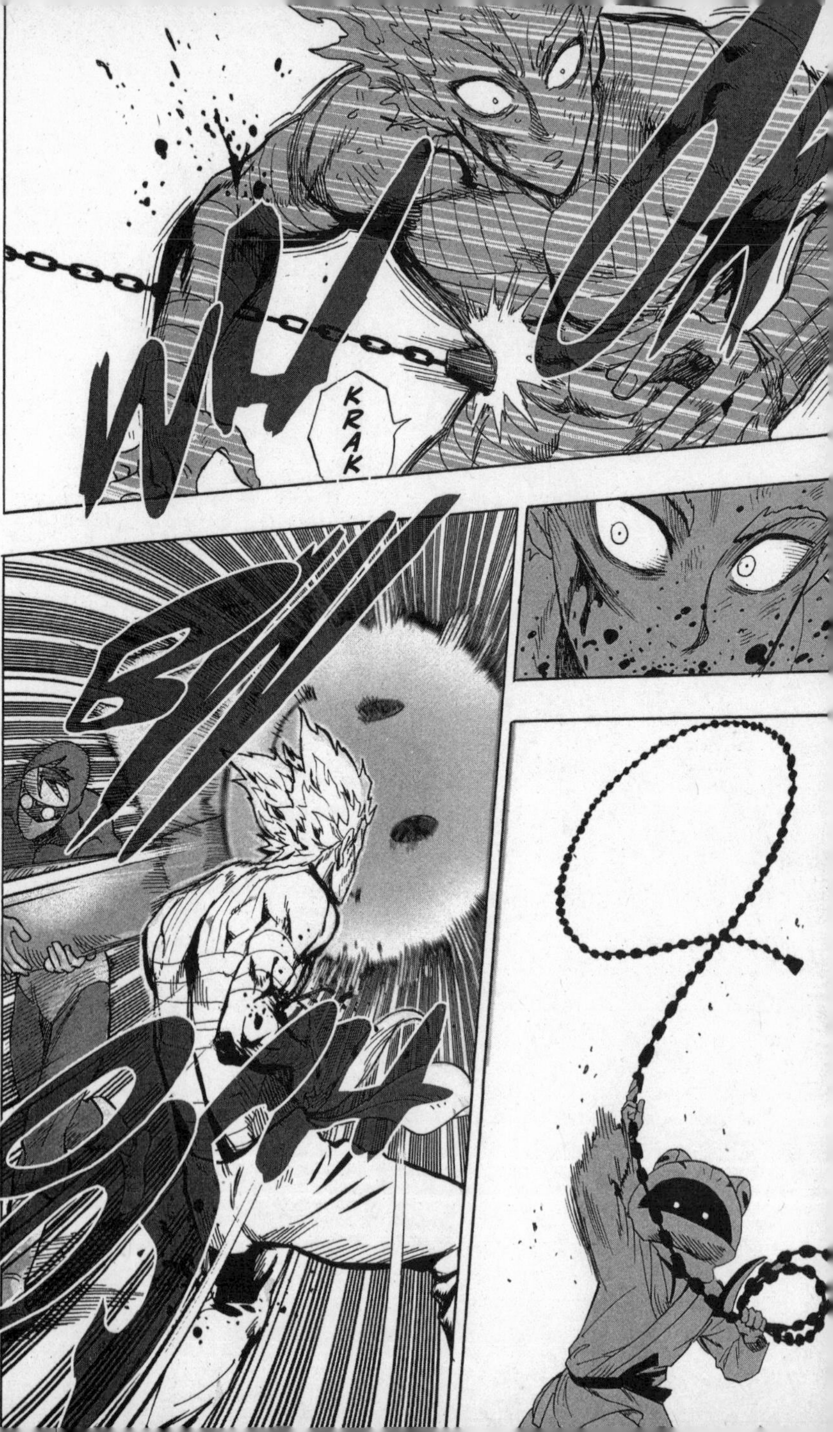
KRAK

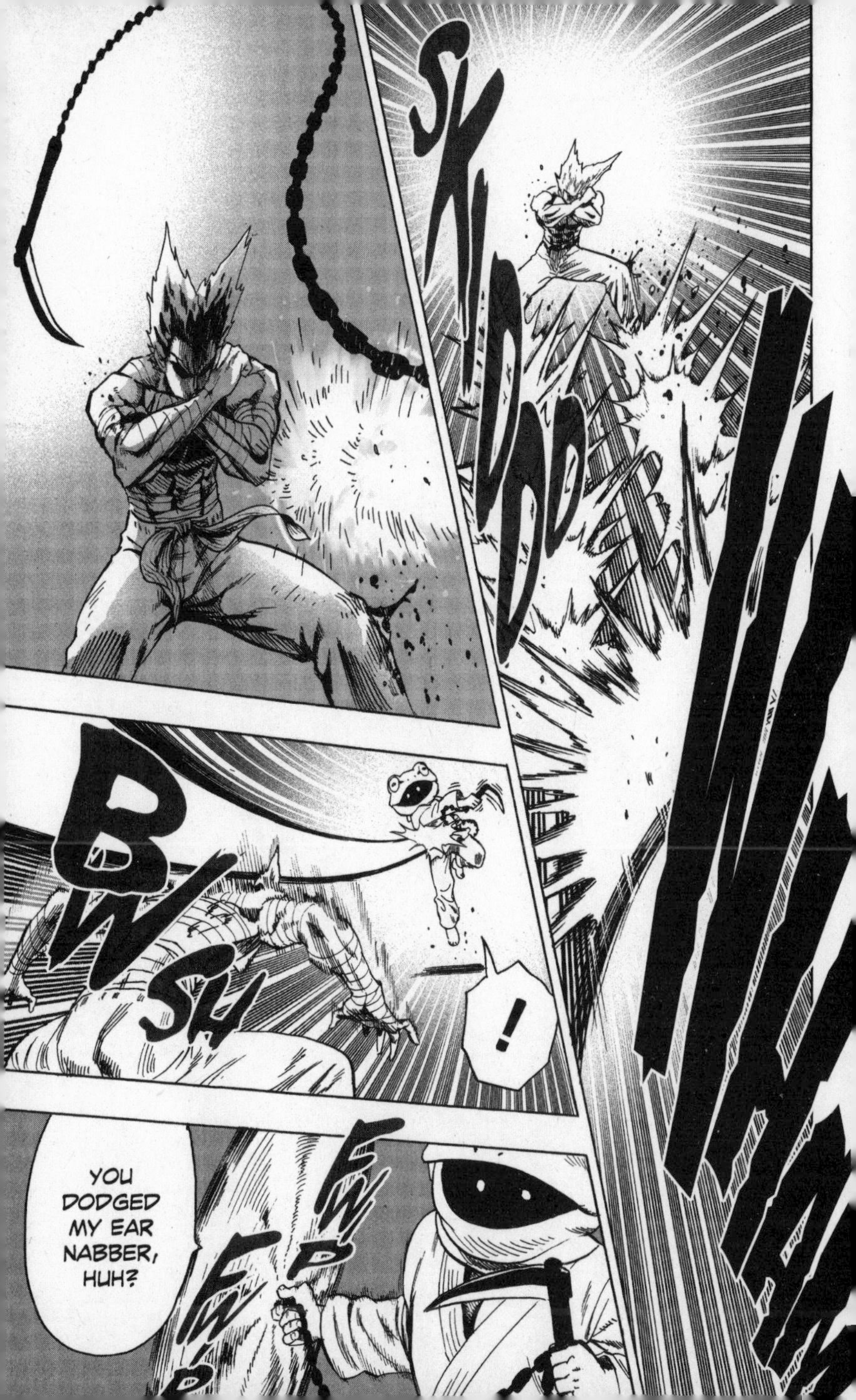
BWSH
!
YOU DODGED MY EAR NABBER, HUH?

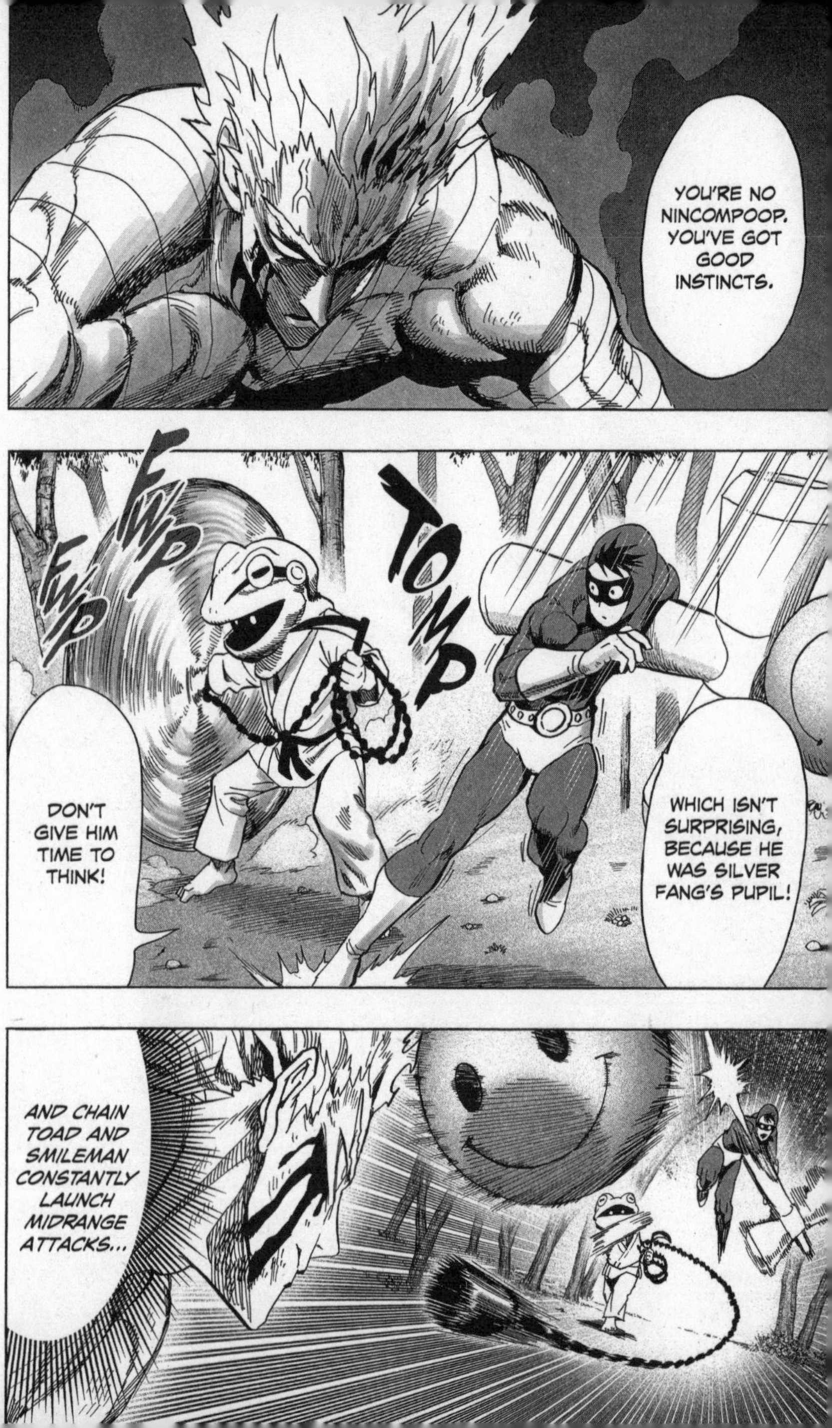
YOU'RE NO NINCOMPOOP. YOU'VE GOT GOOD INSTINCTS.
WHICH ISN'T SURPRISING, BECAUSE HE WAS SILVER FANG'S PUPIL!
TOMP
FWIP
FWIP
DON'T GIVE HIM TIME TO THINK!
AND CHAIN TOAD AND SMILEMAN CONSTANTLY LAUNCH MIDRANGE ATTACKS...

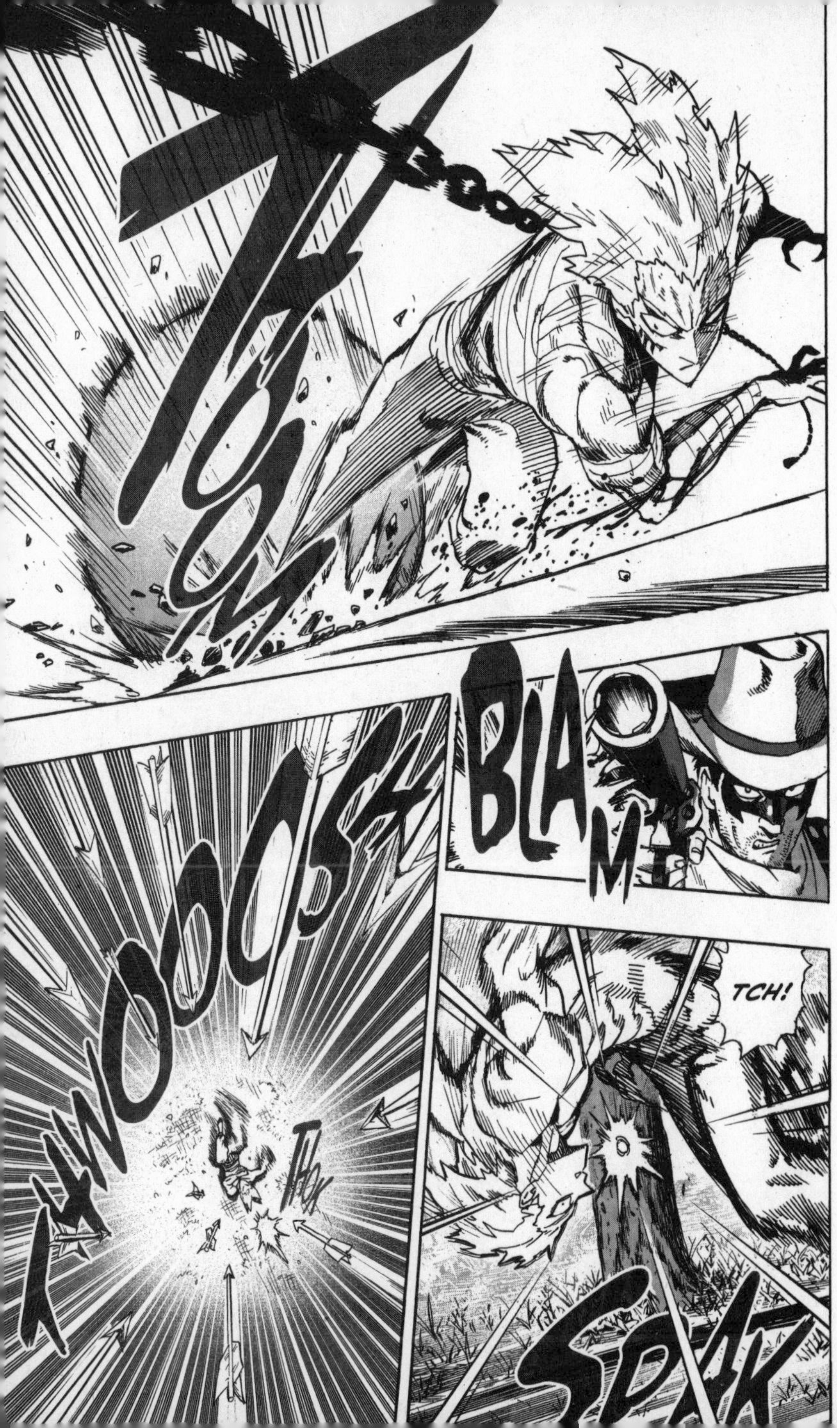
BLAM
THWOOOSH
TCH!

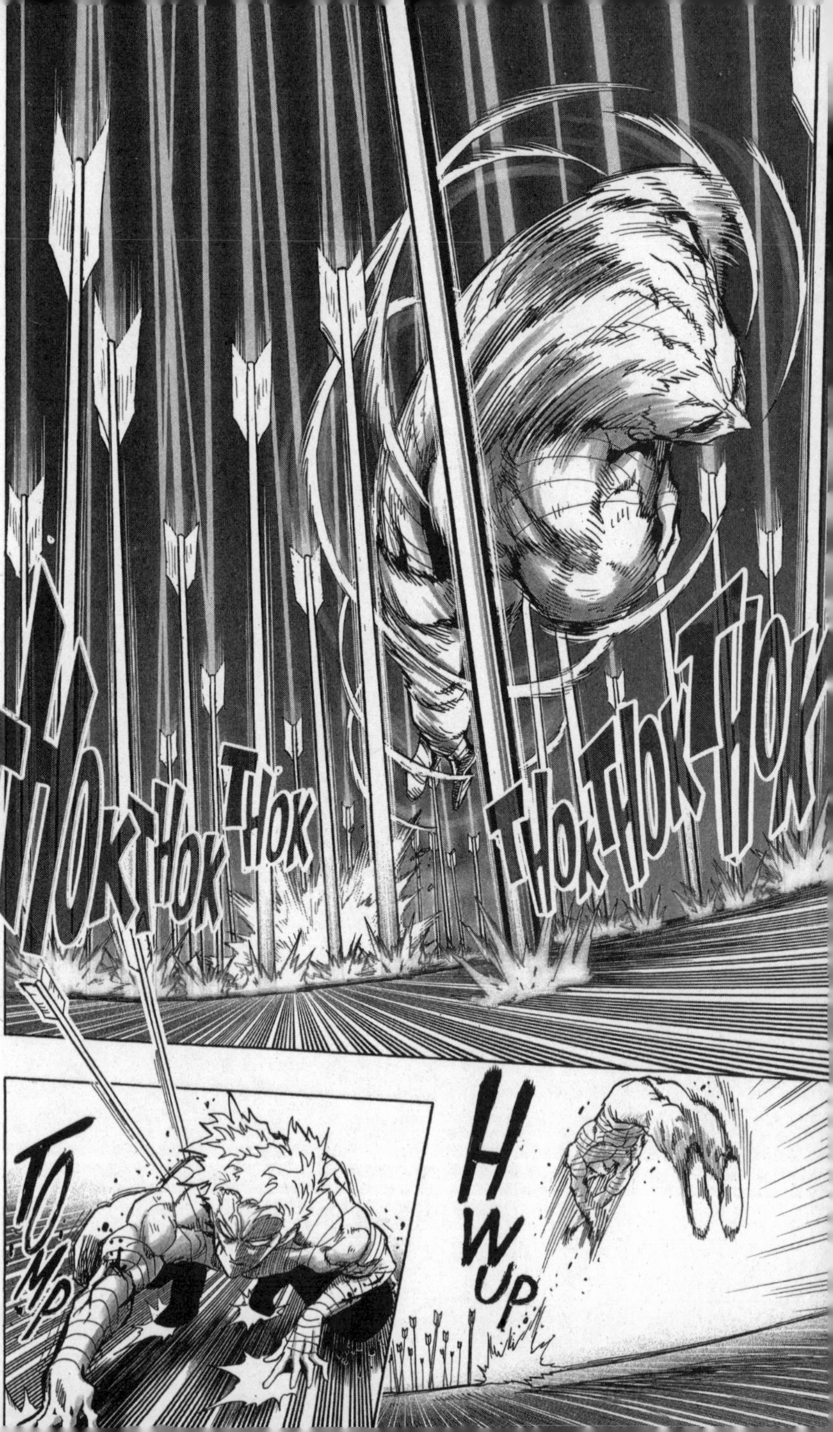
THOK THOK THOK
THOK THOK THOK
HWUP
TOMP

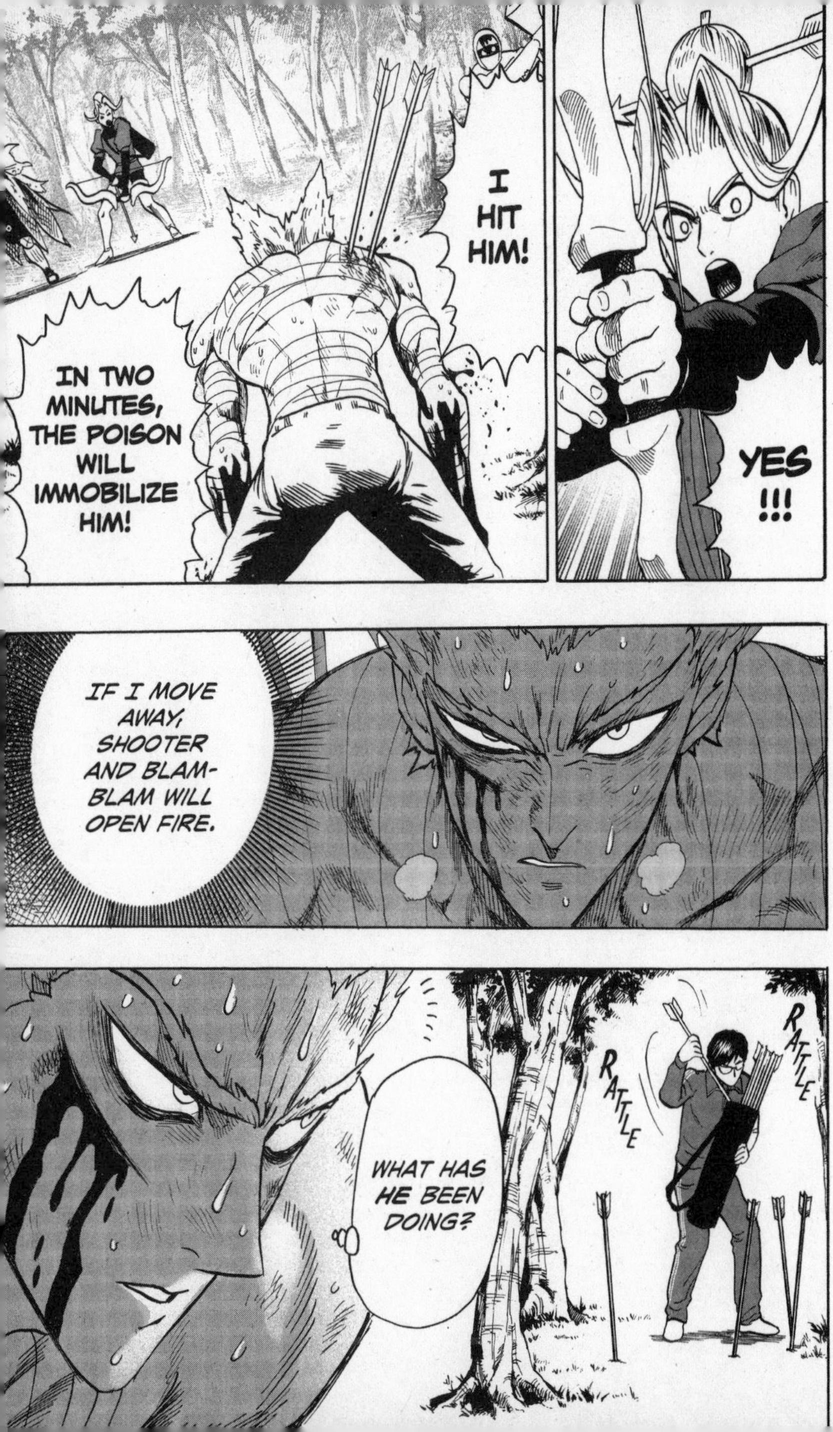
YES!!!
I HIT HIM!
IN TWO MINUTES, THE POISON WILL IMMOBILIZE HIM!
IF I MOVE AWAY, SHOOTER AND BLAM-BLAM WILL OPEN FIRE.
RATTLE
RATTLE
WHAT HAS HE BEEN DOING?

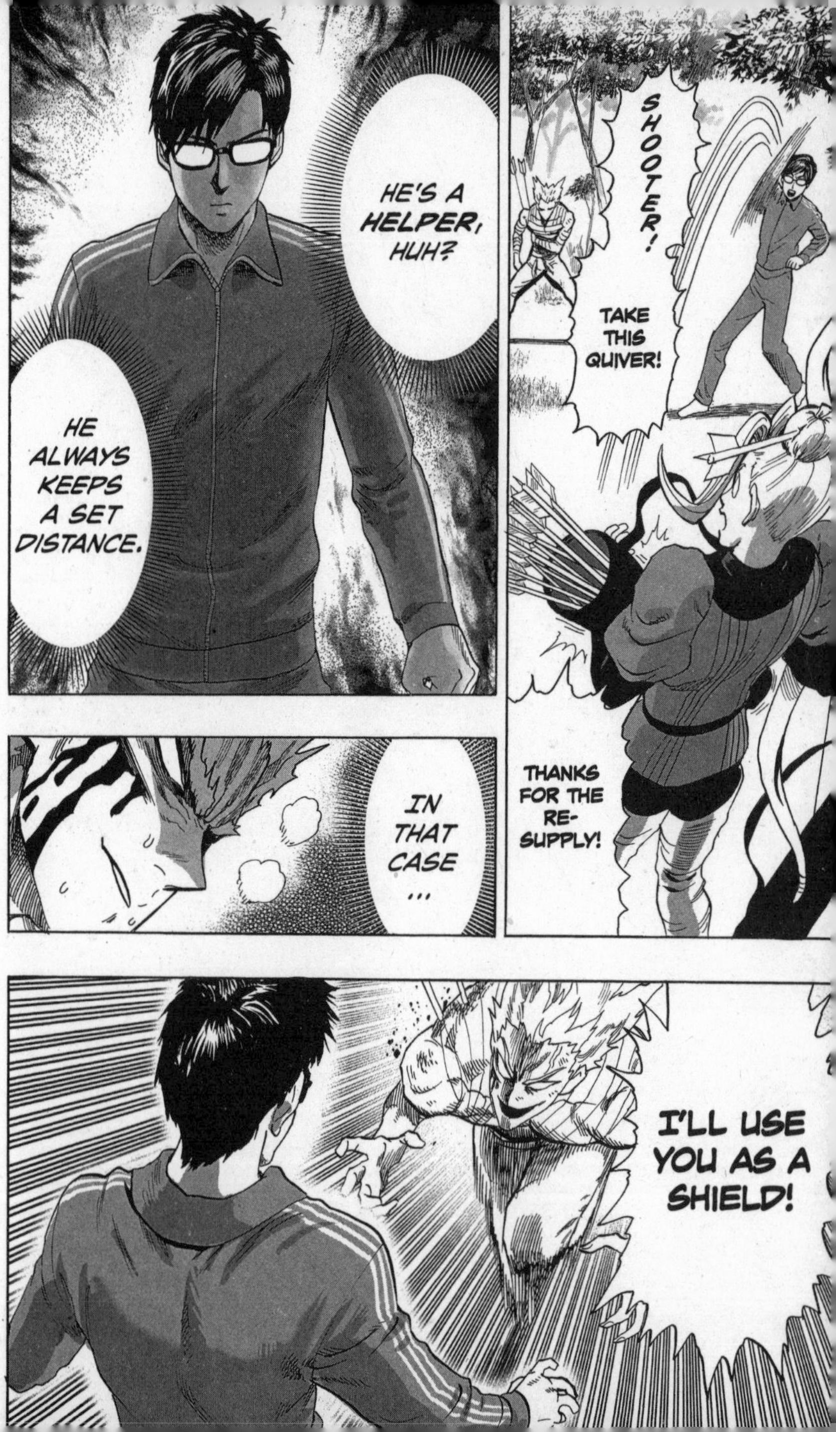
SHOOTER!
TAKE THIS QUIVER!
THANKS FOR THE RE-SUPPLY!
HE'S A HELPER, HUH?
HE ALWAYS KEEPS A SET DISTANCE.
IN THAT CASE...
I'LL USE YOU AS A SHIELD!

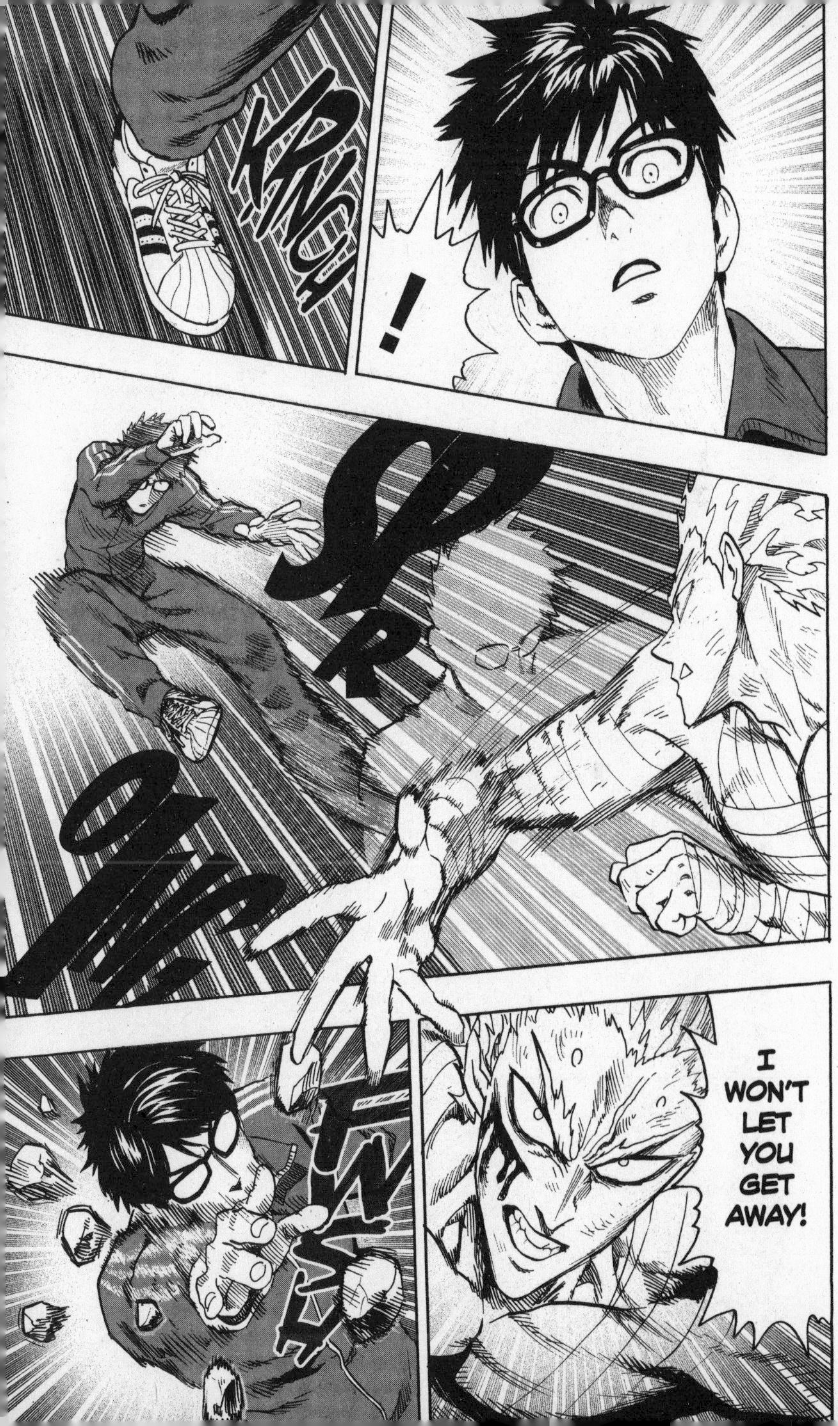
!
KRNCH!
I WON'T LET YOU GET AWAY!

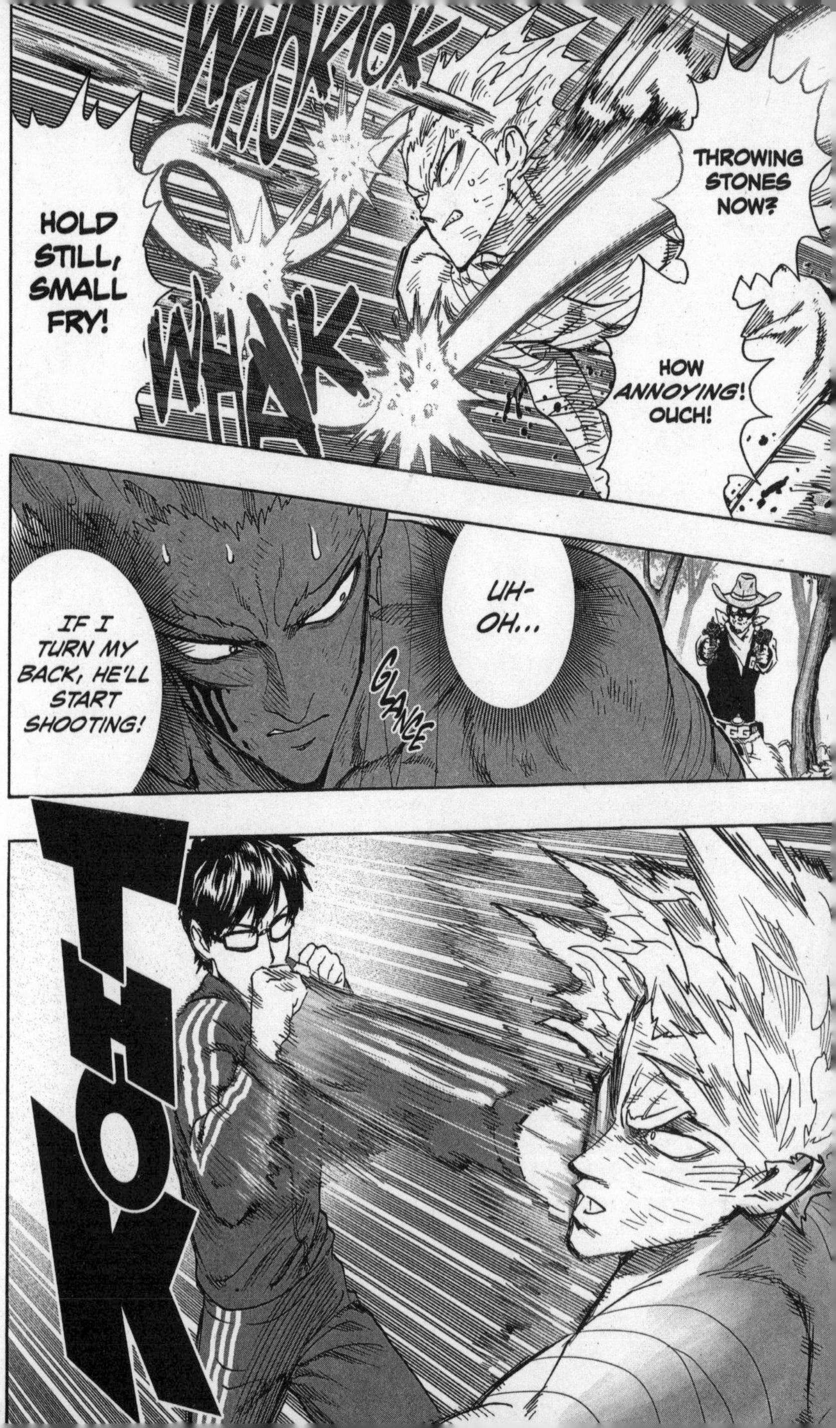
THROWING STONES NOW?
HOW ANNOYING! OUCH!
WHAK
HOLD STILL, SMALL FRY!
UH-OH...
GLANCE
IF I TURN MY BACK, HE'LL START SHOOTING!
THOK

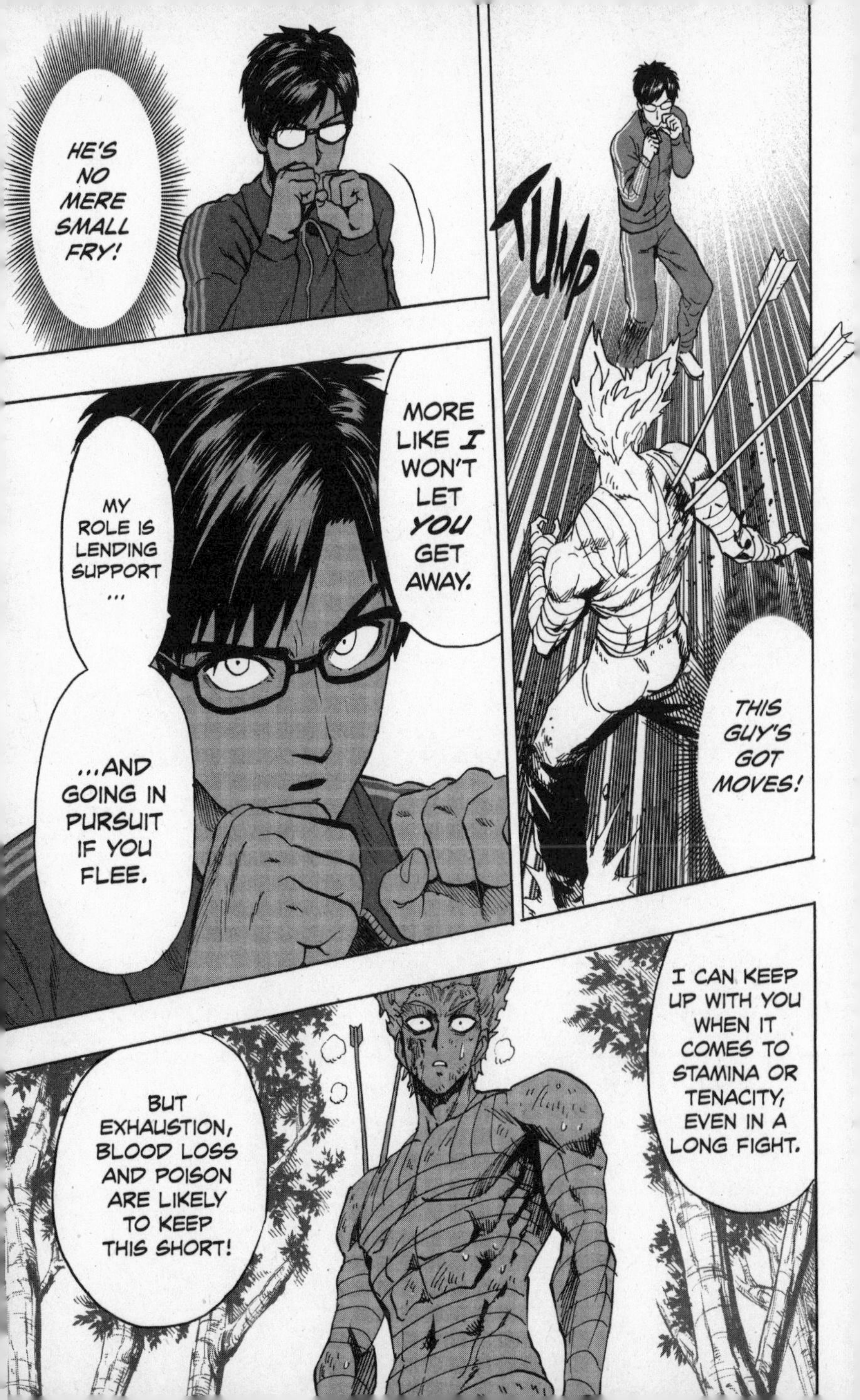
TUMP
THIS GUY'S GOT MOVES!
HE'S NO MERE SMALL FRY!
MORE LIKE I WON'T LET YOU GET AWAY.
MY ROLE IS LENDING SUPPORT...
...AND GOING IN PURSUIT IF YOU FLEE.
I CAN KEEP UP WITH YOU WHEN IT COMES TO STAMINA OR TENACITY, EVEN IN A LONG FIGHT.
BUT EXHAUSTION, BLOOD LOSS AND POISON ARE LIKELY TO KEEP THIS SHORT!

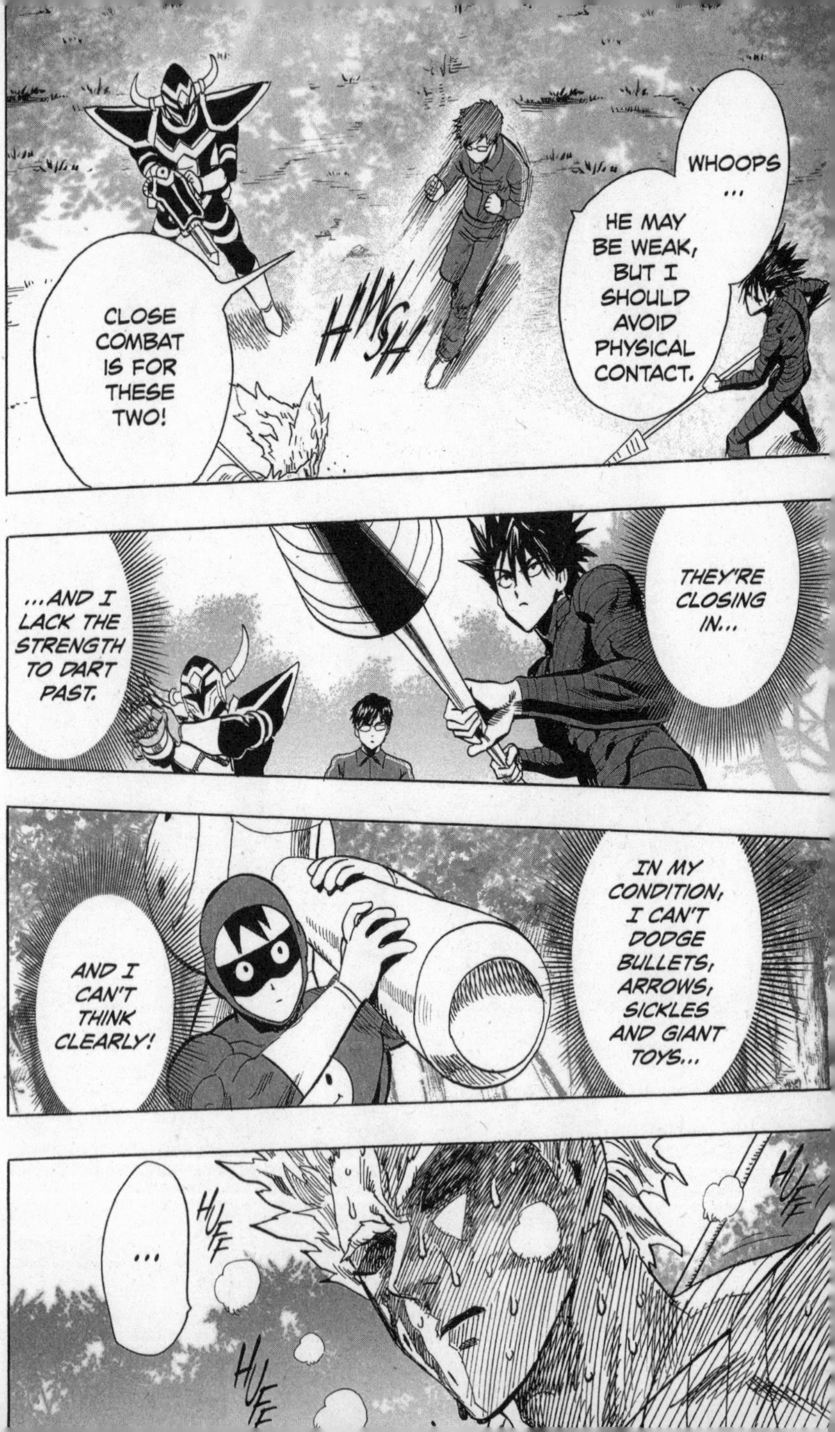
WHOOPS ... HE MAY BE WEAK, BUT I SHOULD AVOID PHYSICAL CONTACT.
HWSH
CLOSE COMBAT IS FOR THESE TWO!
THEY'RE CLOSING IN...
...AND I LACK THE STRENGTH TO DART PAST.
IN MY CONDITION, I CAN'T DODGE BULLETS, ARROWS, SICKLES AND GIANT TOYS...
AND I CAN'T THINK CLEARLY!
HUFF
HUFF
...
HUFF

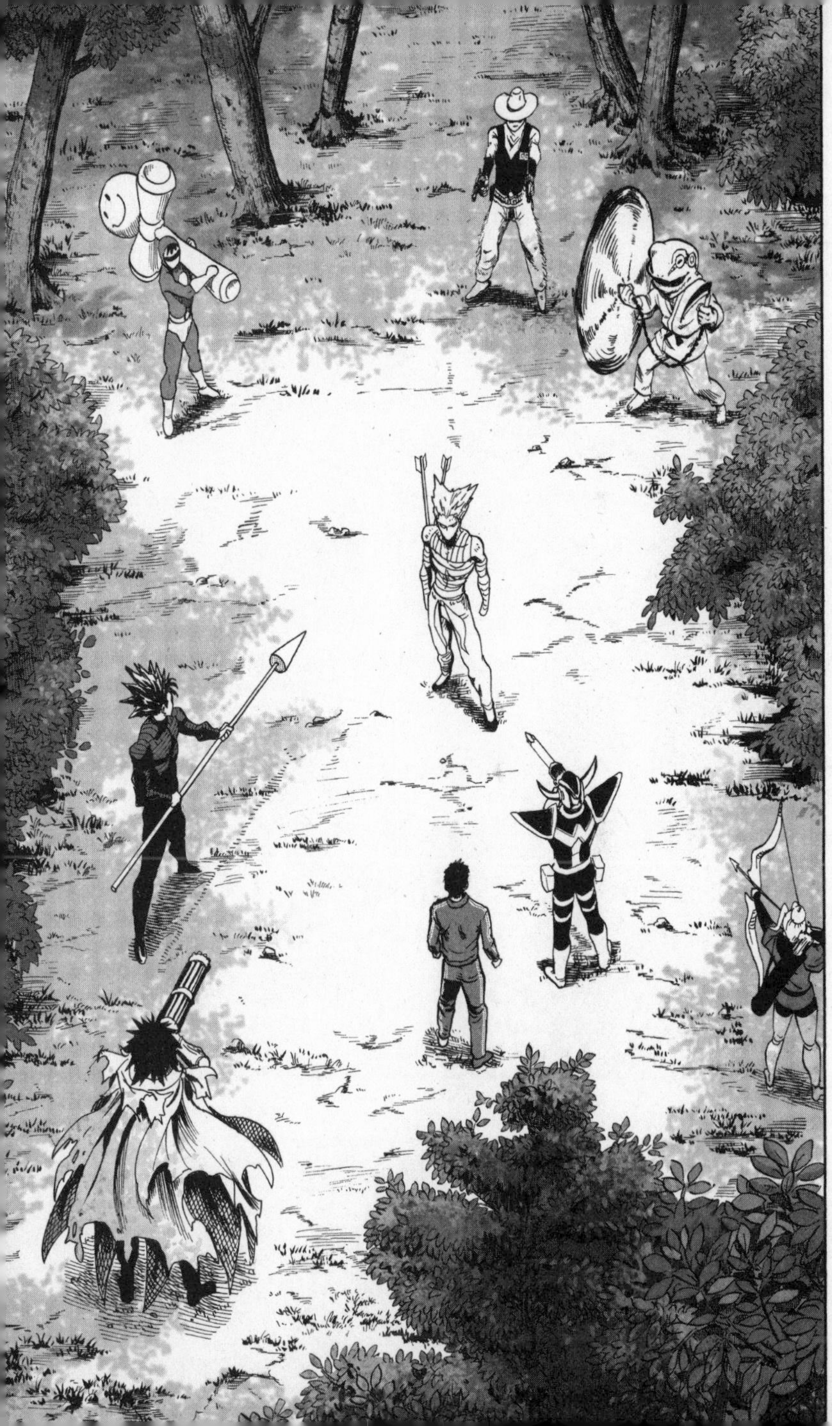

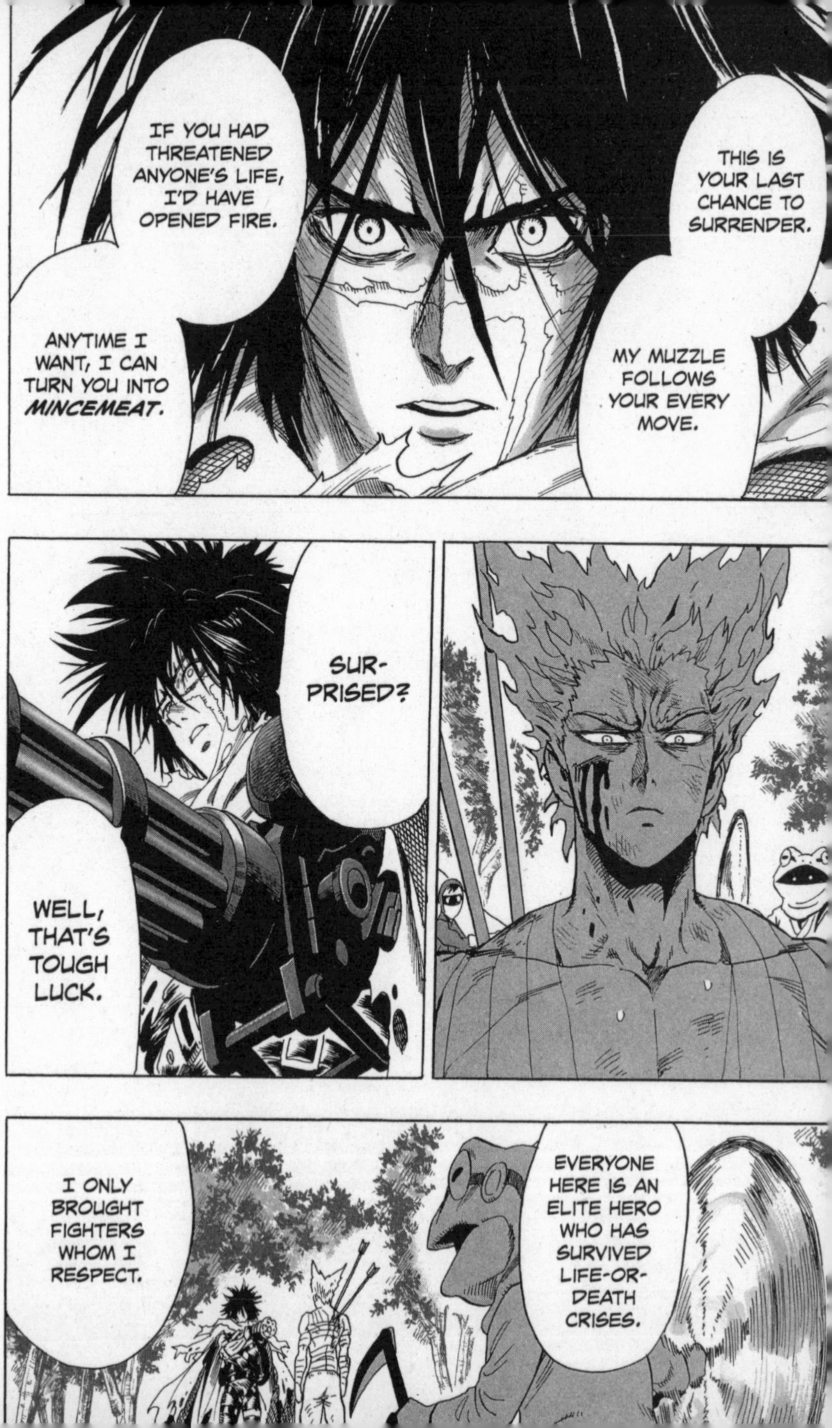
THIS IS YOUR LAST CHANCE TO SURRENDER.
MY MUZZLE FOLLOWS YOUR EVERY MOVE.
IF YOU HAD THREATENED ANYONE'S LIFE, I'D HAVE OPENED FIRE.
ANYTIME I WANT, I CAN TURN YOU INTO *MINCEMEAT*.
SUR-PRISED?
WELL, THAT'S TOUGH LUCK.
EVERYONE HERE IS AN ELITE HERO WHO HAS SURVIVED LIFE-OR-DEATH CRISES.
I ONLY BROUGHT FIGHTERS WHOM I RESPECT.

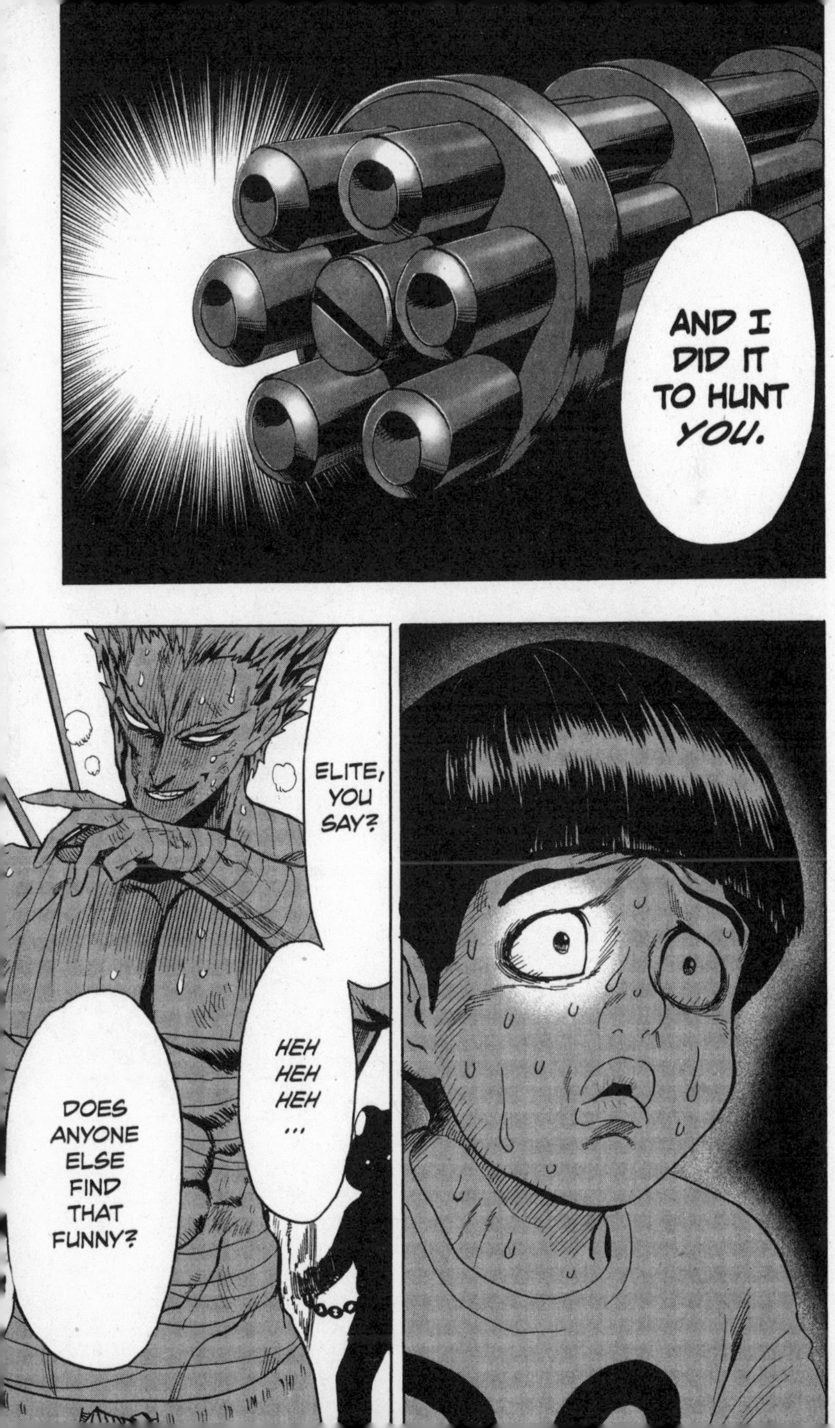
AND I DID IT TO HUNT *YOU.*
ELITE, YOU SAY?
HEH HEH HEH ...
DOES ANYONE ELSE FIND THAT FUNNY?

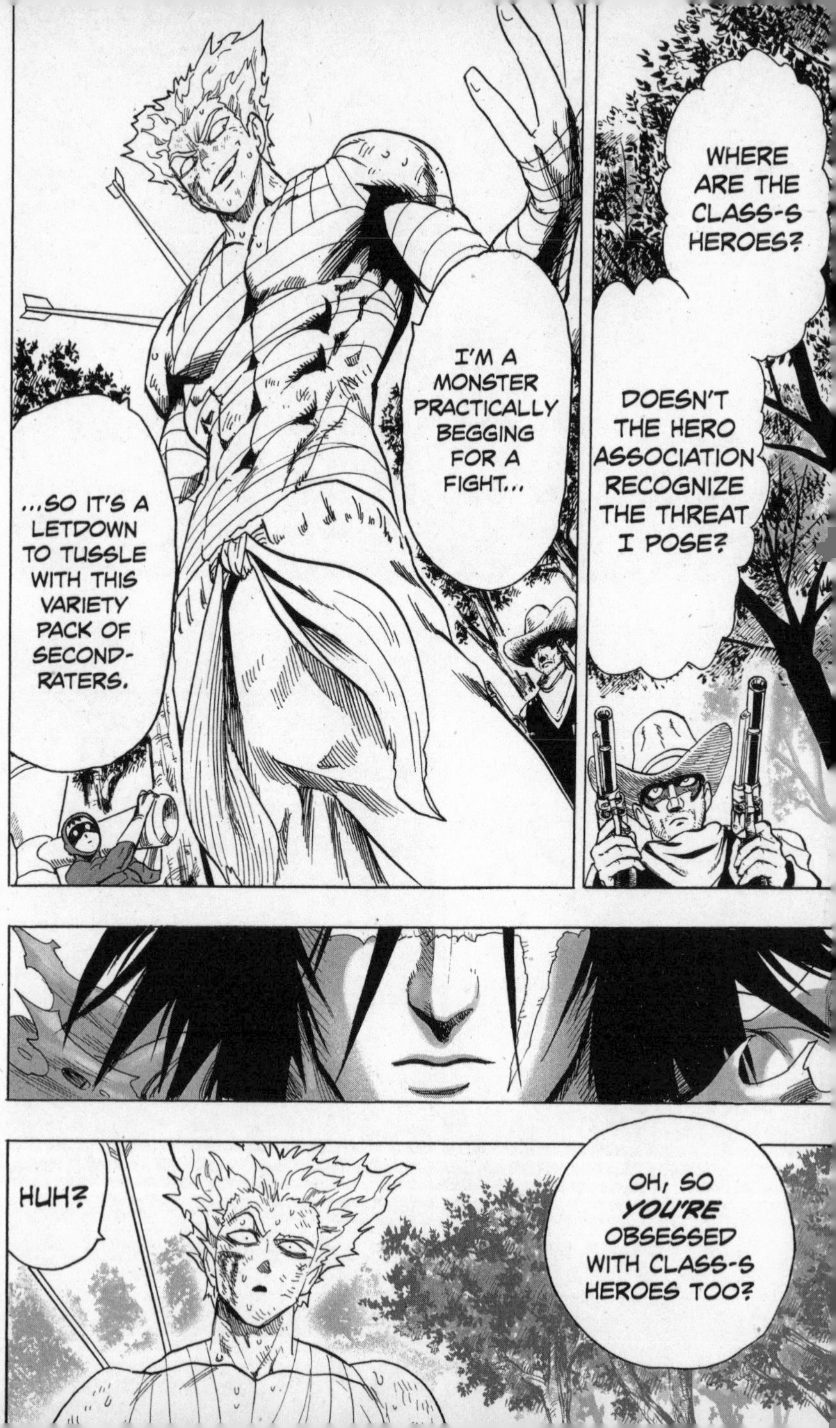
WHERE ARE THE CLASS-S HEROES?
DOESN'T THE HERO ASSOCIATION RECOGNIZE THE THREAT I POSE?
I'M A MONSTER PRACTICALLY BEGGING FOR A FIGHT...
...SO IT'S A LETDOWN TO TUSSLE WITH THIS VARIETY PACK OF SECOND-RATERS.
OH, SO *YOU'RE* OBSESSED WITH CLASS-S HEROES TOO?
HUH?

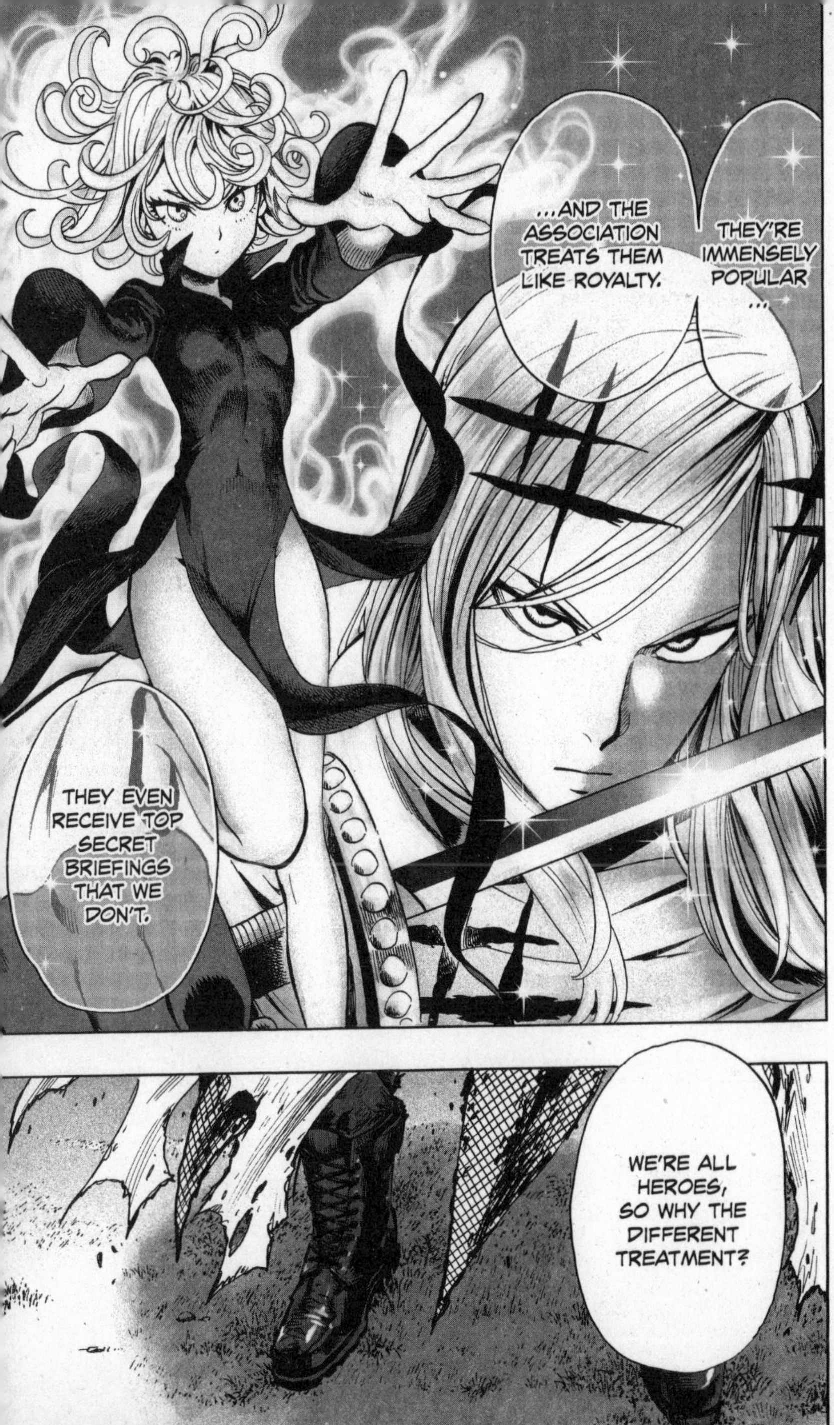
THEY'RE IMMENSELY POPULAR ...
...AND THE ASSOCIATION TREATS THEM LIKE ROYALTY.
THEY EVEN RECEIVE TOP SECRET BRIEFINGS THAT WE DON'T.
WE'RE ALL HEROES, SO WHY THE DIFFERENT TREATMENT?

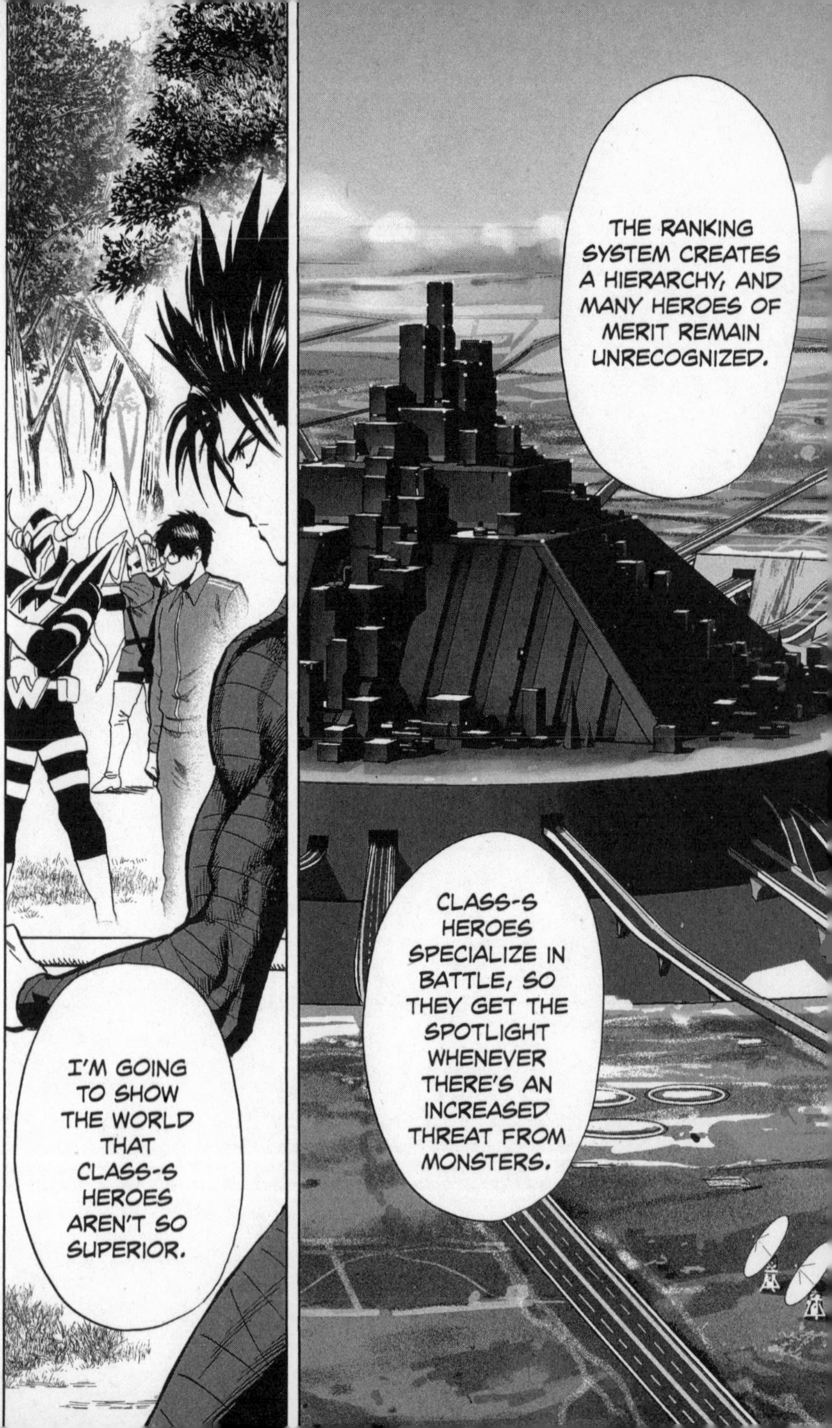
THE RANKING SYSTEM CREATES A HIERARCHY, AND MANY HEROES OF MERIT REMAIN UNRECOGNIZED.
CLASS-S HEROES SPECIALIZE IN BATTLE, SO THEY GET THE SPOTLIGHT WHENEVER THERE'S AN INCREASED THREAT FROM MONSTERS.
I'M GOING TO SHOW THE WORLD THAT CLASS-S HEROES AREN'T SO SUPERIOR.

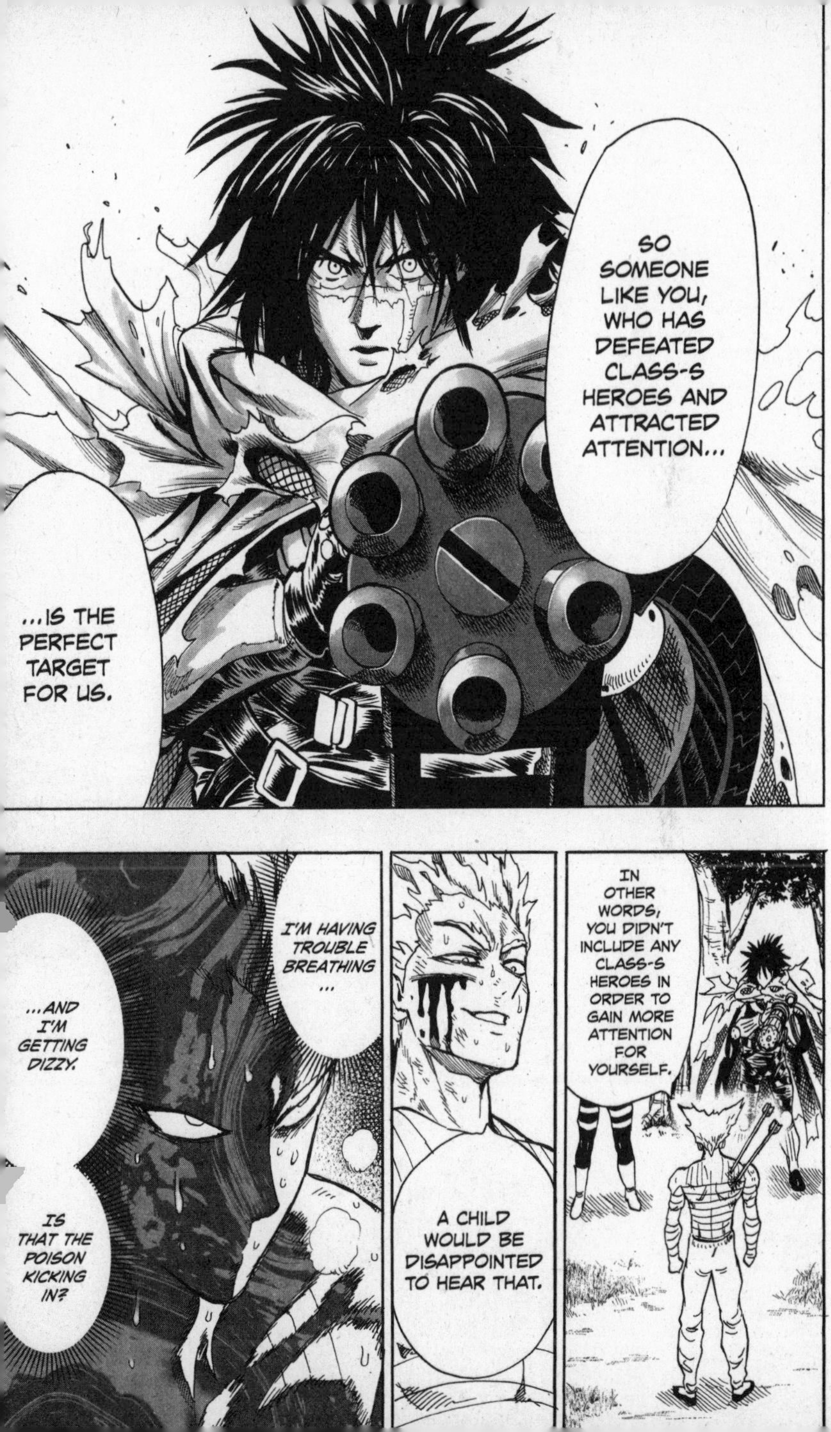
SO SOMEONE LIKE YOU, WHO HAS DEFEATED CLASS-S HEROES AND ATTRACTED ATTENTION...
...IS THE PERFECT TARGET FOR US.
IN OTHER WORDS, YOU DIDN'T INCLUDE ANY CLASS-S HEROES IN ORDER TO GAIN MORE ATTENTION FOR YOURSELF.
A CHILD WOULD BE DISAPPOINTED TO HEAR THAT.
I'M HAVING TROUBLE BREATHING...
...AND I'M GETTING DIZZY.
IS THAT THE POISON KICKING IN?

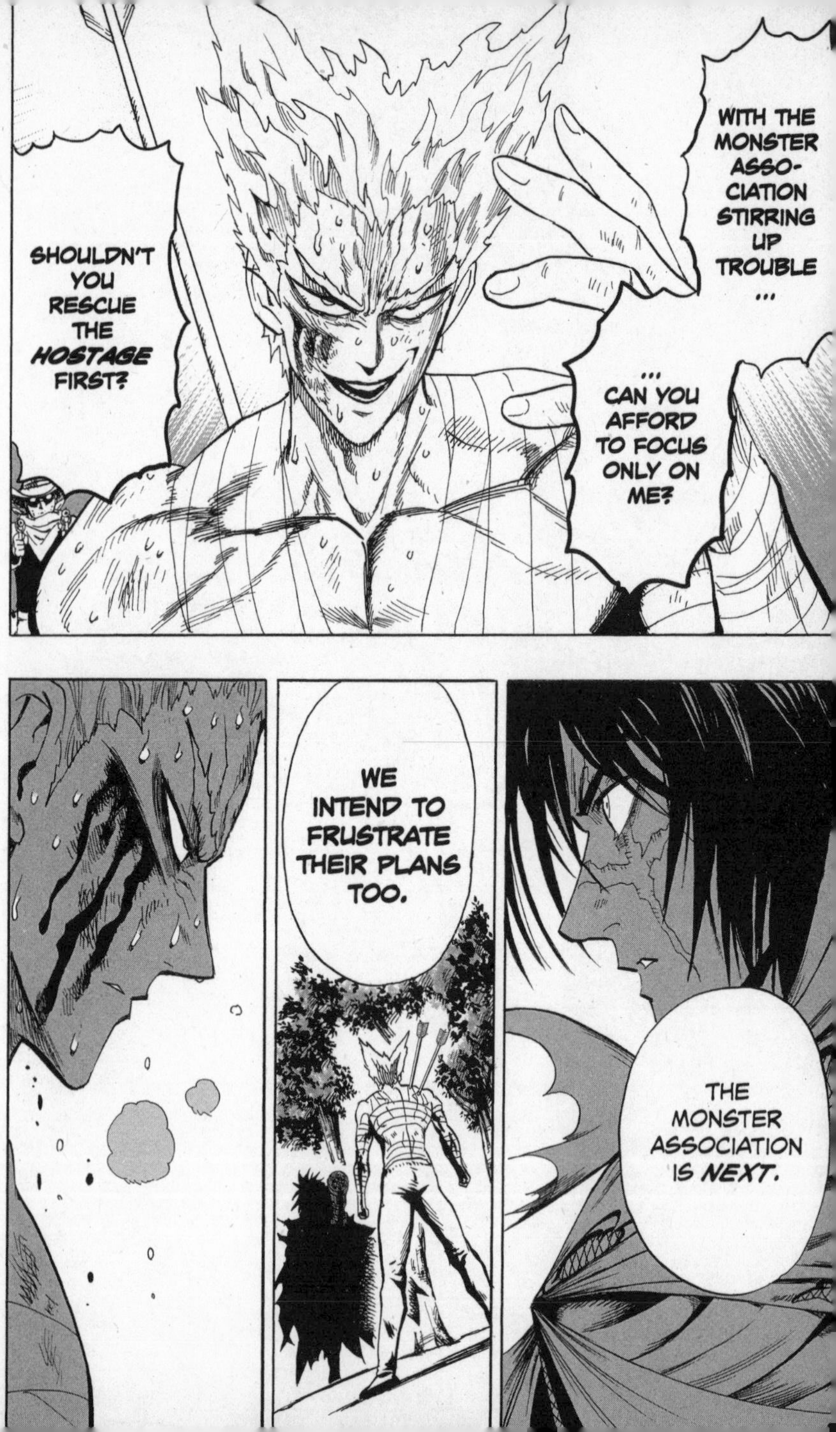
WITH THE MONSTER ASSO-CIATION STIRRING UP TROUBLE ...
... CAN YOU AFFORD TO FOCUS ONLY ON ME?
SHOULDN'T YOU RESCUE THE *HOSTAGE* FIRST?
THE MONSTER ASSOCIATION IS *NEXT*.
WE INTEND TO FRUSTRATE THEIR PLANS TOO.

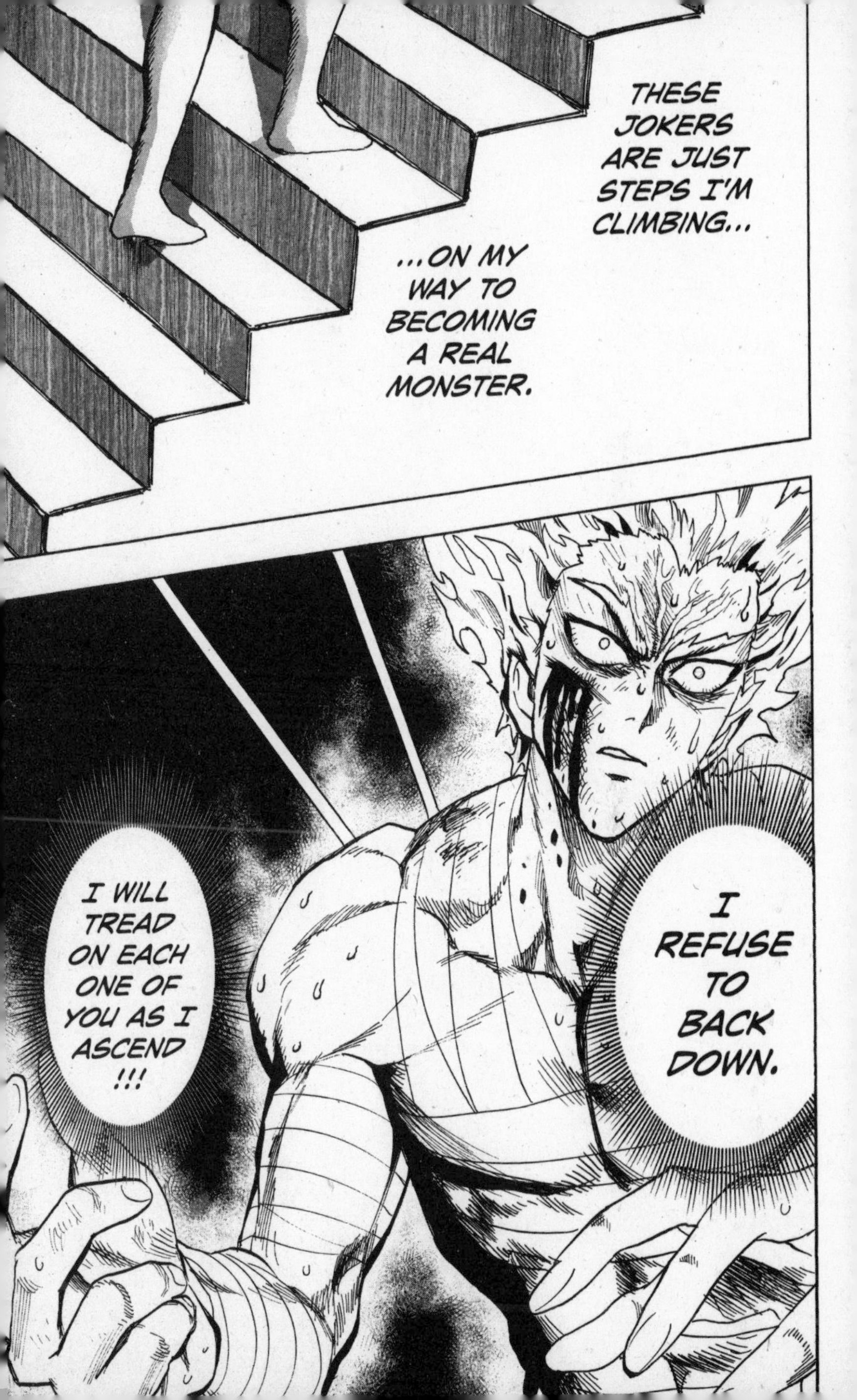
THESE JOKERS ARE JUST STEPS I'M CLIMBING...
...ON MY WAY TO BECOMING A REAL MONSTER.
I REFUSE TO BACK DOWN.
I WILL TREAD ON EACH ONE OF YOU AS I ASCEND !!!

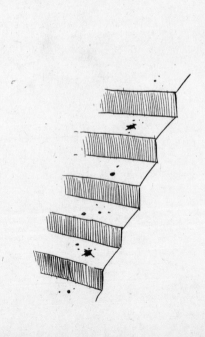

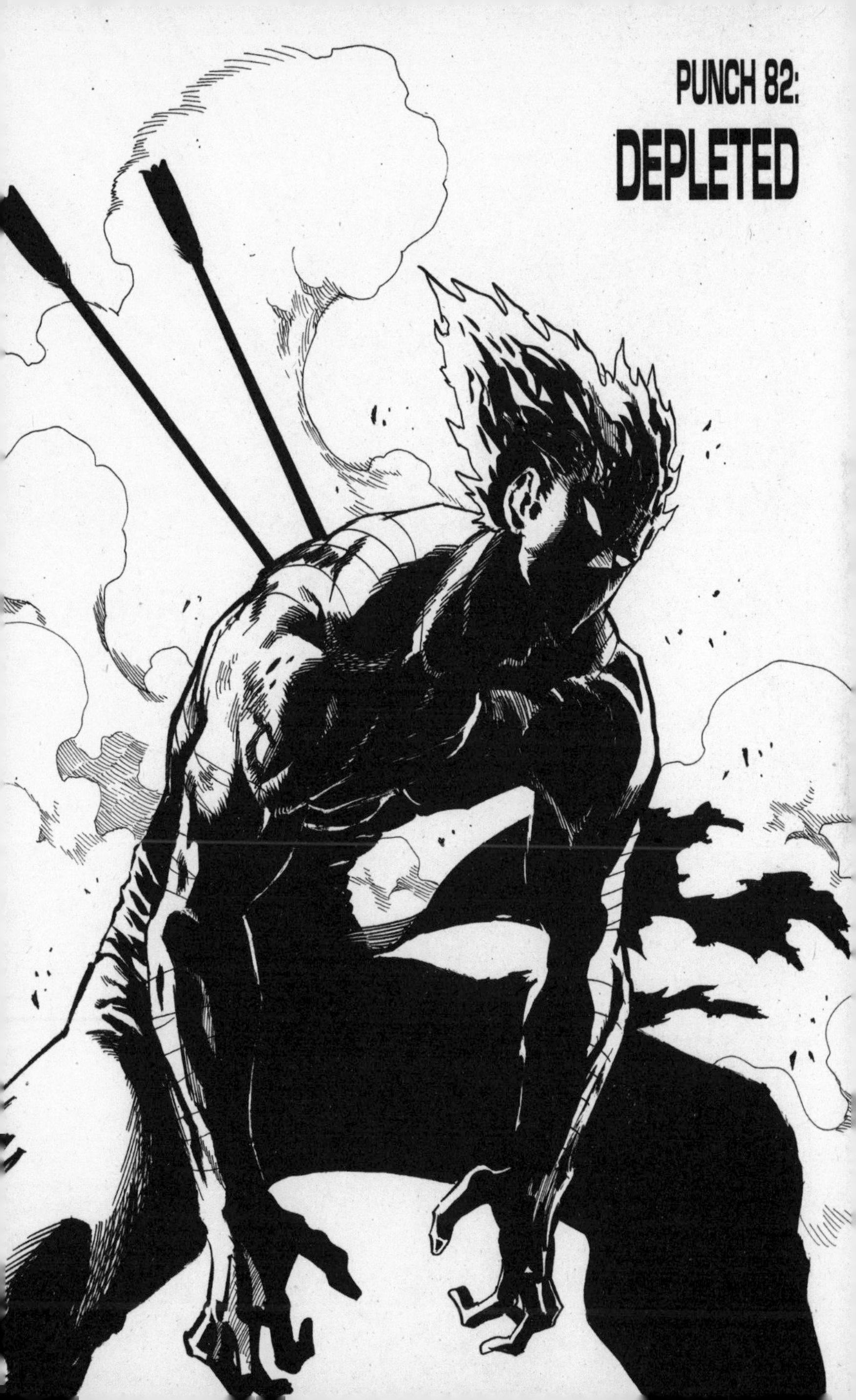
PUNCH 82:
DEPLETED

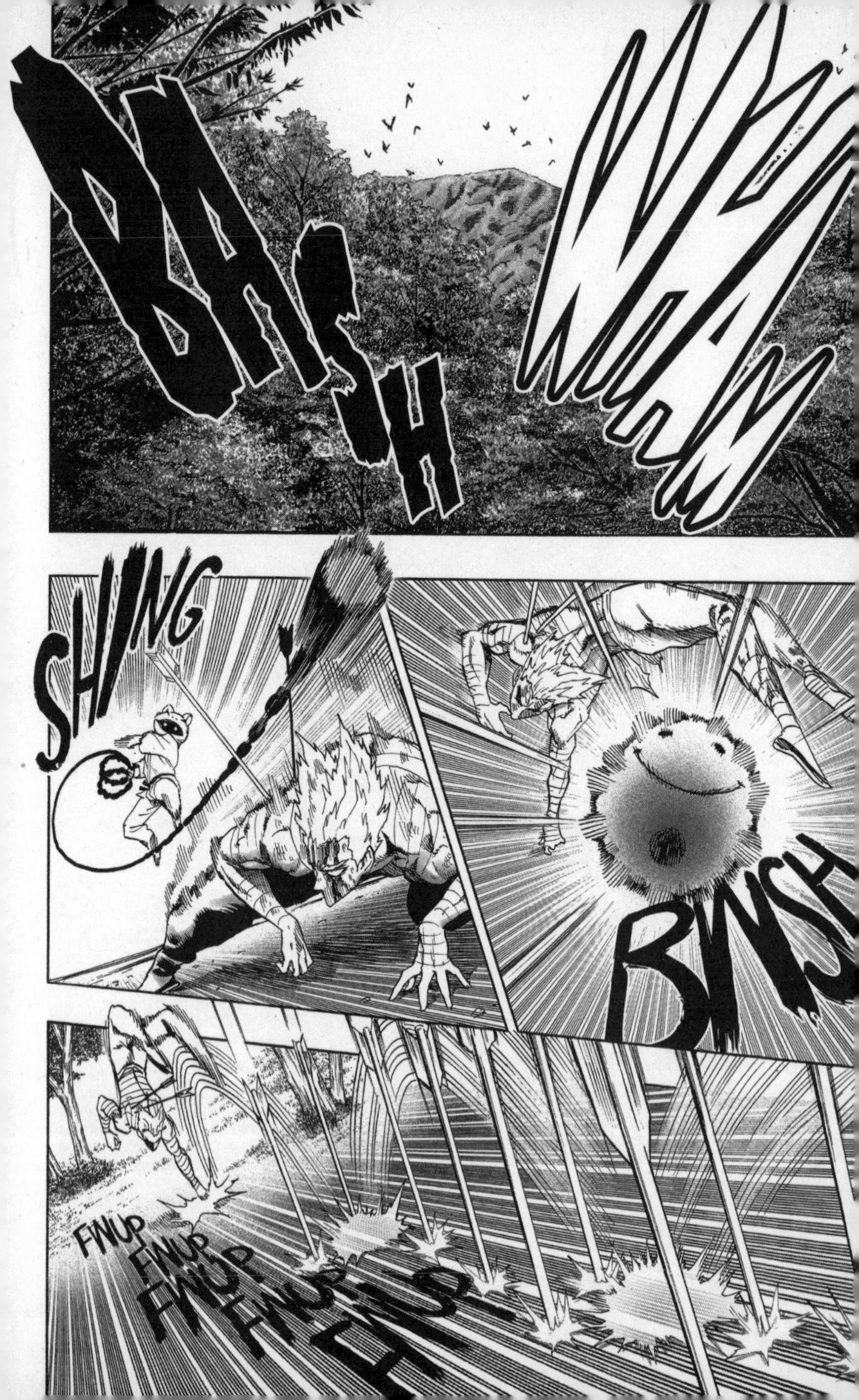
SHING
FWUP
FWUP
FWUP

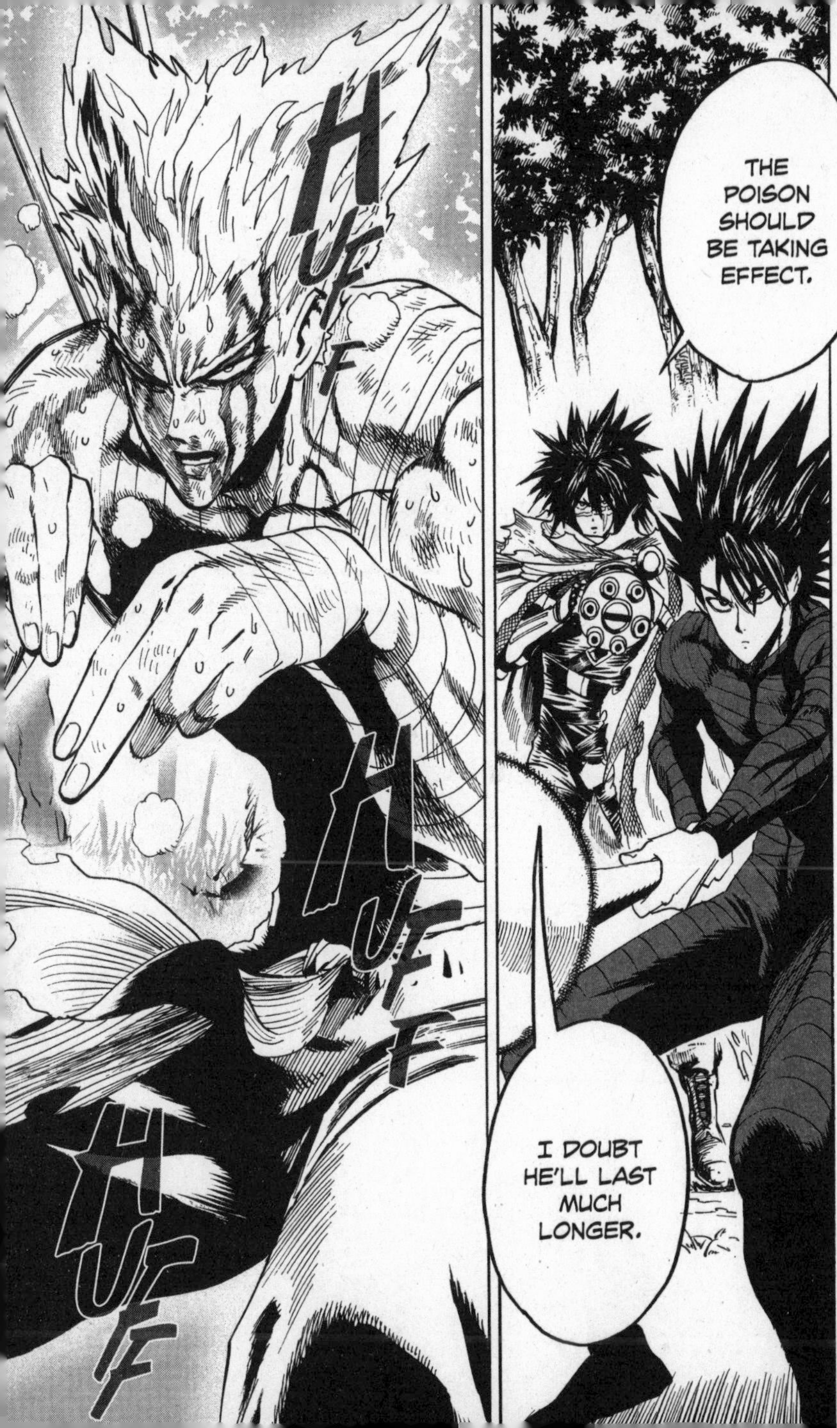
THE POISON SHOULD BE TAKING EFFECT.
I DOUBT HE'LL LAST MUCH LONGER.
HUFF
HUFF
HUFF

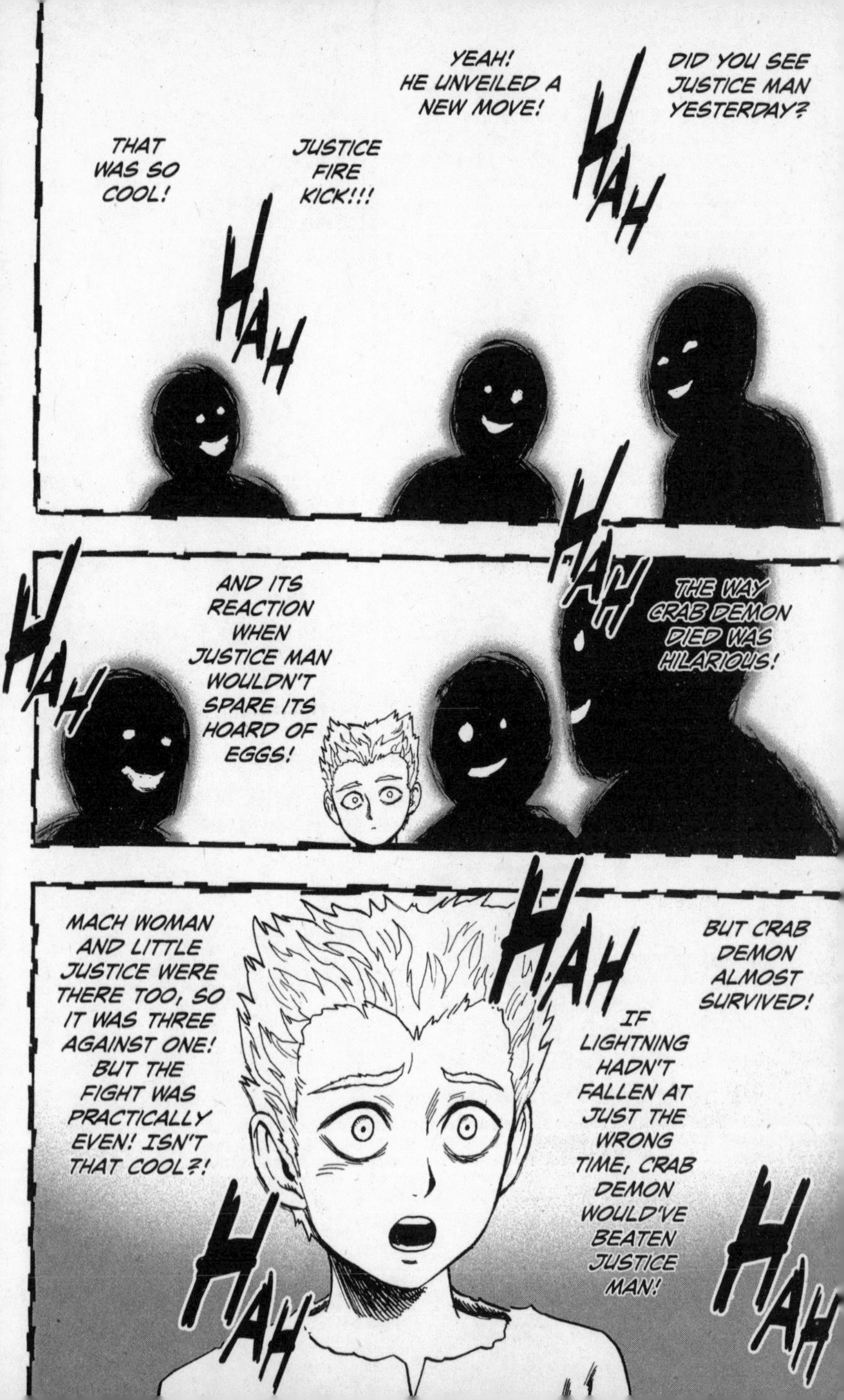
DID YOU SEE JUSTICE MAN YESTERDAY?
HAH
YEAH! HE UNVEILED A NEW MOVE!
JUSTICE FIRE KICK!!!
THAT WAS SO COOL!
HAH
HAH
THE WAY CRAB DEMON DIED WAS HILARIOUS!
AND ITS REACTION WHEN JUSTICE MAN WOULDN'T SPARE ITS HOARD OF EGGS!
HAH
BUT CRAB DEMON ALMOST SURVIVED!
HAH
IF LIGHTNING HADN'T FALLEN AT JUST THE WRONG TIME, CRAB DEMON WOULD'VE BEATEN JUSTICE MAN!
MACH WOMAN AND LITTLE JUSTICE WERE THERE TOO, SO IT WAS THREE AGAINST ONE! BUT THE FIGHT WAS PRACTICALLY EVEN! ISN'T THAT COOL?!
HAH
HAH

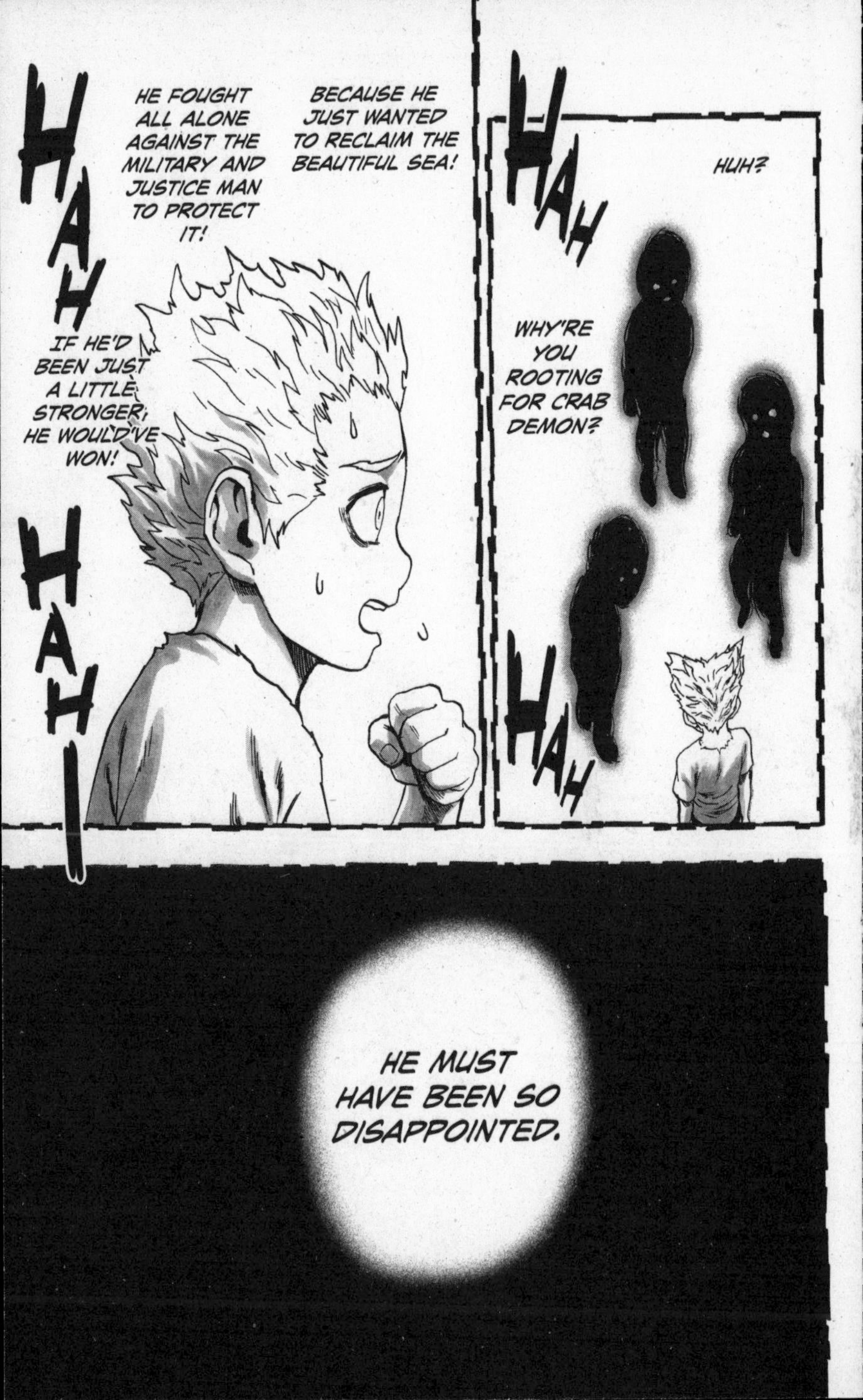
HAH HAH
HUH?
WHY'RE YOU ROOTING FOR CRAB DEMON?
HAH HAH
BECAUSE HE JUST WANTED TO RECLAIM THE BEAUTIFUL SEA!
HE FOUGHT ALL ALONE AGAINST THE MILITARY AND JUSTICE MAN TO PROTECT IT!
HAH HAH
IF HE'D BEEN JUST A LITTLE STRONGER, HE WOULD'VE WON!
HAH HAH
HE MUST HAVE BEEN SO DISAPPOINTED.

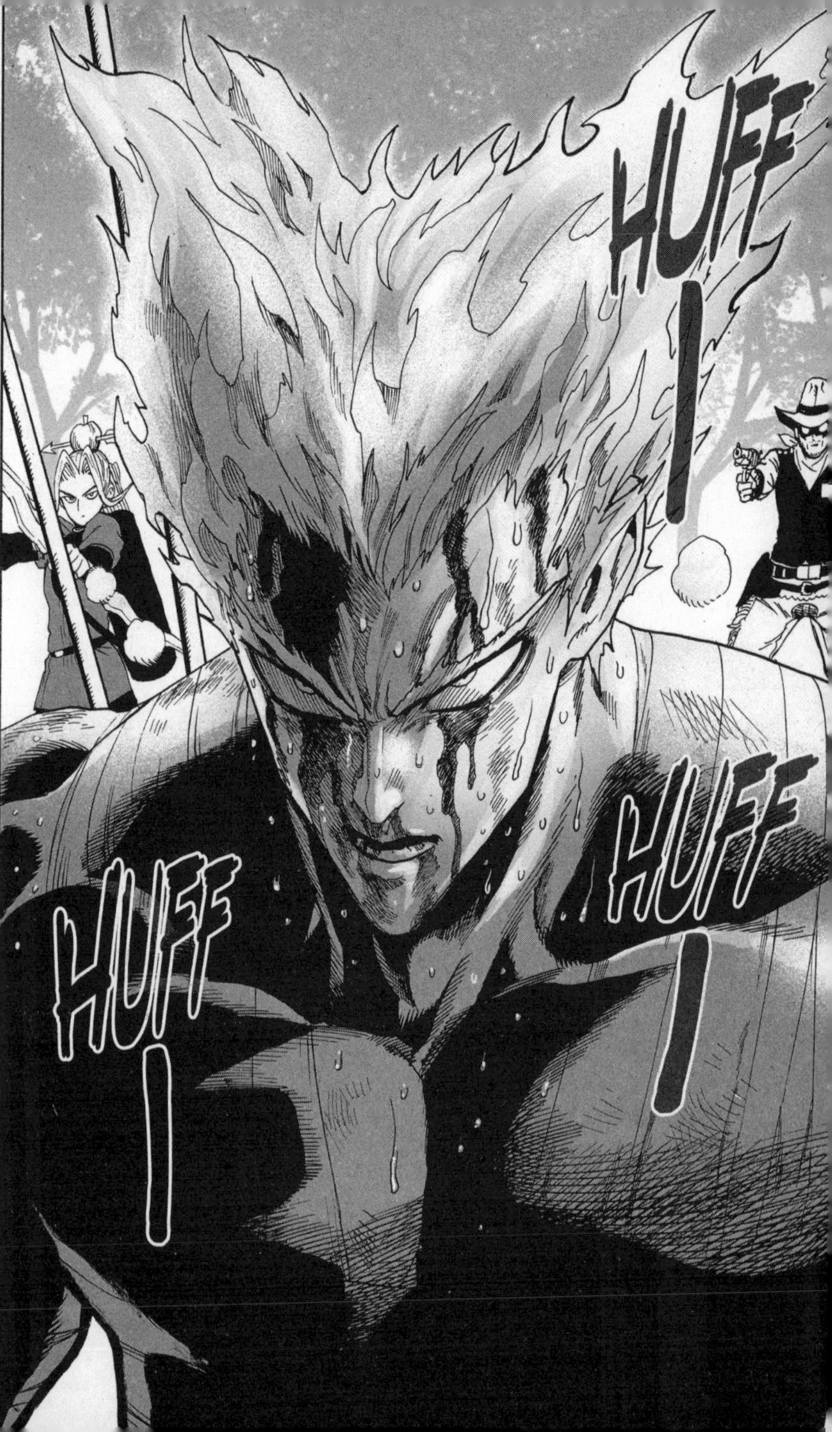
HUFF
HUFF
HUFF

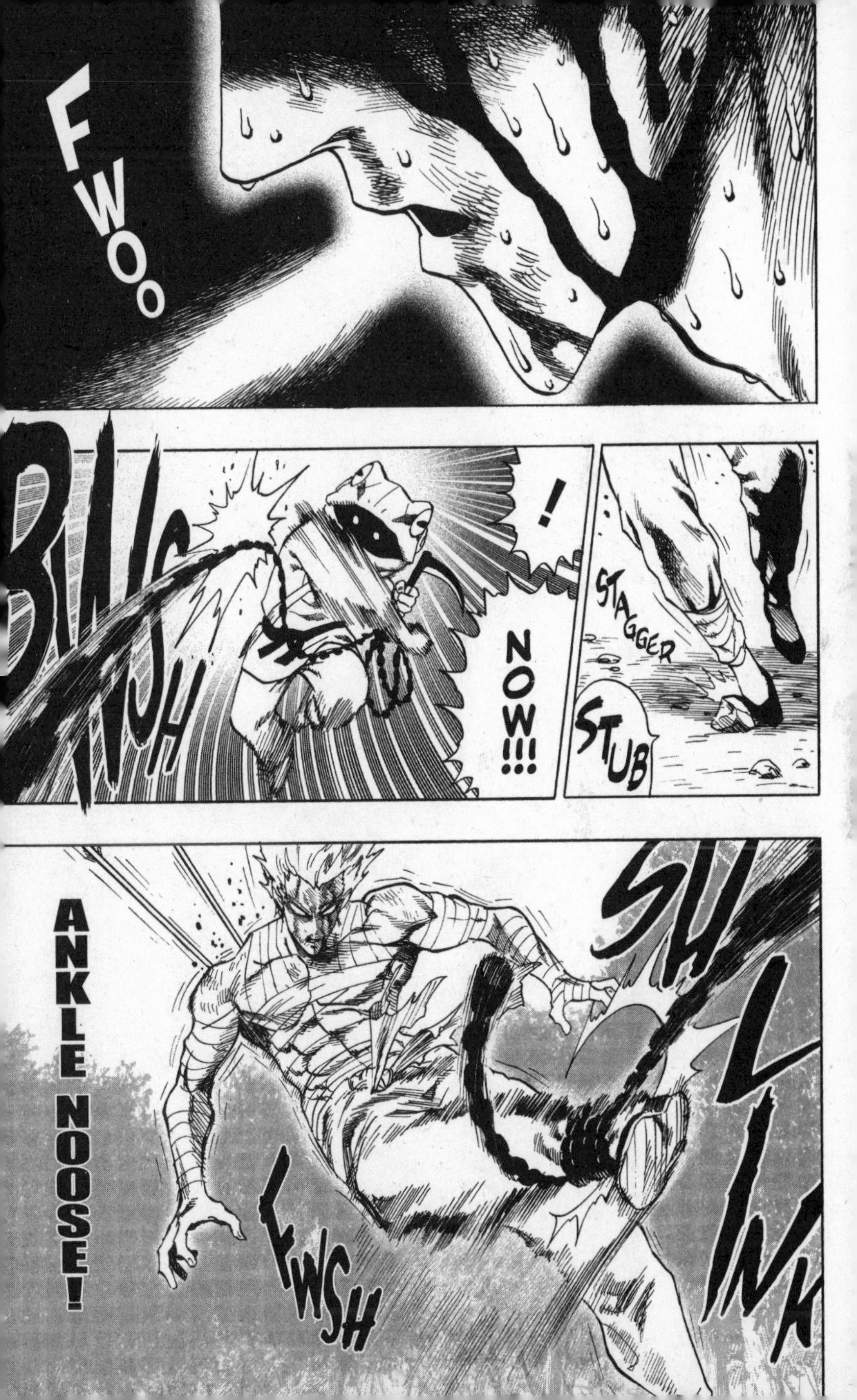
FWOO
STAGGER
STUB
!
NOW!!!
ANKLE NOOSE!
FWSH

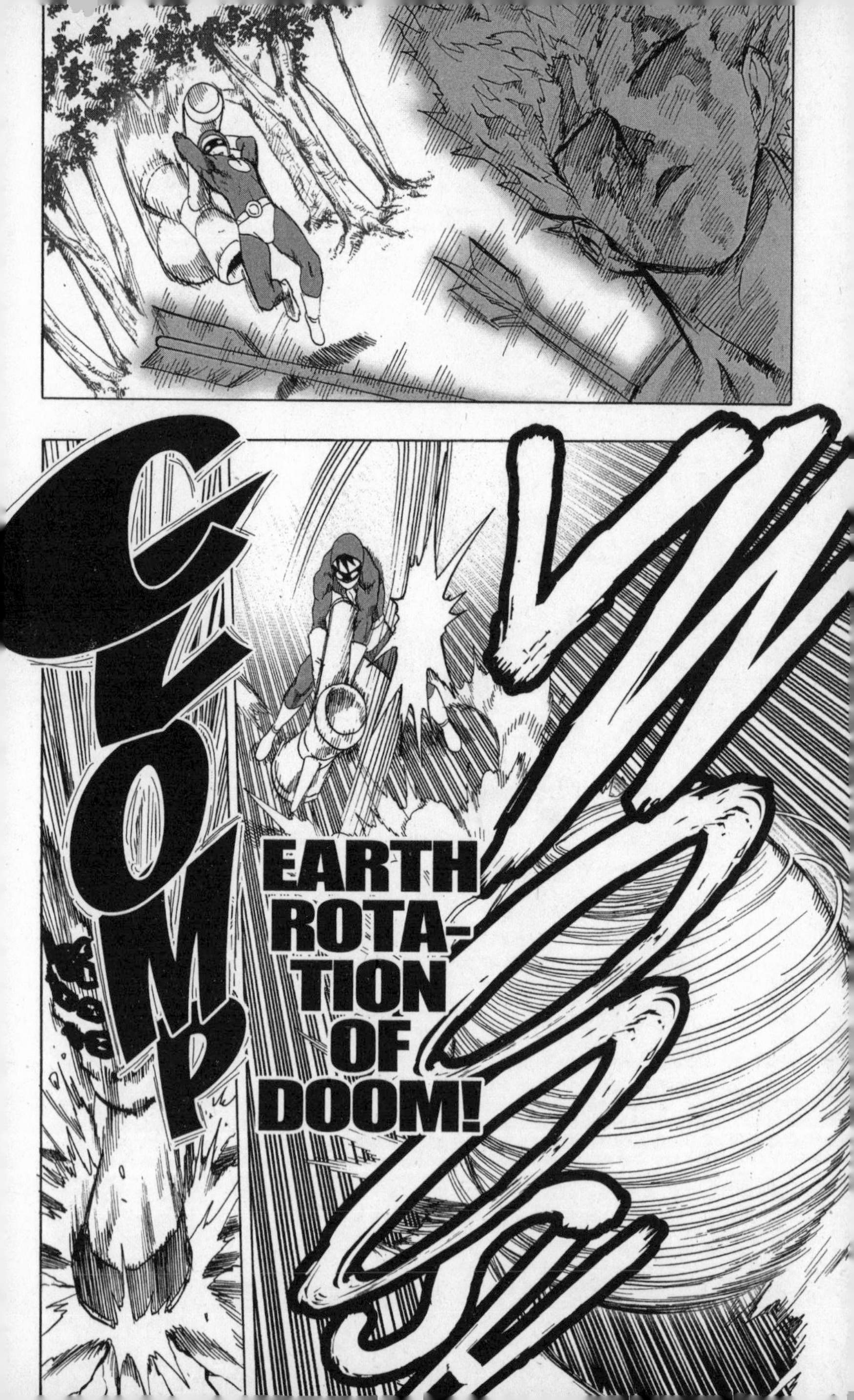
CHOMP
EARTH ROTATION OF DOOM!

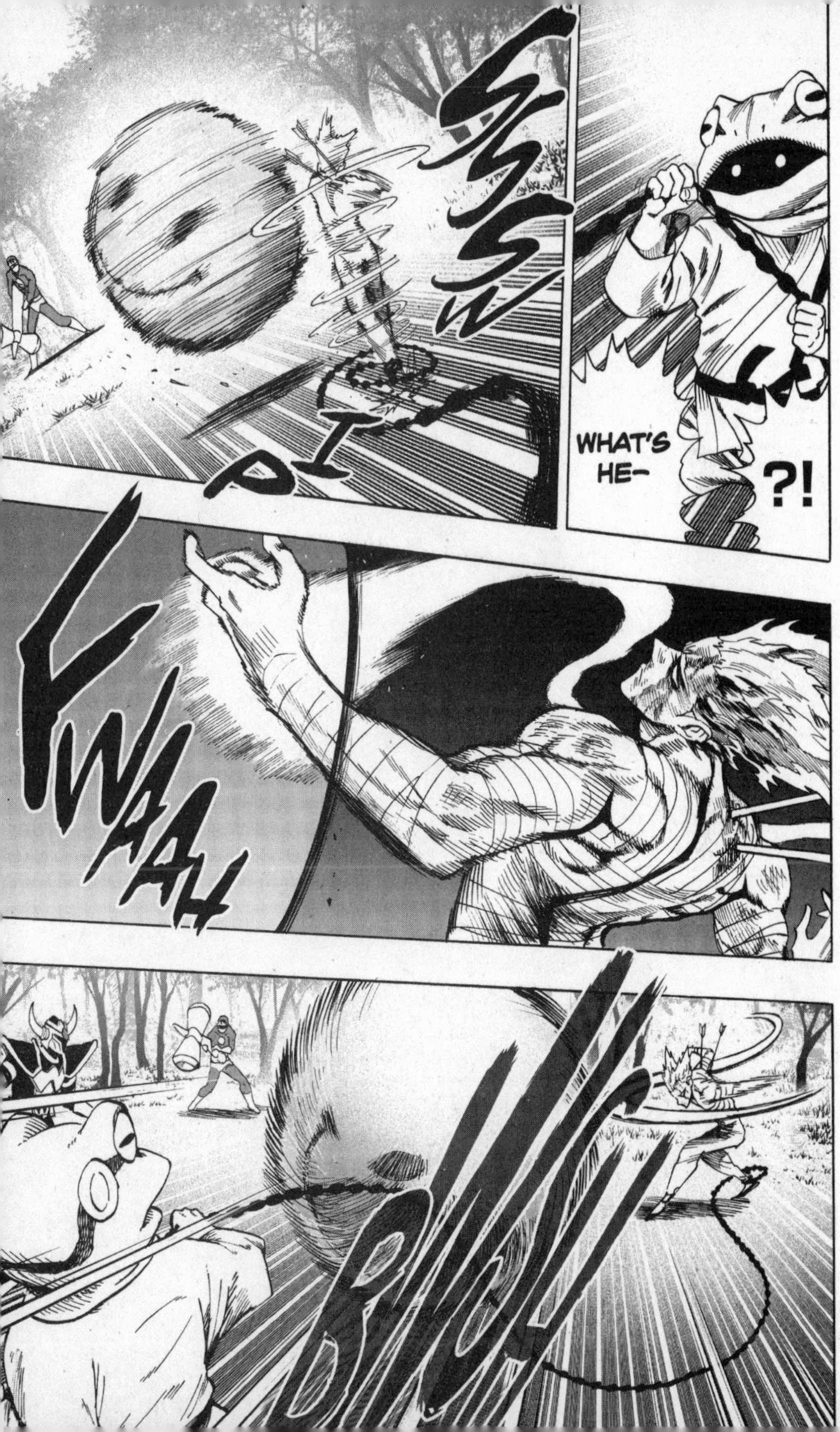
WHAT'S HE-
?!

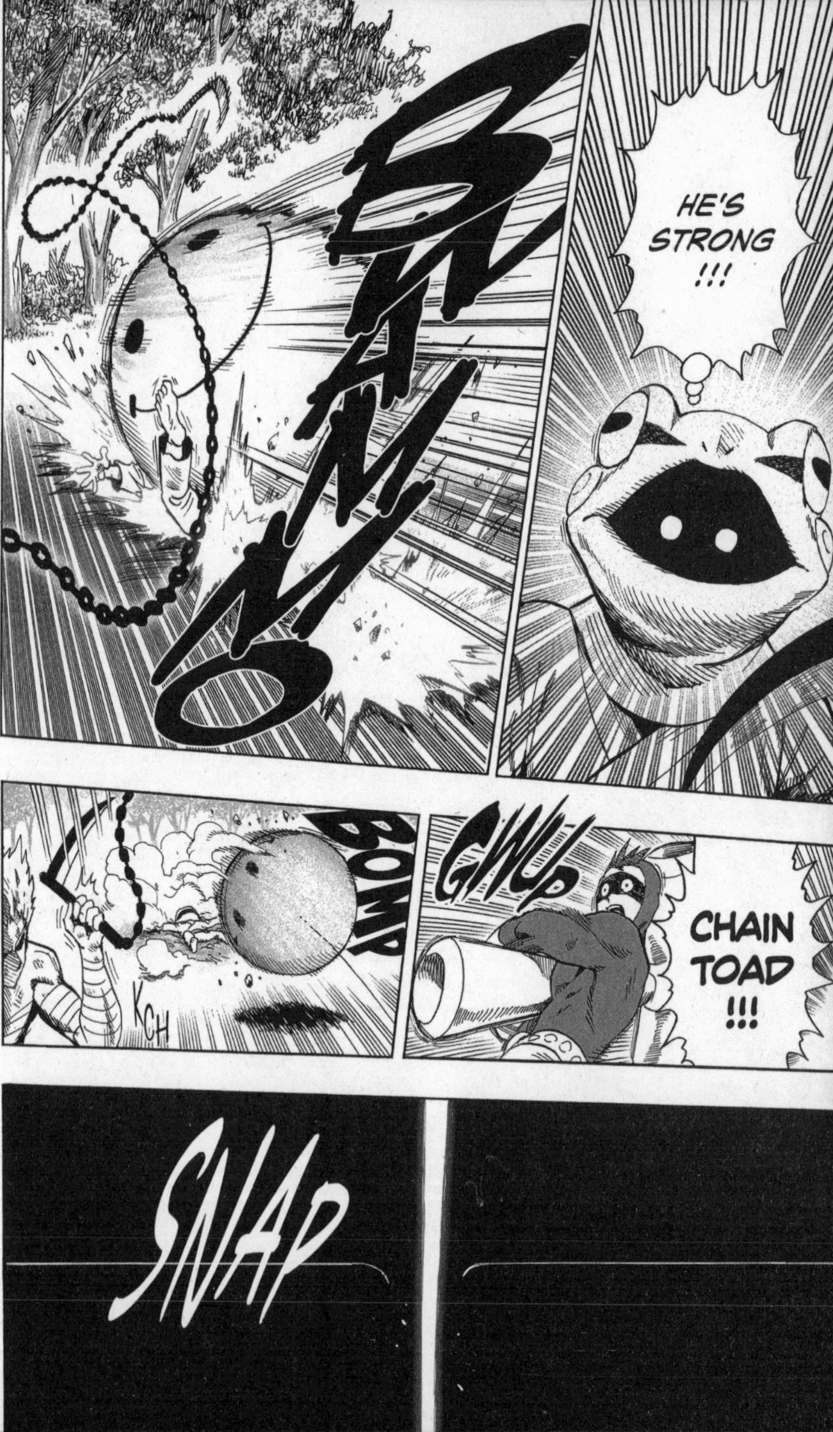
HE'S STRONG !!!
GWUP
CHAIN TOAD !!!
BOMP
KCH
SNAP

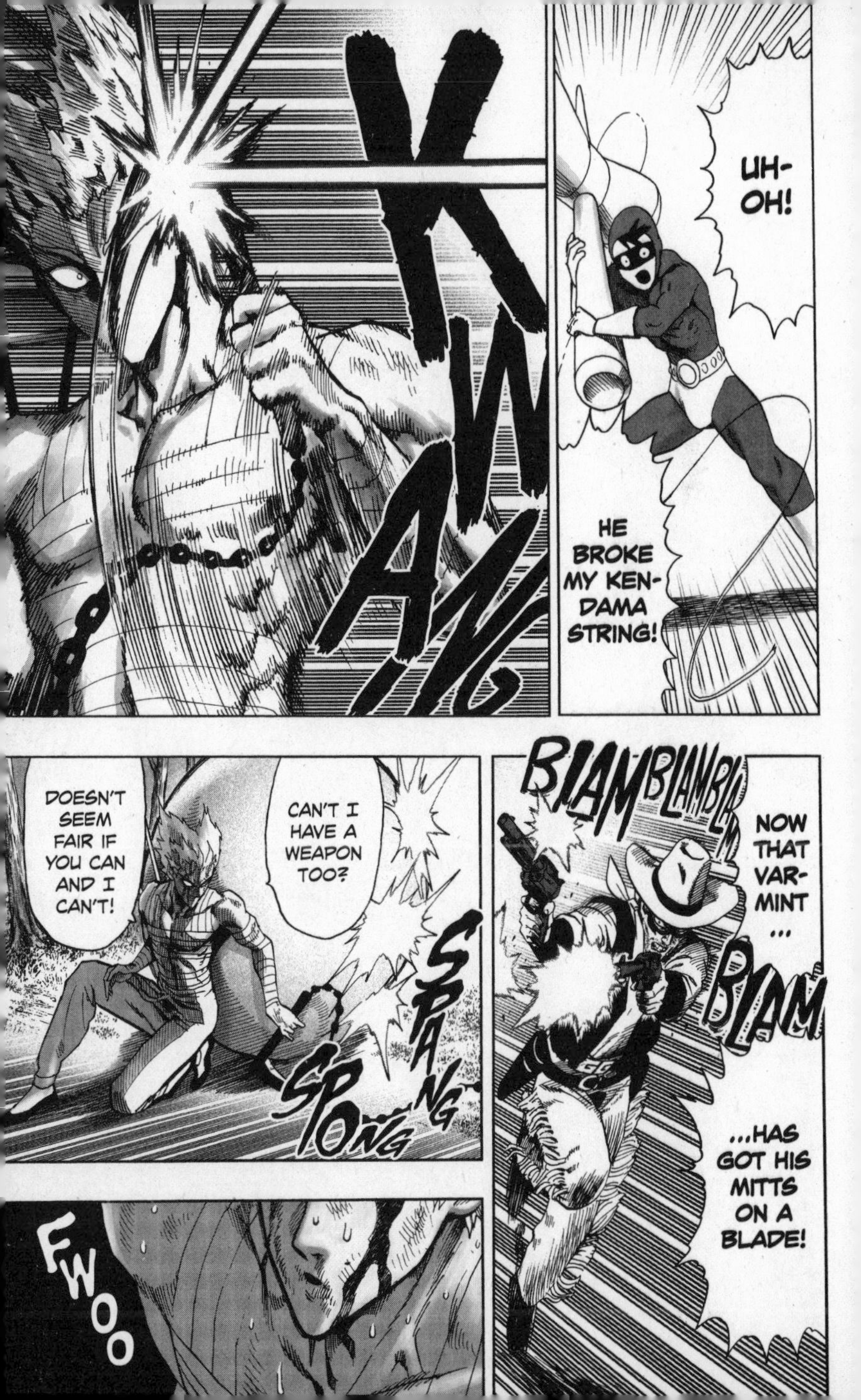
UH-OH!
HE BROKE MY KEN-DAMA STRING!
XWANG
BLAMBLAMBLAM
NOW THAT VARMINT...
BLAM
...HAS GOT HIS MITTS ON A BLADE!
CAN'T I HAVE A WEAPON TOO?
DOESN'T SEEM FAIR IF YOU CAN AND I CAN'T!
SPANG
SPONG
FWOO

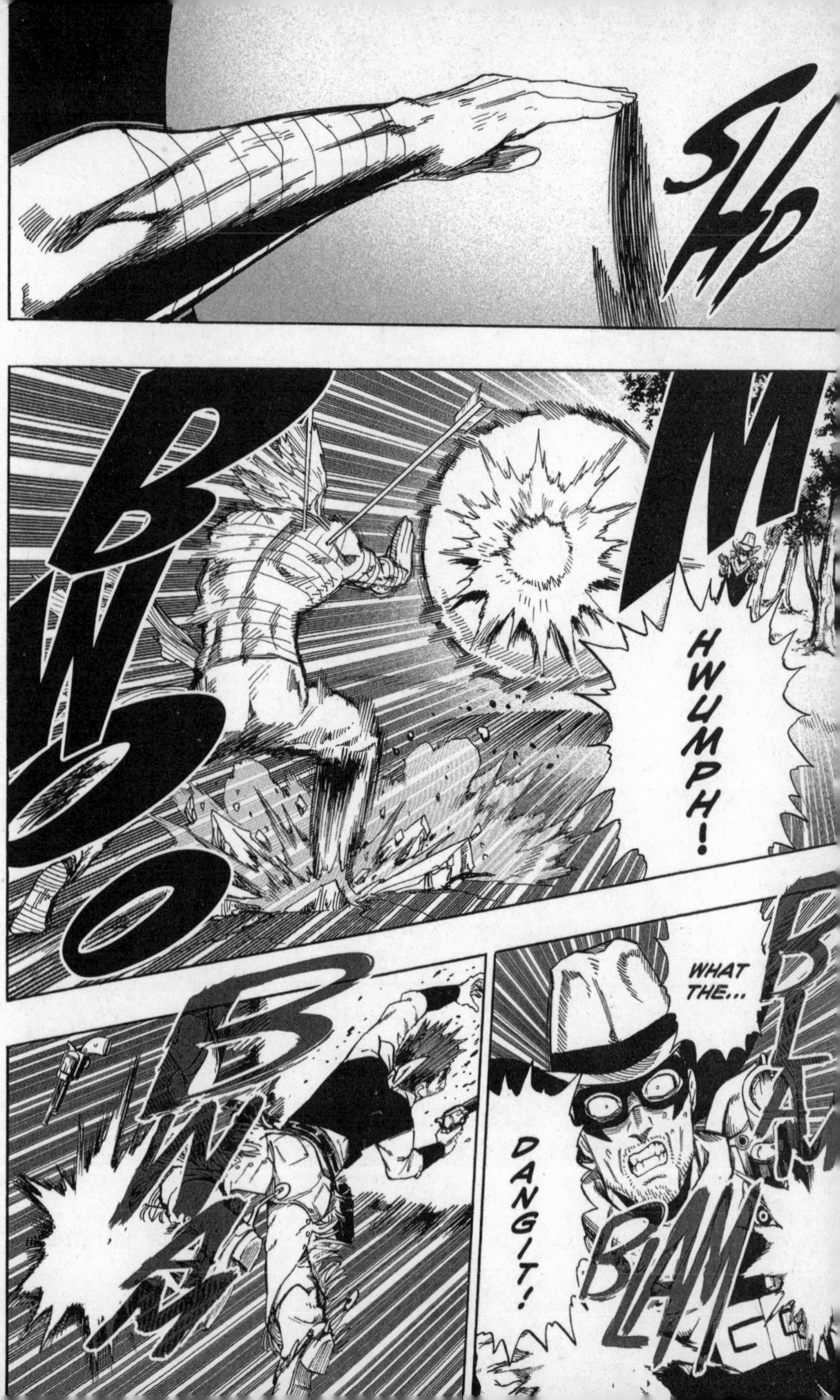
SHP
HWUMPH!
WHAT THE...
DANGIT!
BLAM

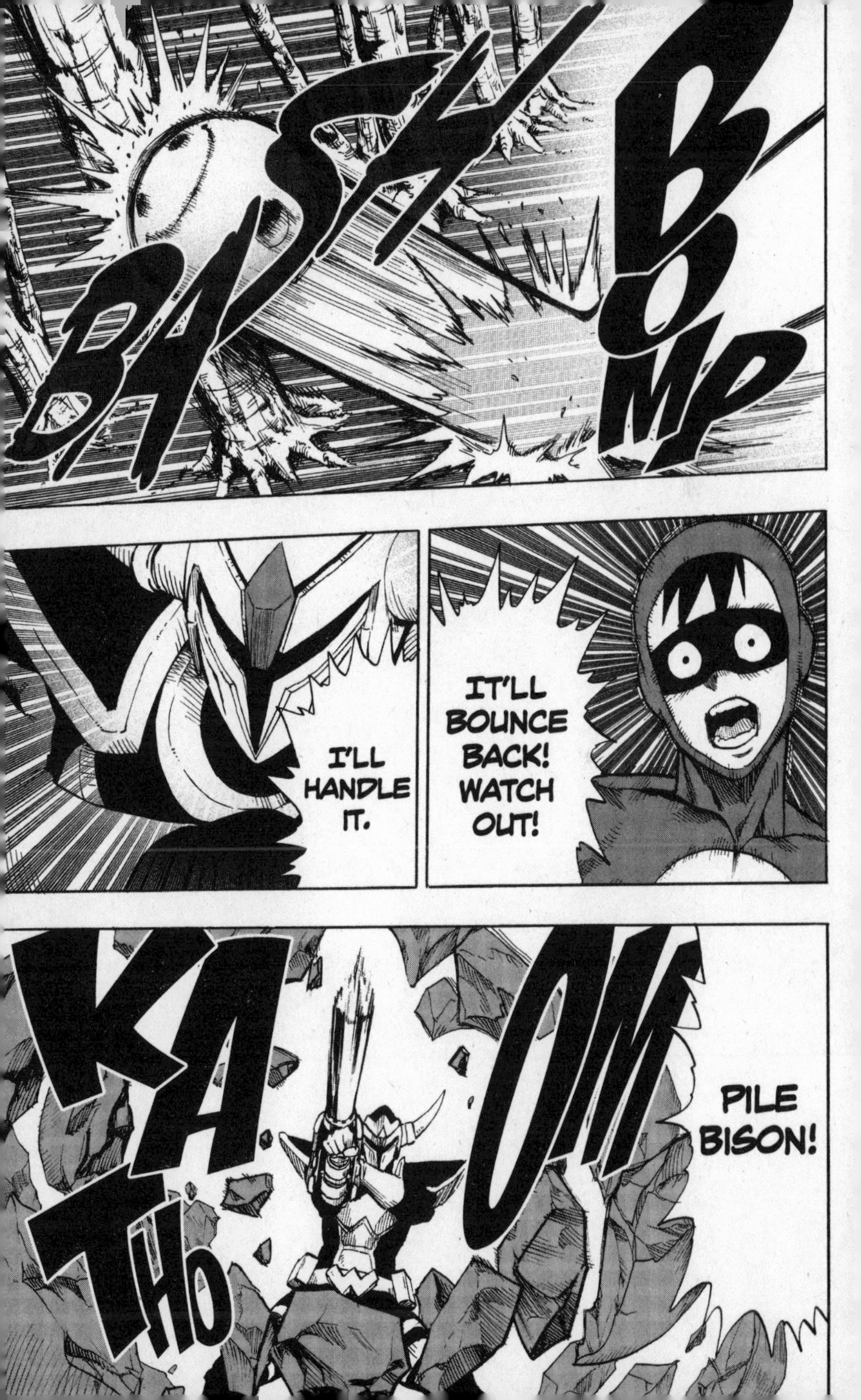
BOMP
BASH
IT'LL BOUNCE BACK! WATCH OUT!
I'LL HANDLE IT.
PILE BISON!
KA-THOOM

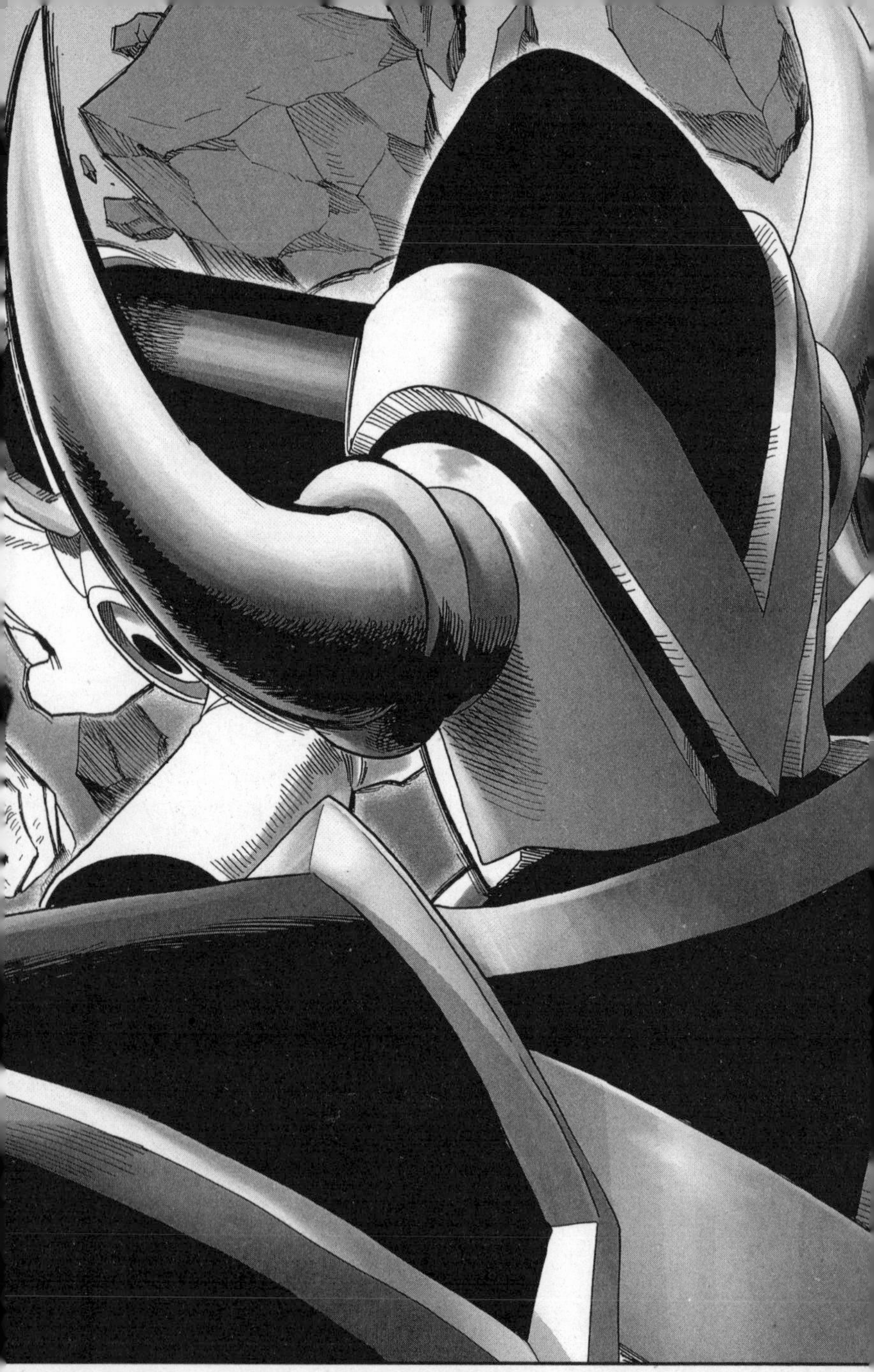

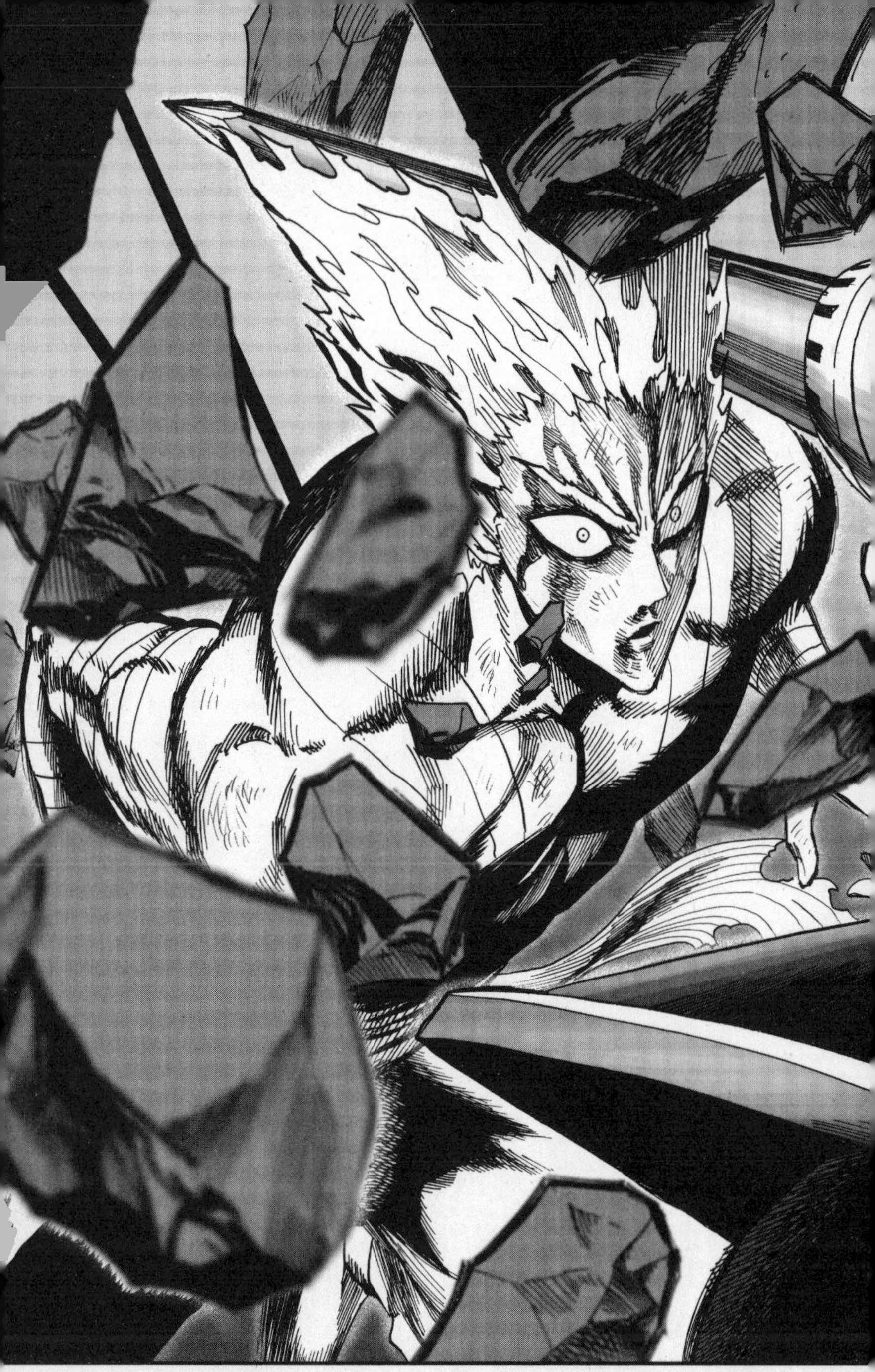

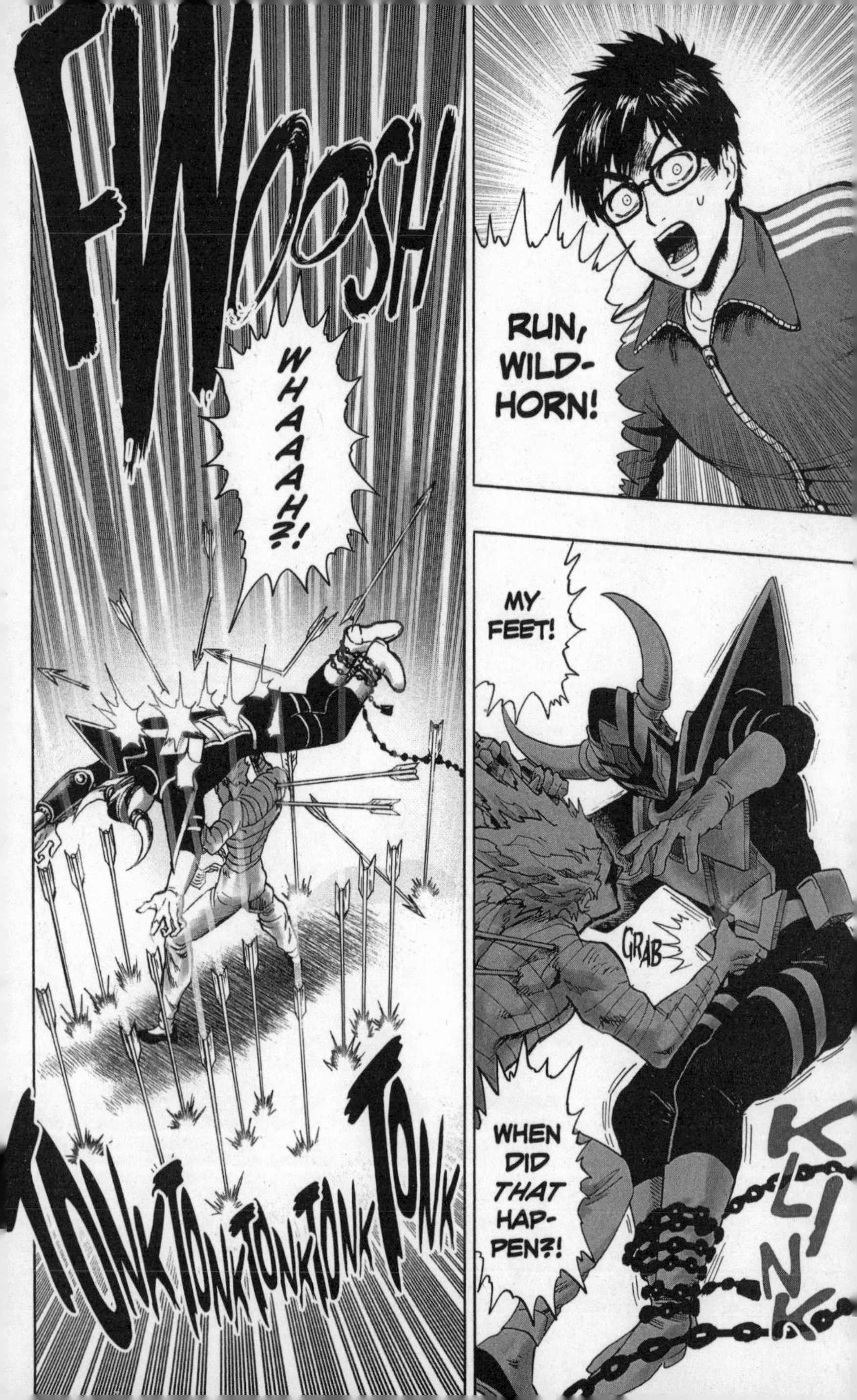
RUN, WILD-HORN!
MY FEET!
GRAB
WHEN DID THAT HAPPEN?!
KLINK
FWOOSH
WHAAAAH?!
TONKTONKTONKTONK TONK

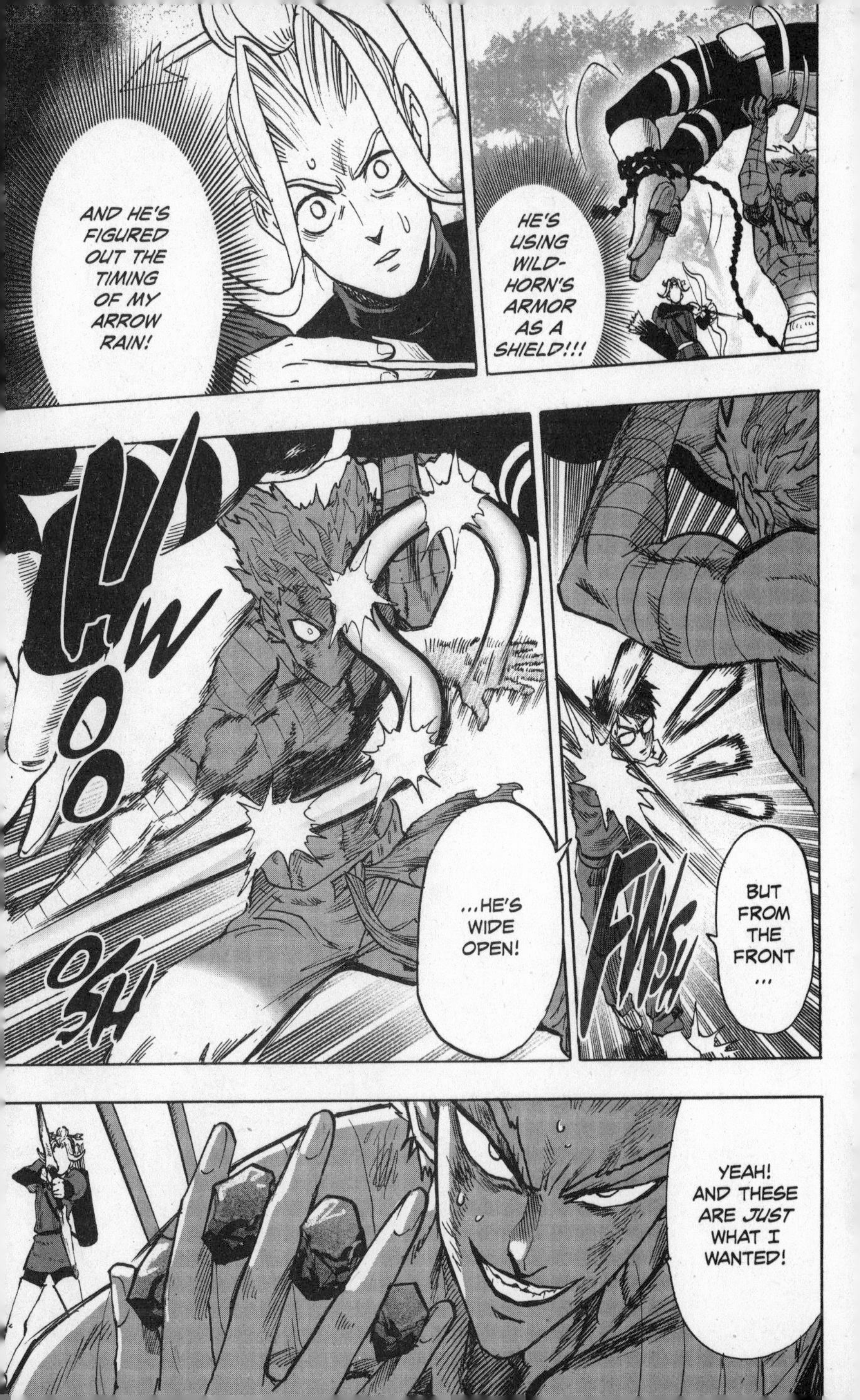
HE'S USING WILD-HORN'S ARMOR AS A SHIELD!!!
AND HE'S FIGURED OUT THE TIMING OF MY ARROW RAIN!
BUT FROM THE FRONT...
FWSH
...HE'S WIDE OPEN!
WHOOOOSH
YEAH! AND THESE ARE *JUST* WHAT I WANTED!

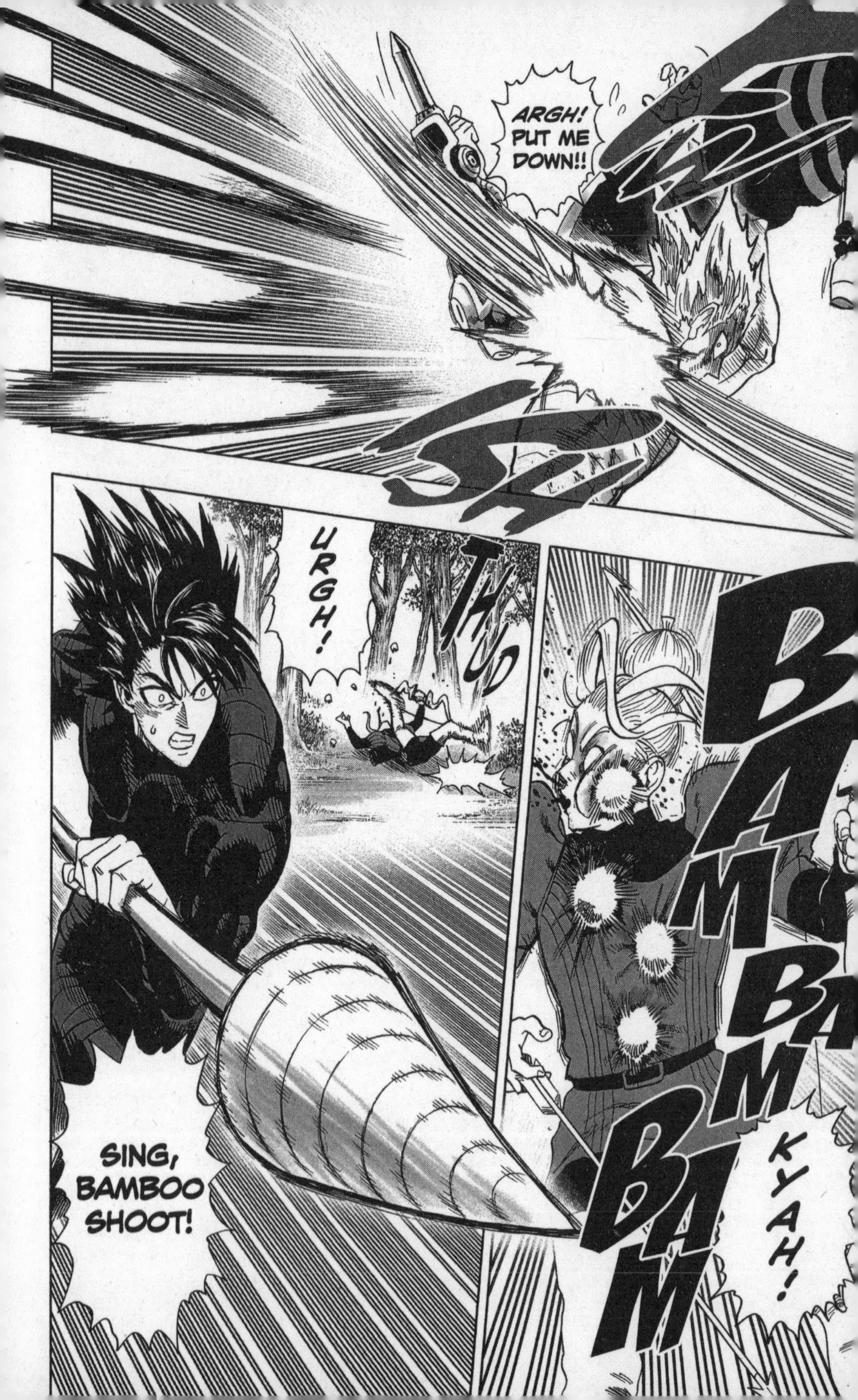
ARGH! PUT ME DOWN!!
BAM BAM BAM BAM
KYAH!
URGH!
THUD
SING, BAMBOO SHOOT!

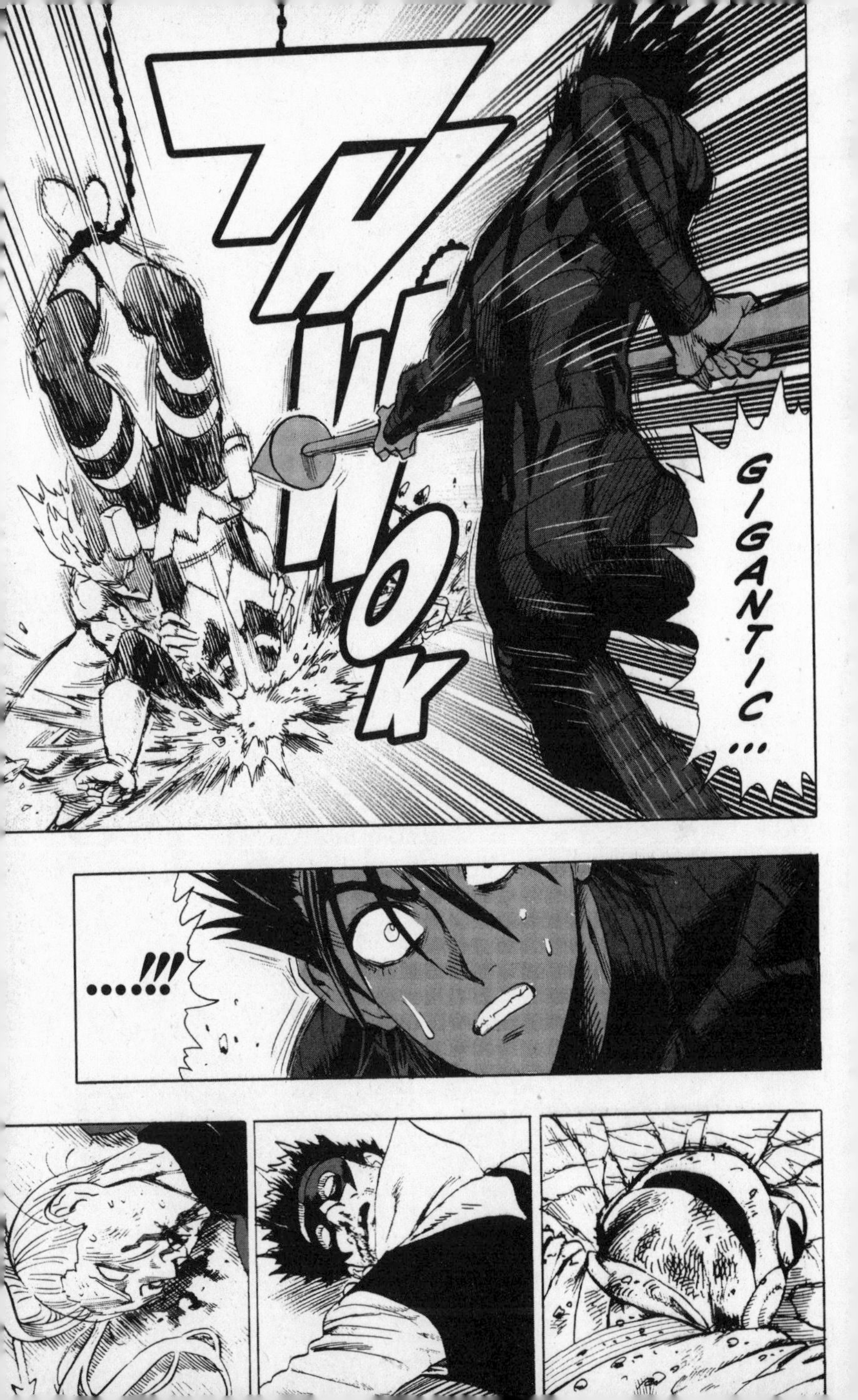

THWOK
GIGANTIC...
.....!!!

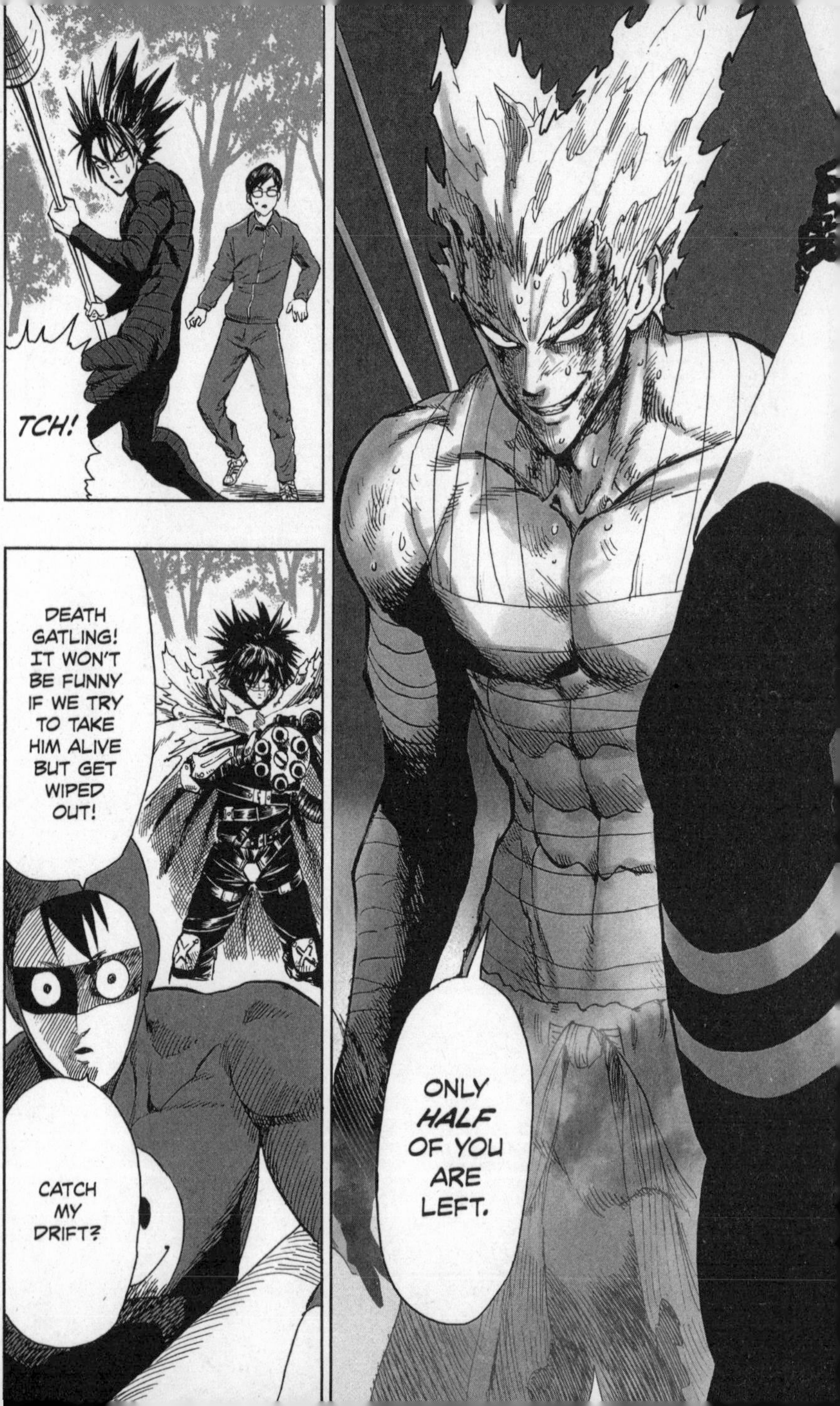
ONLY *HALF* OF YOU ARE LEFT.
TCH!
DEATH GATLING! IT WON'T BE FUNNY IF WE TRY TO TAKE HIM ALIVE BUT GET WIPED OUT!
CATCH MY DRIFT?

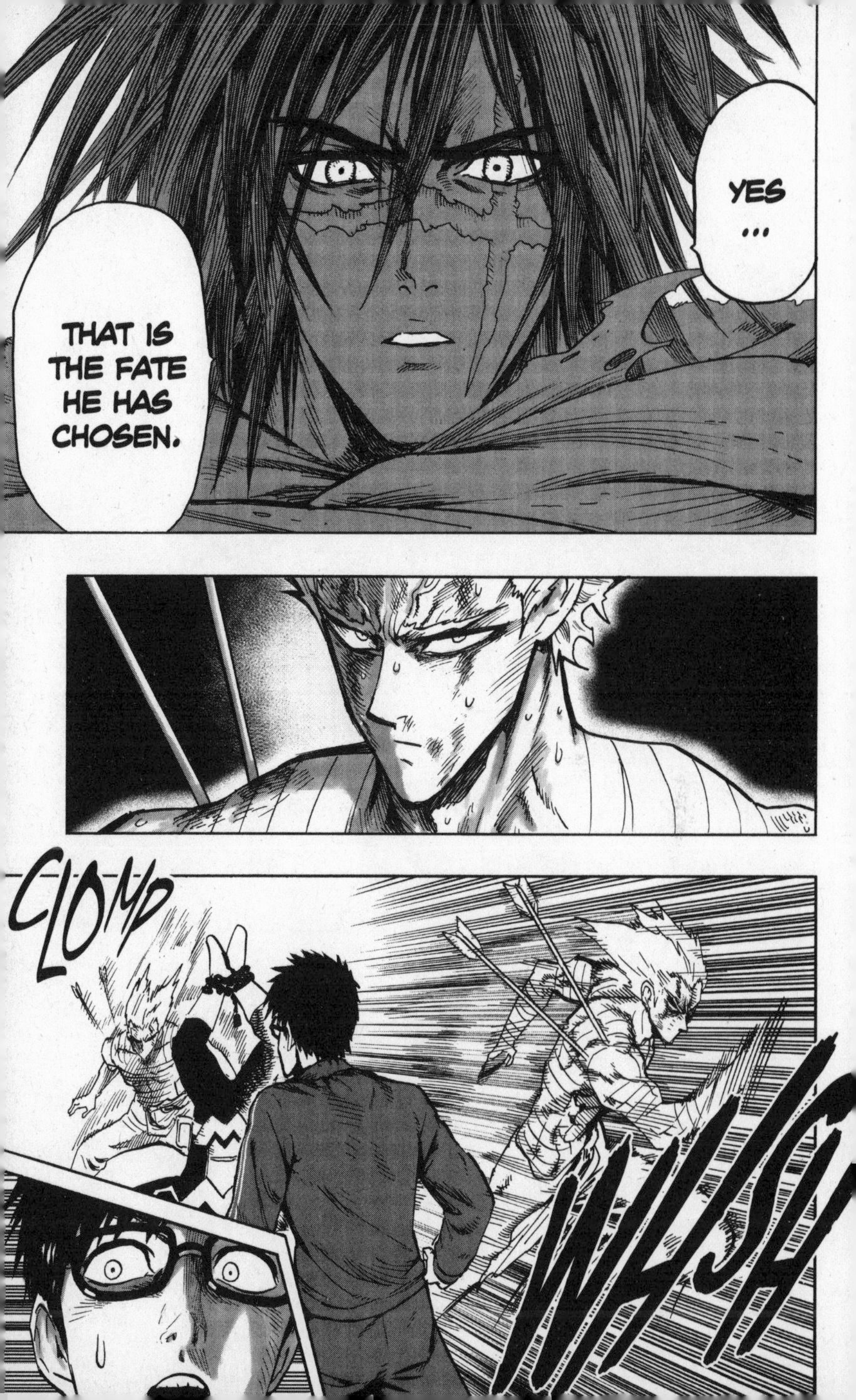
YES ...
THAT IS THE FATE HE HAS CHOSEN.
CLOMP
WHSH

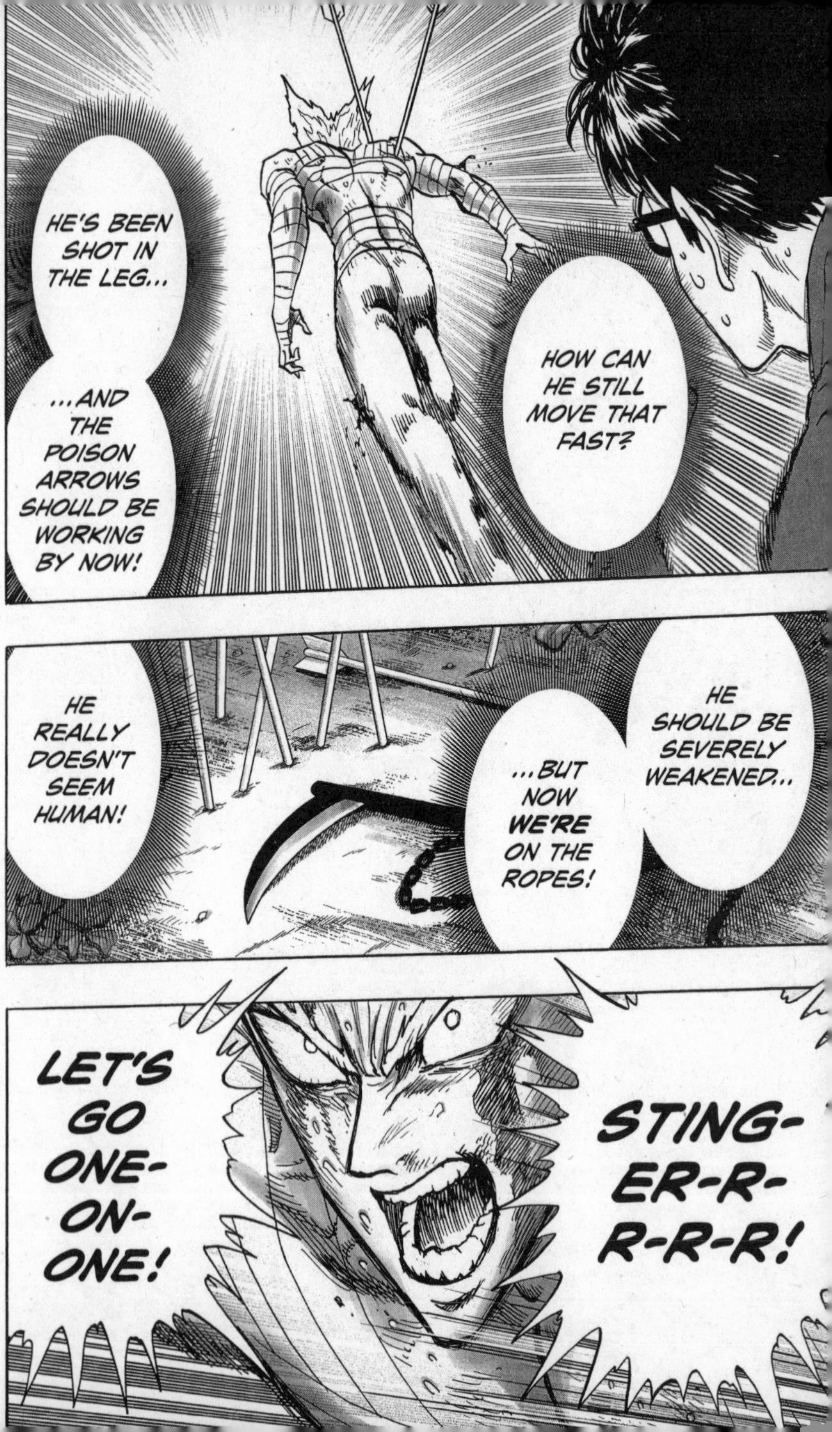
HOW CAN HE STILL MOVE THAT FAST?
HE'S BEEN SHOT IN THE LEG...
...AND THE POISON ARROWS SHOULD BE WORKING BY NOW!
HE SHOULD BE SEVERELY WEAKENED...
...BUT NOW WE'RE ON THE ROPES!
HE REALLY DOESN'T SEEM HUMAN!
STING-ER-R-R-R-R!
LET'S GO ONE-ON-ONE!

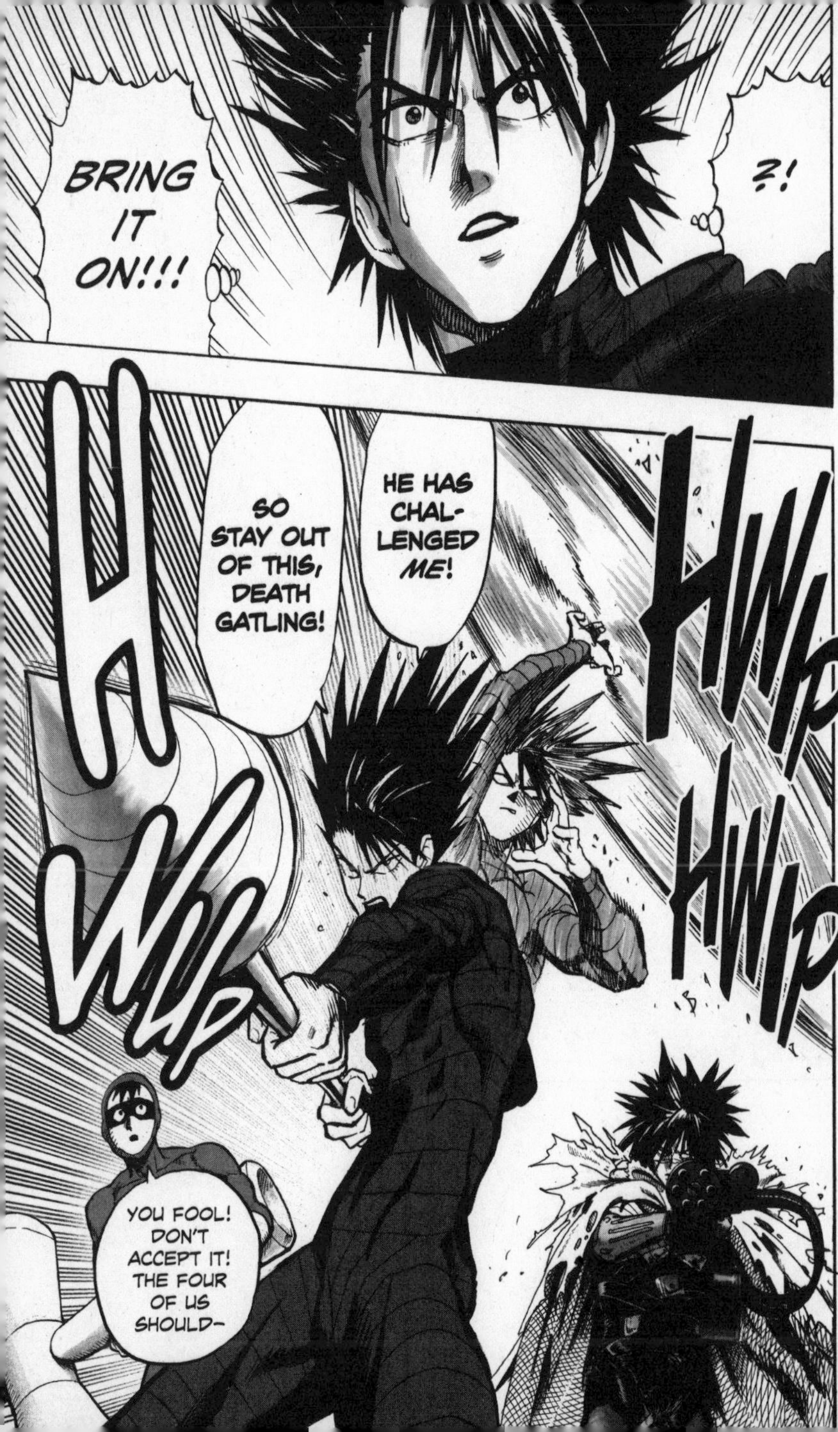
?!
BRING IT ON!!!
HWIP
HWIP
HWIP
HE HAS CHAL-LENGED ME!
SO STAY OUT OF THIS, DEATH GATLING!
YOU FOOL! DON'T ACCEPT IT! THE FOUR OF US SHOULD-

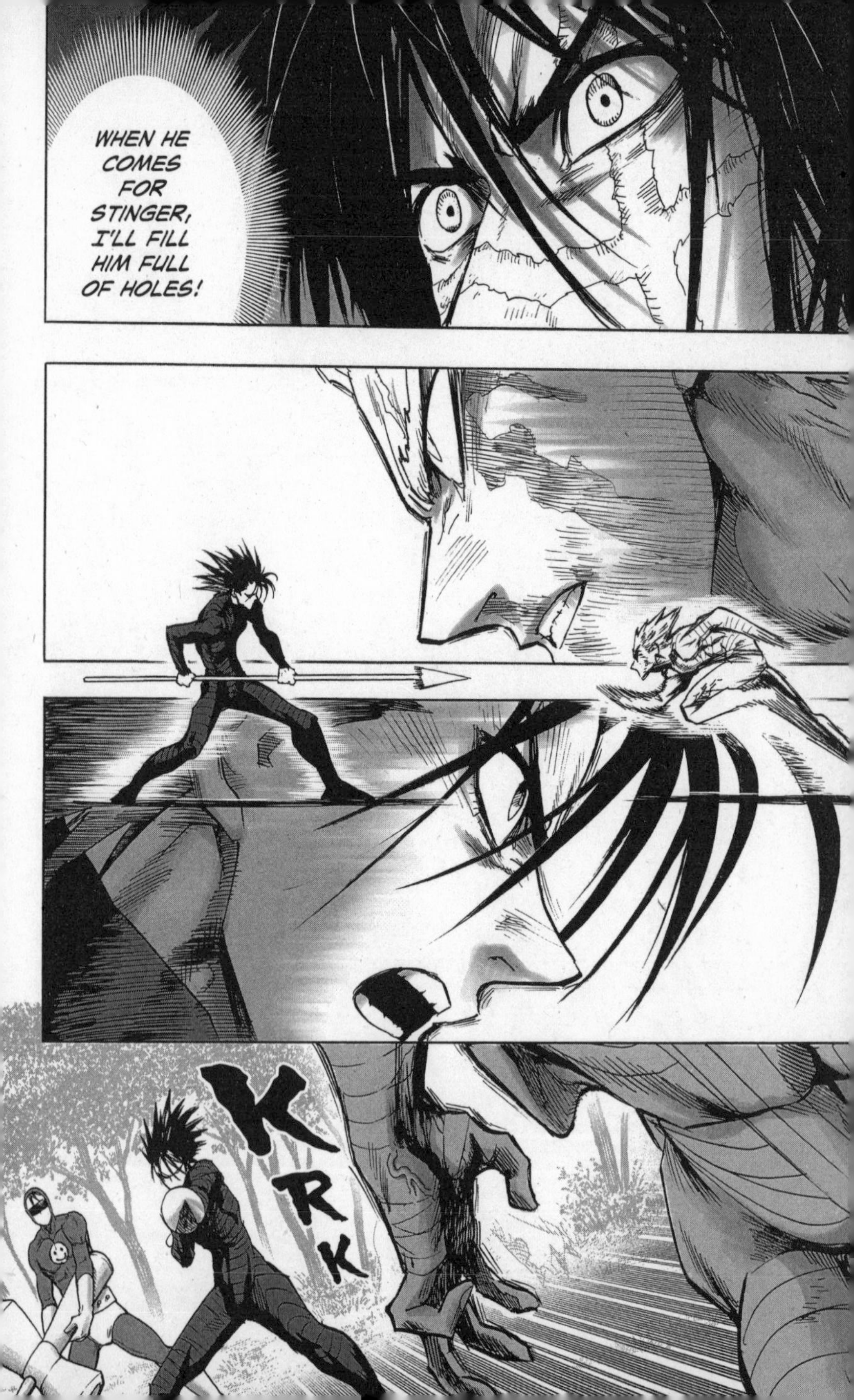
WHEN HE COMES FOR STINGER, I'LL FILL HIM FULL OF HOLES!
KRK

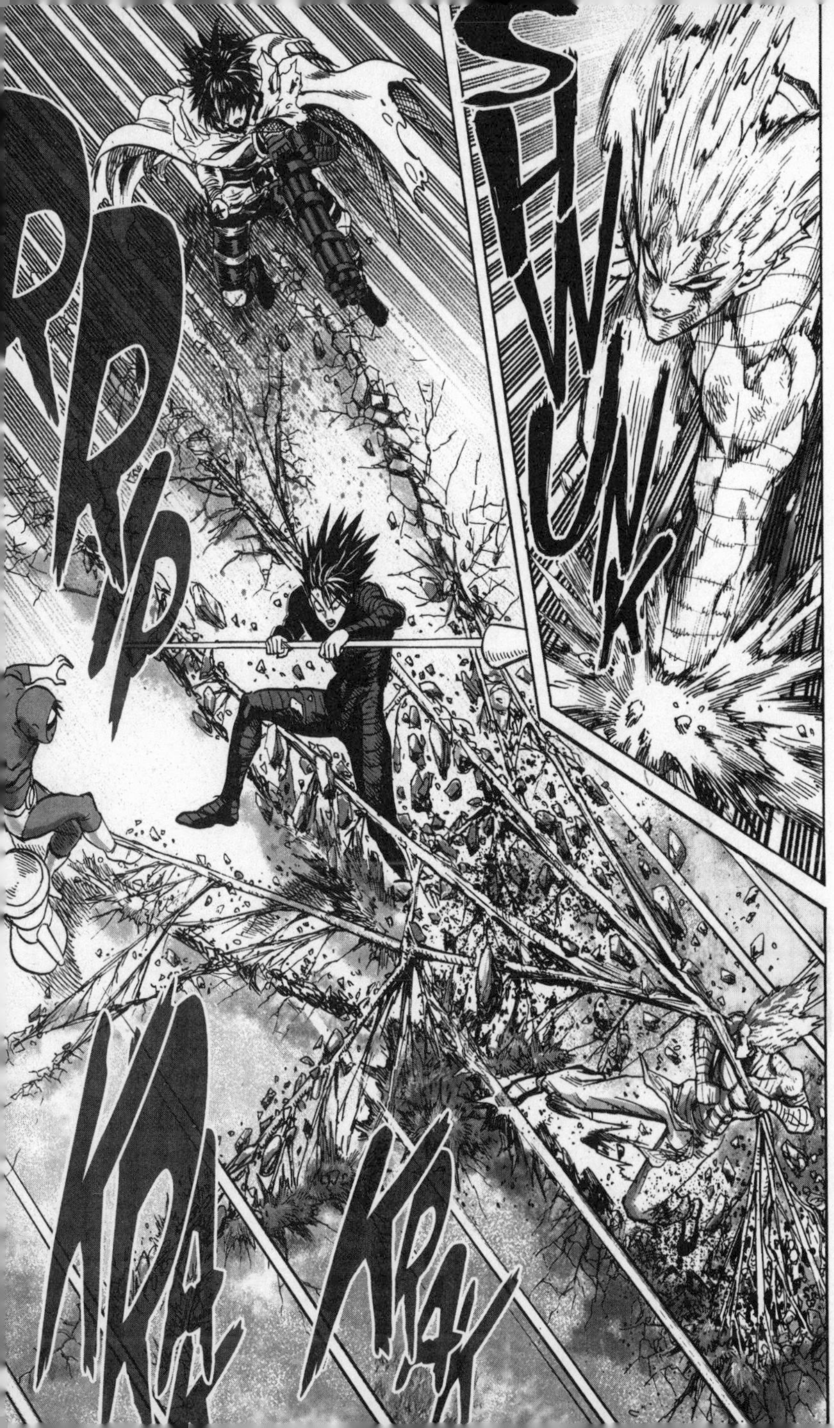
SHWUNK
KRAK KRAK

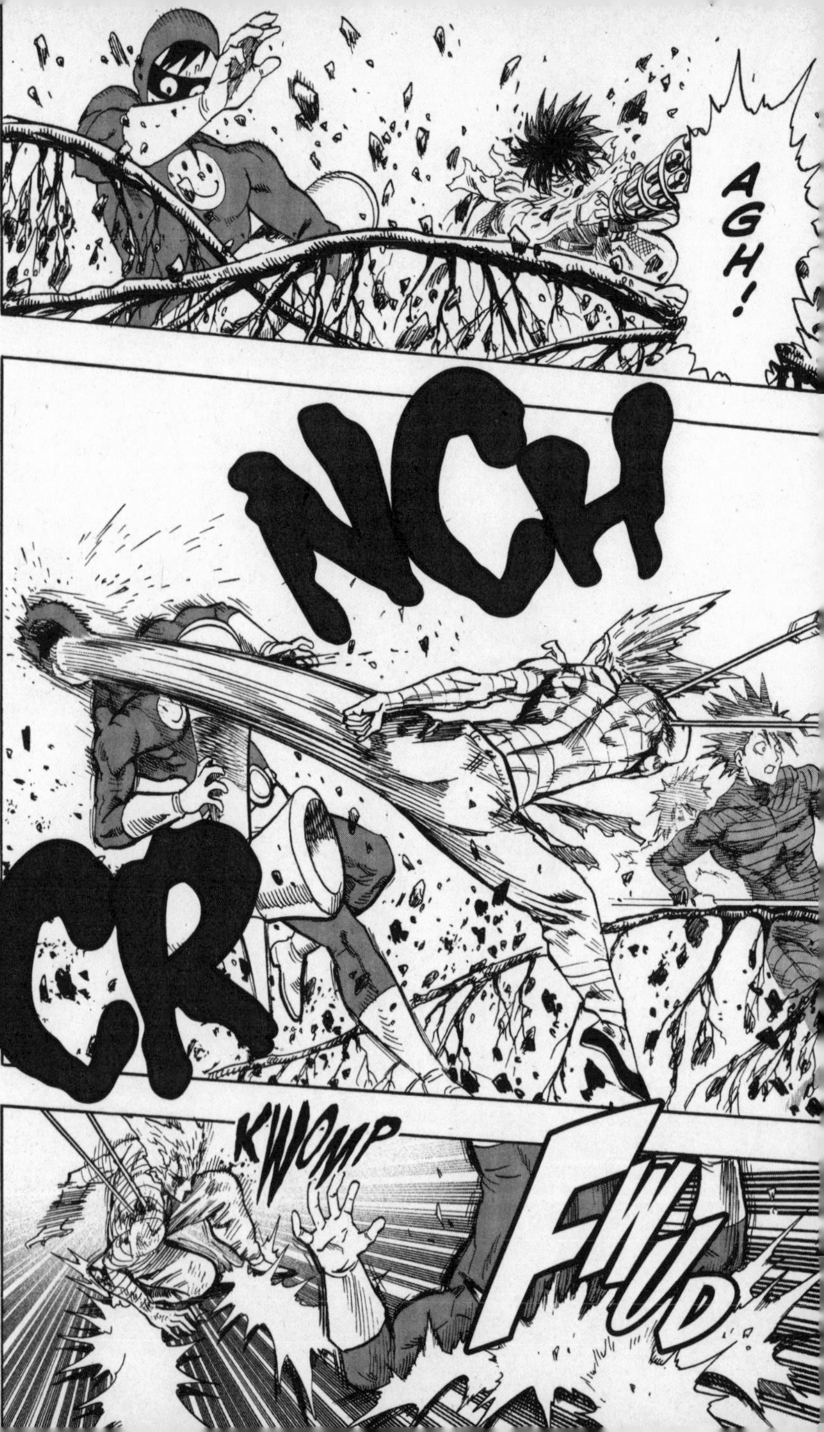
AGH!
CR
NCH
FWUD
KWOMP

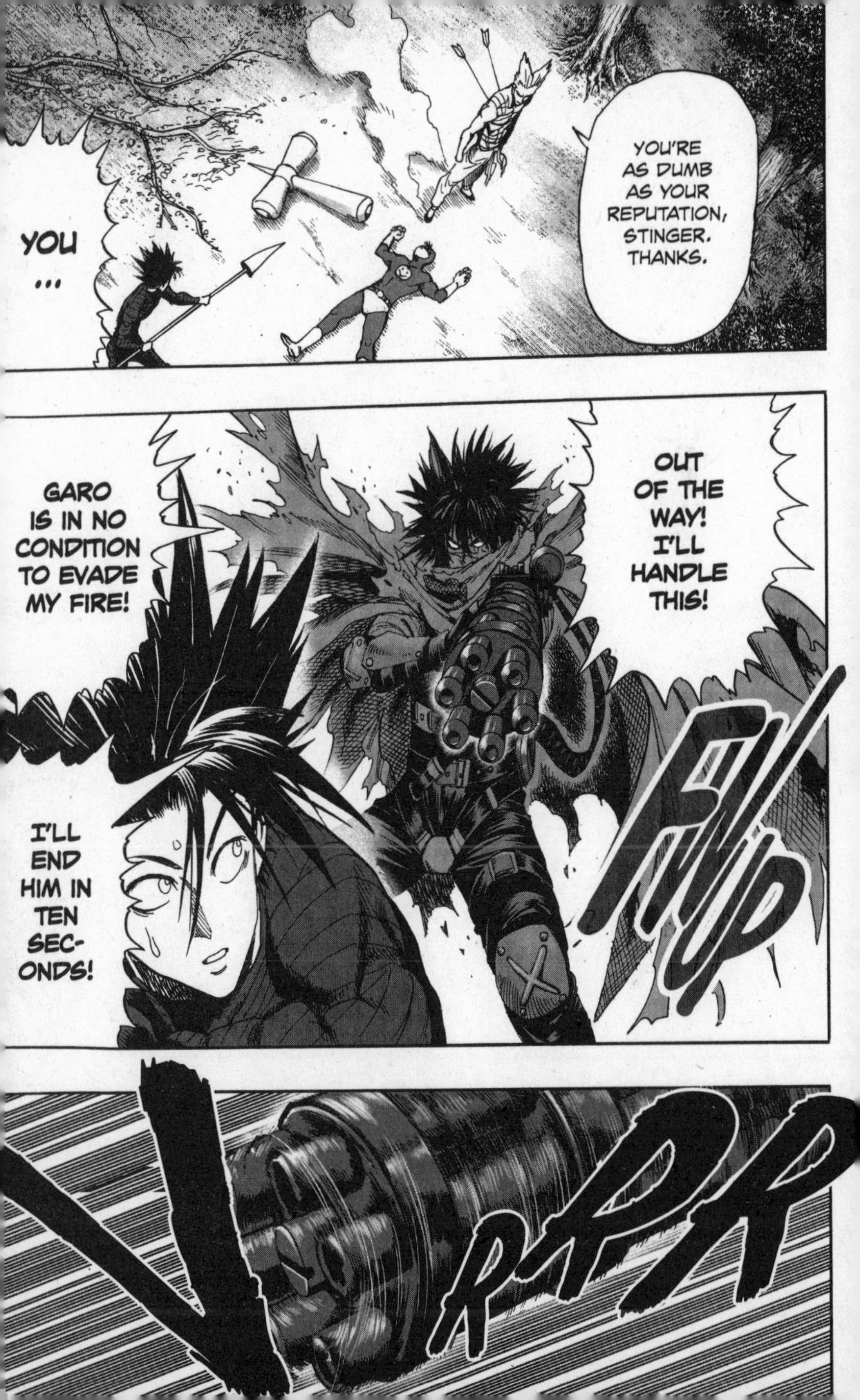
YOU'RE AS DUMB AS YOUR REPUTATION, STINGER. THANKS.
YOU ...
OUT OF THE WAY! I'LL HANDLE THIS!
GARO IS IN NO CONDITION TO EVADE MY FIRE!
I'LL END HIM IN TEN SEC-ONDS!
VRRR

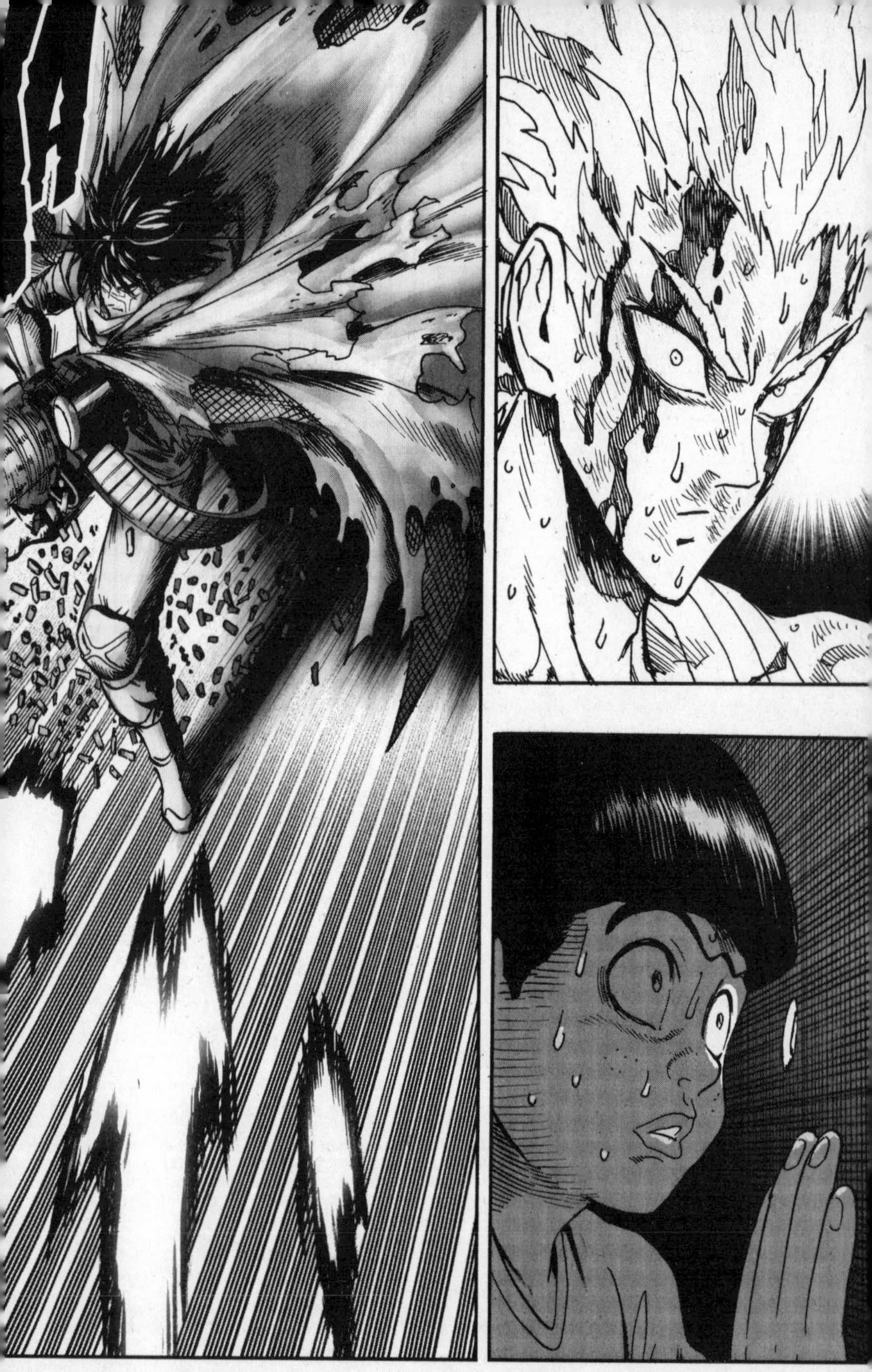

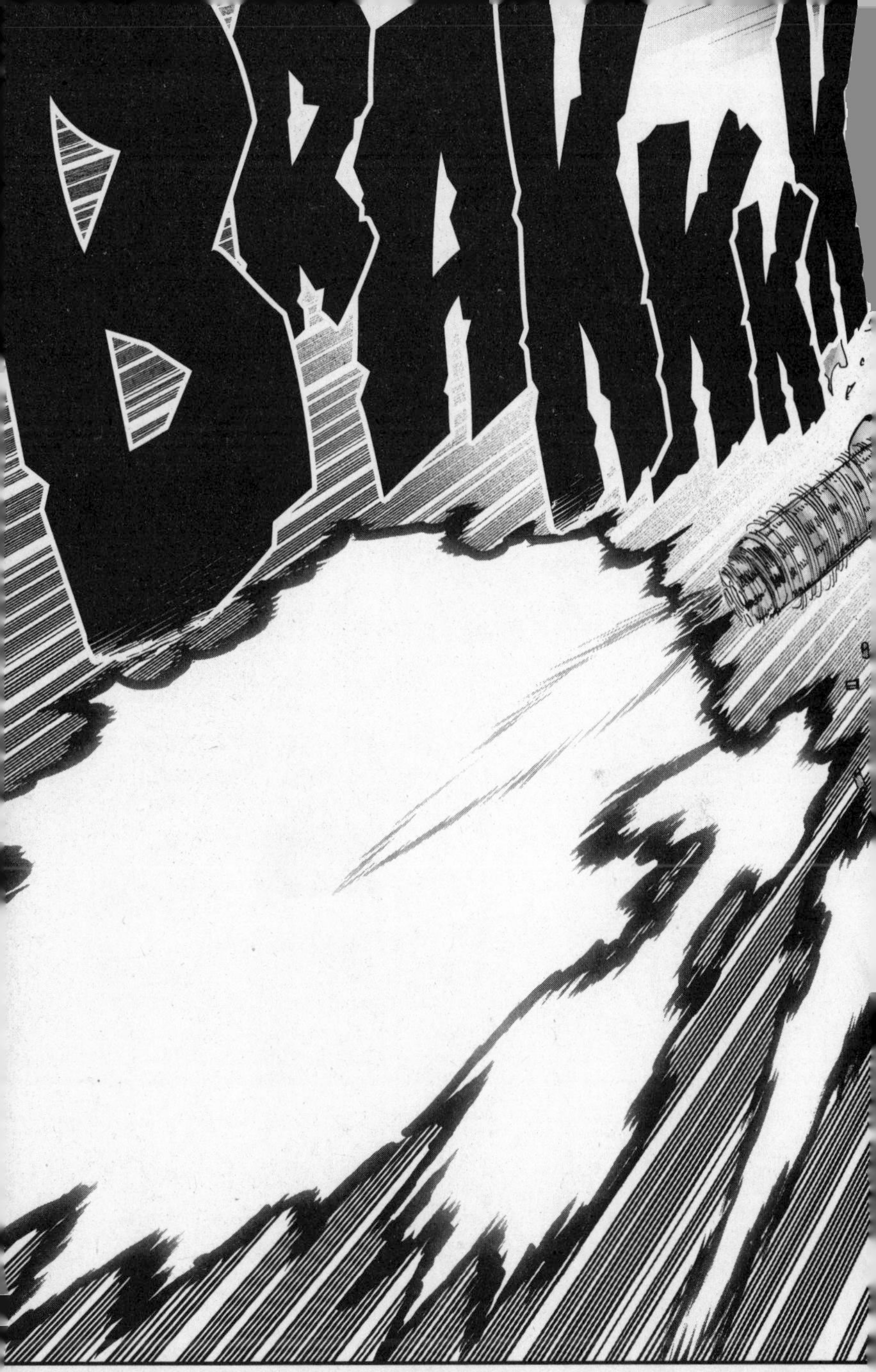

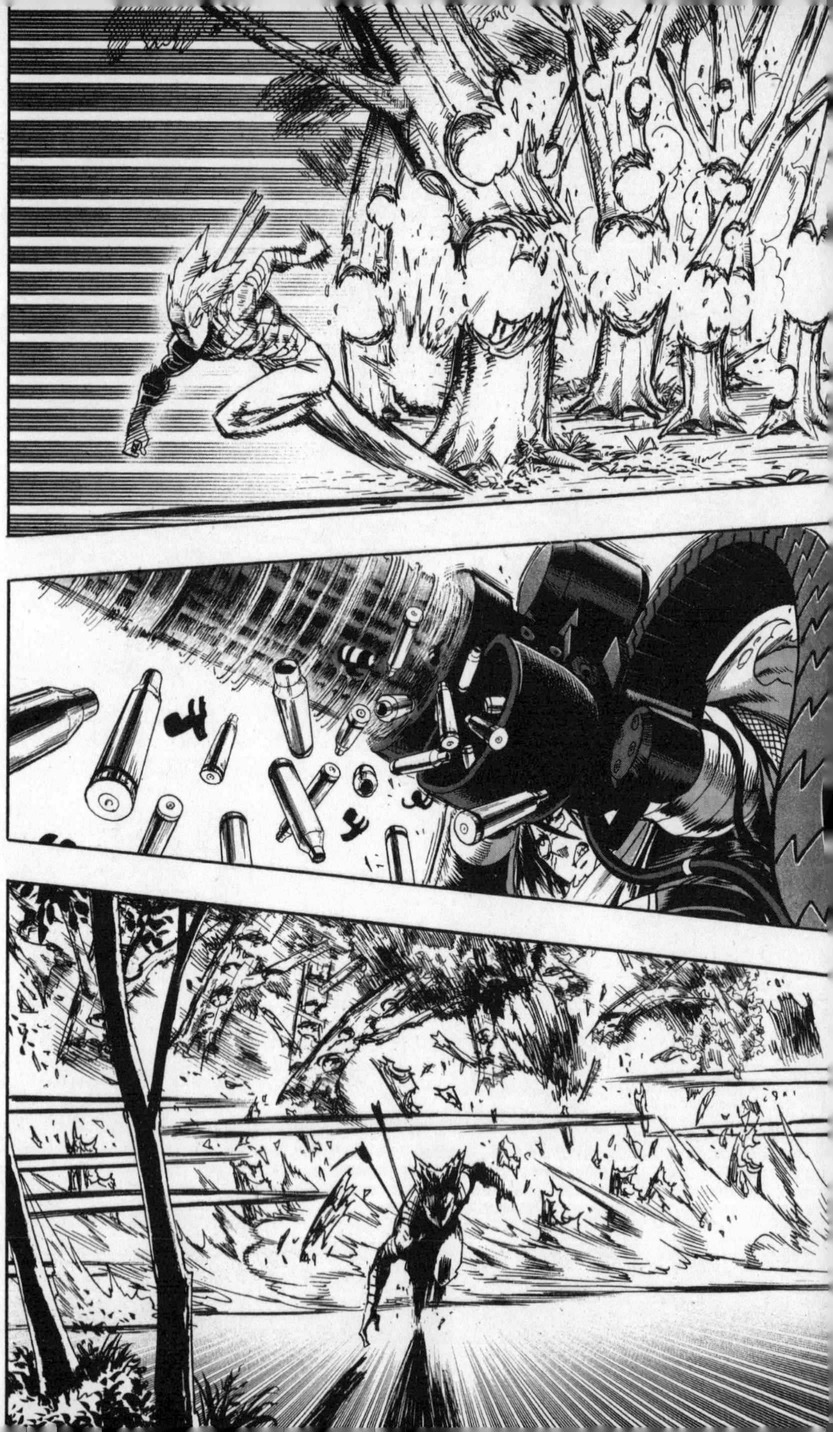

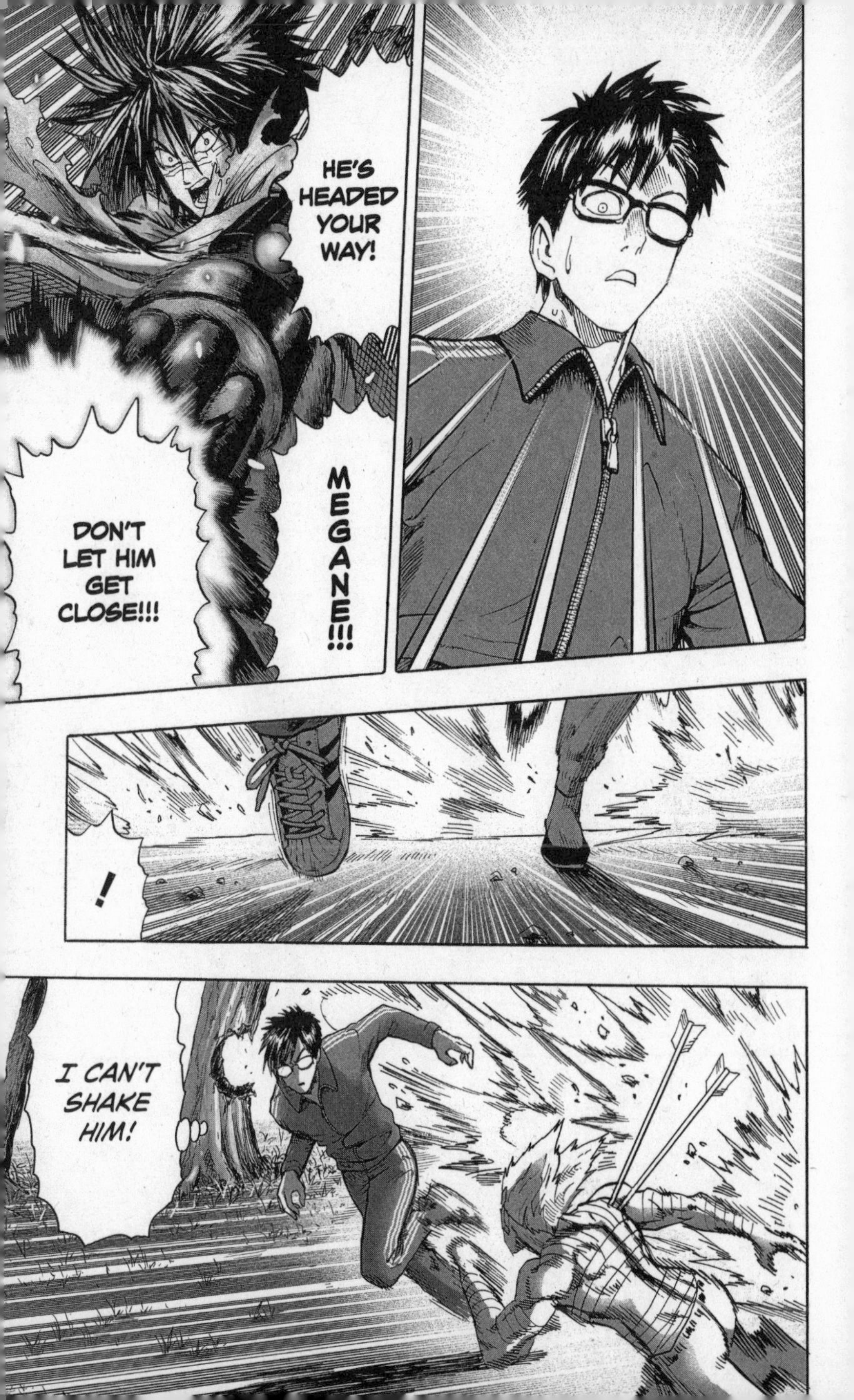
HE'S HEADED YOUR WAY!
MEGANE!!!
DON'T LET HIM GET CLOSE!!!
!
I CAN'T SHAKE HIM!

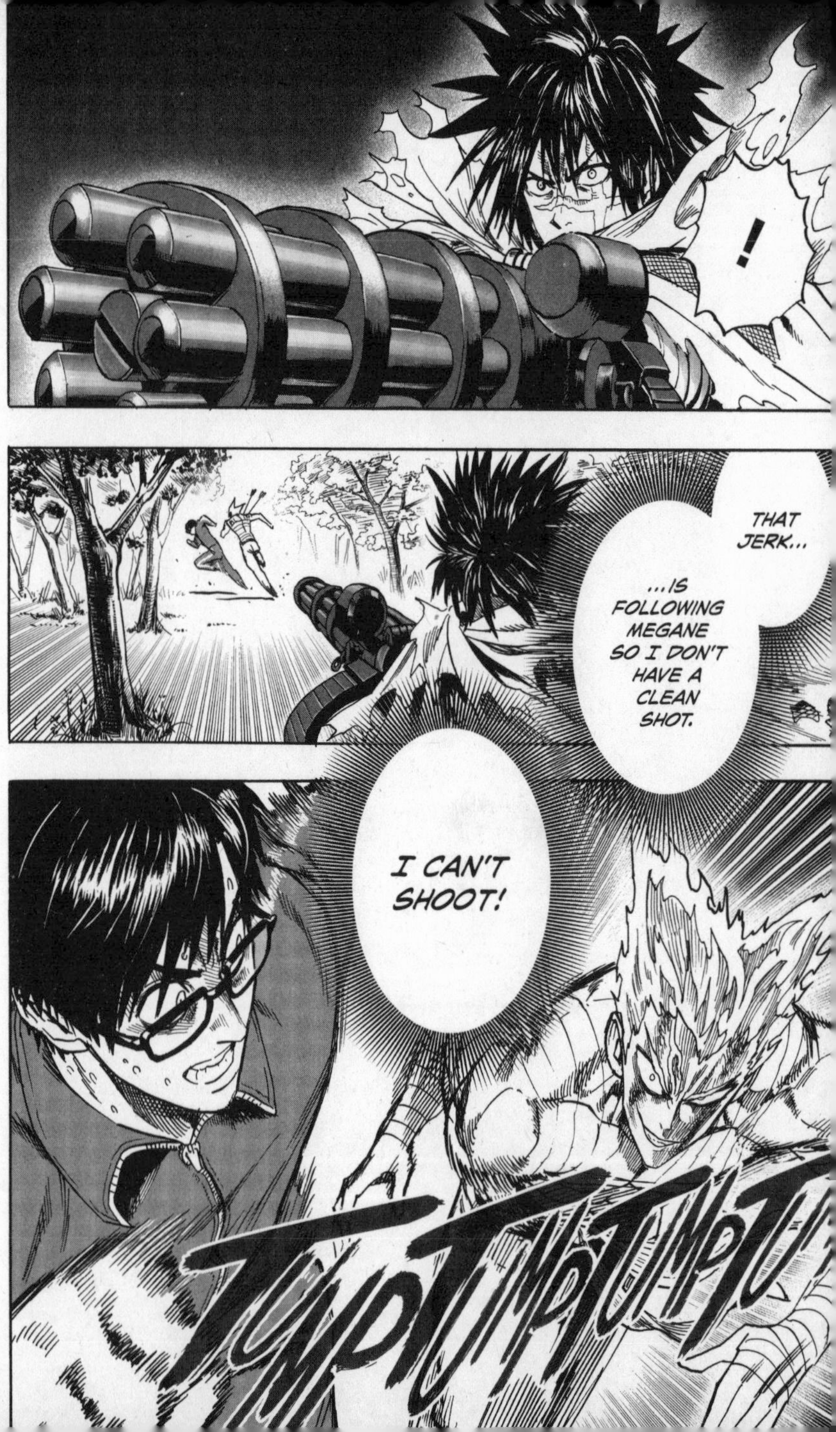
!
THAT JERK...
...IS FOLLOWING MEGANE SO I DON'T HAVE A CLEAN SHOT.
I CAN'T SHOOT!
TUMP TUMP TUMP TU

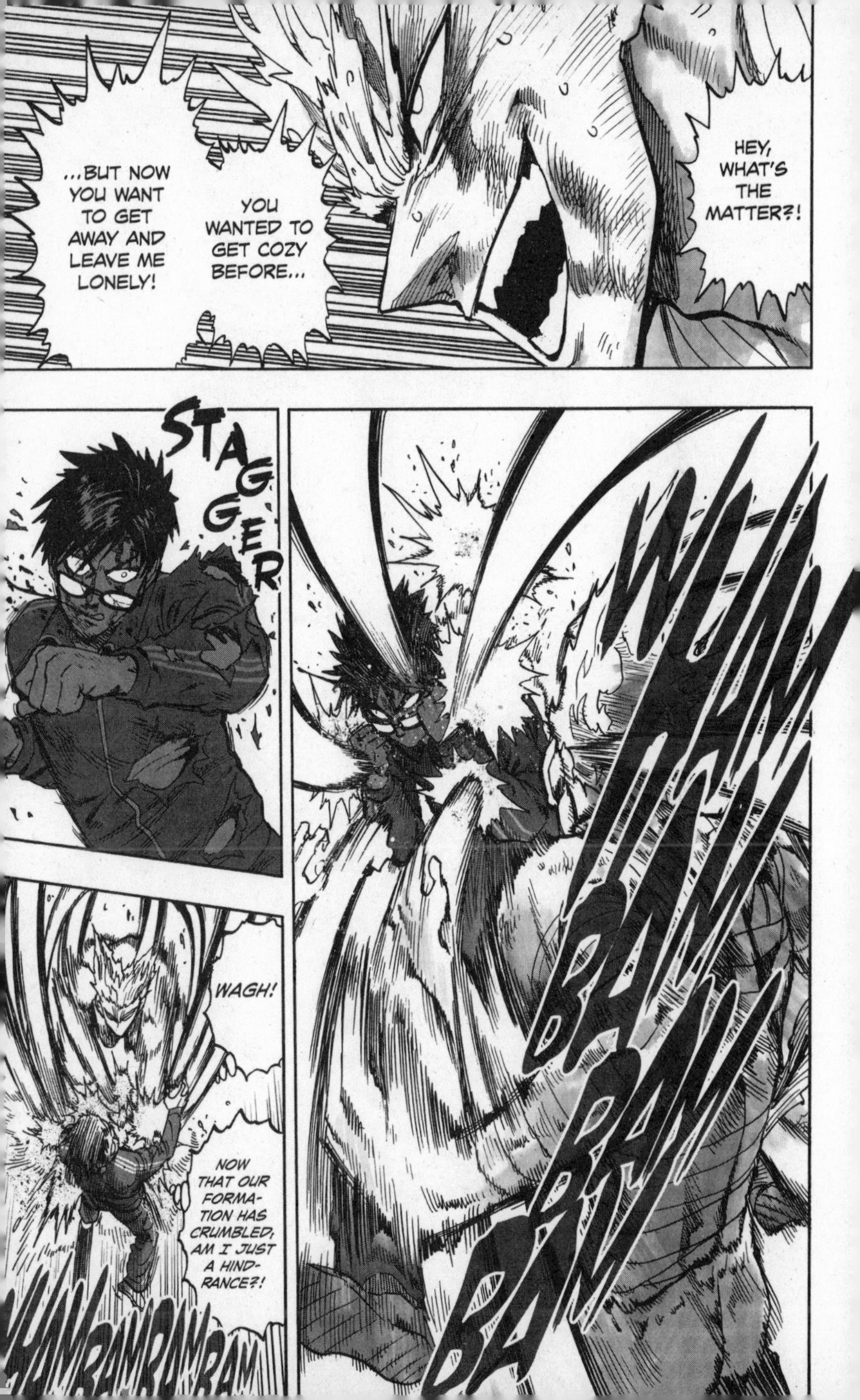
HEY, WHAT'S THE MATTER?!
YOU WANTED TO GET COZY BEFORE...
...BUT NOW YOU WANT TO GET AWAY AND LEAVE ME LONELY!
STAGGER
WAGH!
NOW THAT OUR FORMATION HAS CRUMBLED, AM I JUST A HINDRANCE?!

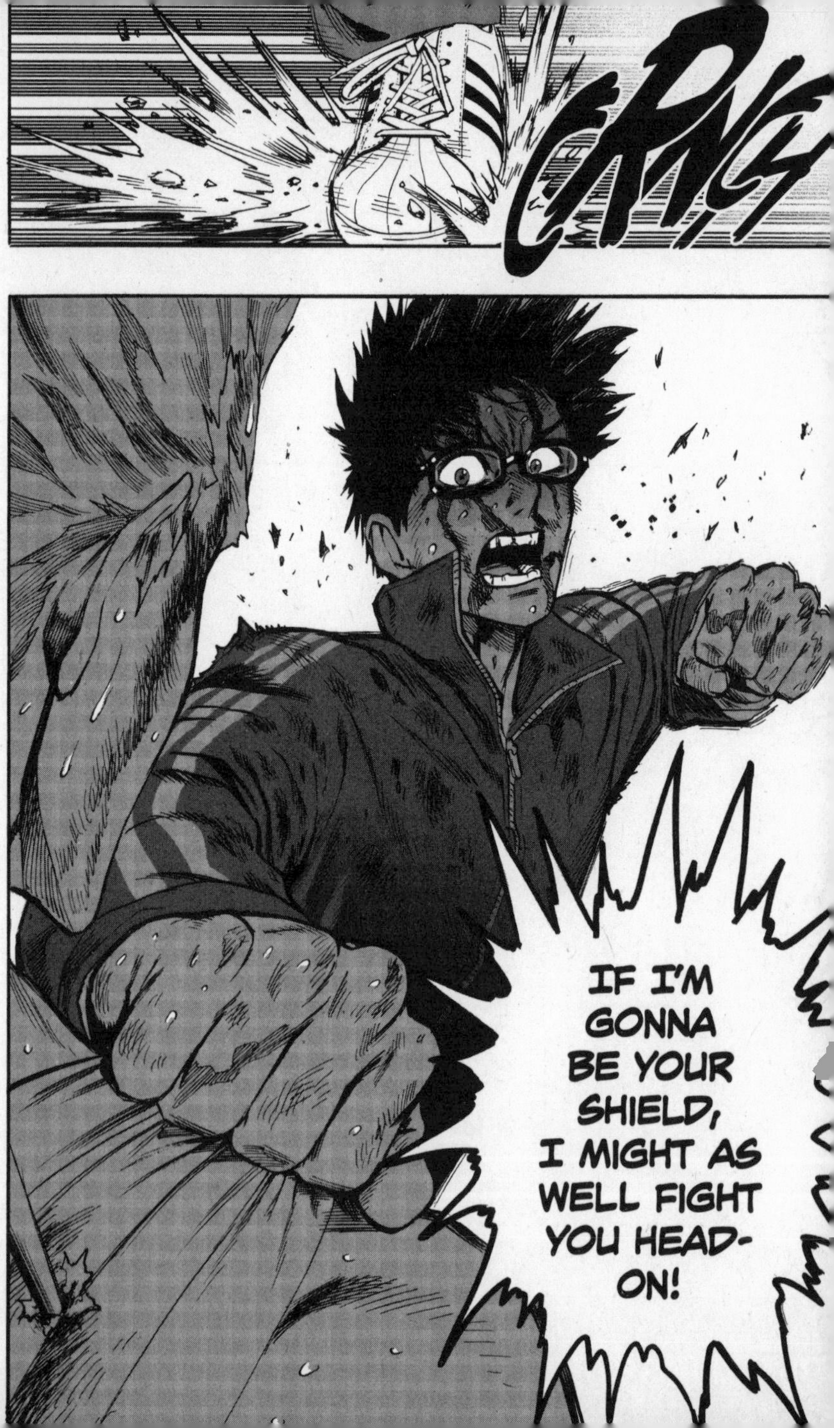
CRNCH
IF I'M GONNA BE YOUR SHIELD, I MIGHT AS WELL FIGHT YOU HEAD-ON!

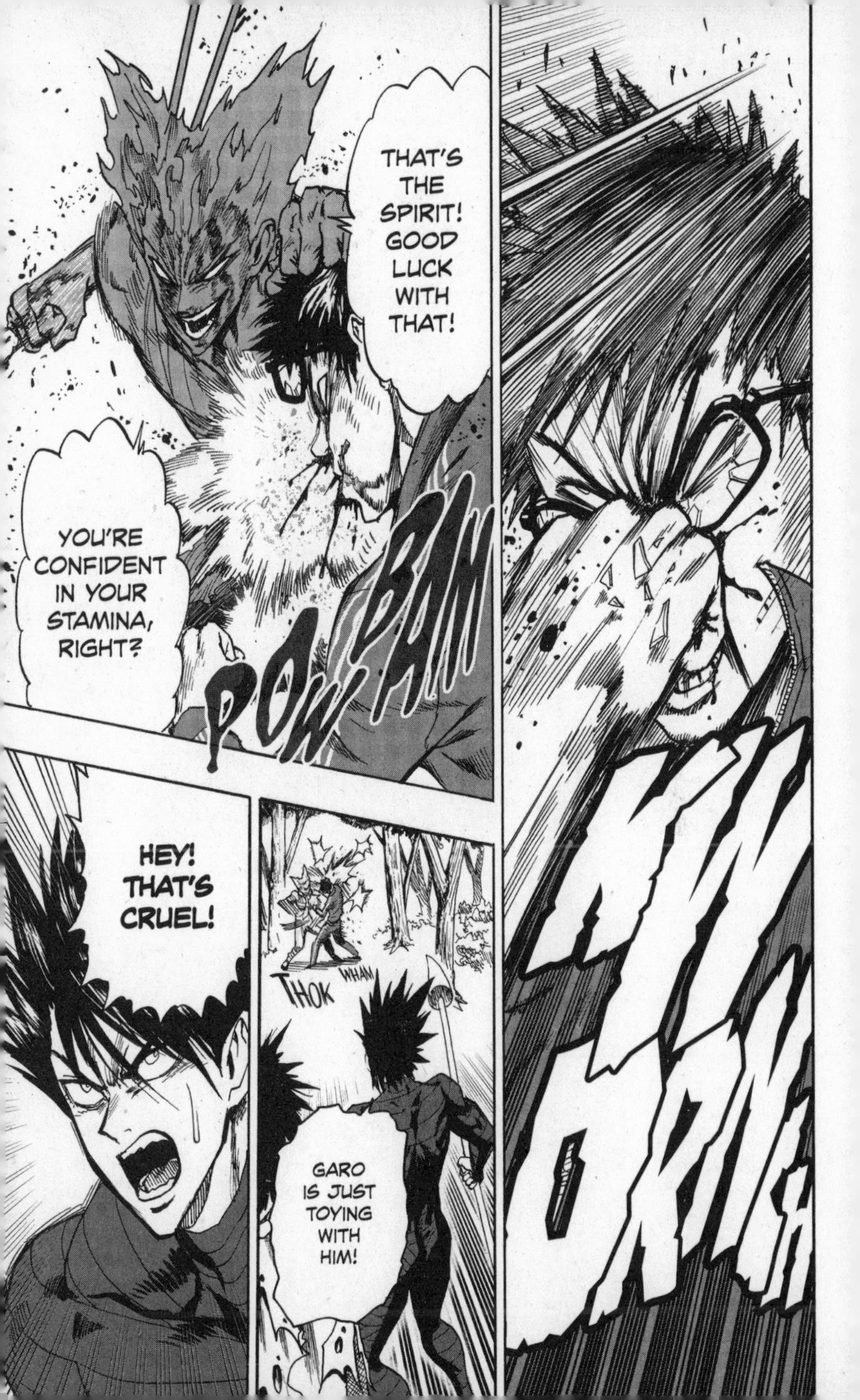
THAT'S THE SPIRIT! GOOD LUCK WITH THAT!
YOU'RE CONFIDENT IN YOUR STAMINA, RIGHT?
POW
BAM
WHAM
THOK
GARO IS JUST TOYING WITH HIM!
HEY! THAT'S CRUEL!

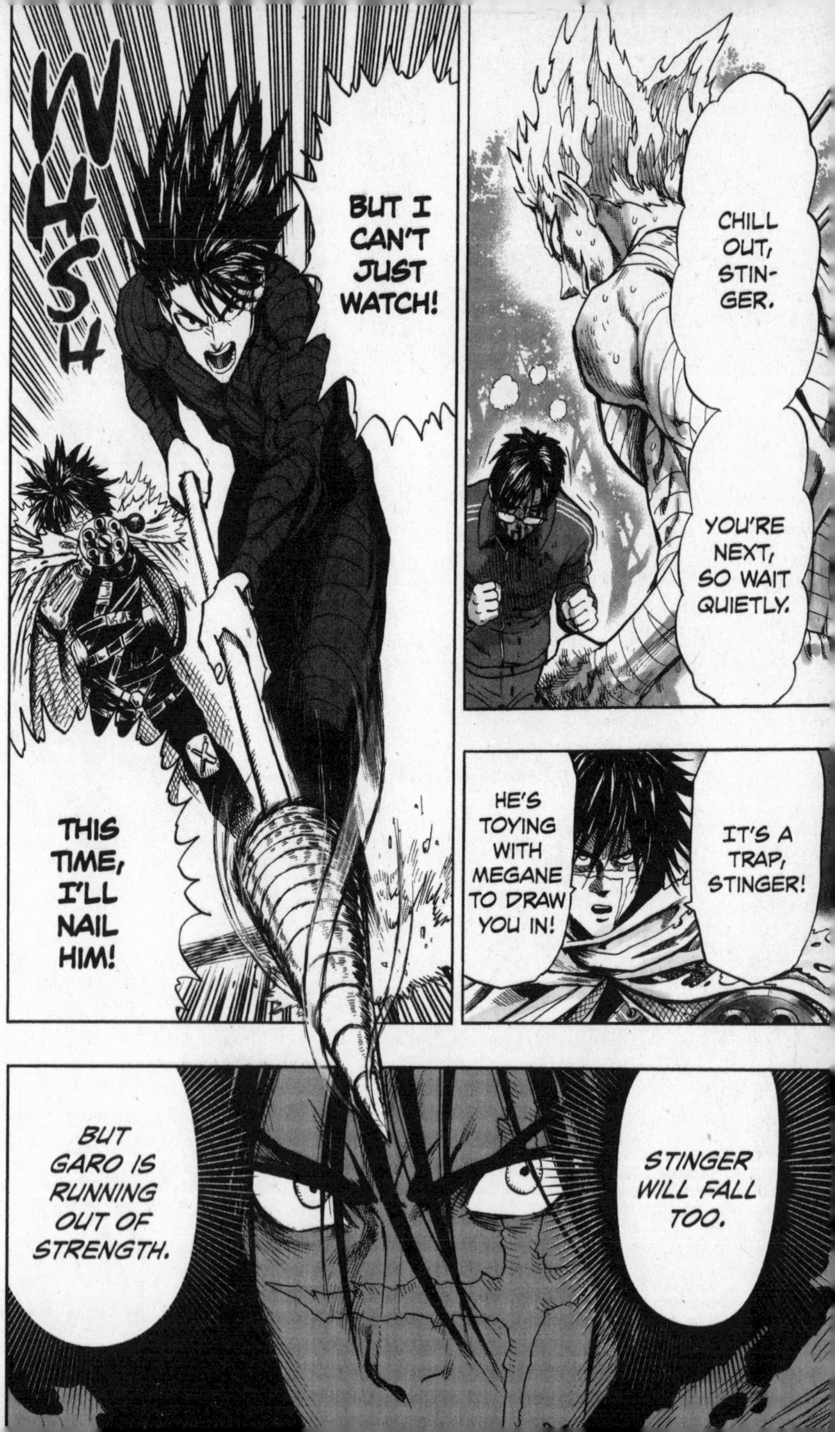
CHILL OUT, STINGER.
YOU'RE NEXT, SO WAIT QUIETLY.
IT'S A TRAP, STINGER!
HE'S TOYING WITH MEGANE TO DRAW YOU IN!
WHSH
BUT I CAN'T JUST WATCH!
THIS TIME, I'LL NAIL HIM!
STINGER WILL FALL TOO.
BUT GARO IS RUNNING OUT OF STRENGTH.

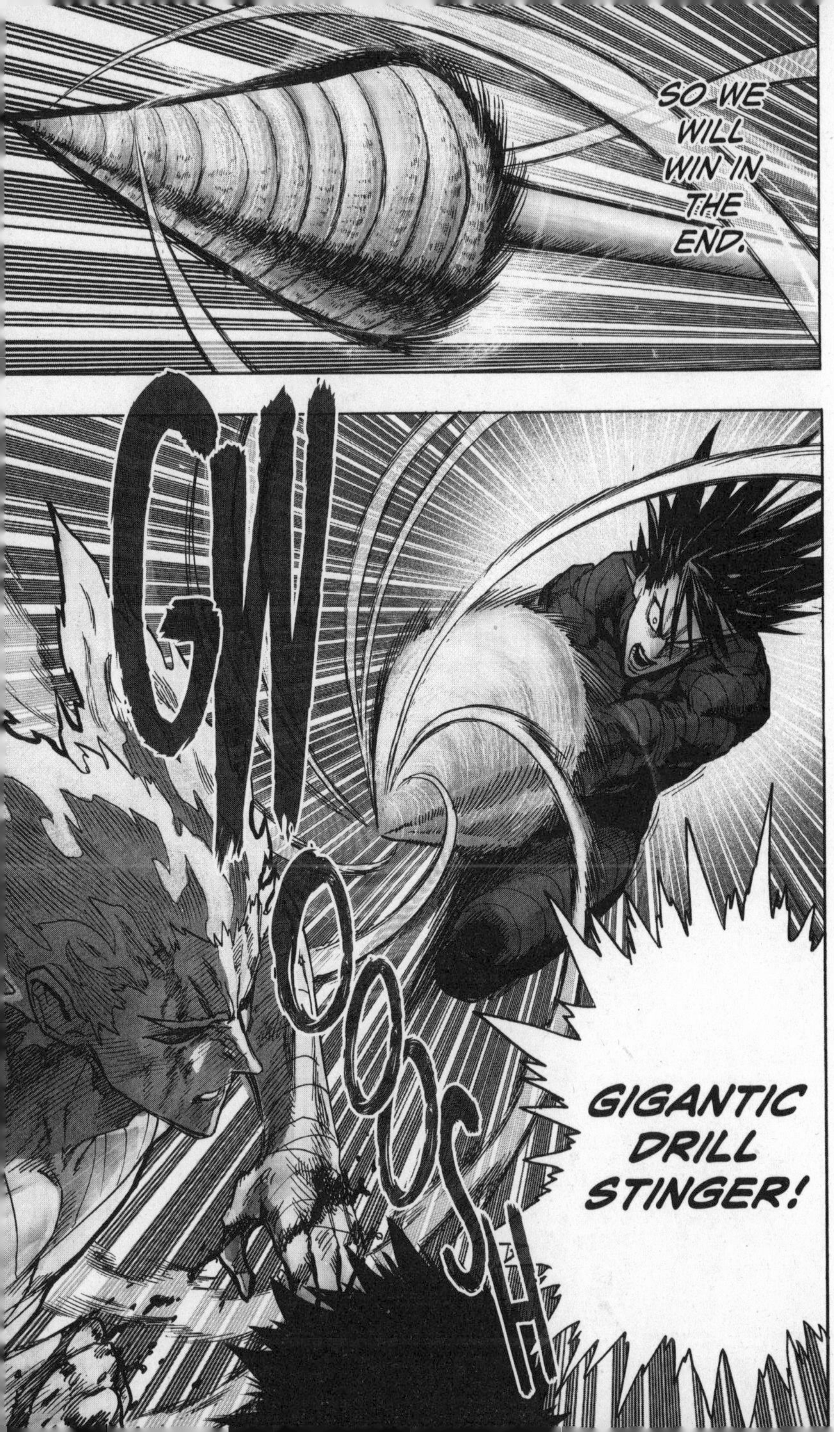
SO WE WILL WIN IN THE END.
GWOOOSH
GIGANTIC DRILL STINGER!

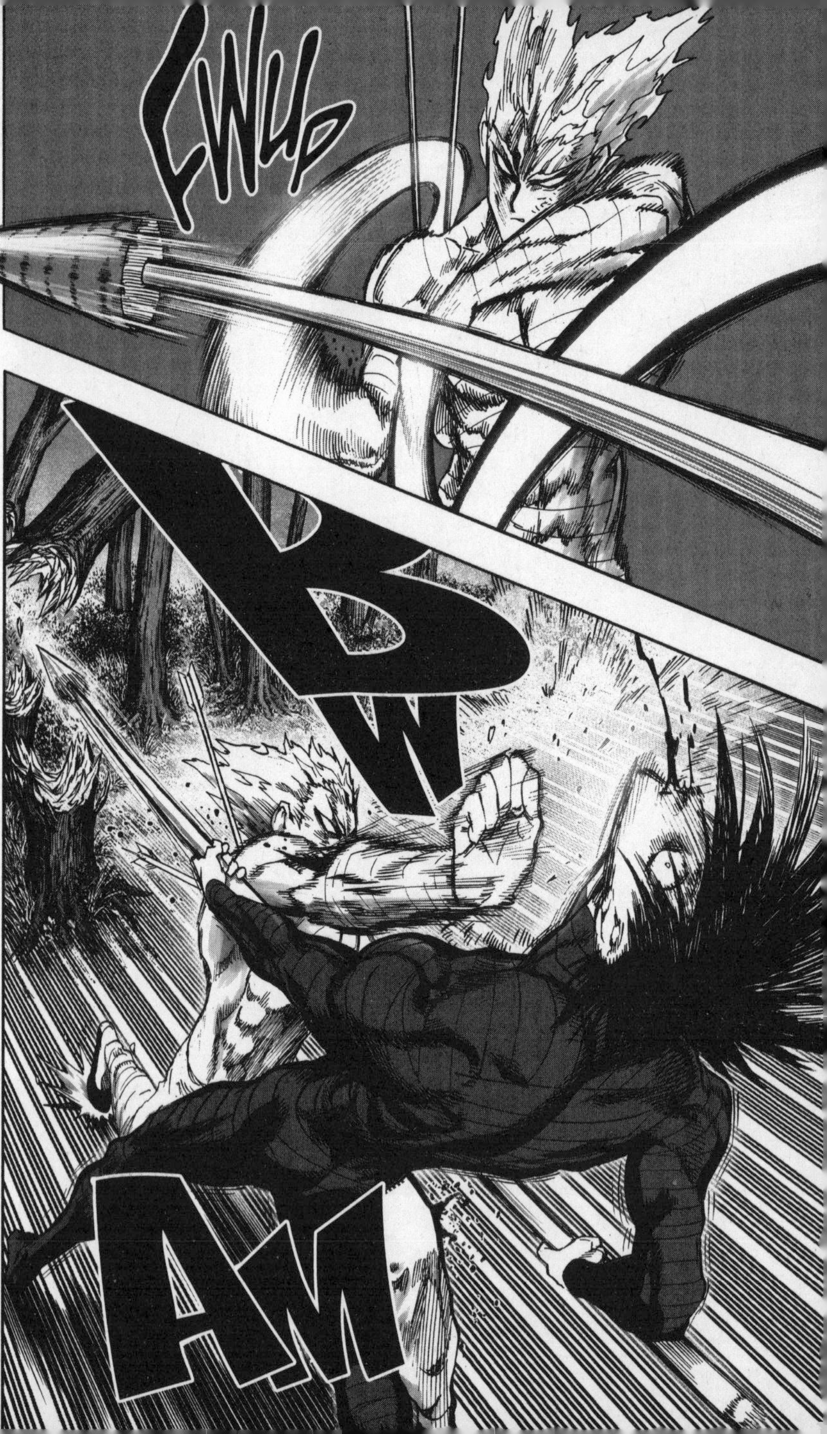
FWUP
BWAM

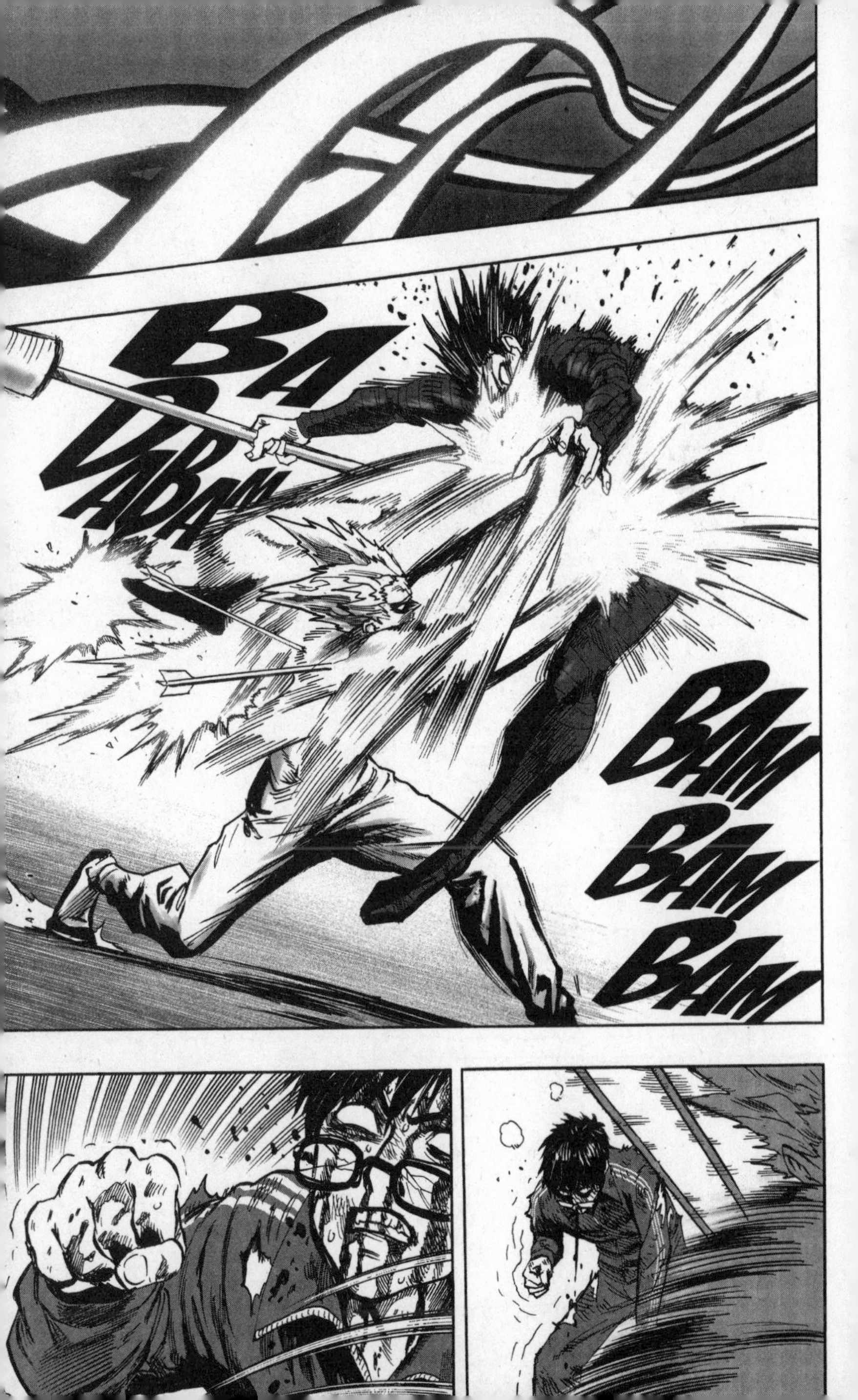
BAM BAM BAM BAM
BADADAM

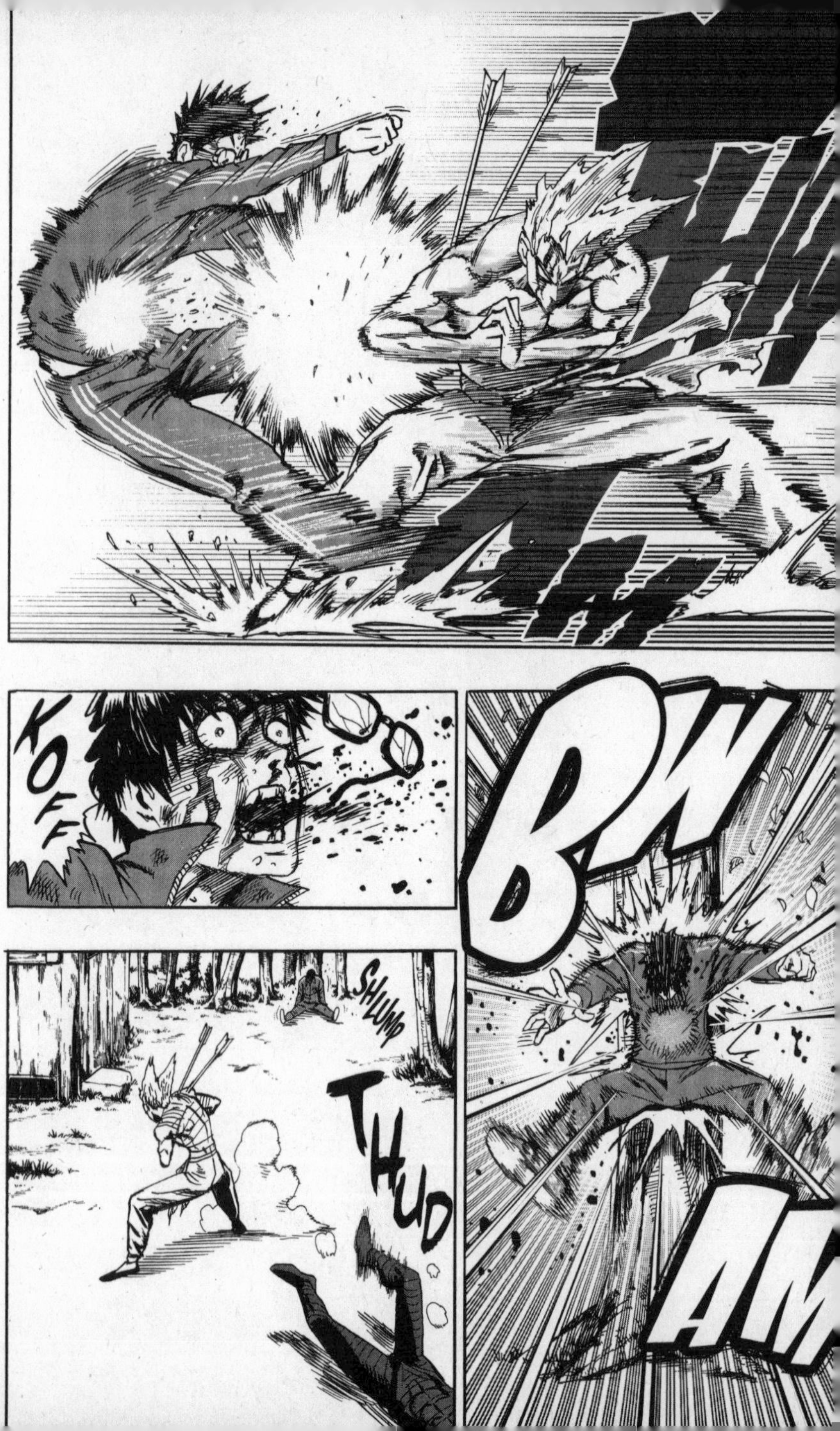
KOFF
SHLUMP
THUD

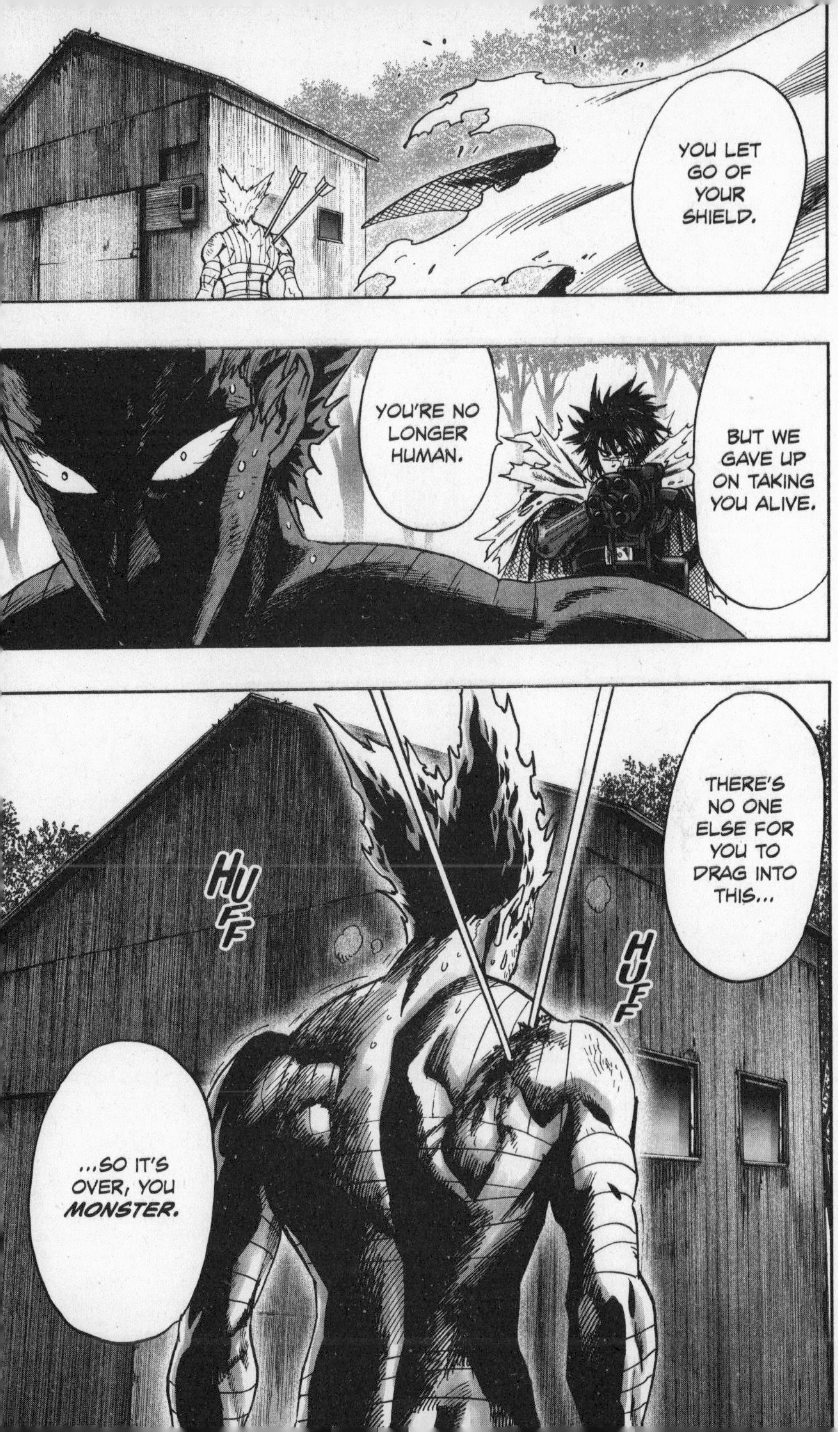
YOU LET GO OF YOUR SHIELD.
BUT WE GAVE UP ON TAKING YOU ALIVE.
YOU'RE NO LONGER HUMAN.
THERE'S NO ONE ELSE FOR YOU TO DRAG INTO THIS...
HUFF
HUFF
...SO IT'S OVER, YOU *MONSTER.*

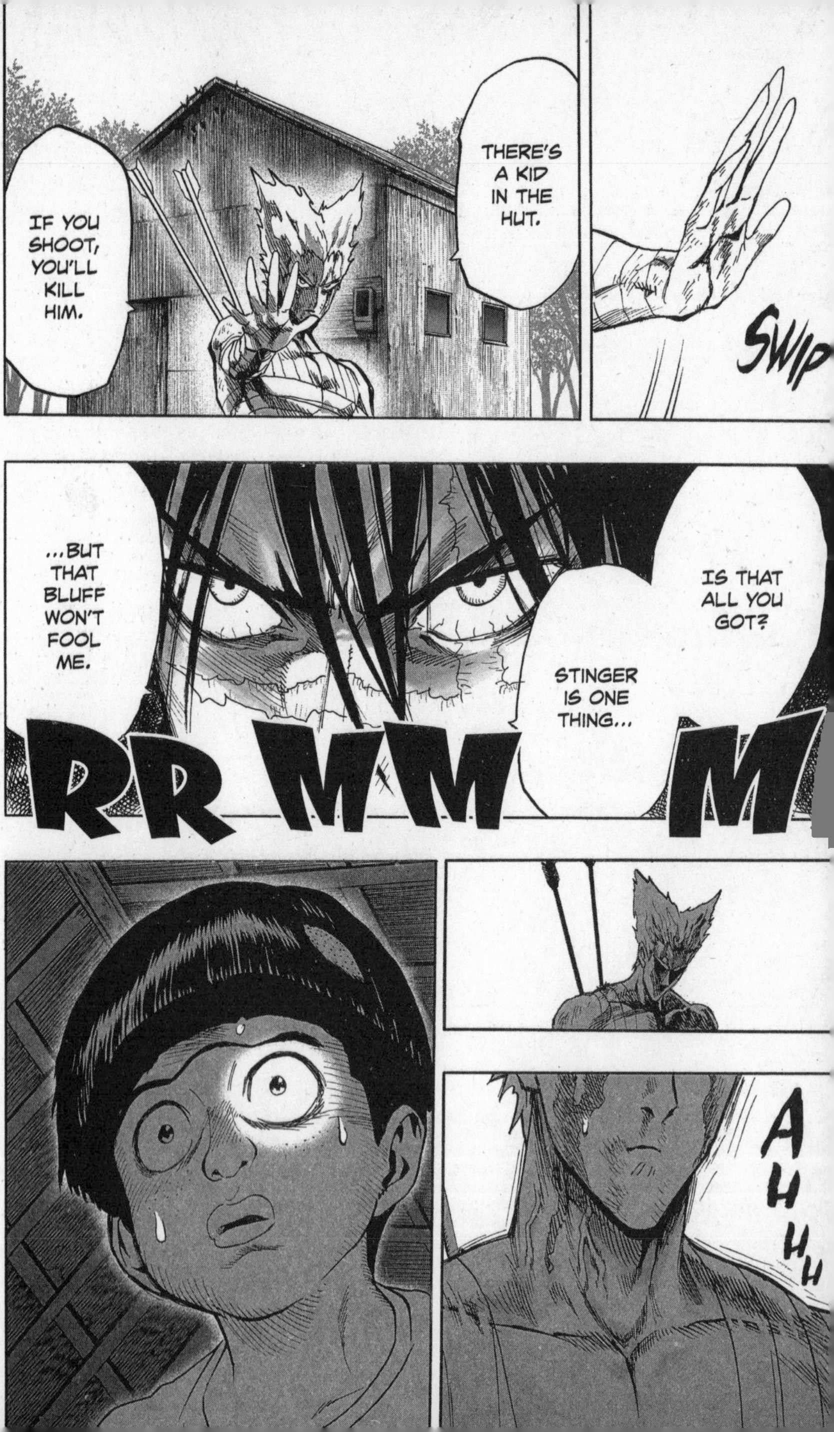
SWIP
THERE'S A KID IN THE HUT.
IF YOU SHOOT, YOU'LL KILL HIM.
IS THAT ALL YOU GOT?
STINGER IS ONE THING...
...BUT THAT BLUFF WON'T FOOL ME.
RRMMM
AHHH

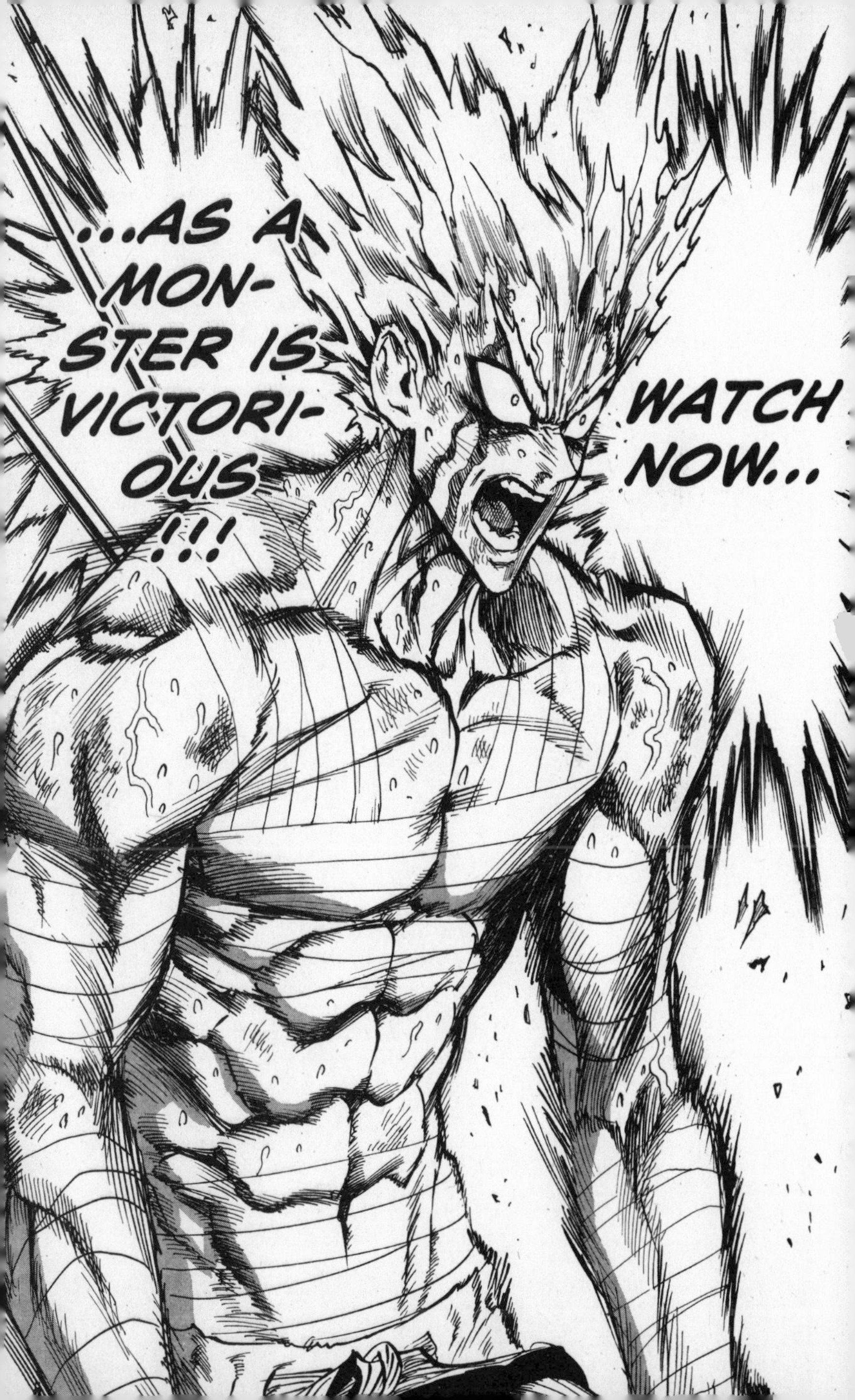
WATCH NOW...
...AS A MONSTER IS VICTORIOUS!!!

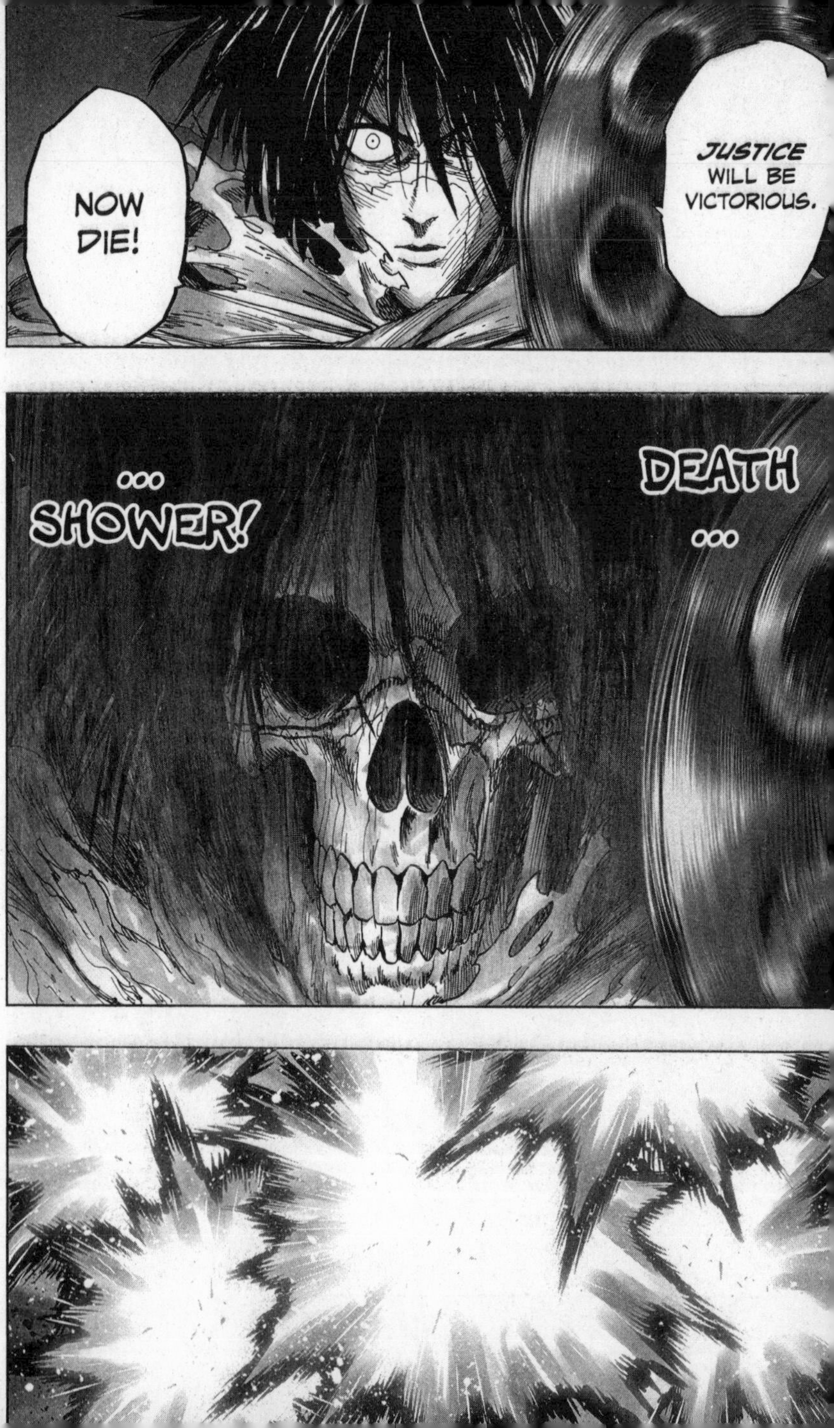
JUSTICE WILL BE VICTORIOUS.
NOW DIE!
DEATH ...
... SHOWER!

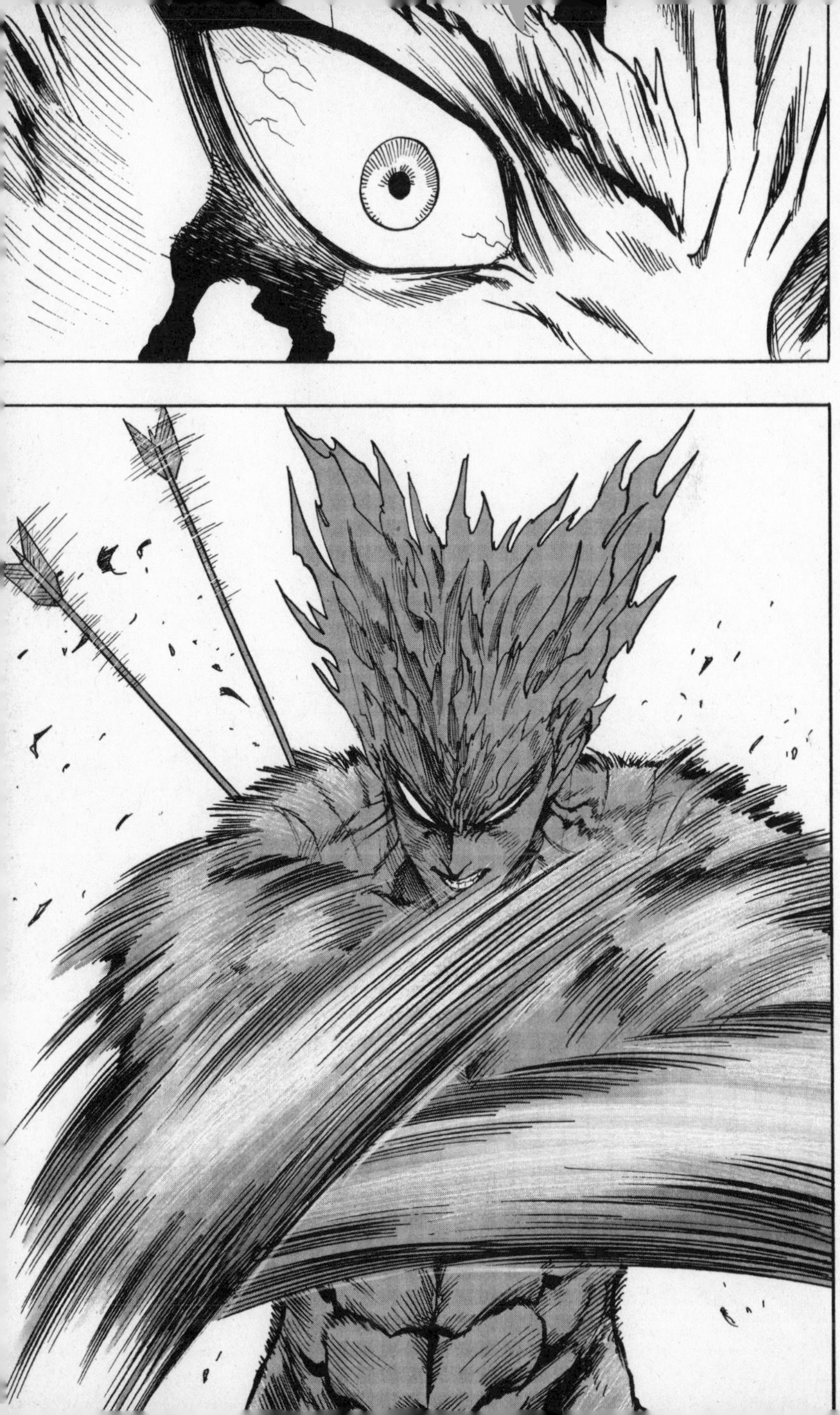

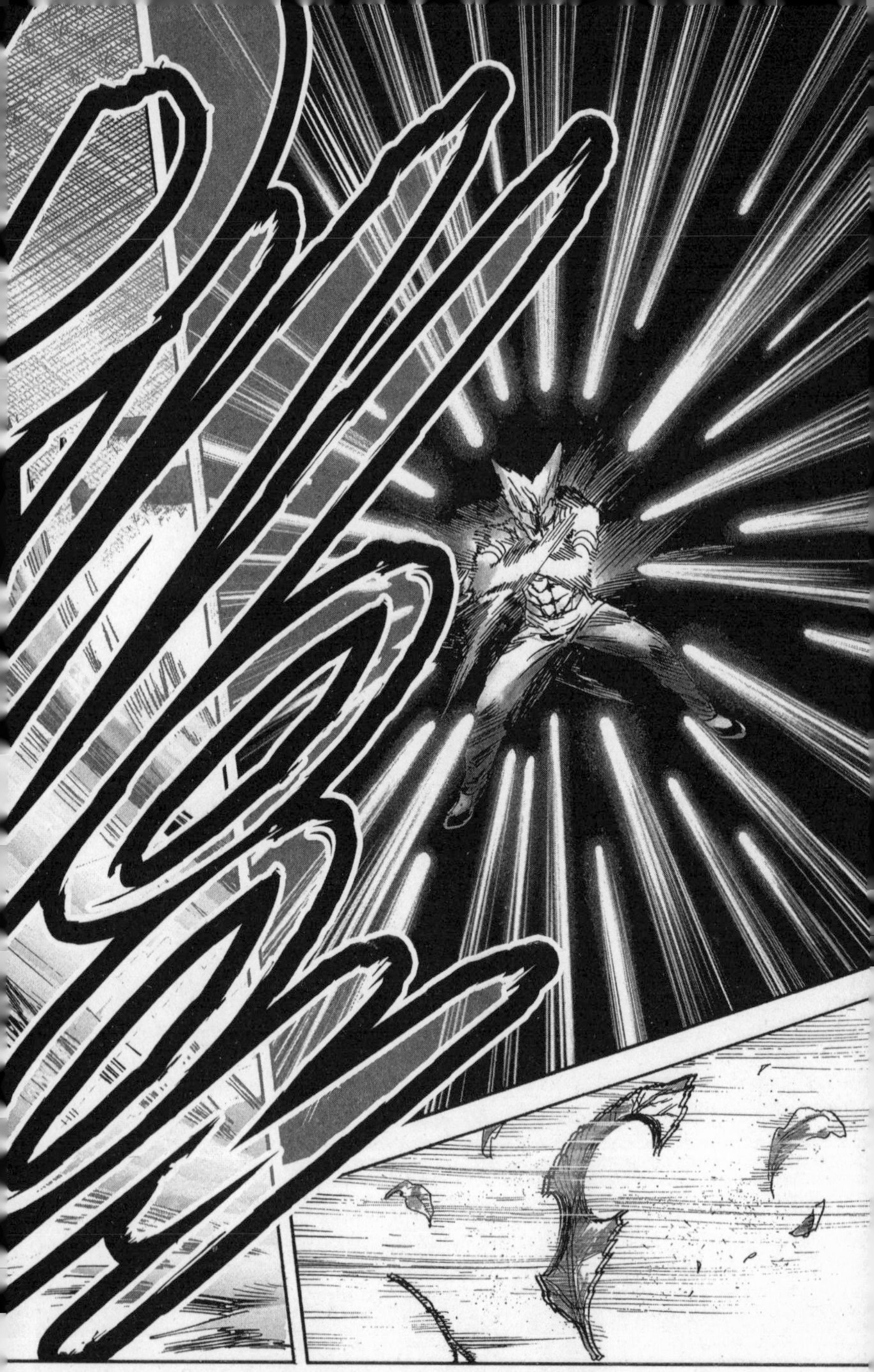

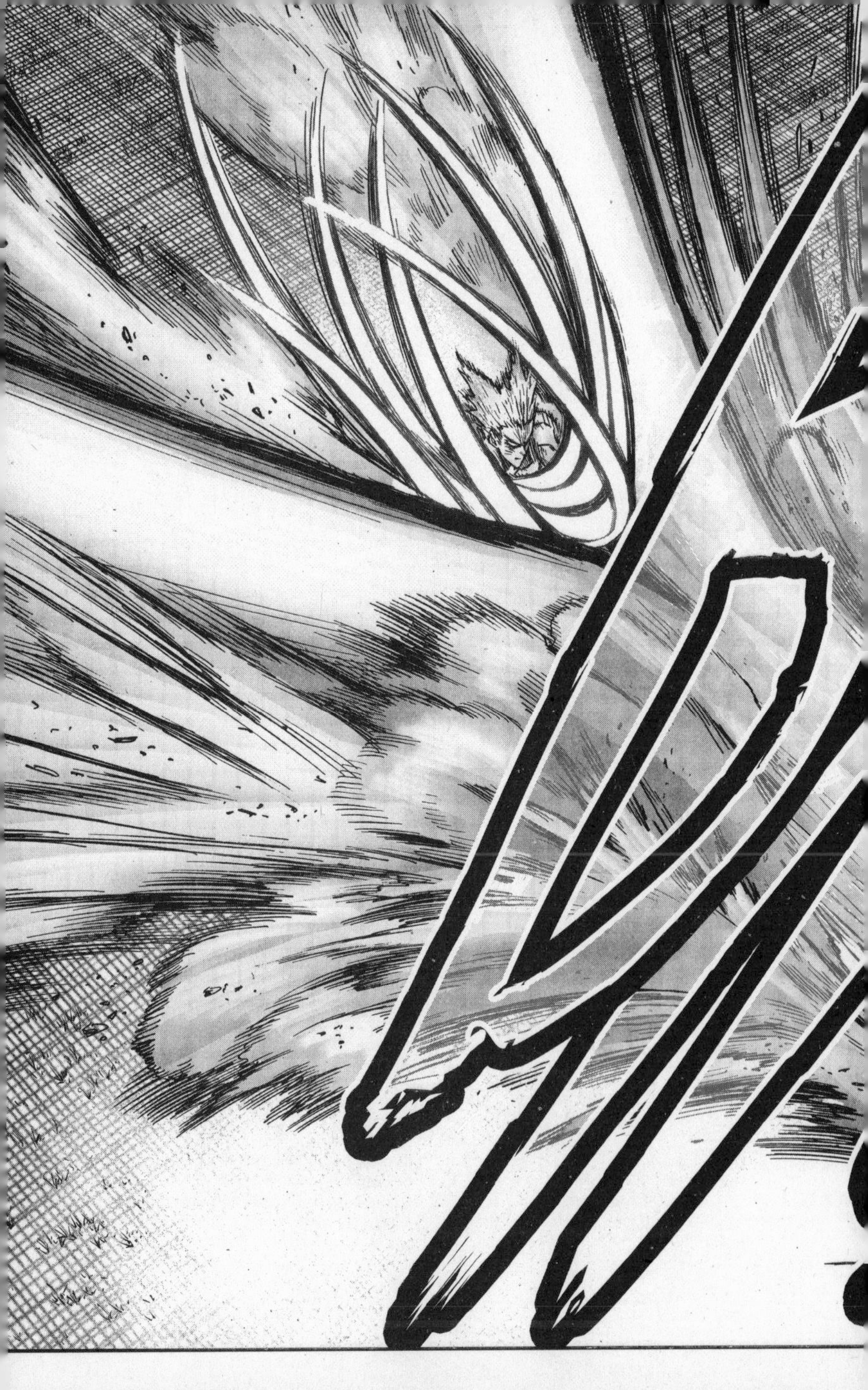

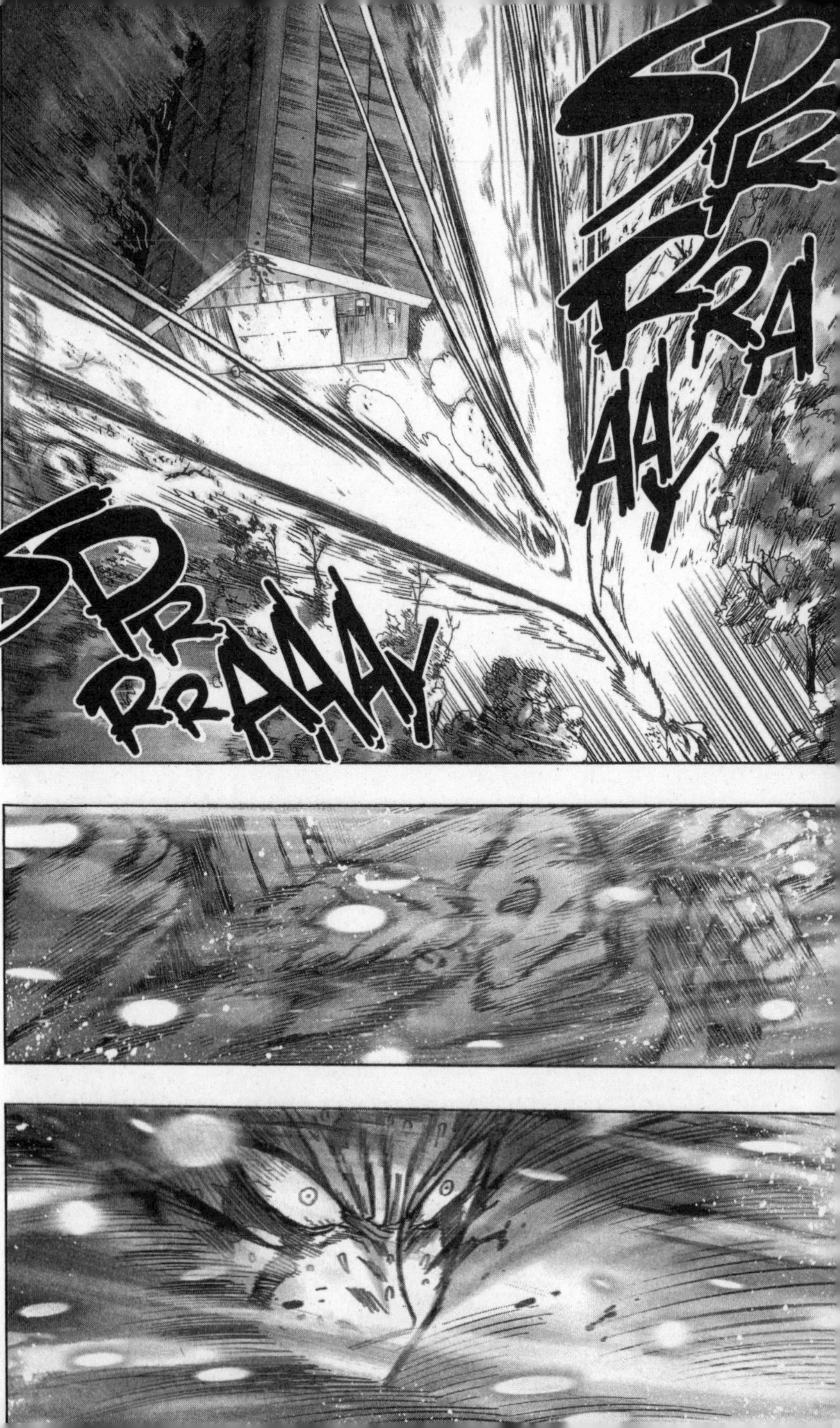
SPRRRAAAY
SPRRRAAAY

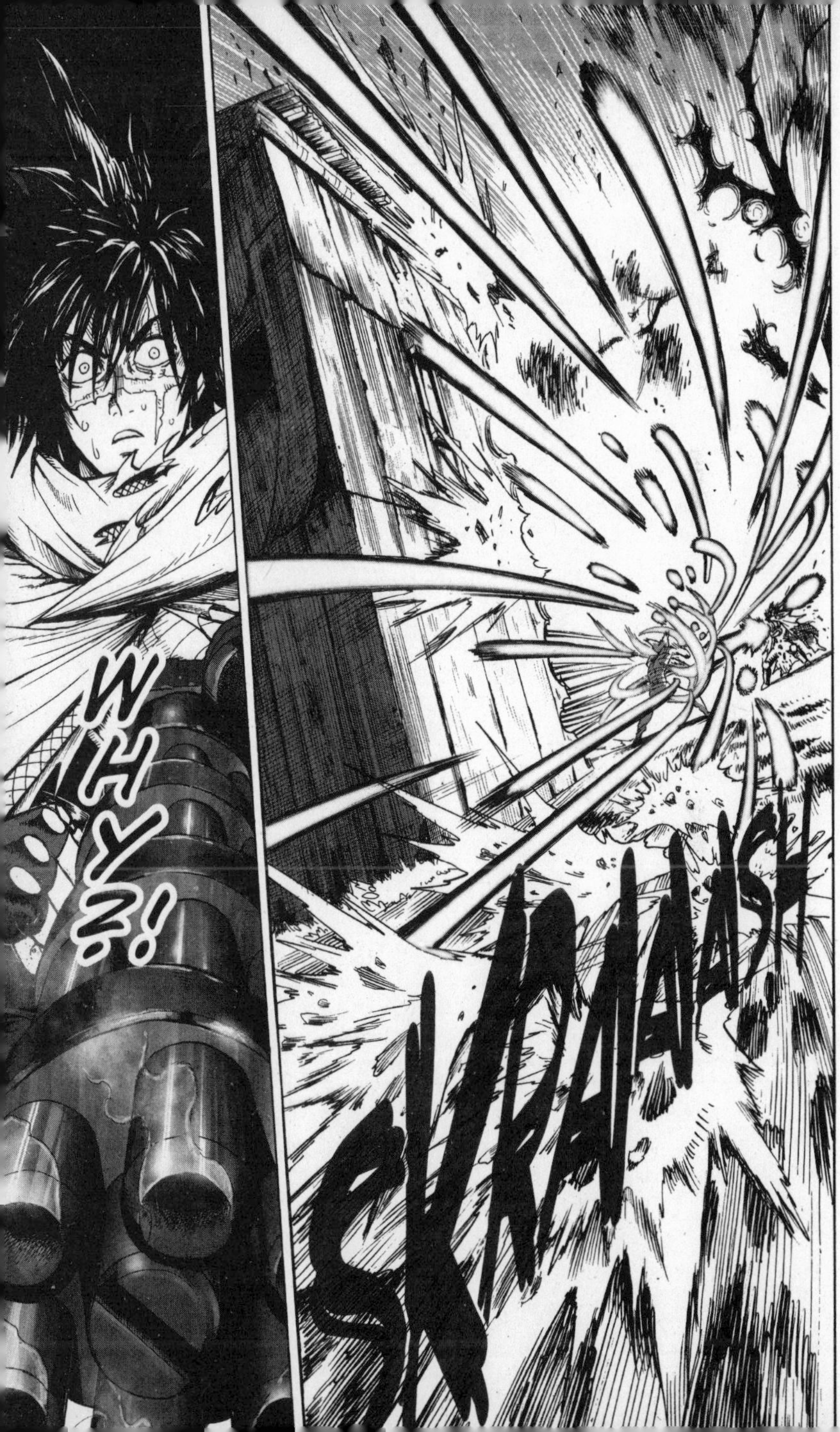
SKRAAASH
WHY?!

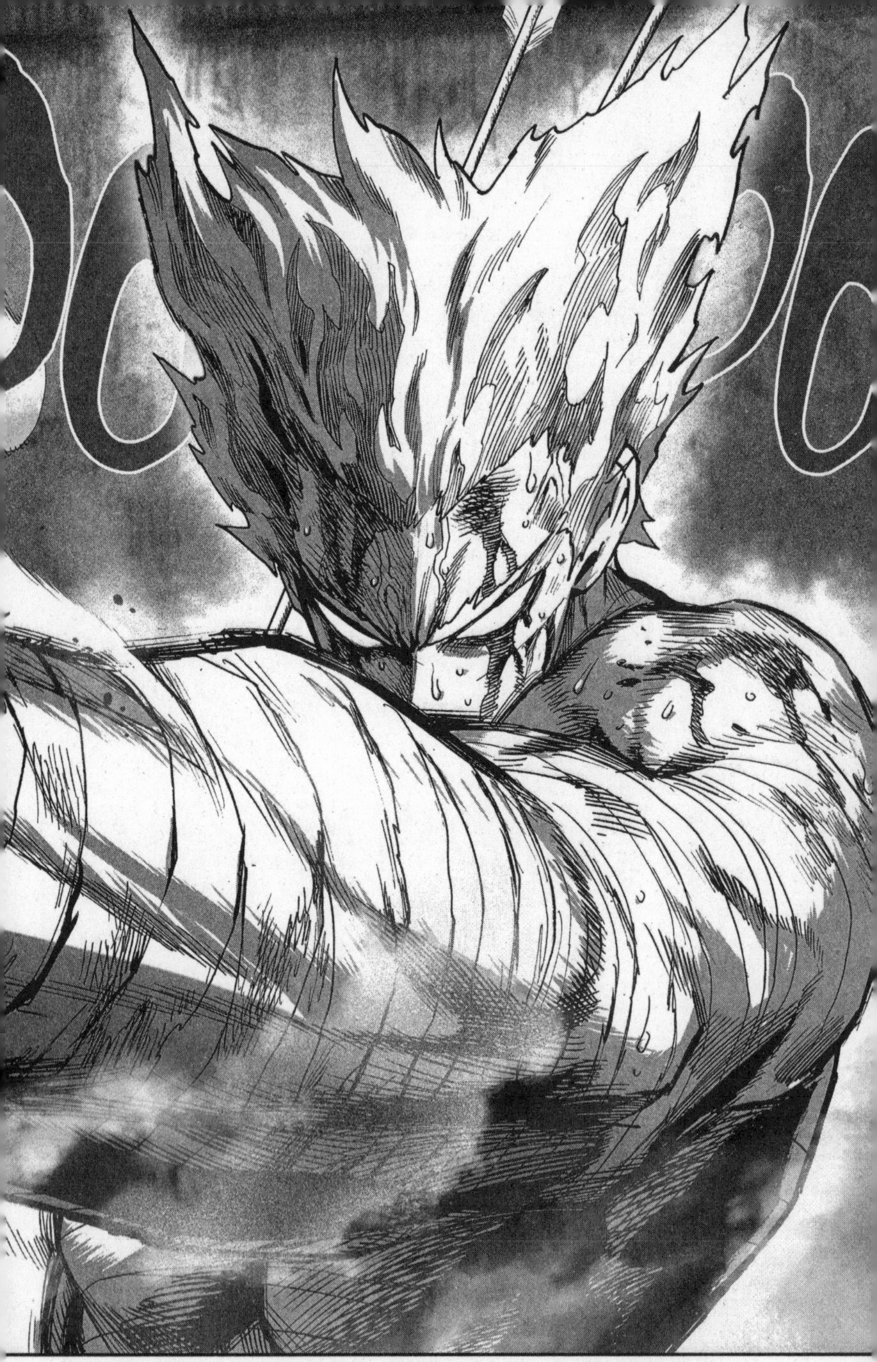

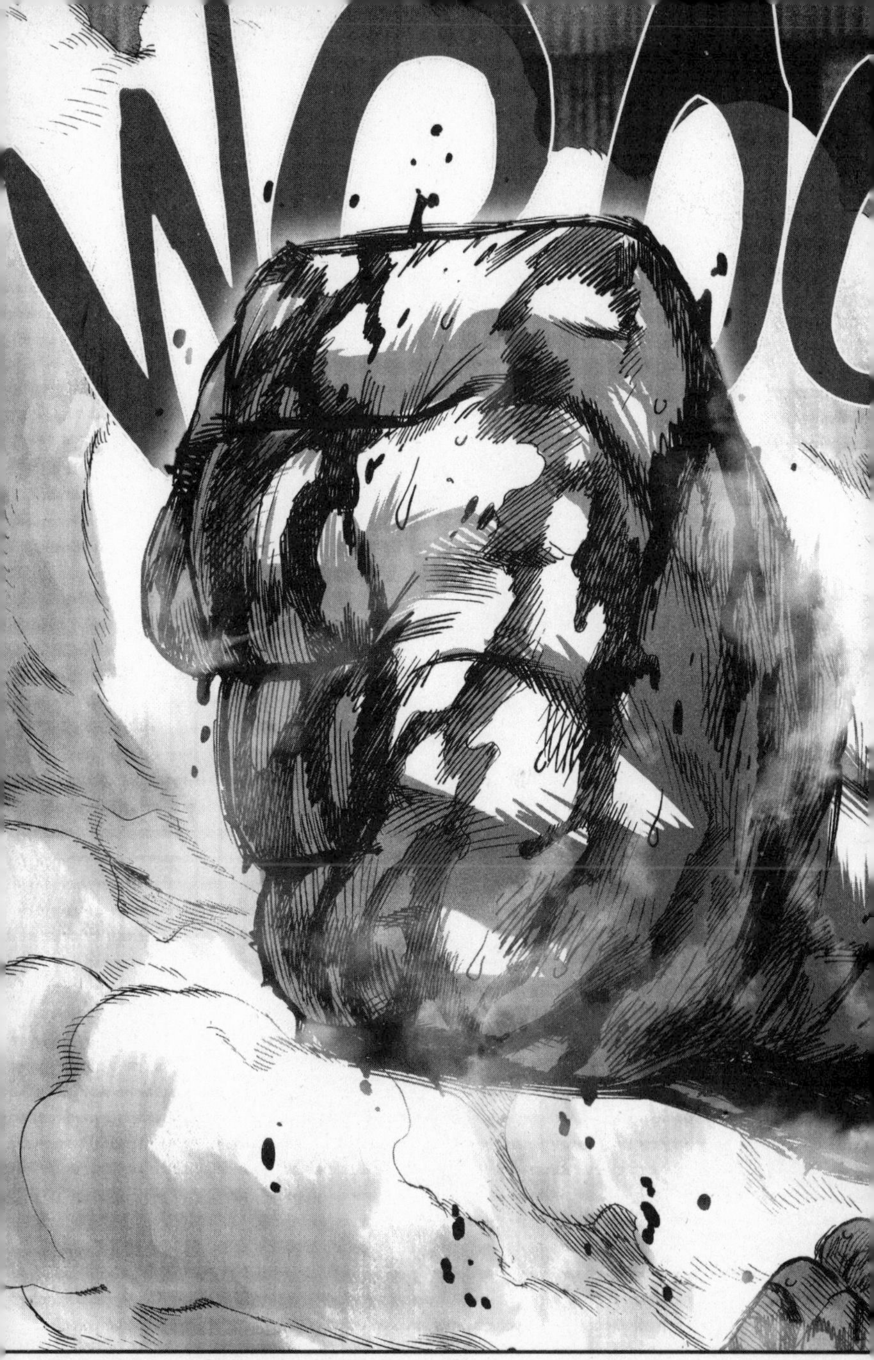
WOO

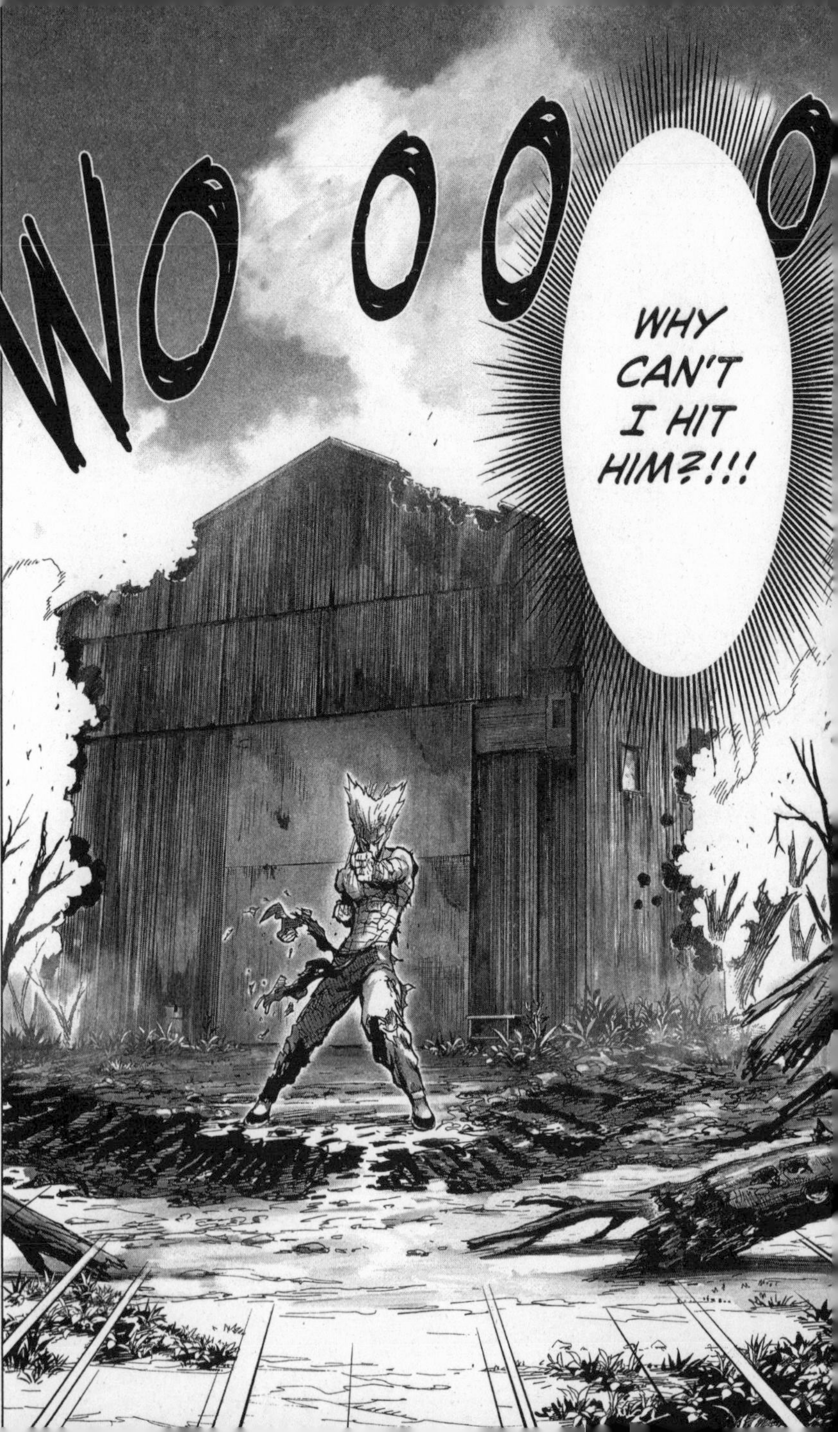
WOOOO
WHY CAN'T I HIT HIM?!!!

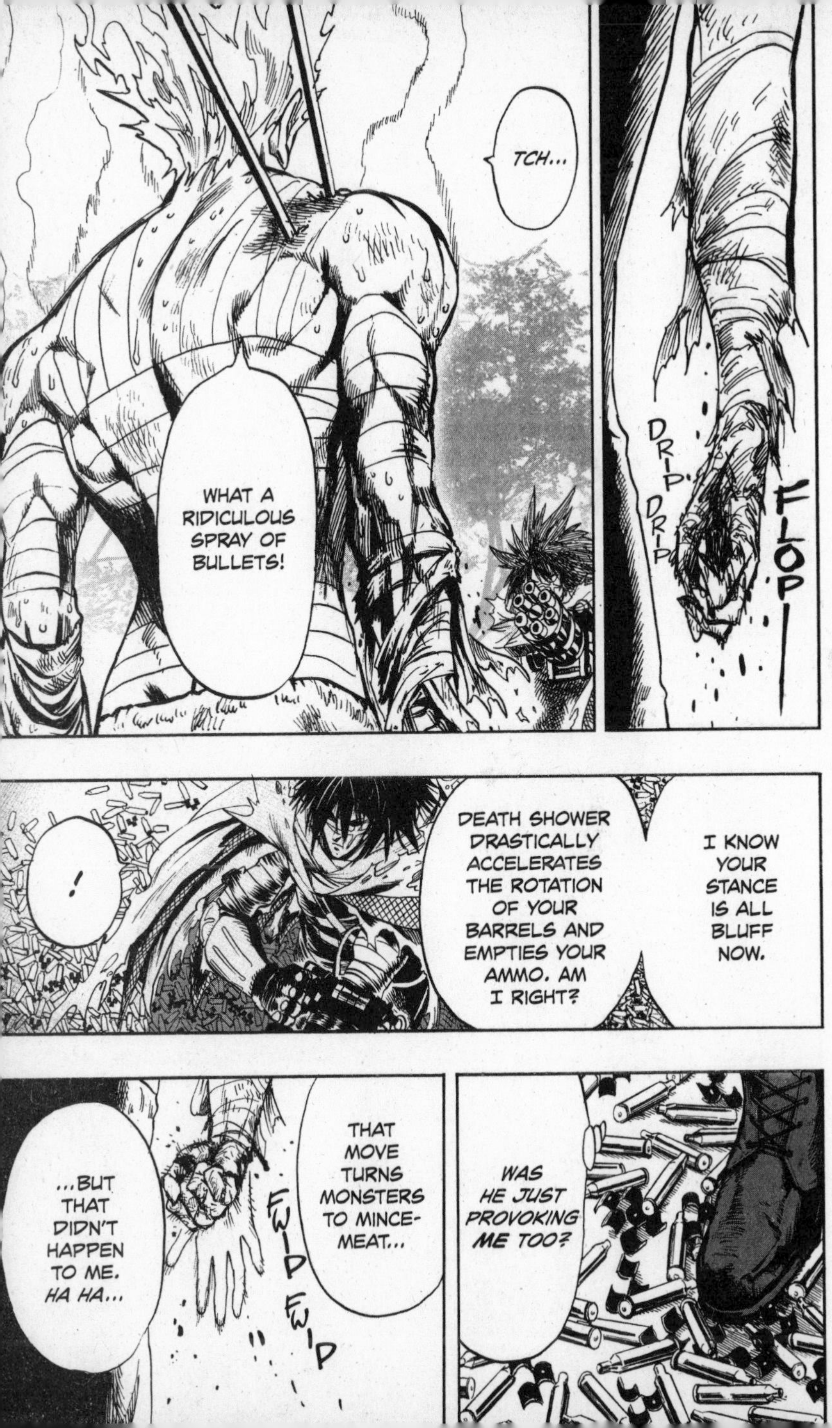
DRIP DRIP
FLOP
TCH...
WHAT A RIDICULOUS SPRAY OF BULLETS!
I KNOW YOUR STANCE IS ALL BLUFF NOW.
DEATH SHOWER DRASTICALLY ACCELERATES THE ROTATION OF YOUR BARRELS AND EMPTIES YOUR AMMO. AM I RIGHT?
!
WAS HE JUST PROVOKING ME TOO?
THAT MOVE TURNS MONSTERS TO MINCE-MEAT...
FWIP FWIP
...BUT THAT DIDN'T HAPPEN TO ME. HA HA...

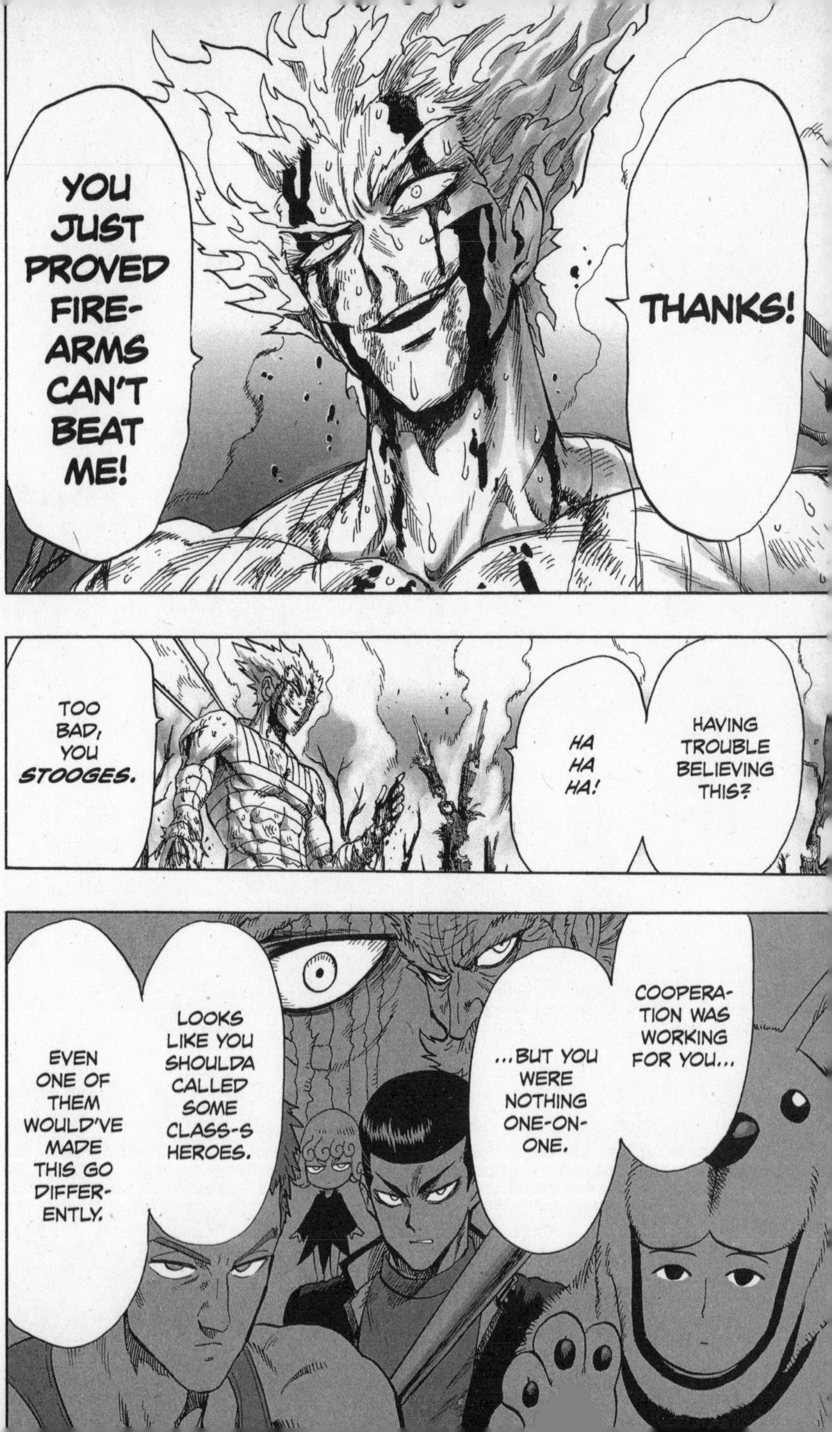
THANKS!
YOU JUST PROVED FIRE-ARMS CAN'T BEAT ME!
HAVING TROUBLE BELIEVING THIS?
HA HA HA!
TOO BAD, YOU *STOOGES*.
COOPERA-TION WAS WORKING FOR YOU...
...BUT YOU WERE NOTHING ONE-ON-ONE.
LOOKS LIKE YOU SHOULDA CALLED SOME CLASS-S HEROES.
EVEN ONE OF THEM WOULD'VE MADE THIS GO DIFFER-ENTLY.

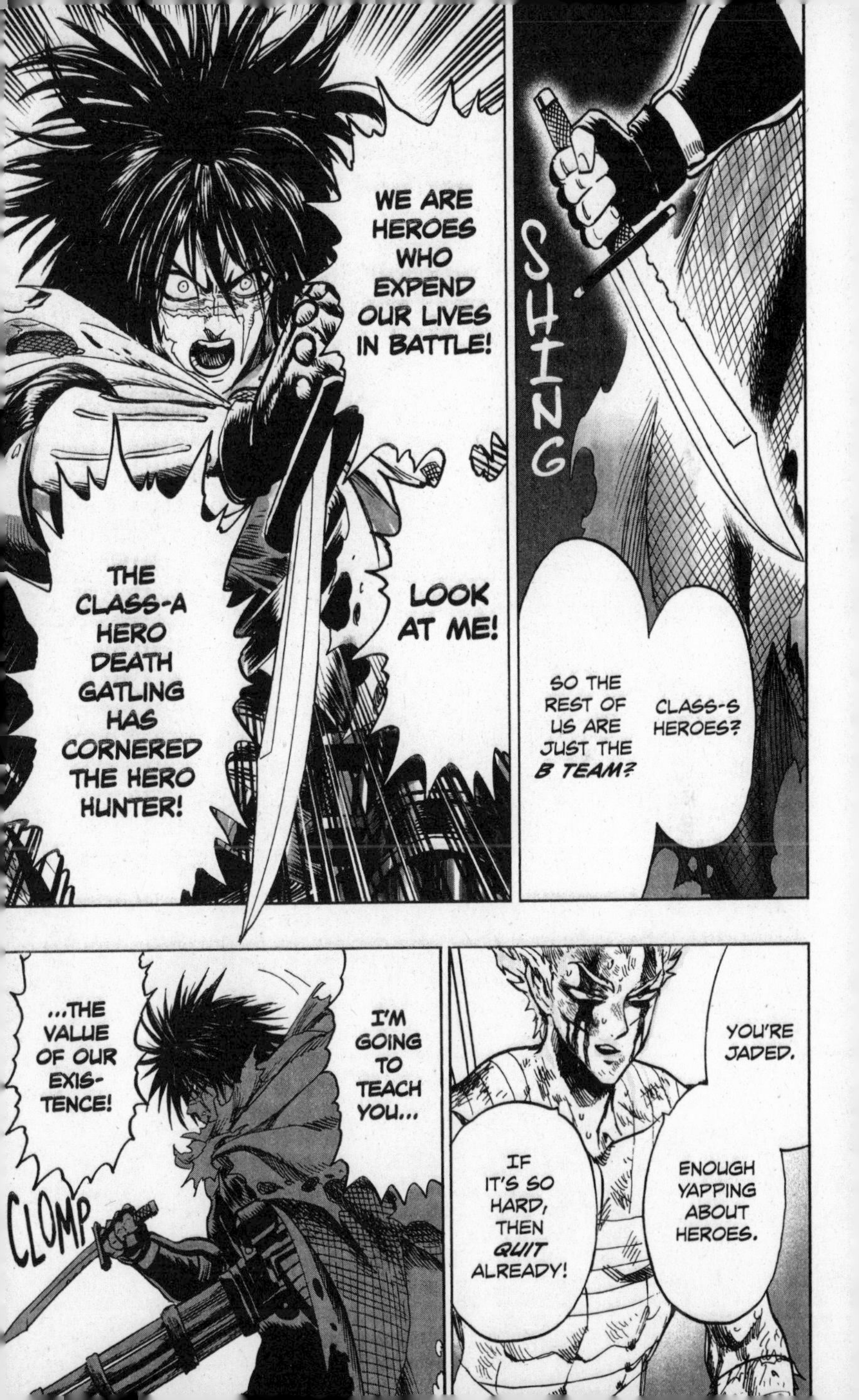
SHING
CLASS-S HEROES?
SO THE REST OF US ARE JUST THE *B TEAM?*
WE ARE HEROES WHO EXPEND OUR LIVES IN BATTLE!
LOOK AT ME!
THE CLASS-A HERO DEATH GATLING HAS CORNERED THE HERO HUNTER!
YOU'RE JADED.
ENOUGH YAPPING ABOUT HEROES.
IF IT'S SO HARD, THEN *QUIT* ALREADY!
I'M GOING TO TEACH YOU...
...THE VALUE OF OUR EXIS-TENCE!
CLOMP

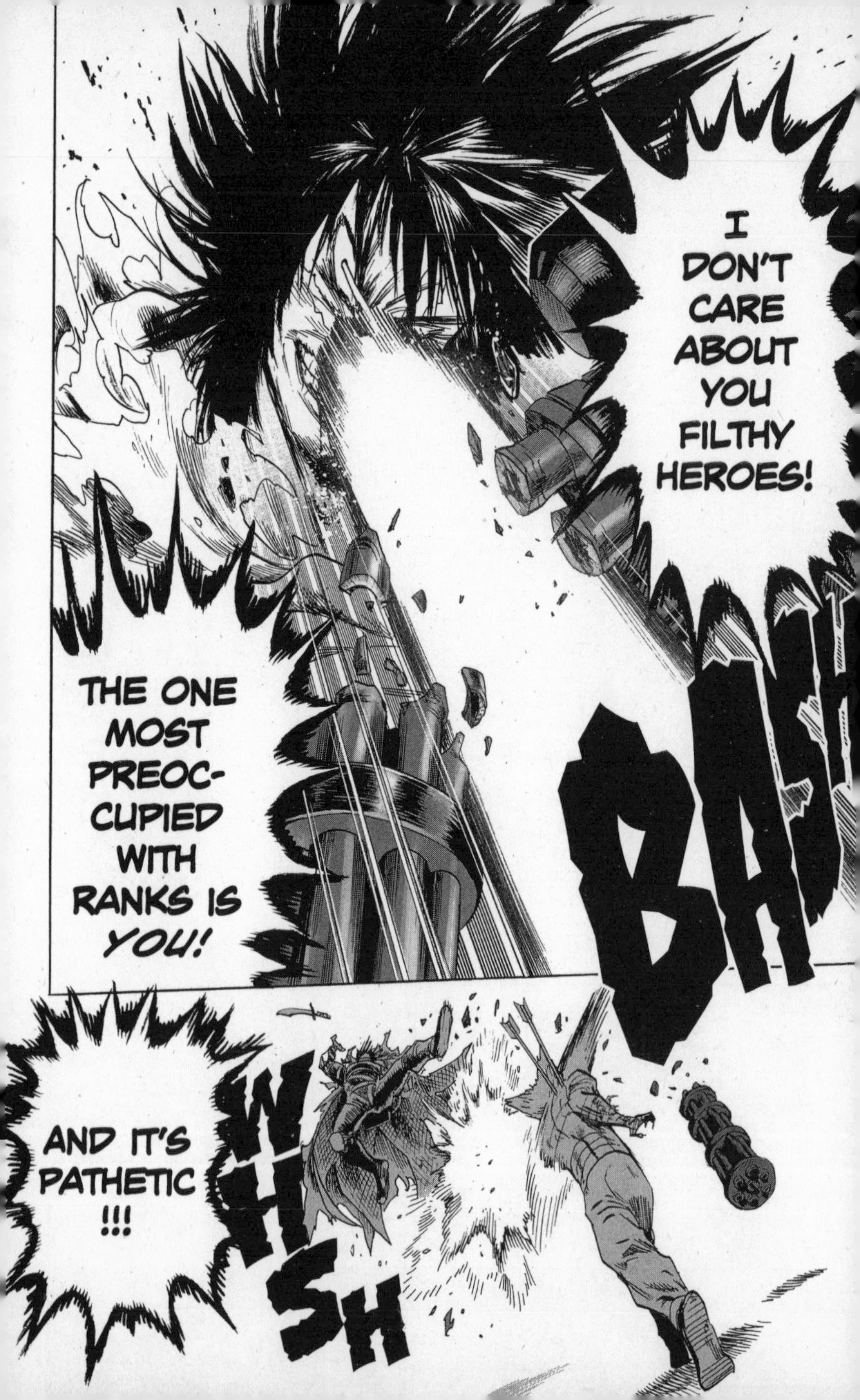
I DON'T CARE ABOUT YOU FILTHY HEROES!
THE ONE MOST PREOCCUPIED WITH RANKS IS *YOU!*
AND IT'S PATHETIC !!!

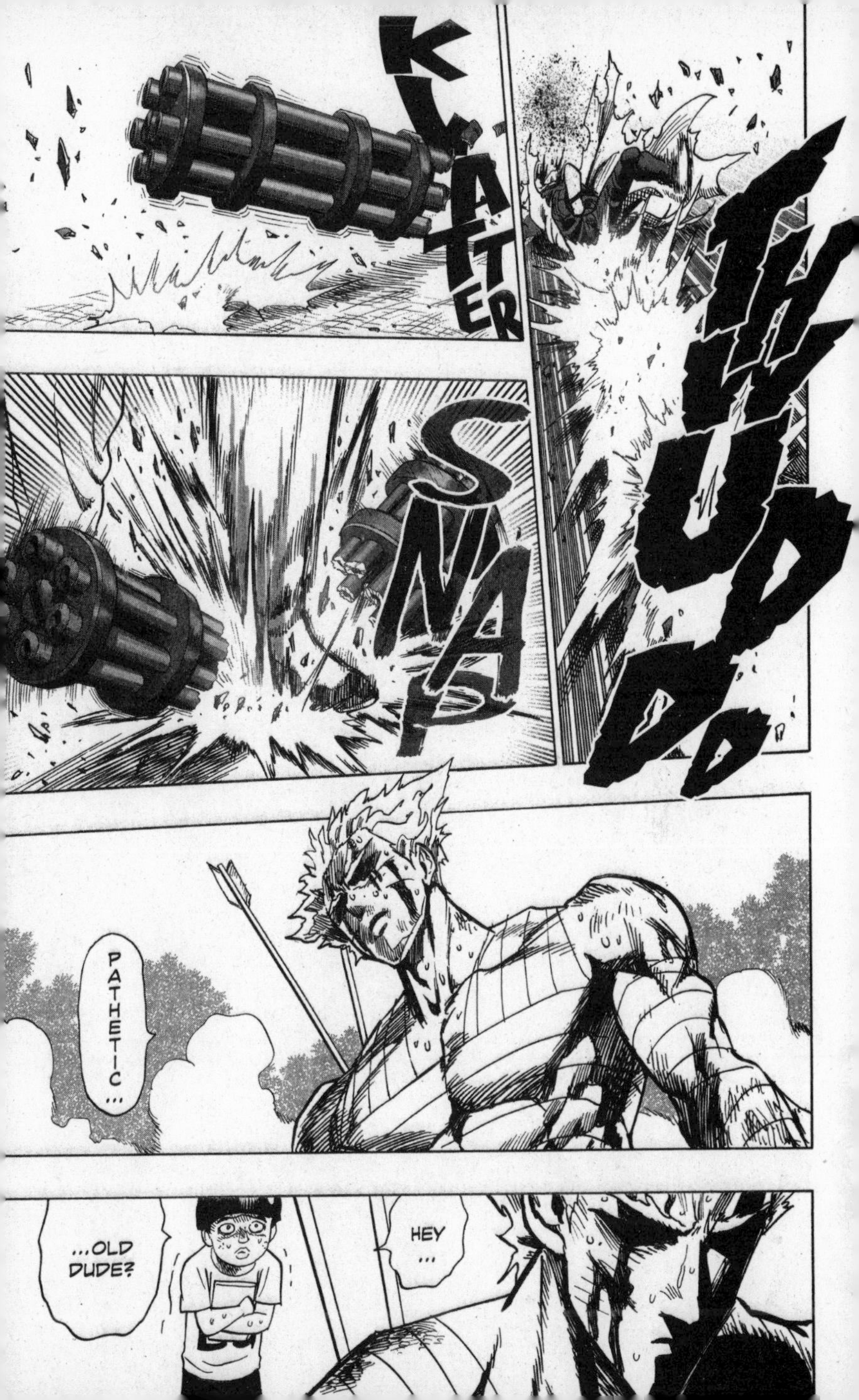
THUDDD
KLATTER
SNAP
PATHETIC...
HEY...
...OLD DUDE?

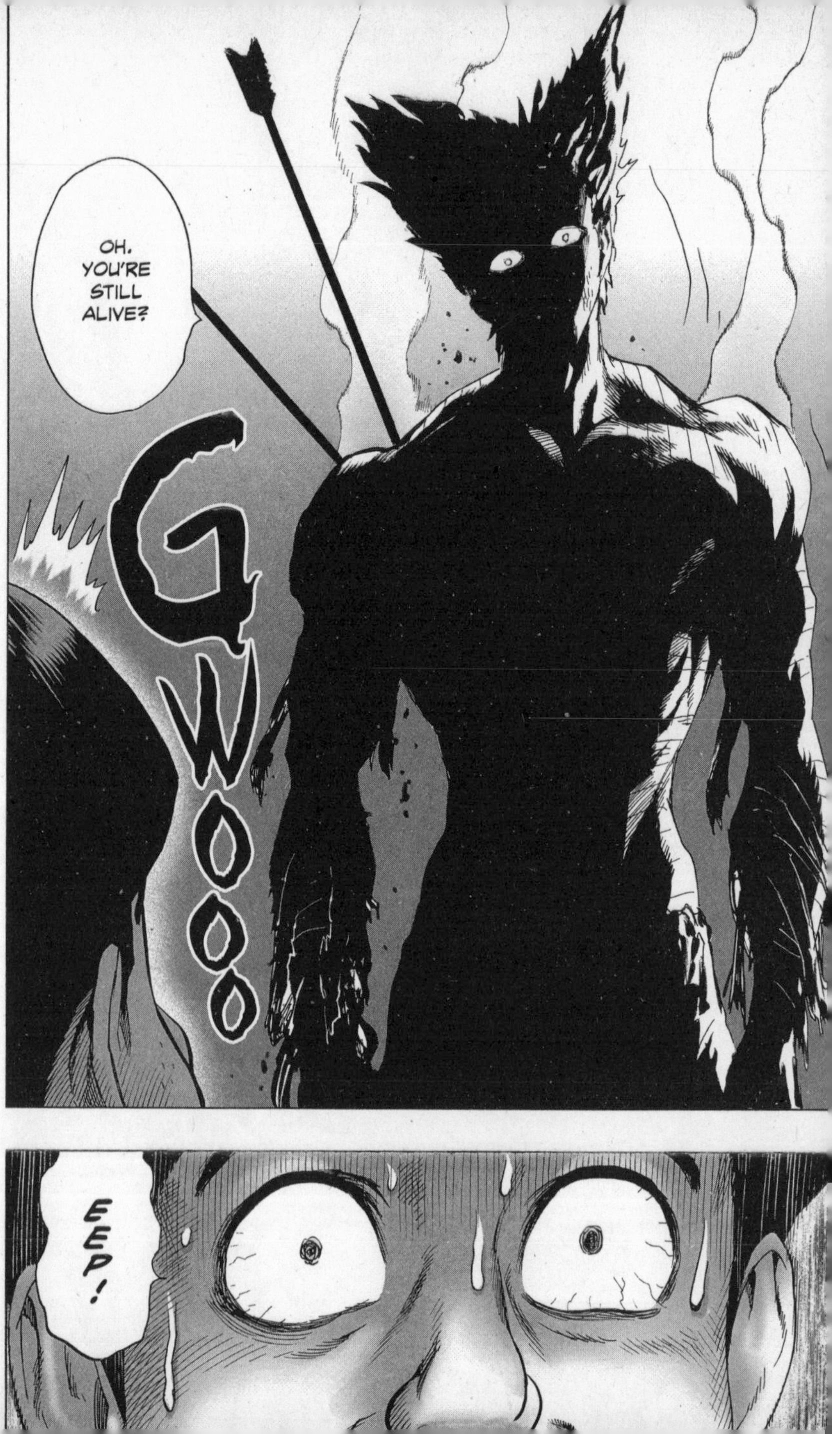
OH. YOU'RE STILL ALIVE?
GWOOO
EEP!

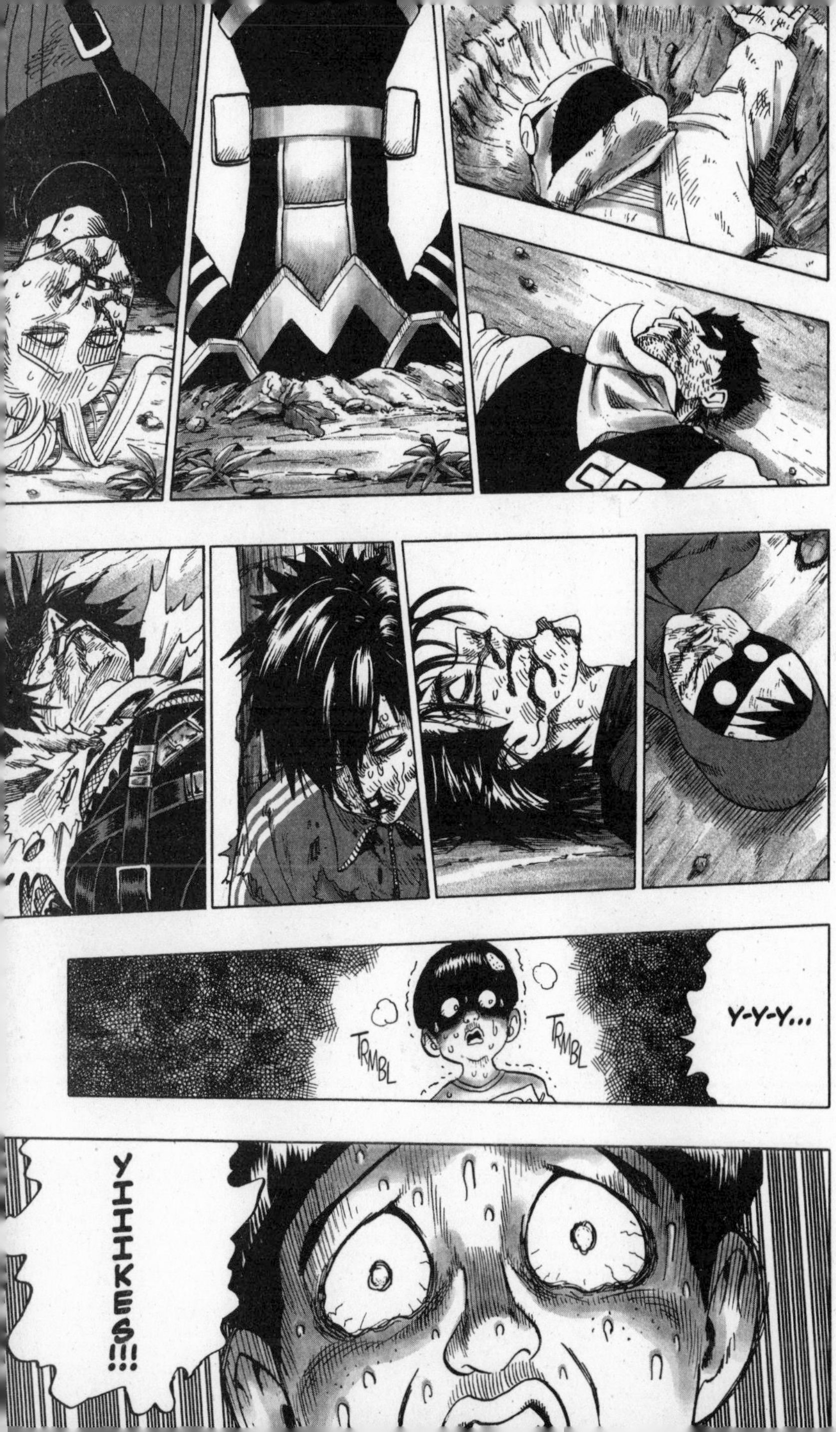

Y-Y-Y...
TRMBL
TRMBL
YIIIIKES!!!

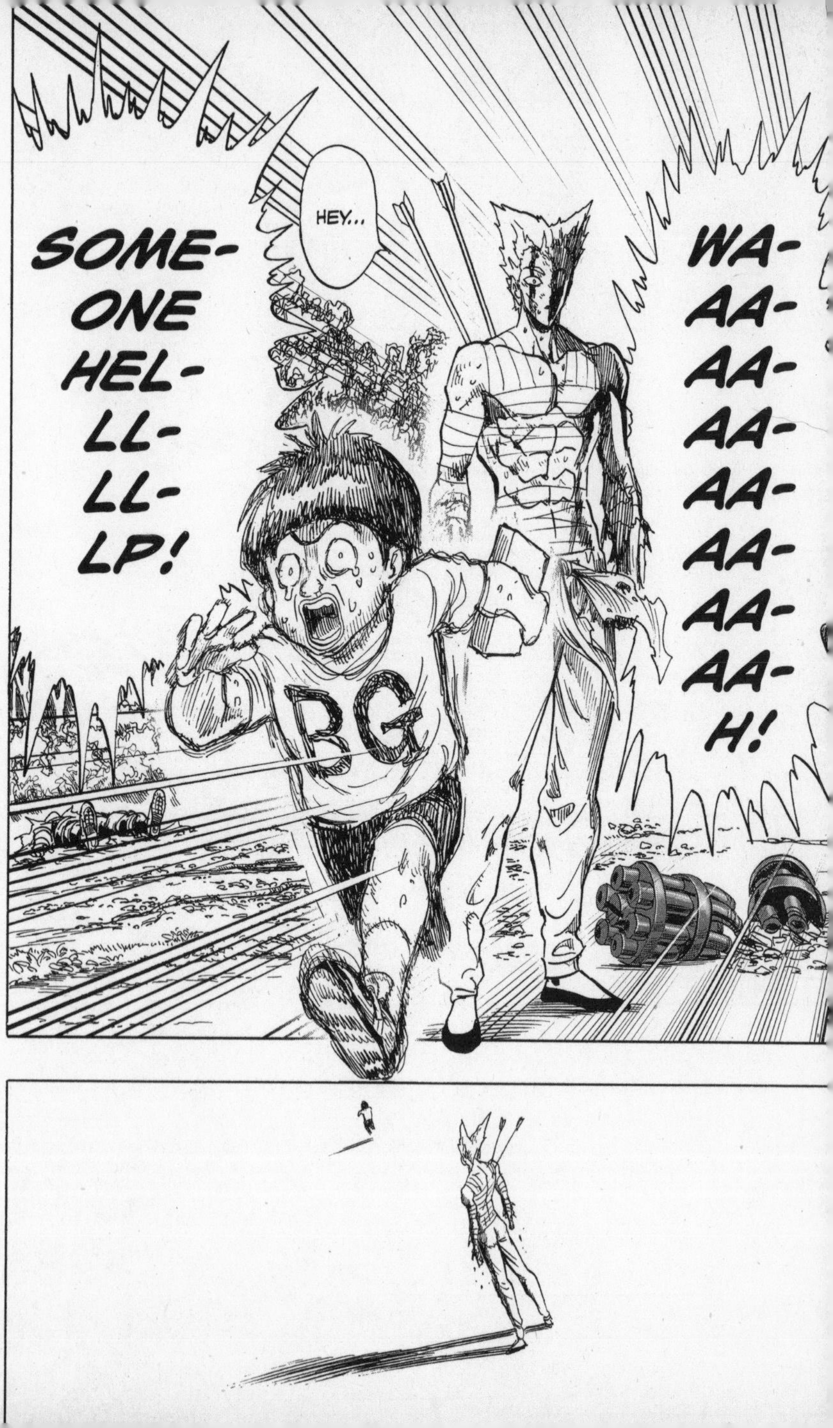
WA-AA-AA-AA-AA-AA-AA-AA-H!
HEY...
SOME-ONE HEL-LL-LL-LP!

HFFFT!

...

GRAB

...

HUF

HUF

I SHOULD TREAT MY WOUNDS...

SHUK

MMM

SHUK

KLUNK

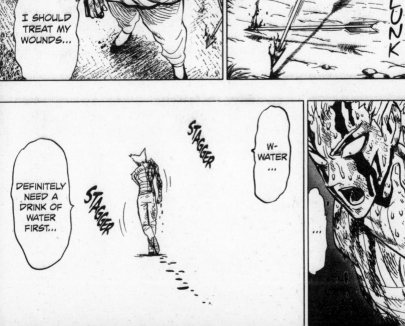

STAGGER

W-WATER...

DEFINITELY NEED A DRINK OF WATER FIRST...

STAGGER

...

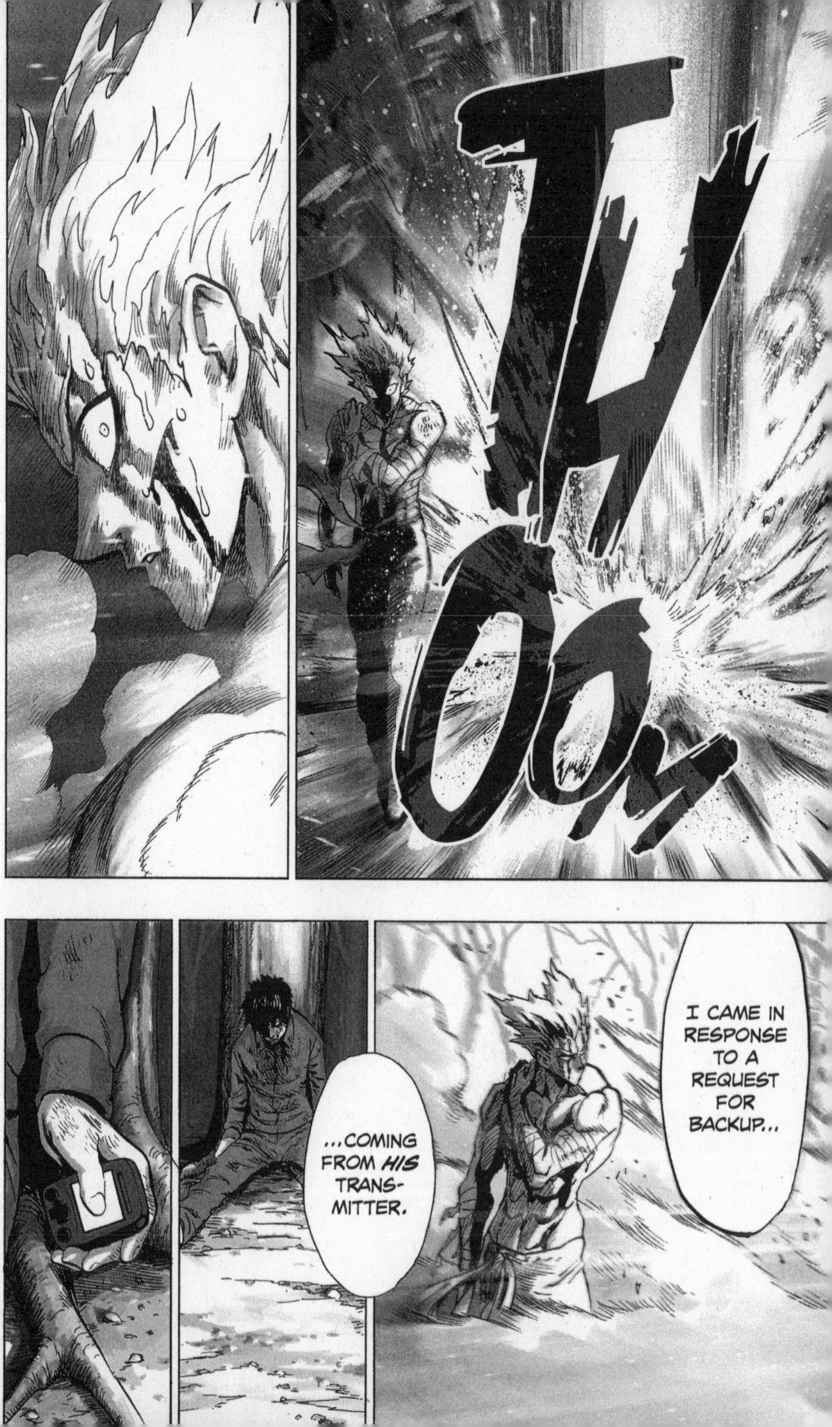
I CAME IN RESPONSE TO A REQUEST FOR BACKUP...
...COMING FROM *HIS* TRANSMITTER.

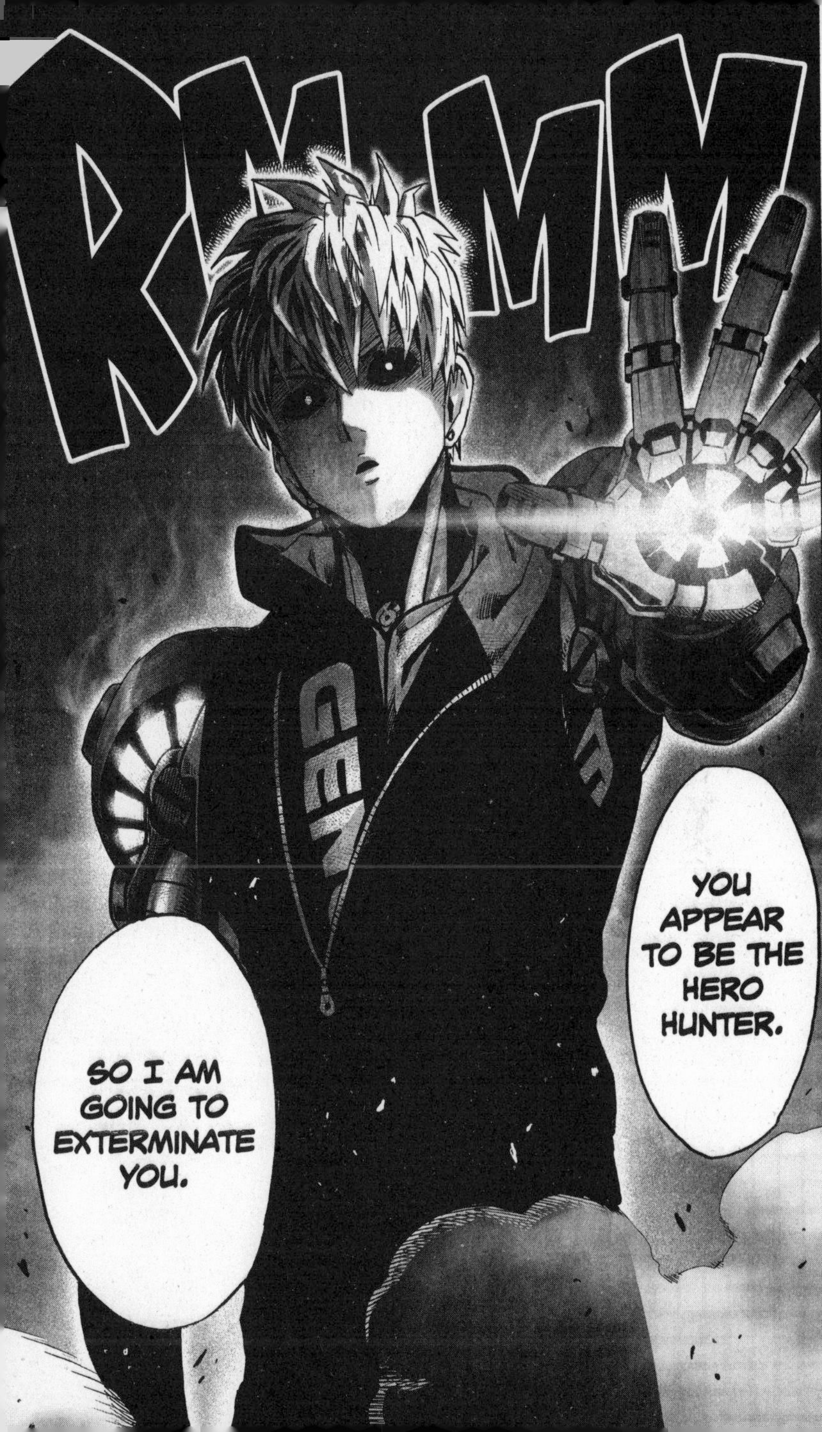
RMMM
YOU APPEAR TO BE THE HERO HUNTER.
SO I AM GOING TO EXTERMINATE YOU.

PUNCH 83: CRUEL STEPS

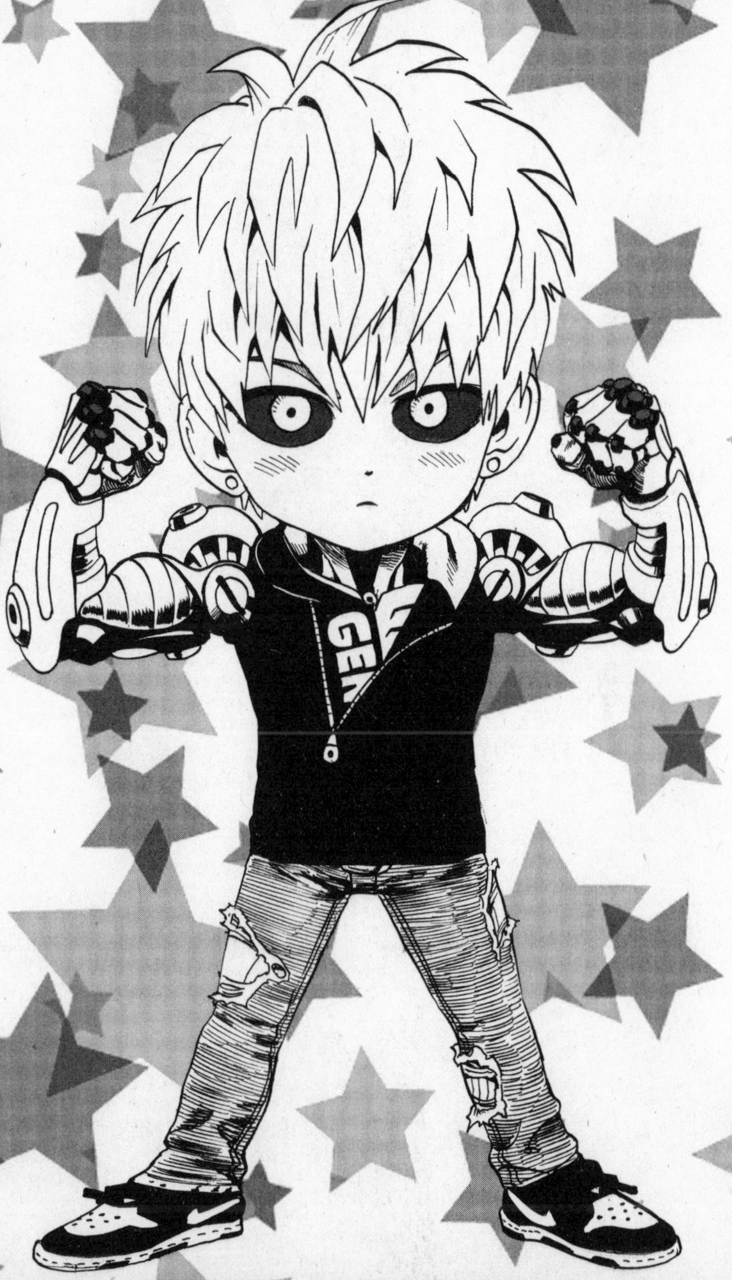

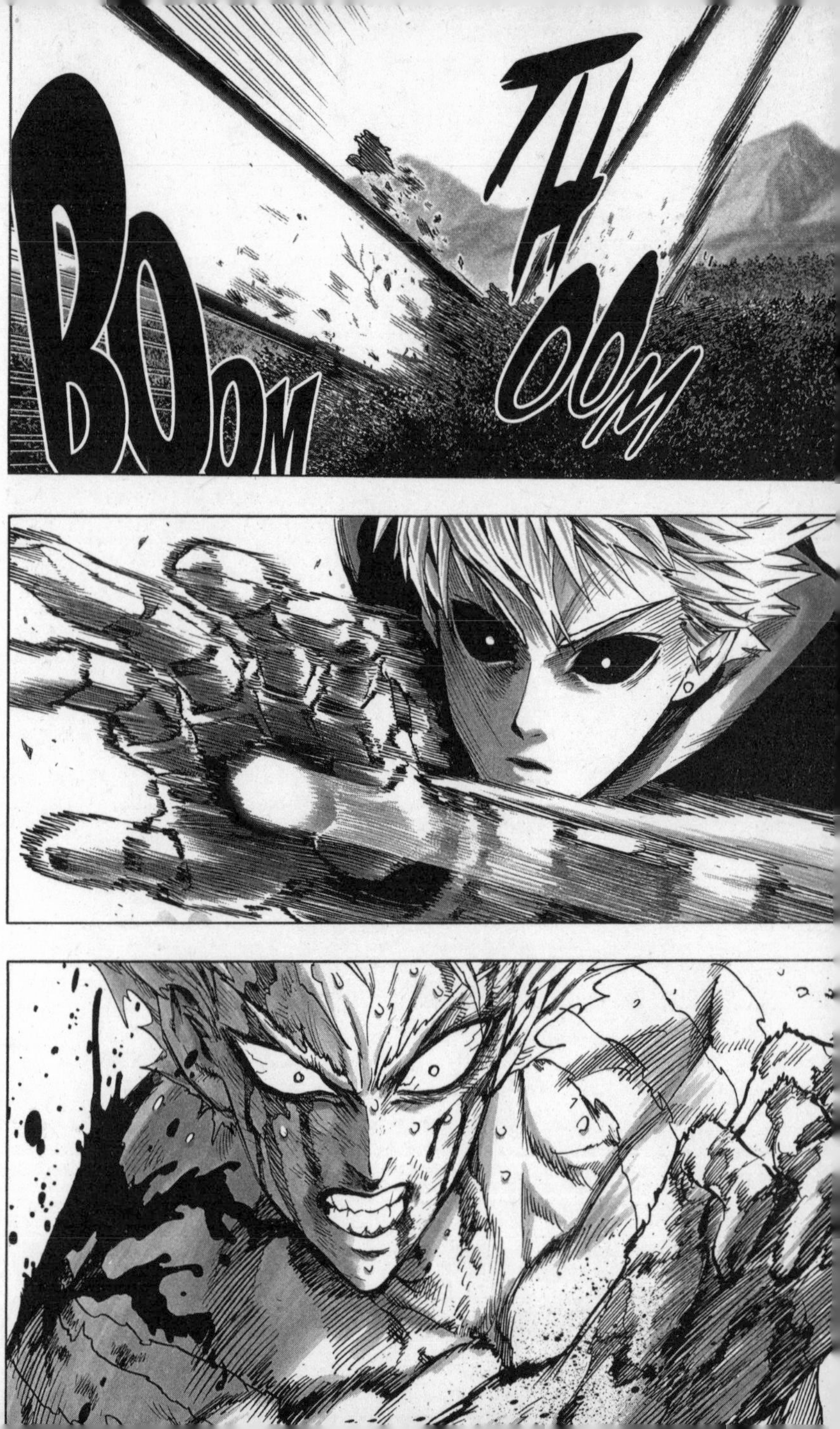
THOOM
BOOM

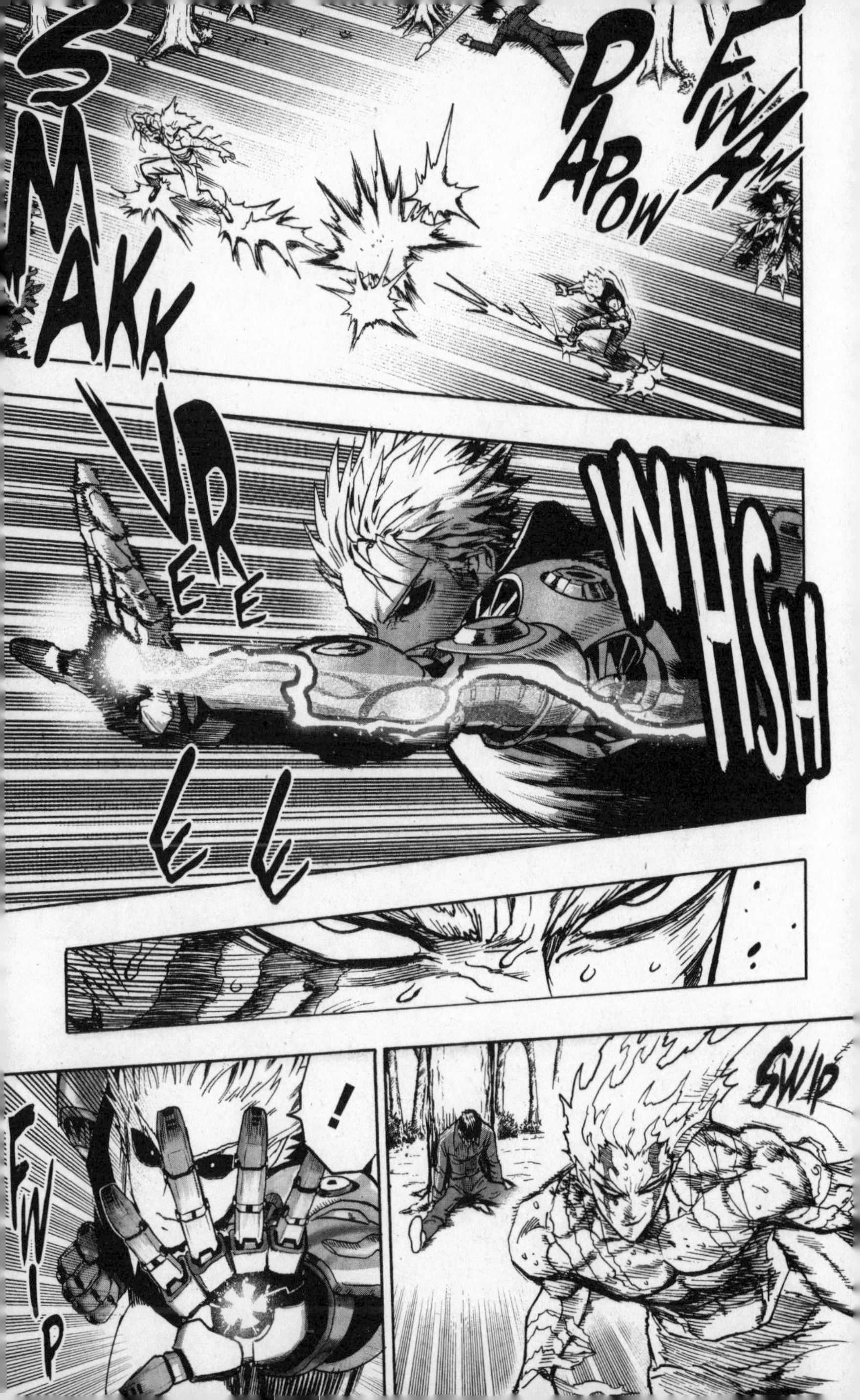
FWAAM
PAPOW
SMAKK
WHSH
VREEEE
SWIP
!
FWIP

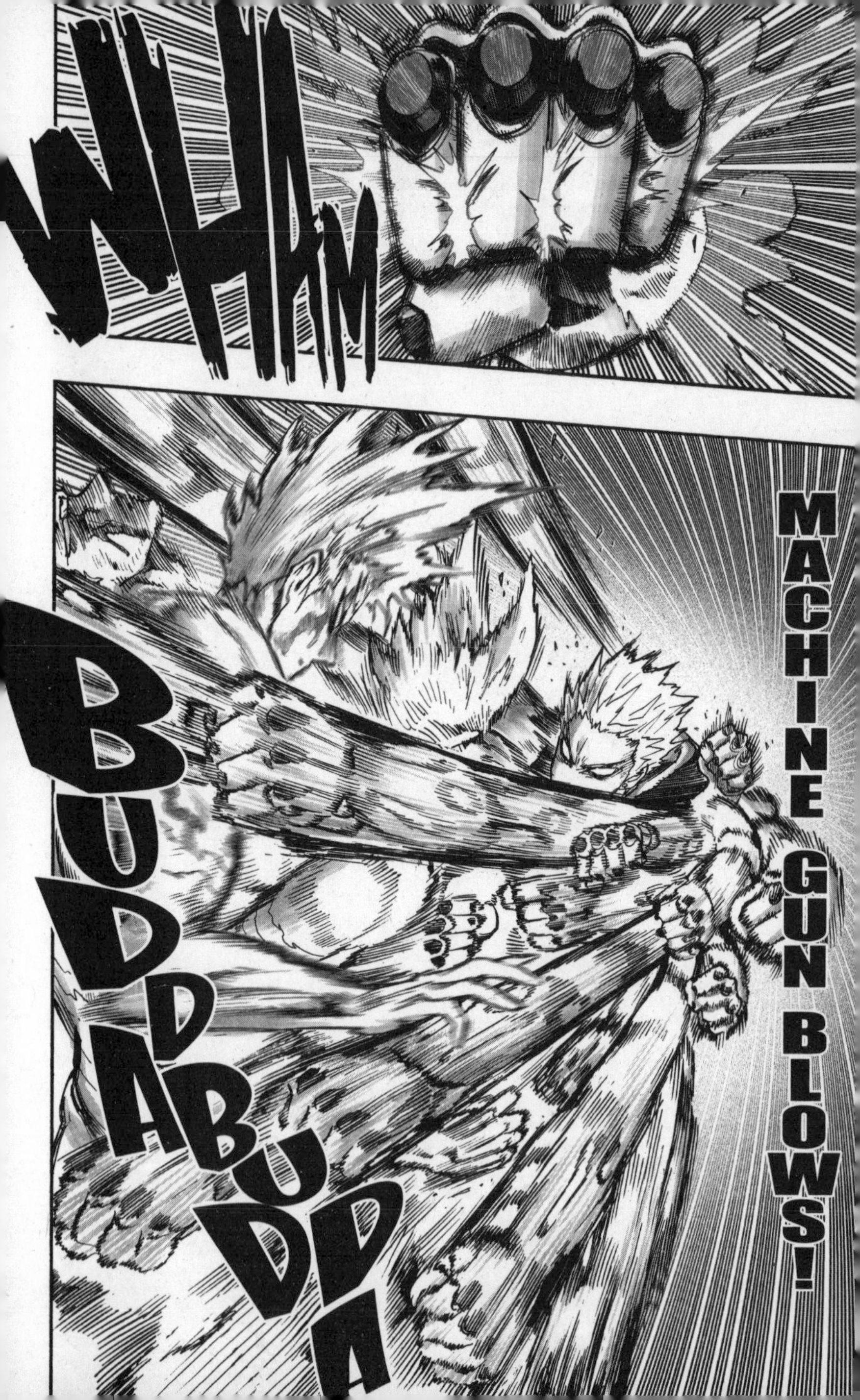
WHAM
MACHINE GUN BLOWS!
BUDDABUDDA

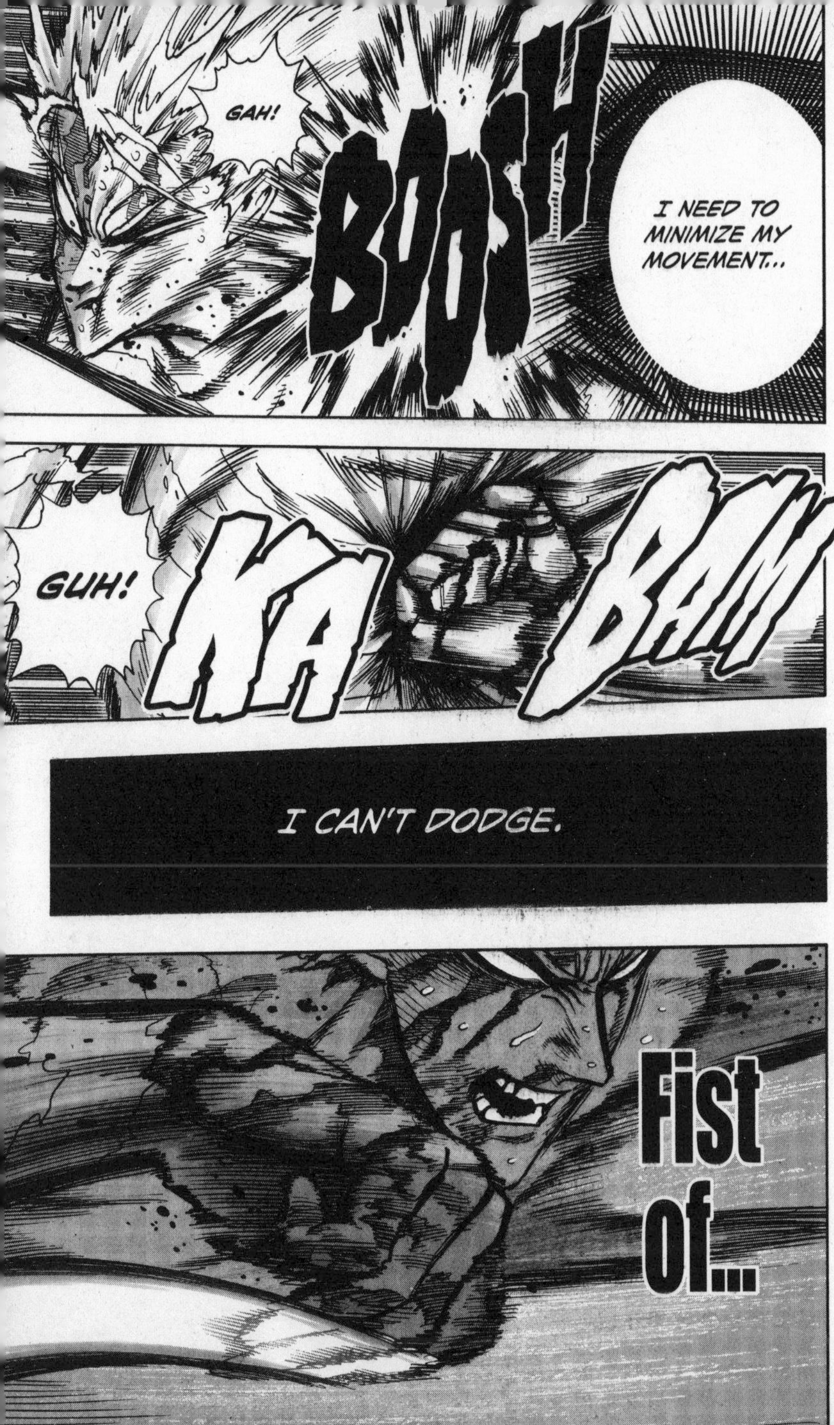
I NEED TO MINIMIZE MY MOVEMENT...
BOOSH
GAH!
KABAM
GUH!
I CAN'T DODGE.
Fist of...

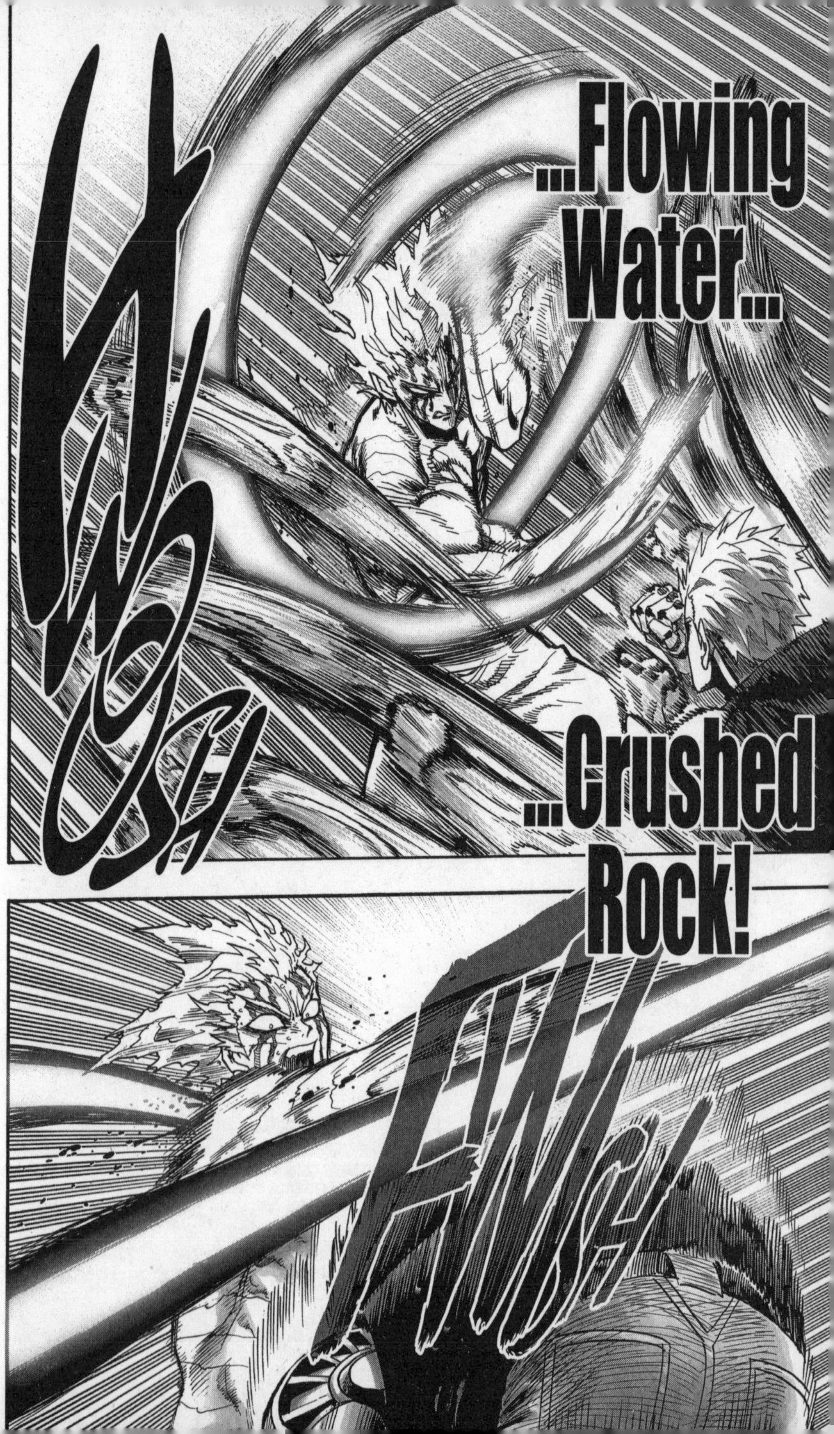
...Flowing Water...
...Crushed Rock!

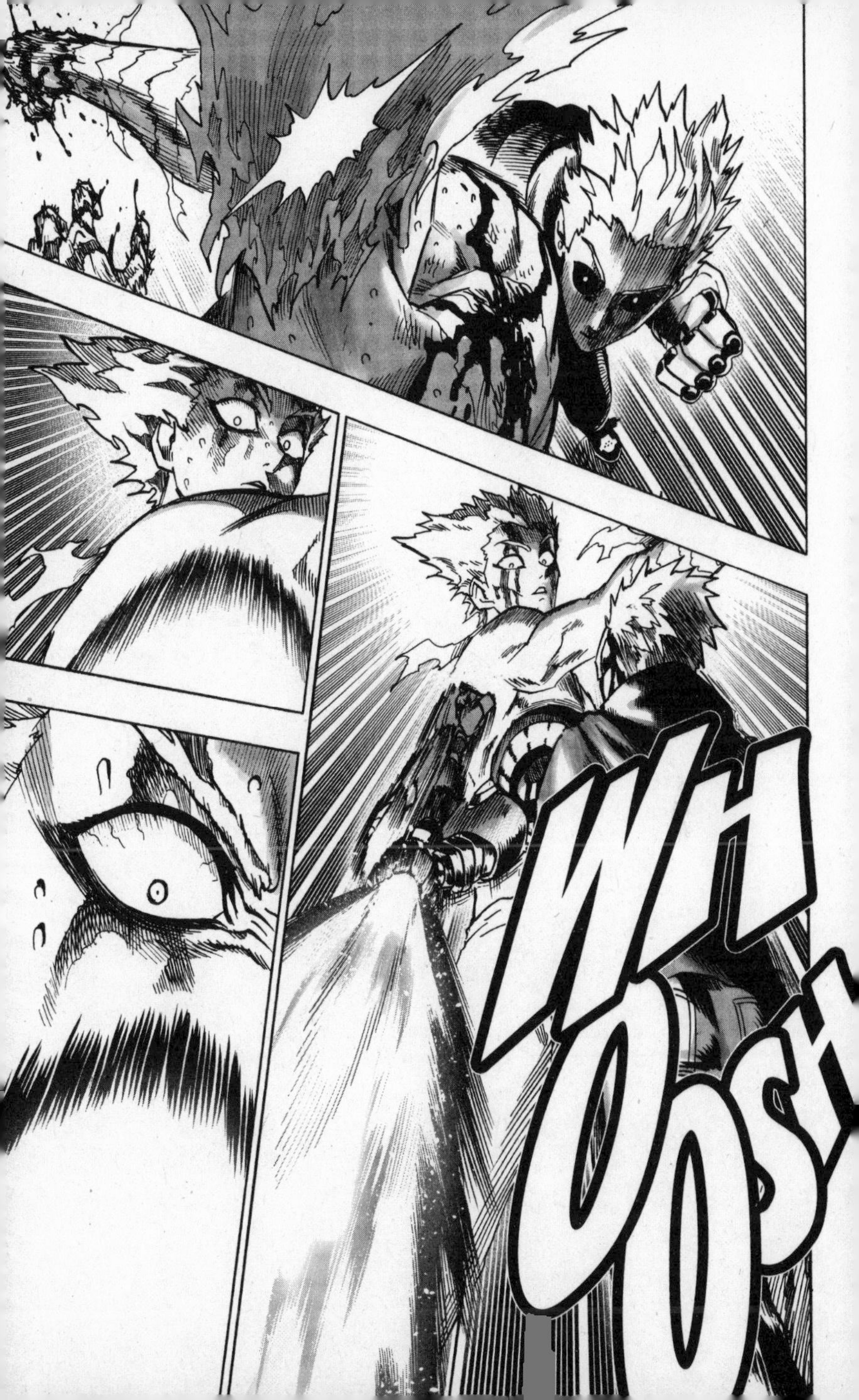
WHOOSH

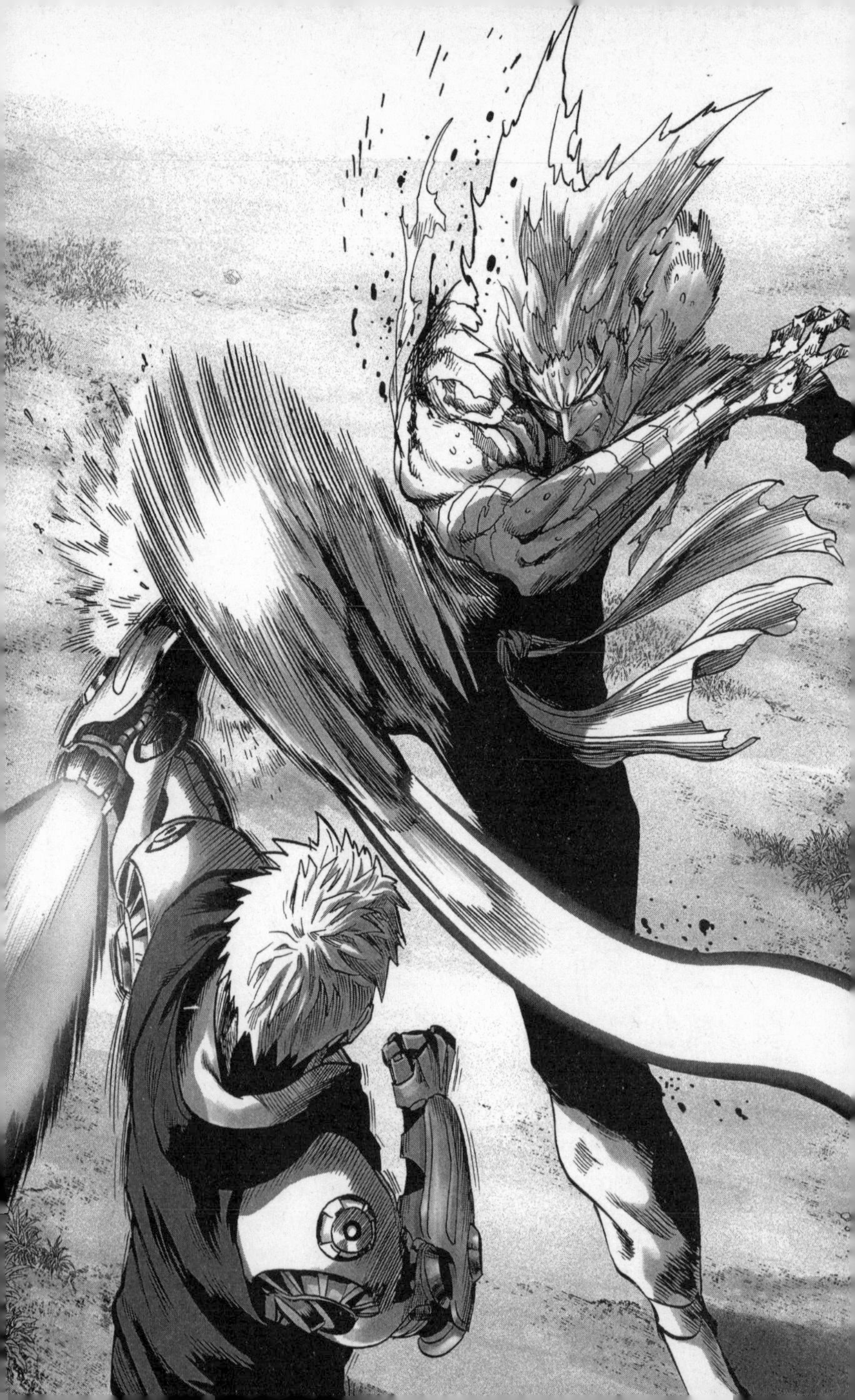

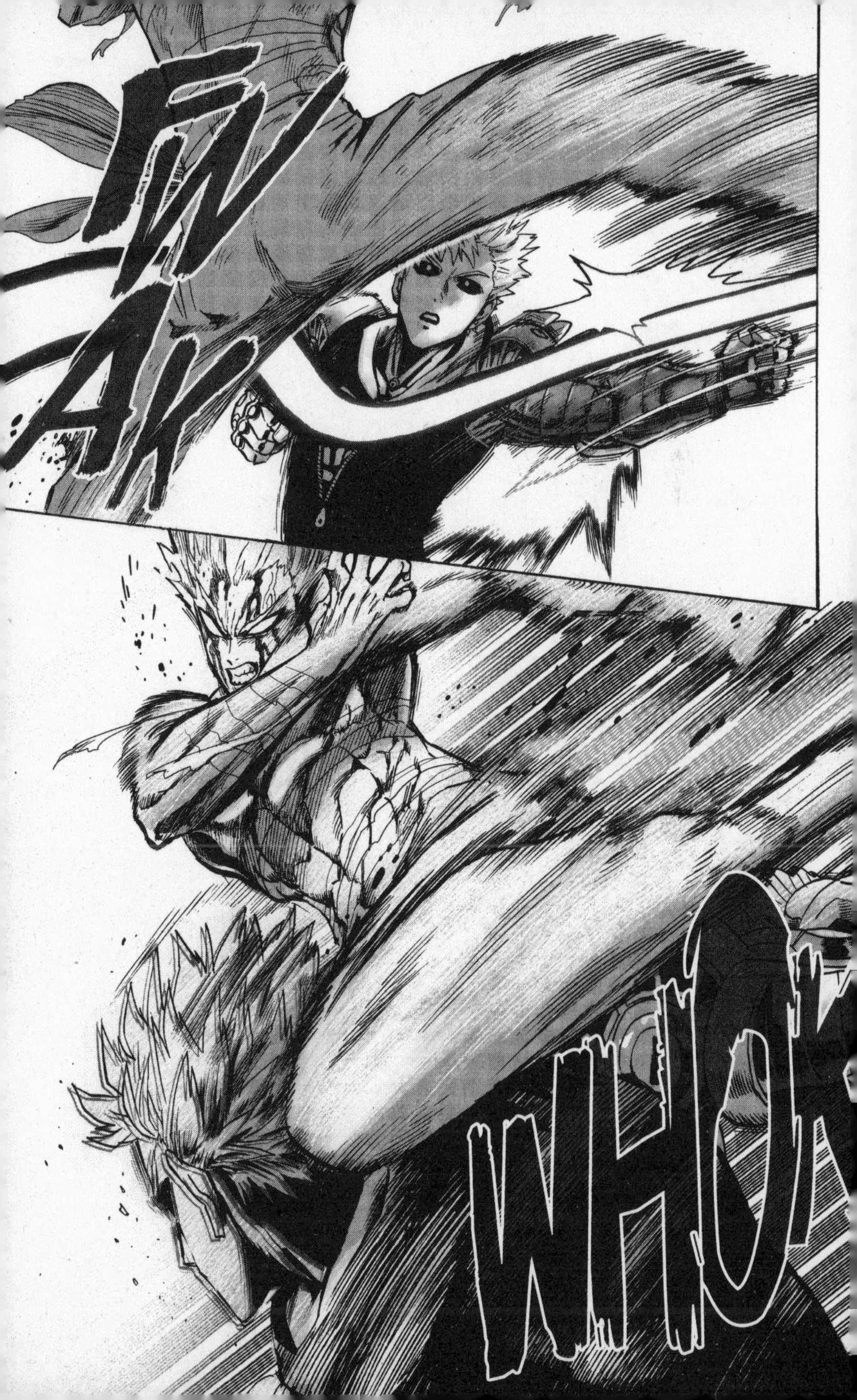
FWAK
WHOK

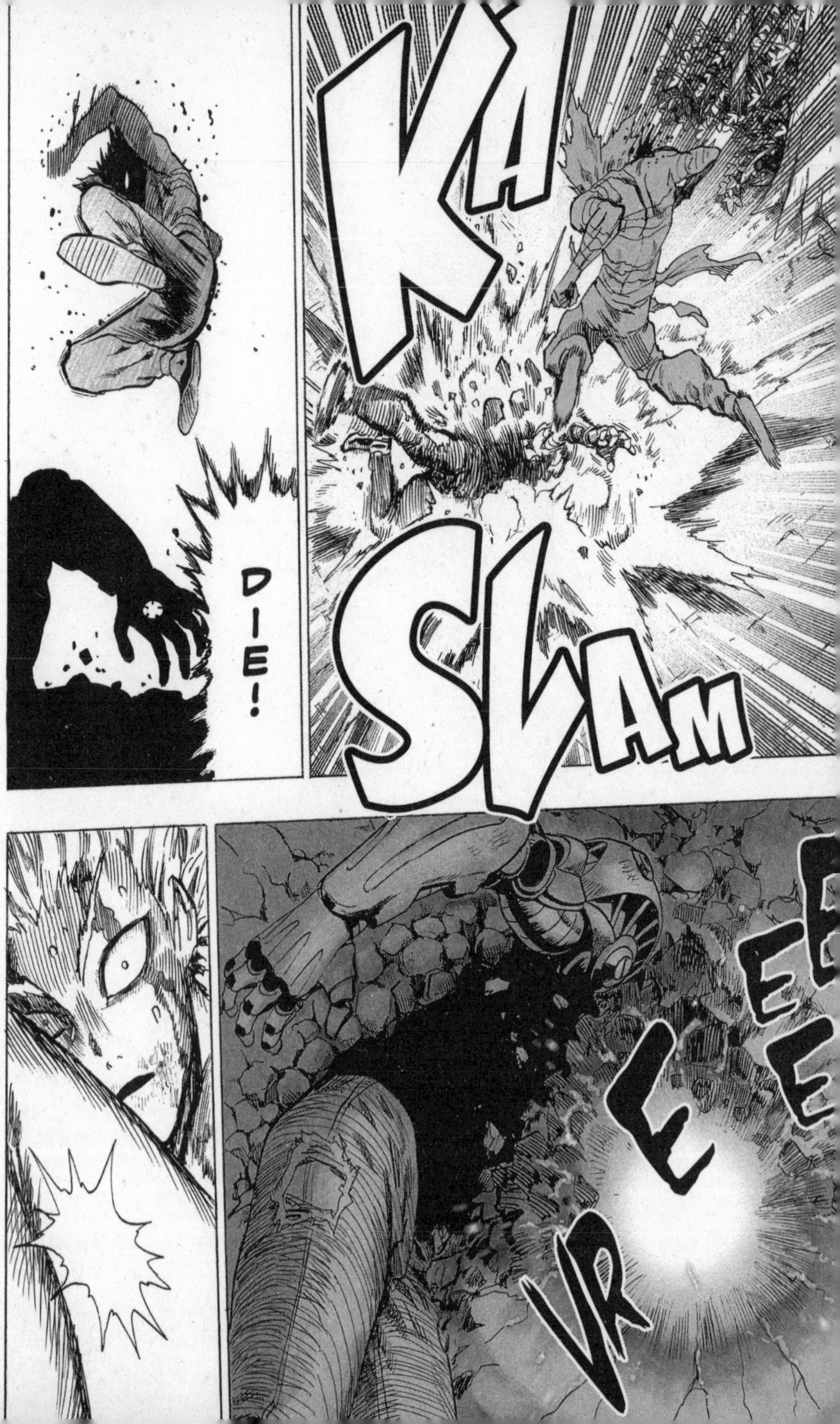
KA
SLAM
DIE!
VREEEE

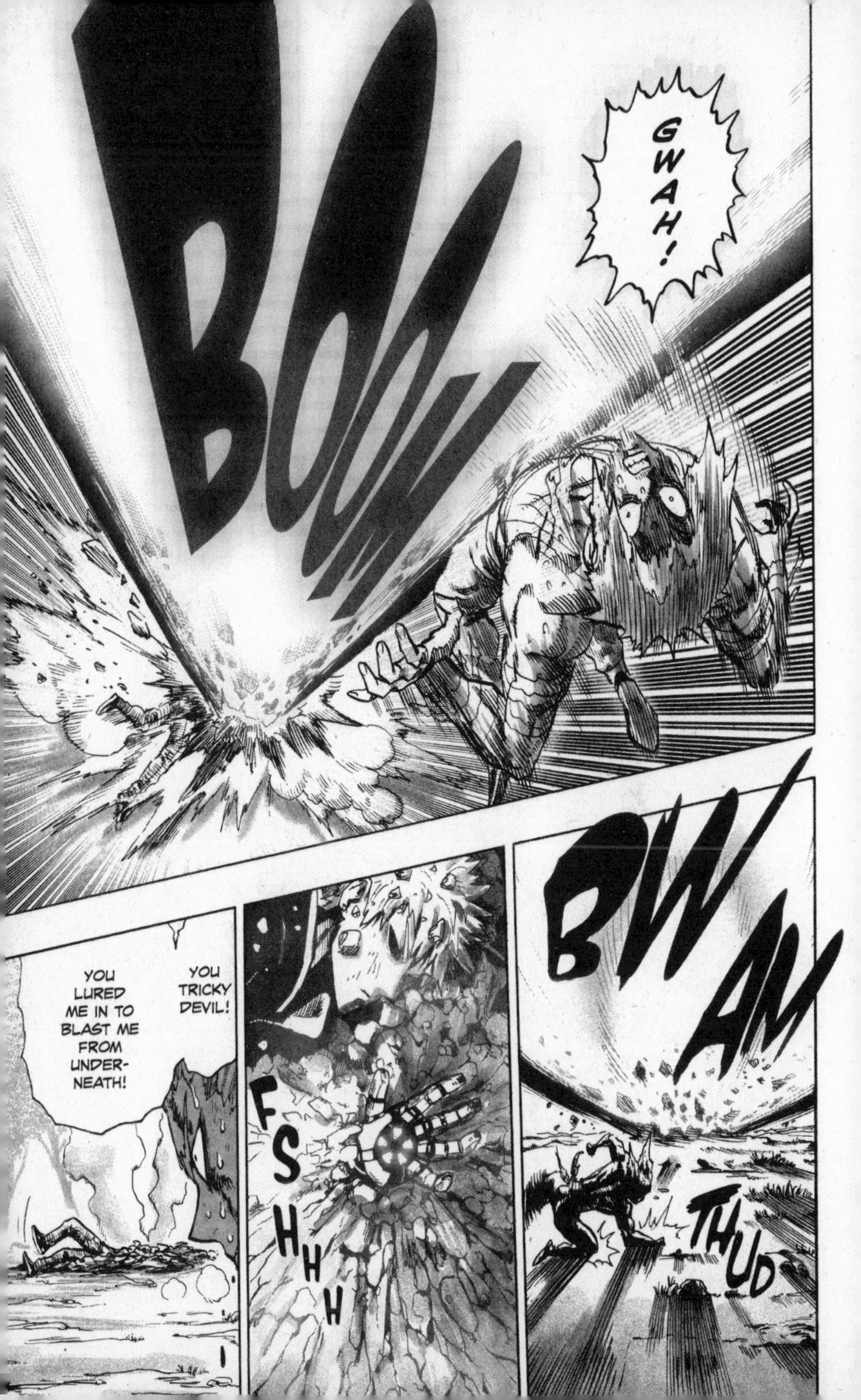
GWAH!
BOOM
BWAM
THUD
FSHHHH
YOU TRICKY DEVIL!
YOU LURED ME IN TO BLAST ME FROM UNDER-NEATH!

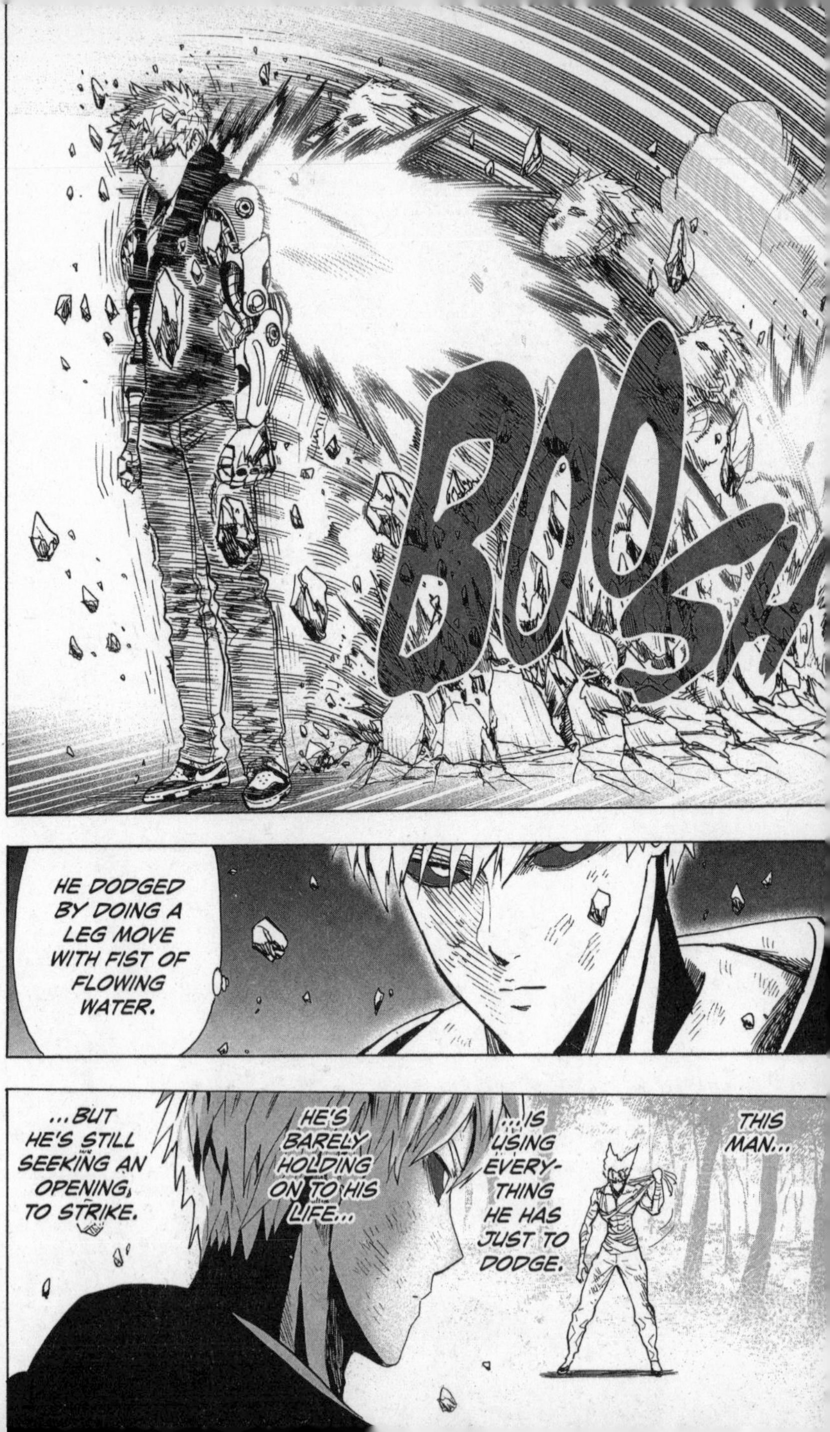
BOOSH
HE DODGED BY DOING A LEG MOVE WITH FIST OF FLOWING WATER.
THIS MAN...
...IS USING EVERY-THING HE HAS JUST TO DODGE.
HE'S BARELY HOLDING ON TO HIS LIFE...
...BUT HE'S STILL SEEKING AN OPENING TO STRIKE.

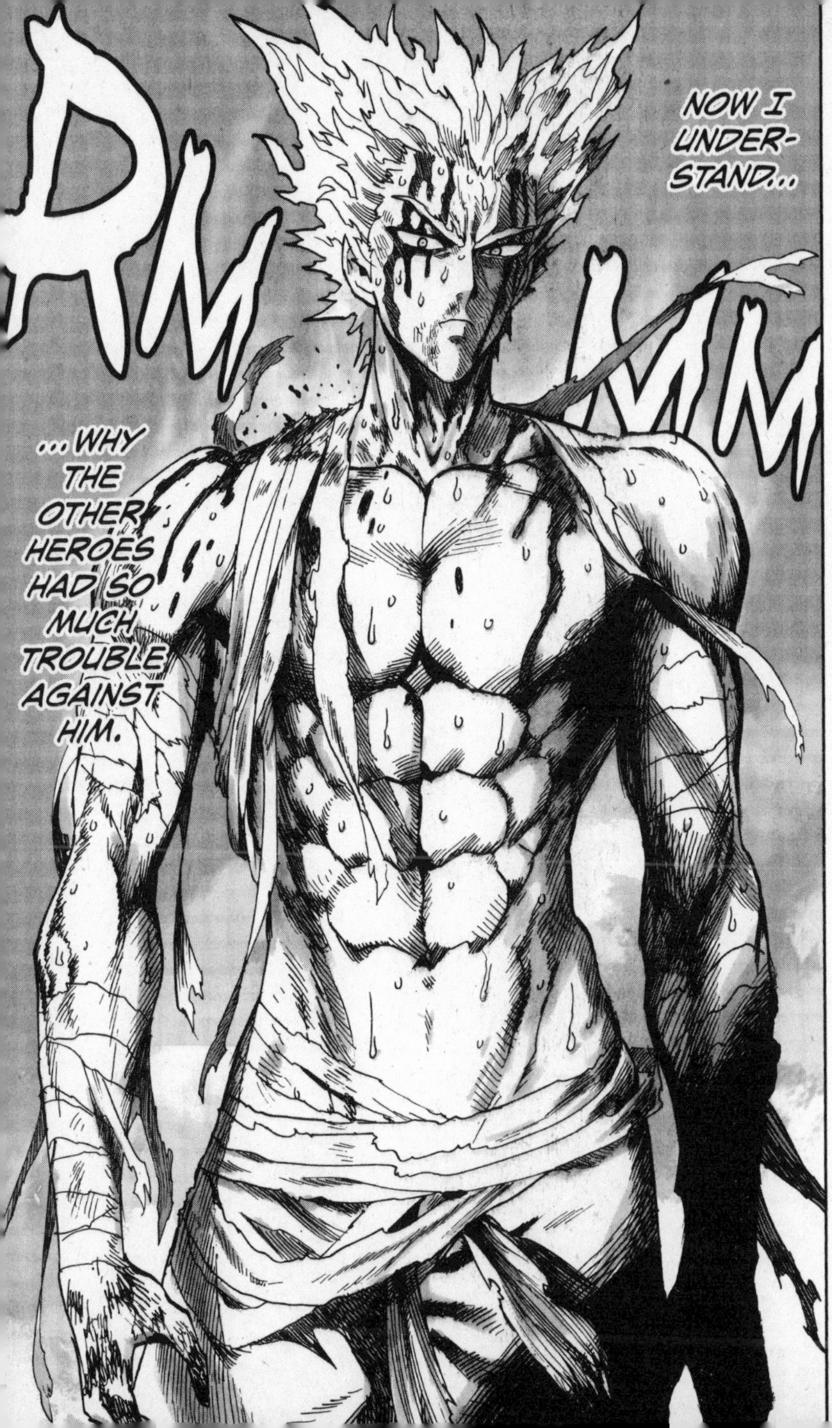
NOW I UNDER-STAND...
...WHY THE OTHER HEROES HAD SO MUCH TROUBLE AGAINST HIM.

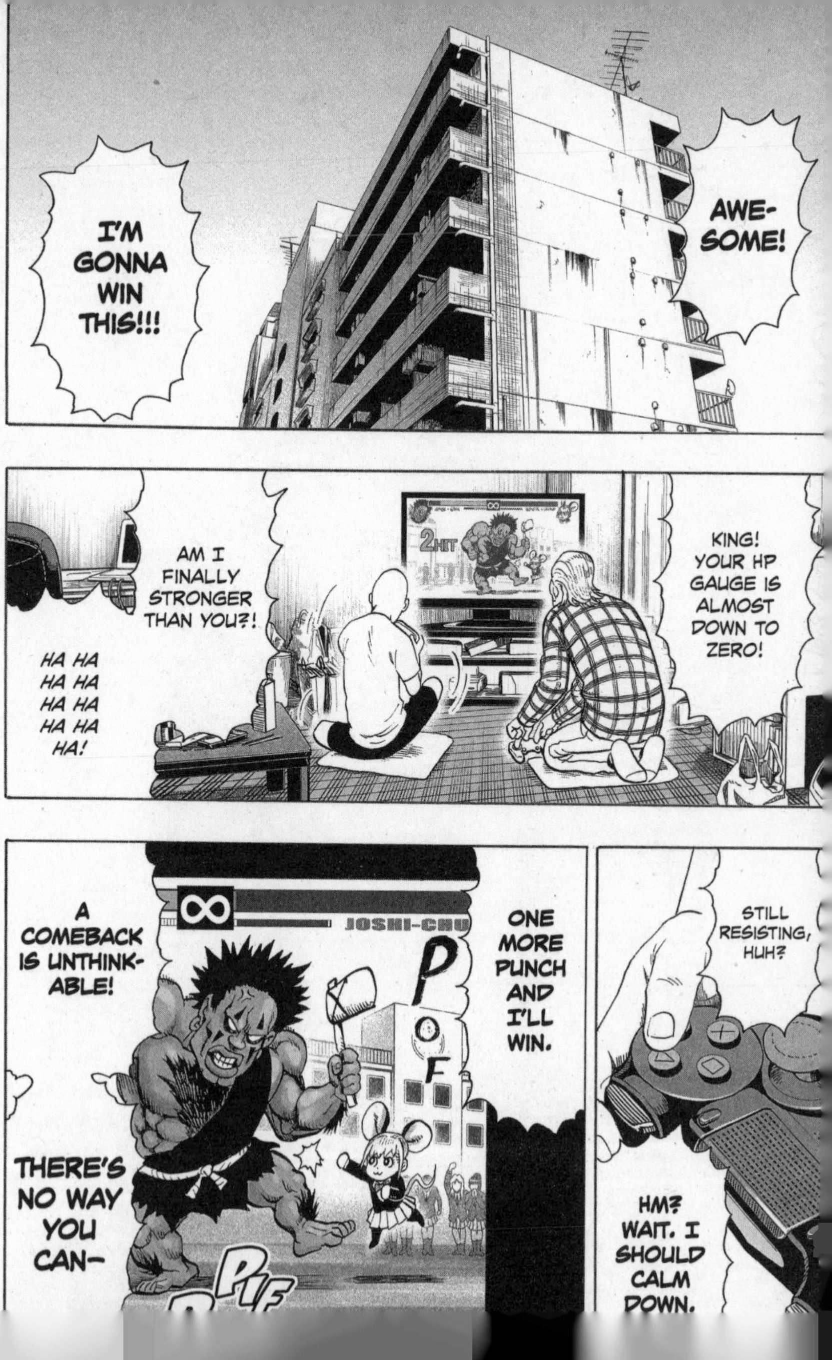
AWE-SOME!
I'M GONNA WIN THIS!!!
KING! YOUR HP GAUGE IS ALMOST DOWN TO ZERO!
2HIT
AM I FINALLY STRONGER THAN YOU?!
HA HA HA HA HA HA HA HA HA!
STILL RESISTING, HUH?
HM? WAIT. I SHOULD CALM DOWN.
JOSHI-CHU
ONE MORE PUNCH AND I'LL WIN.
POF
A COMEBACK IS UNTHINKABLE!
THERE'S NO WAY YOU CAN–

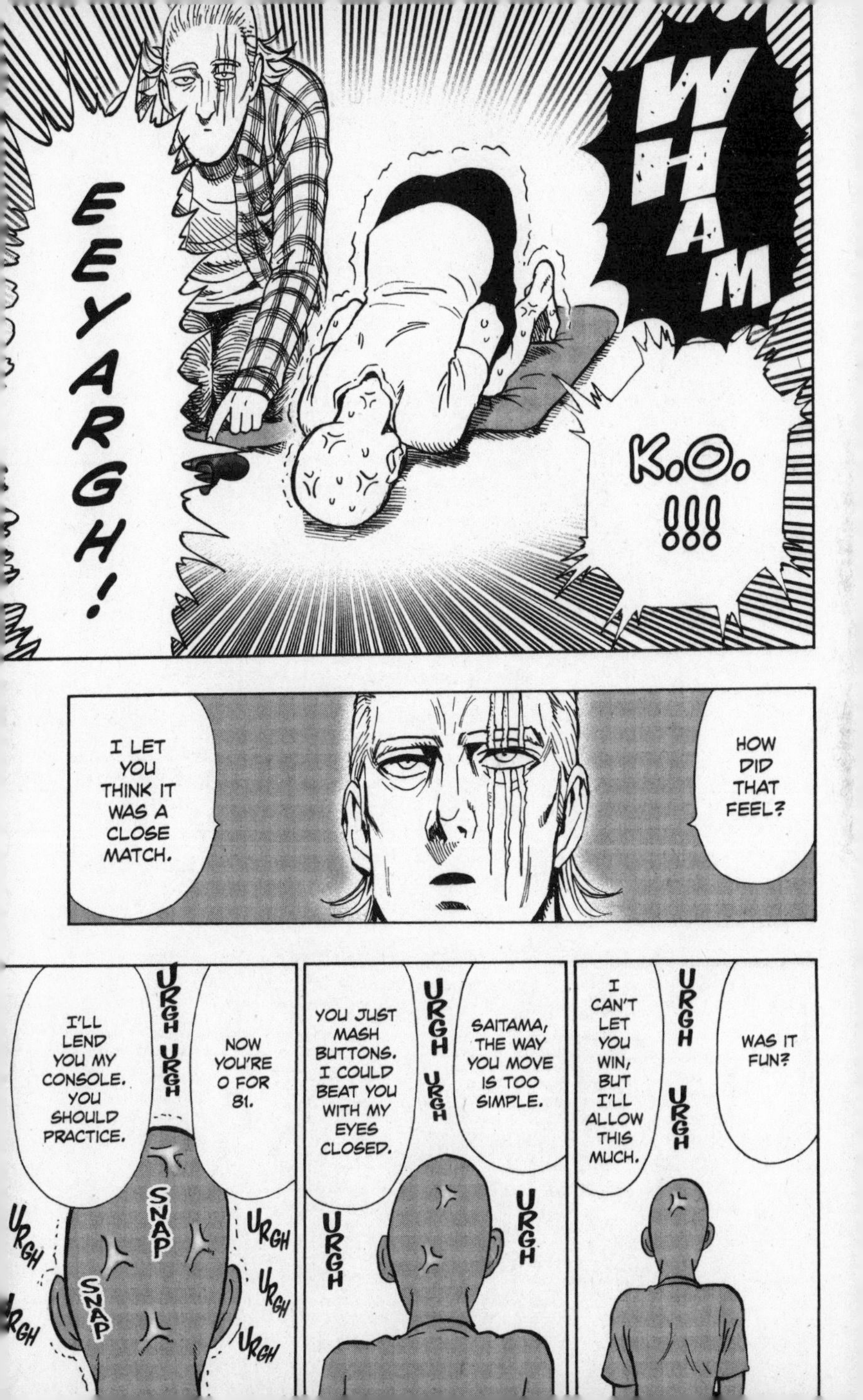
WHAM
K.O.!!!
EEYARGH!
HOW DID THAT FEEL?
I LET YOU THINK IT WAS A CLOSE MATCH.
WAS IT FUN?
URGH
URGH
I CAN'T LET YOU WIN, BUT I'LL ALLOW THIS MUCH.
SAITAMA, THE WAY YOU MOVE IS TOO SIMPLE.
URGH
URGH
YOU JUST MASH BUTTONS. I COULD BEAT YOU WITH MY EYES CLOSED.
URGH
URGH
NOW YOU'RE 0 FOR 81.
URGH URGH
I'LL LEND YOU MY CONSOLE. YOU SHOULD PRACTICE.
SNAP
URGH
URGH
URGH
SNAP
URGH

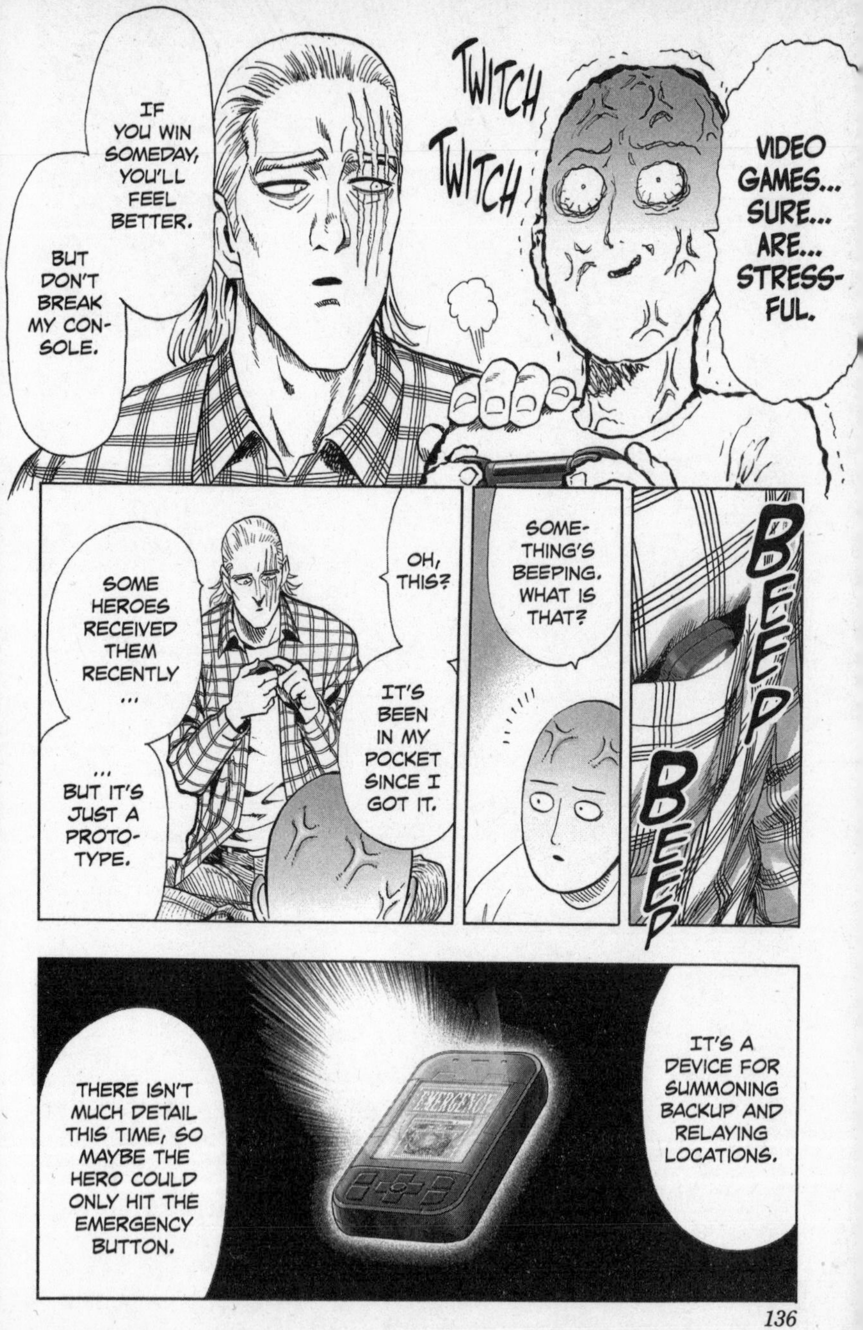
VIDEO GAMES... SURE... ARE... STRESSFUL.
TWITCH
TWITCH
IF YOU WIN SOMEDAY, YOU'LL FEEL BETTER.
BUT DON'T BREAK MY CONSOLE.
BEEP
BEEP
SOMETHING'S BEEPING. WHAT IS THAT?
OH, THIS?
IT'S BEEN IN MY POCKET SINCE I GOT IT.
SOME HEROES RECEIVED THEM RECENTLY...
...BUT IT'S JUST A PROTOTYPE.
IT'S A DEVICE FOR SUMMONING BACKUP AND RELAYING LOCATIONS.
EMERGENCY
THERE ISN'T MUCH DETAIL THIS TIME, SO MAYBE THE HERO COULD ONLY HIT THE EMERGENCY BUTTON.

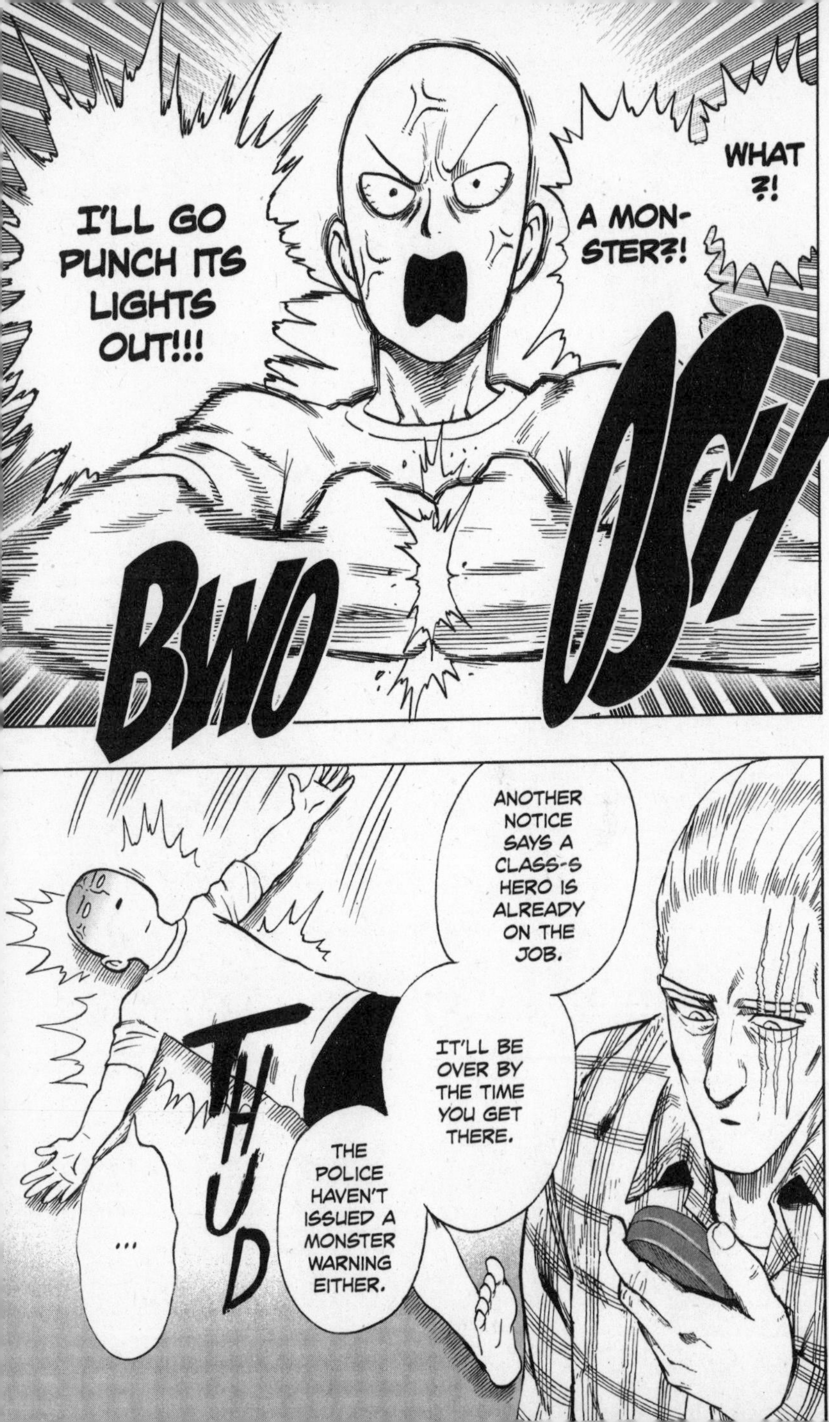
WHAT?!
A MONSTER?!
I'LL GO PUNCH ITS LIGHTS OUT!!!
BWOOSH
ANOTHER NOTICE SAYS A CLASS-S HERO IS ALREADY ON THE JOB.
IT'LL BE OVER BY THE TIME YOU GET THERE.
THE POLICE HAVEN'T ISSUED A MONSTER WARNING EITHER.
THUD
...

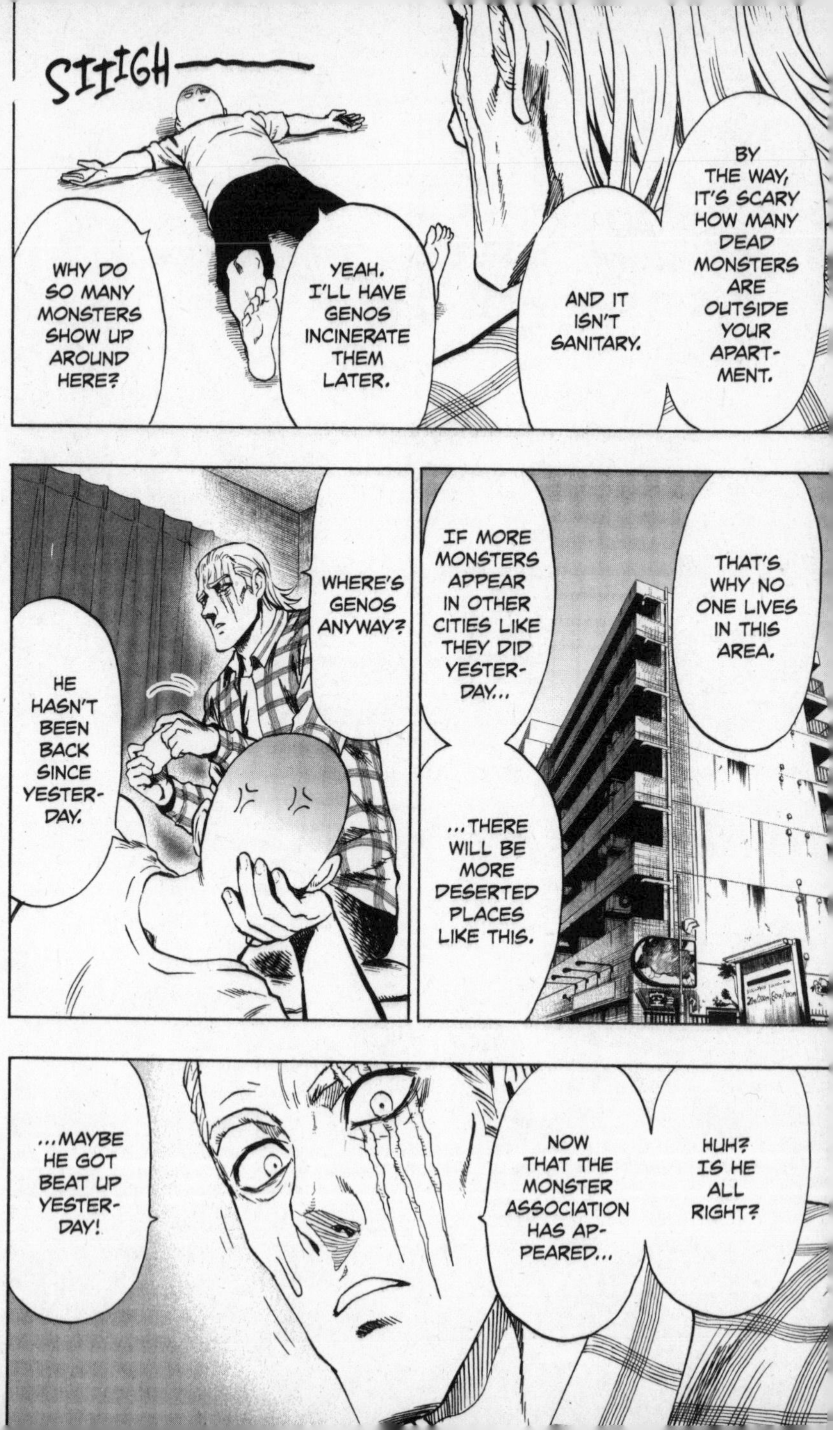
BY THE WAY, IT'S SCARY HOW MANY DEAD MONSTERS ARE OUTSIDE YOUR APART-MENT.
AND IT ISN'T SANITARY.
SIIIGH——
YEAH. I'LL HAVE GENOS INCINERATE THEM LATER.
WHY DO SO MANY MONSTERS SHOW UP AROUND HERE?
THAT'S WHY NO ONE LIVES IN THIS AREA.
IF MORE MONSTERS APPEAR IN OTHER CITIES LIKE THEY DID YESTER-DAY...
...THERE WILL BE MORE DESERTED PLACES LIKE THIS.
WHERE'S GENOS ANYWAY?
HE HASN'T BEEN BACK SINCE YESTER-DAY.
HUH? IS HE ALL RIGHT?
NOW THAT THE MONSTER ASSOCIATION HAS AP-PEARED...
...MAYBE HE GOT BEAT UP YESTER-DAY!

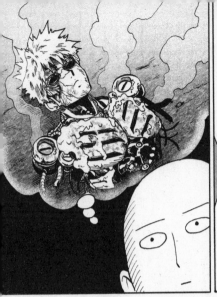

I'M SURE GENOS IS FINE!

NO. I SHOULD GO.

KING! TELL ME WHERE THAT ALERT CAME FROM!

HWOOO

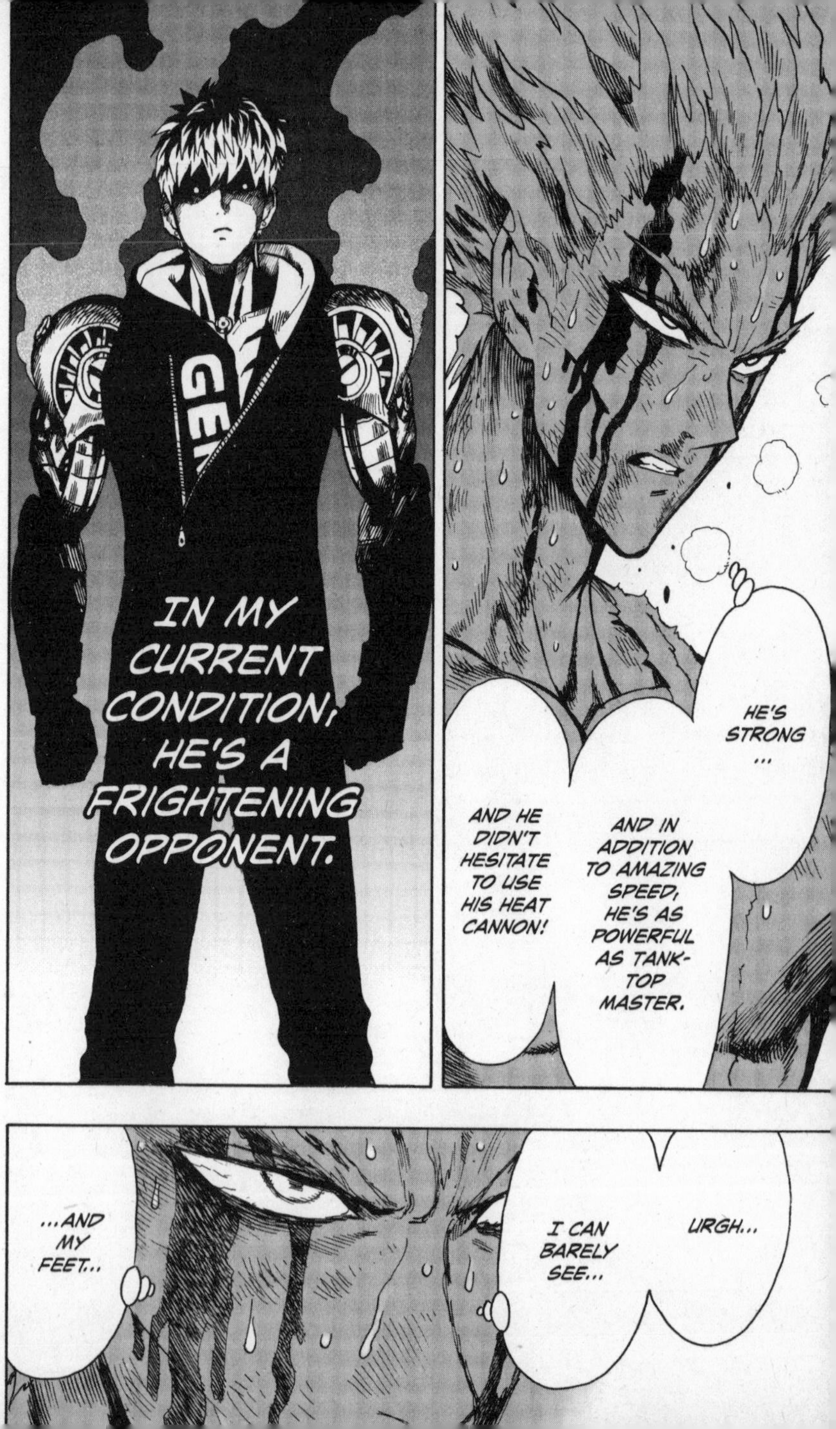
HE'S STRONG ...
AND IN ADDITION TO AMAZING SPEED, HE'S AS POWERFUL AS TANK-TOP MASTER.
AND HE DIDN'T HESITATE TO USE HIS HEAT CANNON!
IN MY CURRENT CONDITION, HE'S A FRIGHTENING OPPONENT.
URGH...
I CAN BARELY SEE...
...AND MY FEET...

SKRRRIK

YOU CANNOT ESCAPE ME LIKE THAT.

GIVE UP.

STAGGER

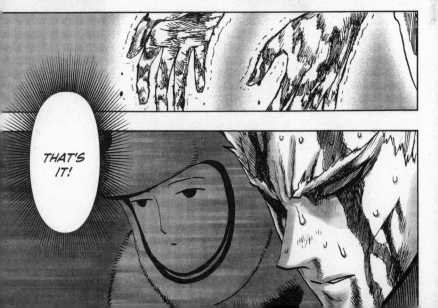

THAT'S IT!

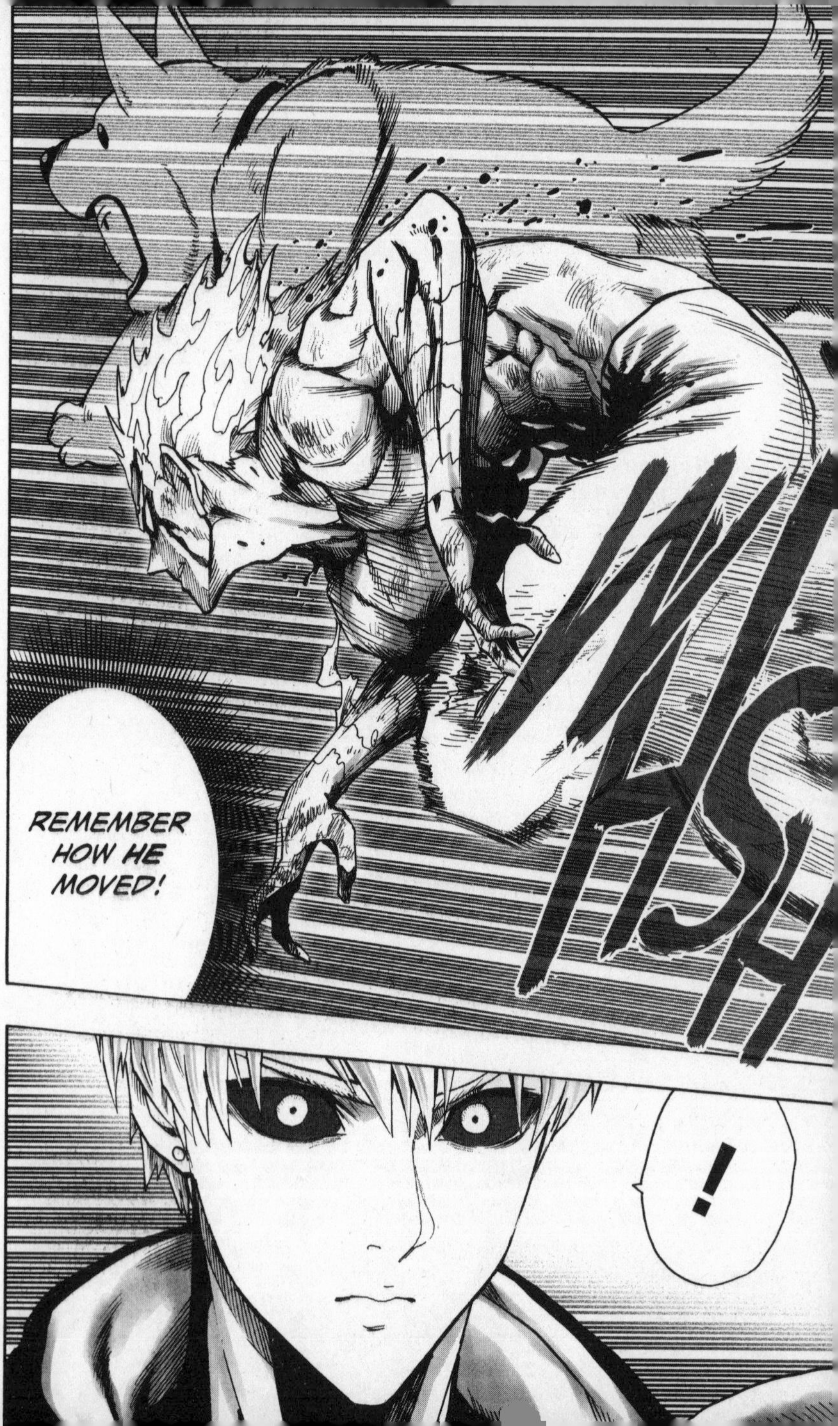
REMEMBER HOW HE MOVED!
!

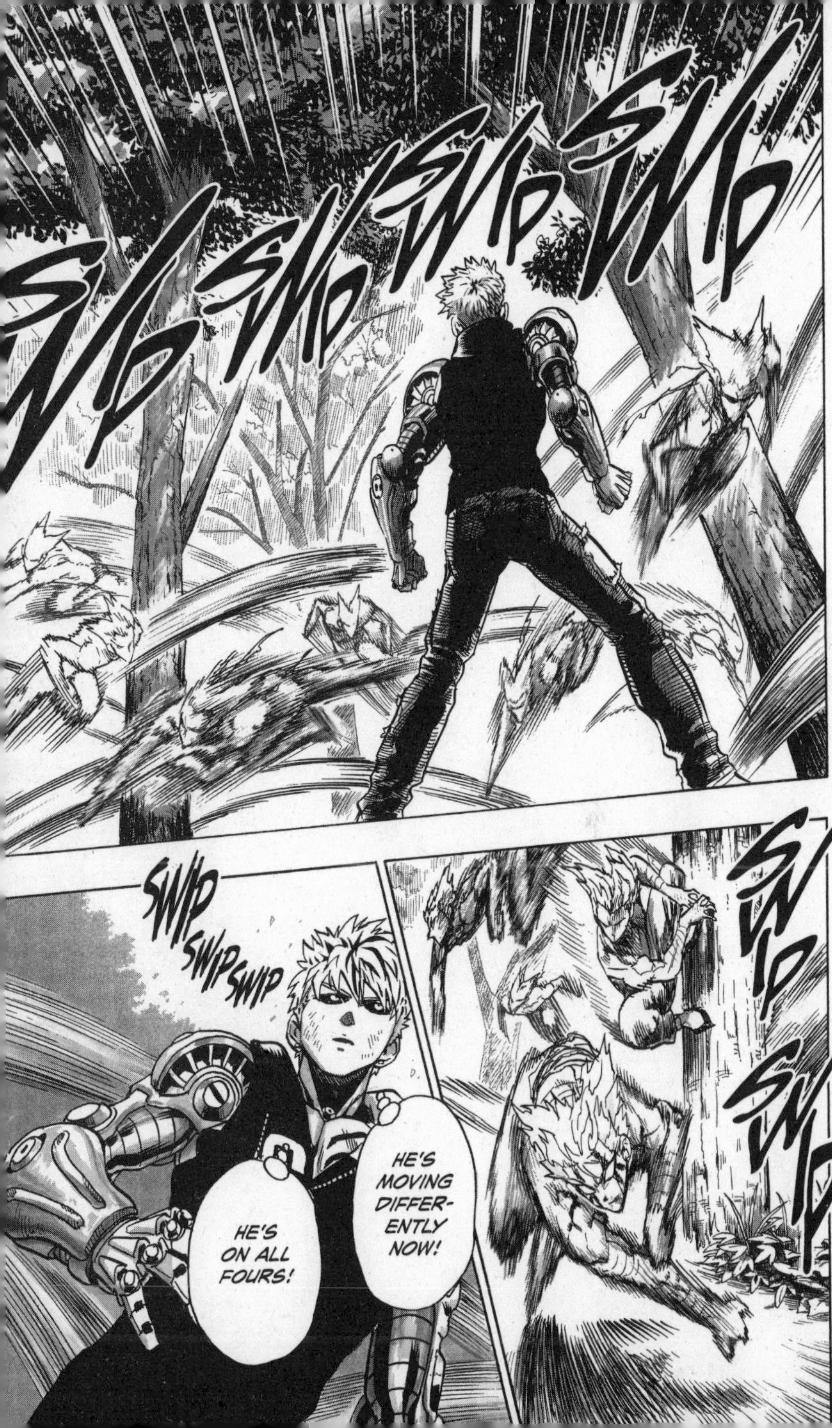
SWIP SWIP SWIP SWIP
SWIP SWIP
SWIP SWIP SWIP
HE'S MOVING DIFFER-ENTLY NOW!
HE'S ON ALL FOURS!

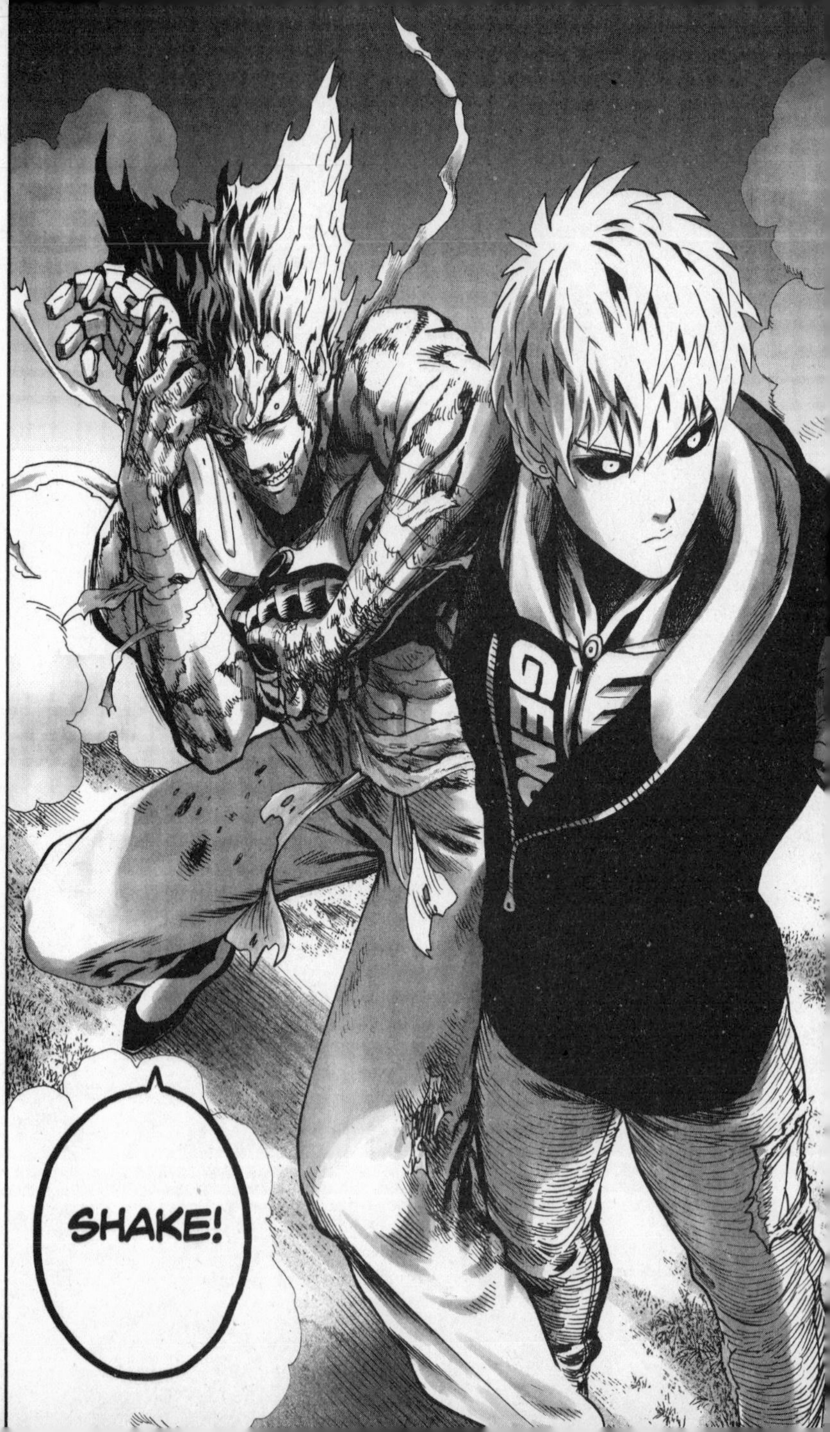
SHAKE!

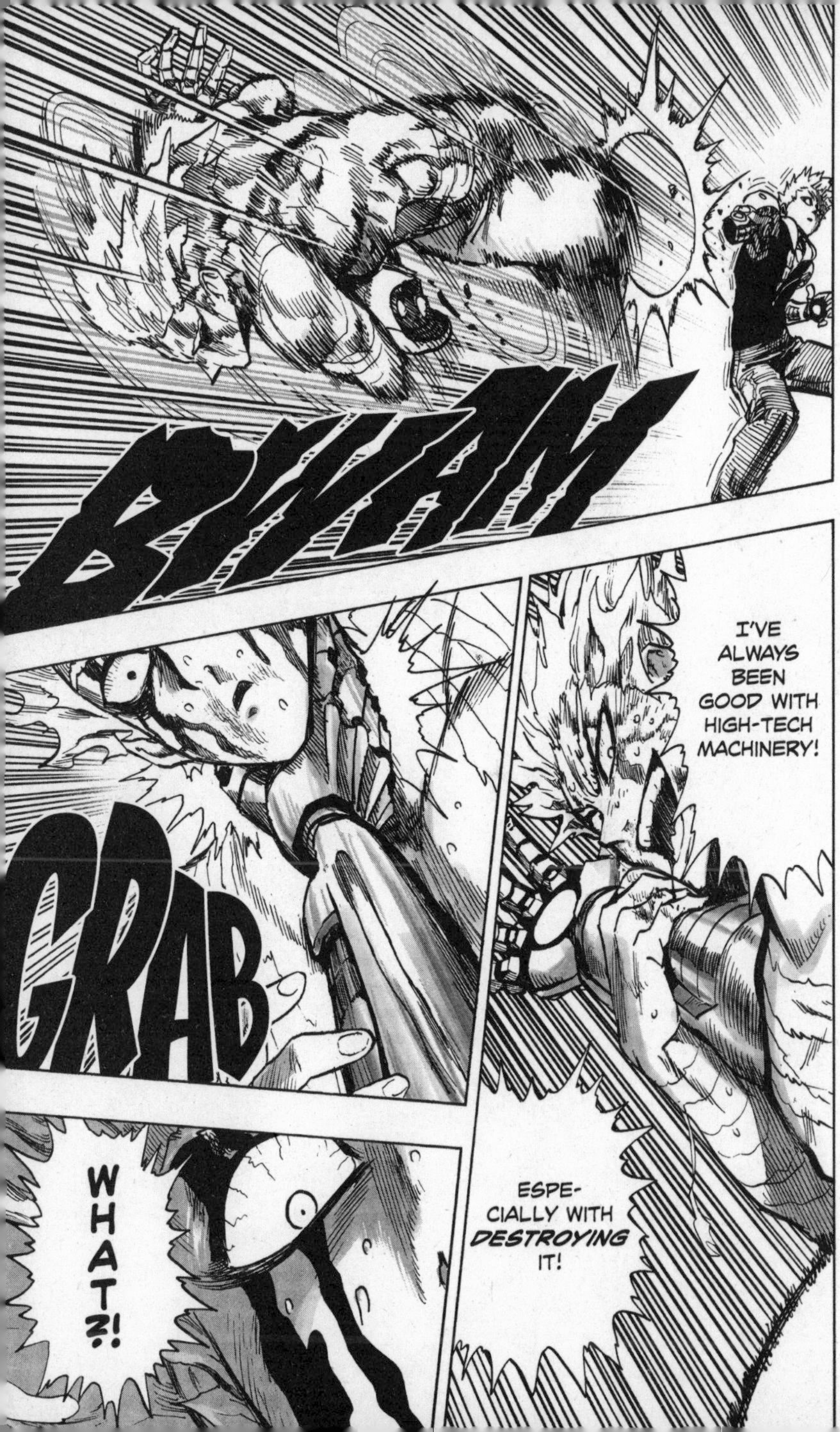
BWAM
I'VE ALWAYS BEEN GOOD WITH HIGH-TECH MACHINERY!
ESPE-CIALLY WITH *DESTROYING* IT!
GRAB
WHAT?!

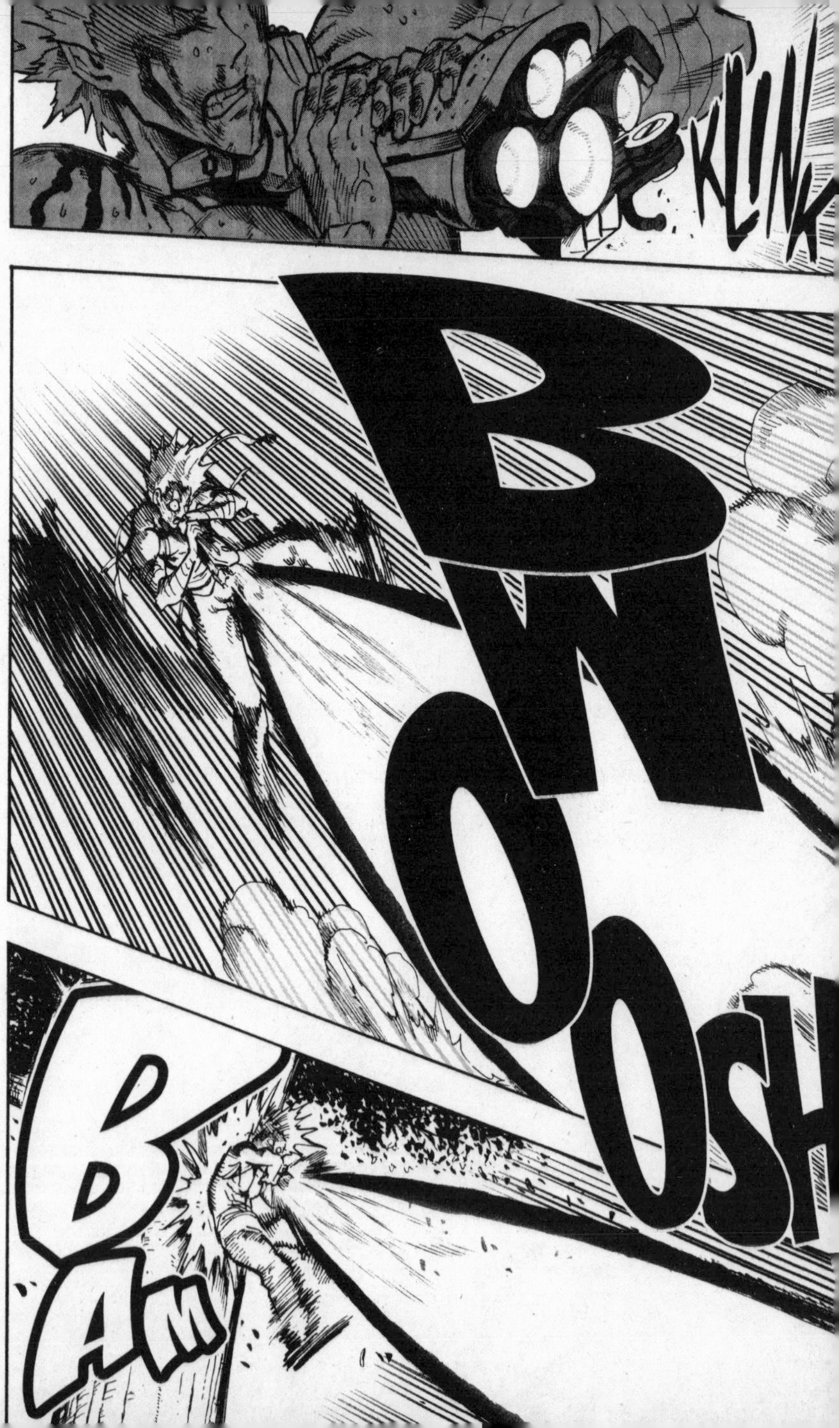
KLINK
BWOOSH
BAM

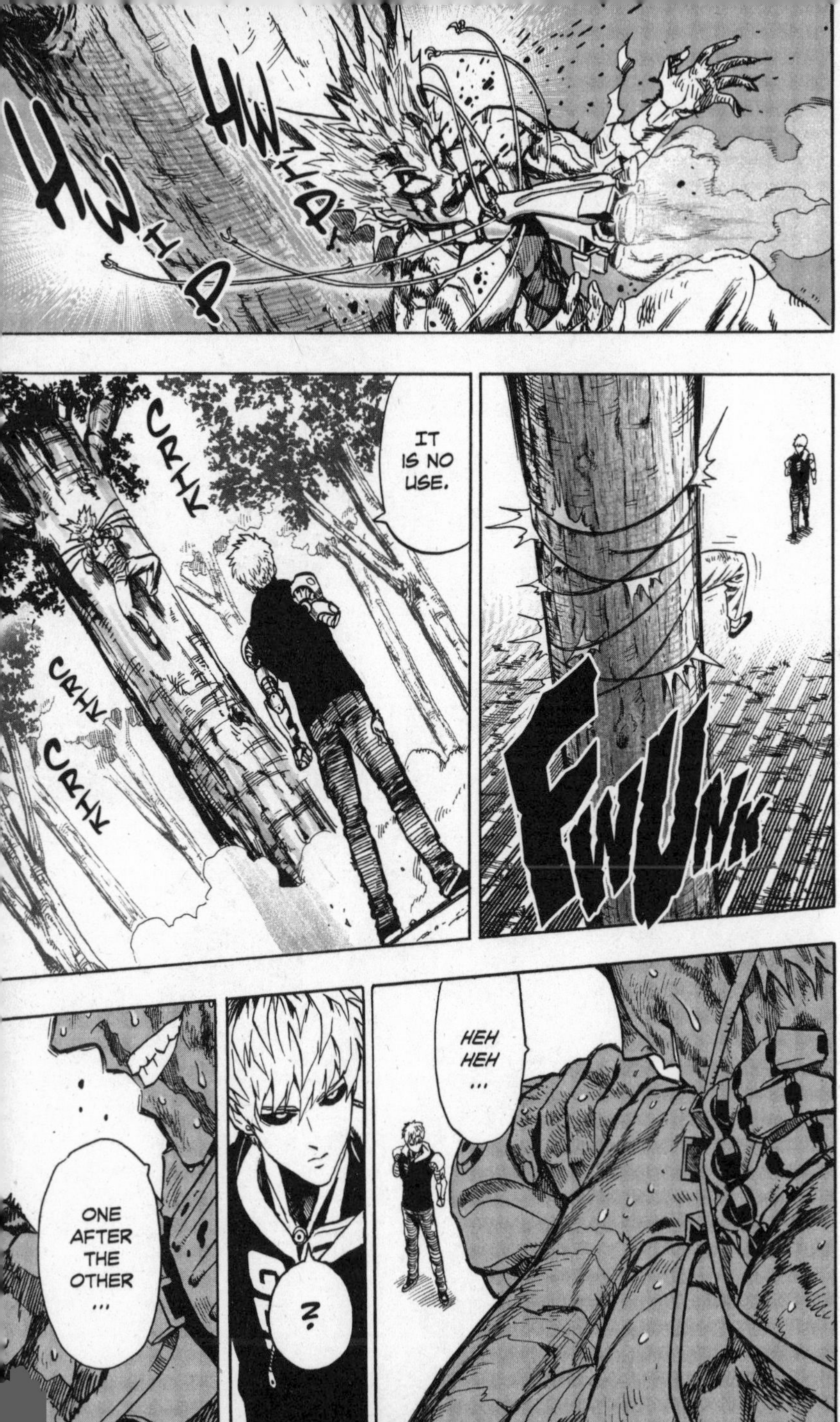
HWIP!
HWIP
FWUNK
IT IS NO USE.
CRIK
CRIK
CRIK
HEH HEH ...
?
ONE AFTER THE OTHER ...

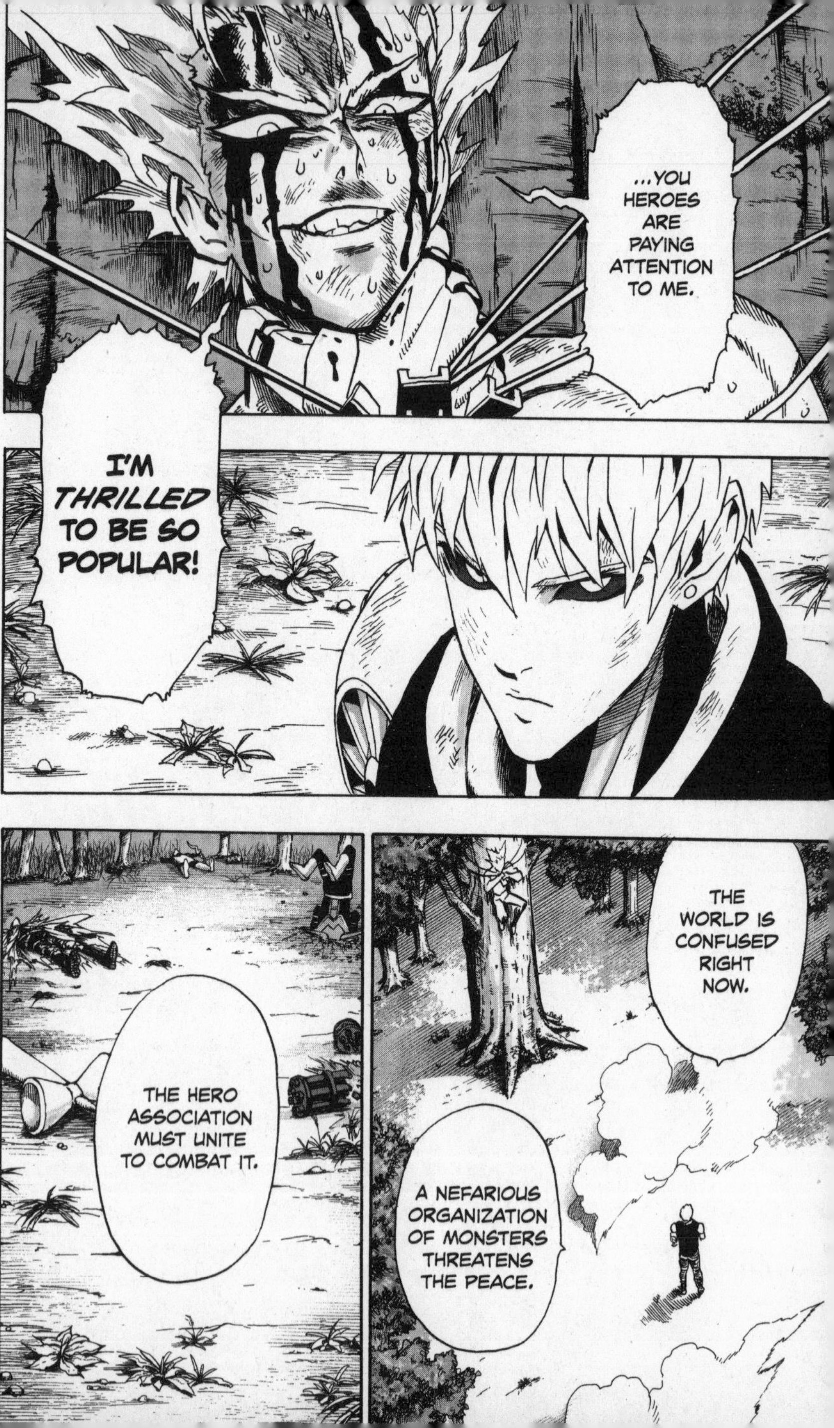
...YOU HEROES ARE PAYING ATTENTION TO ME.
I'M *THRILLED* TO BE SO POPULAR!
THE WORLD IS CONFUSED RIGHT NOW.
A NEFARIOUS ORGANIZATION OF MONSTERS THREATENS THE PEACE.
THE HERO ASSOCIATION MUST UNITE TO COMBAT IT.

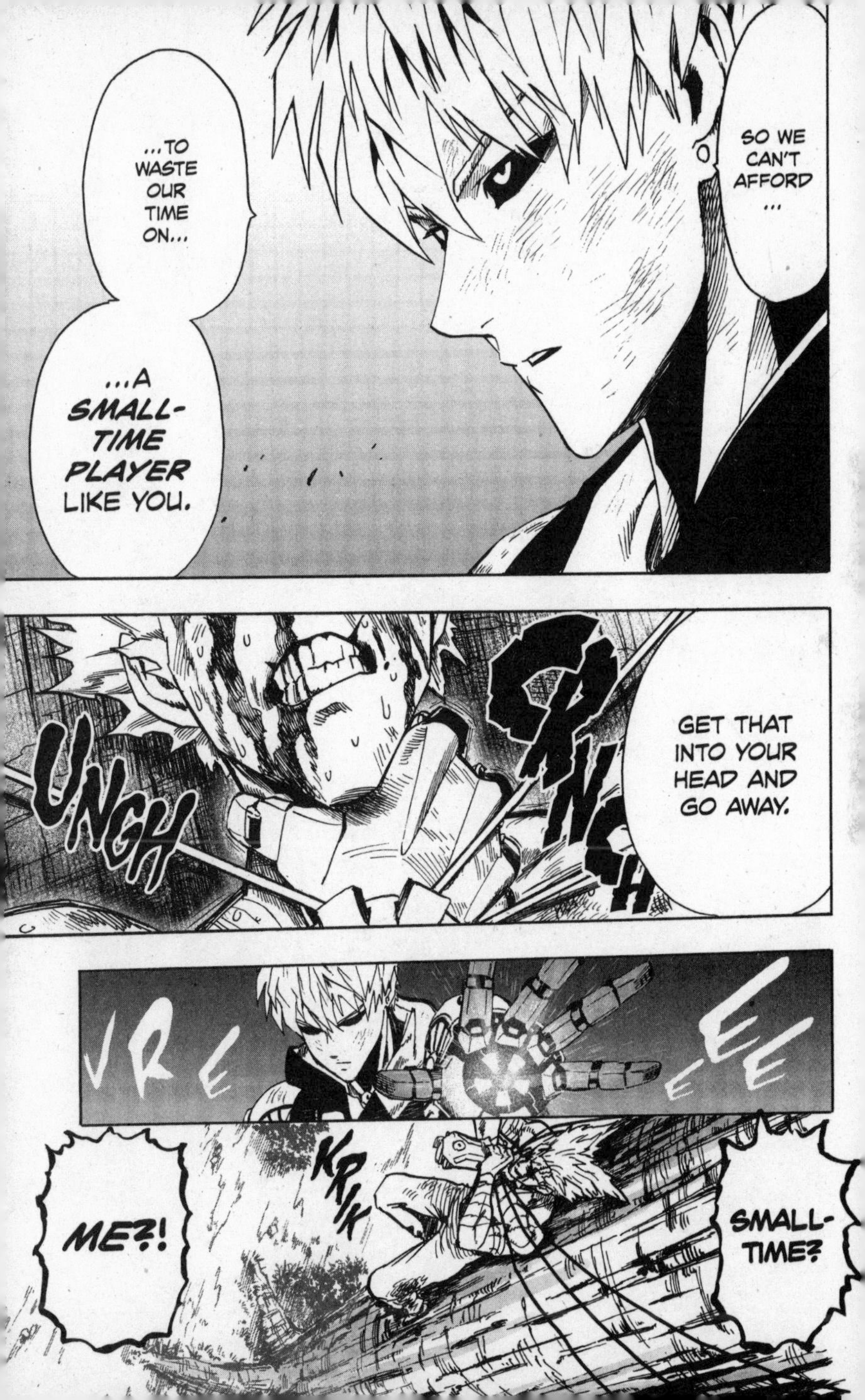
SO WE CAN'T AFFORD ...
...TO WASTE OUR TIME ON...
...A SMALL-TIME PLAYER LIKE YOU.
GET THAT INTO YOUR HEAD AND GO AWAY.
UNGH
SMALL-TIME?
KRIK
ME?!

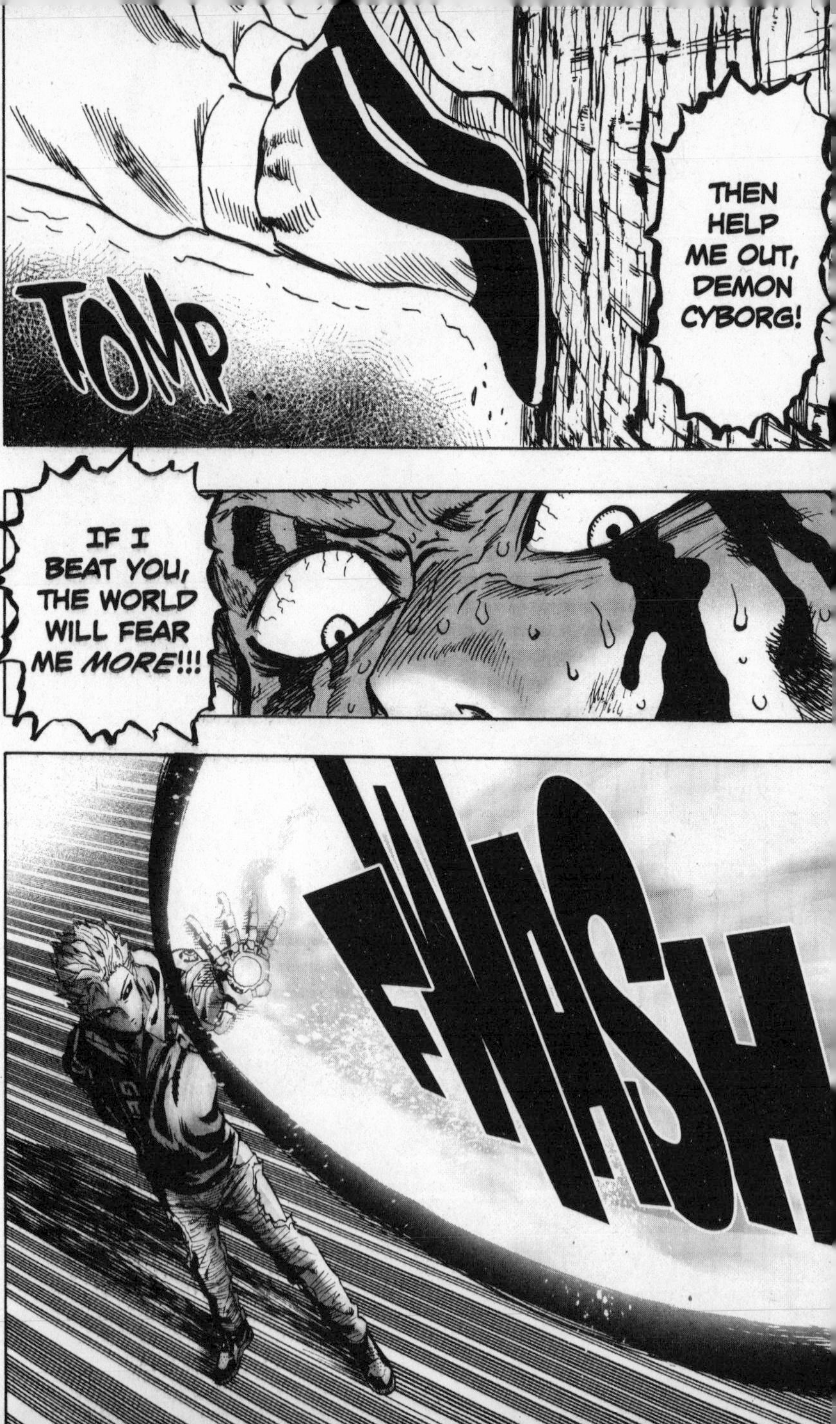
THEN HELP ME OUT, DEMON CYBORG!
TOMP
IF I BEAT YOU, THE WORLD WILL FEAR ME *MORE*!!!
FWASH

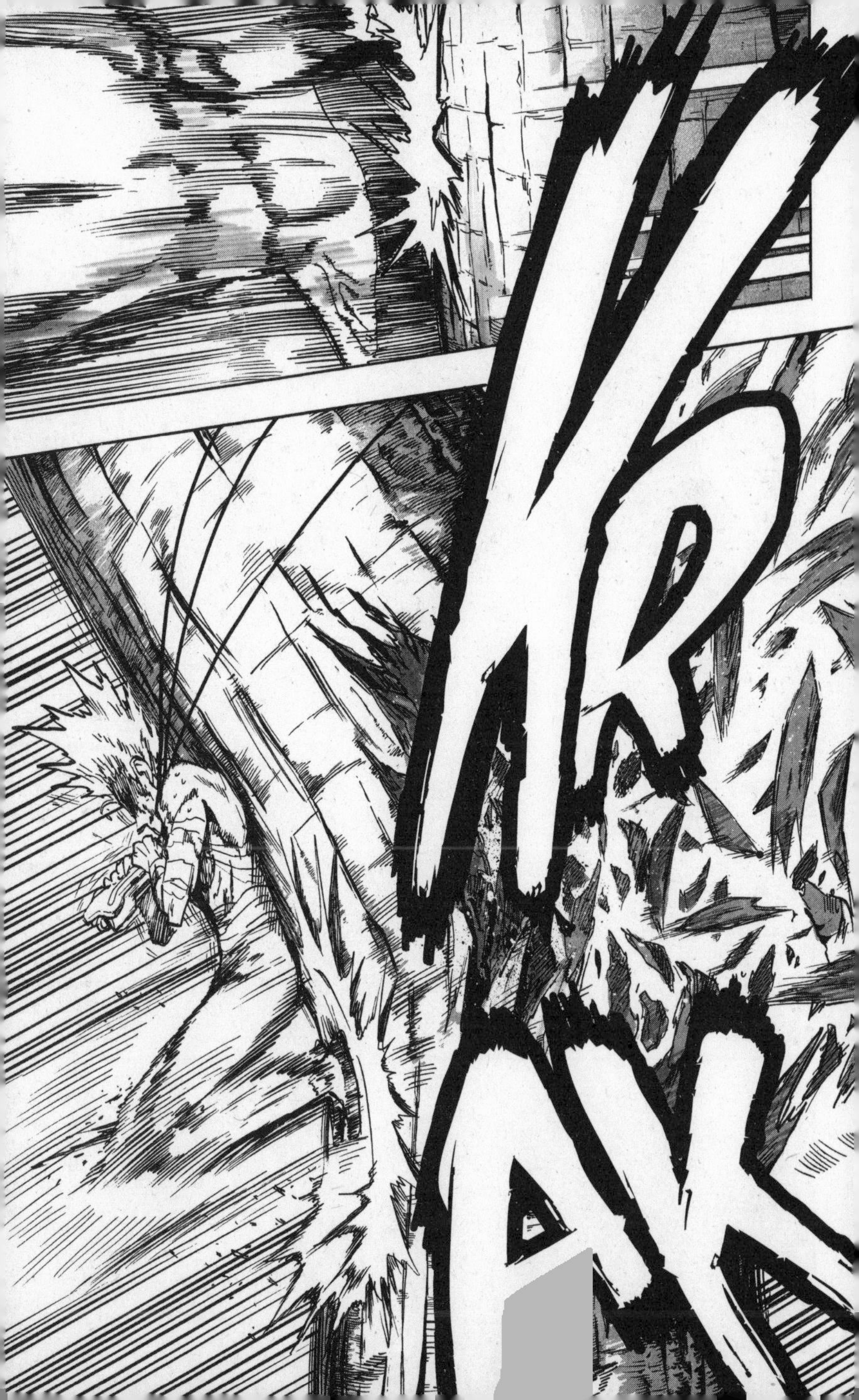

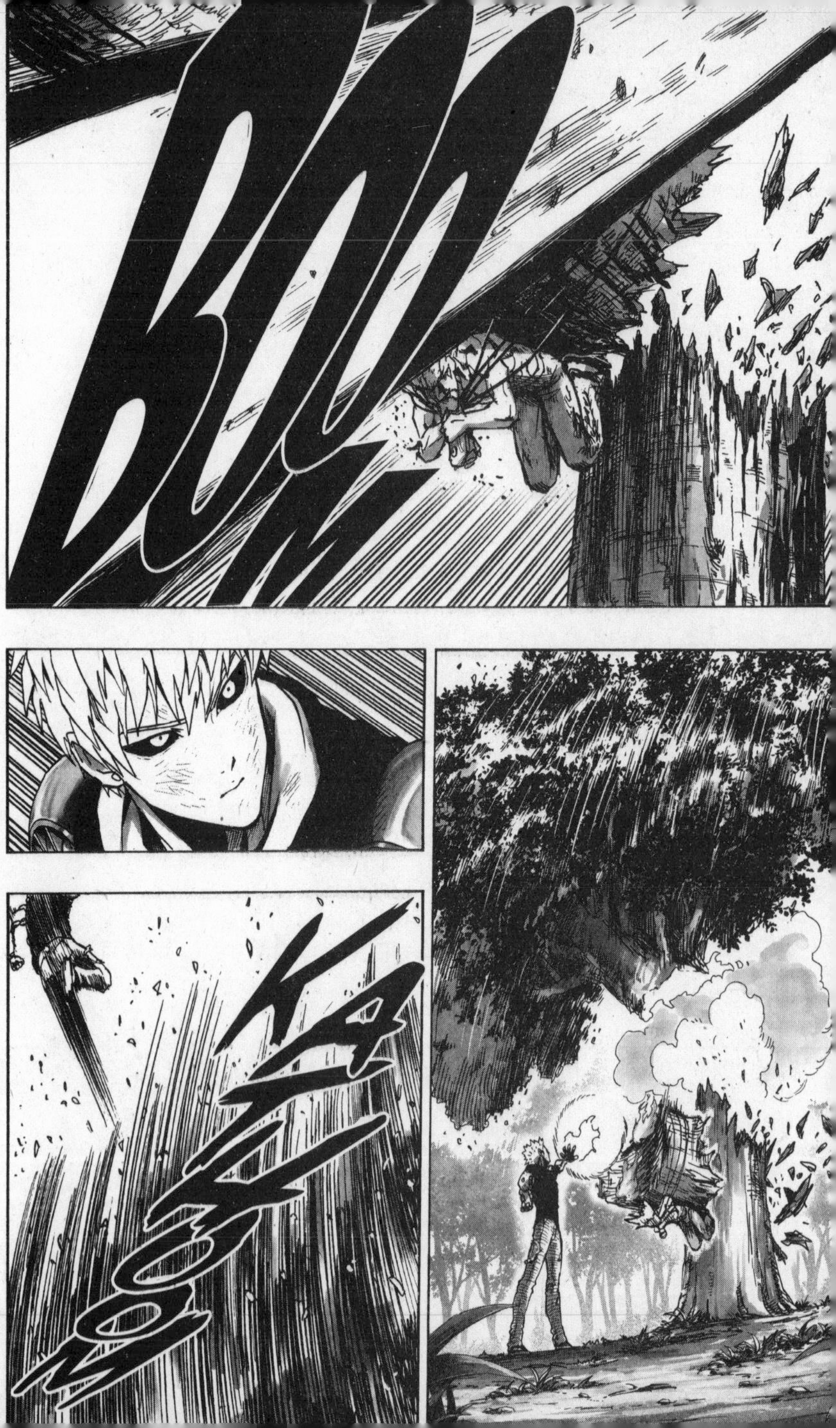
BOOM
KABOOM

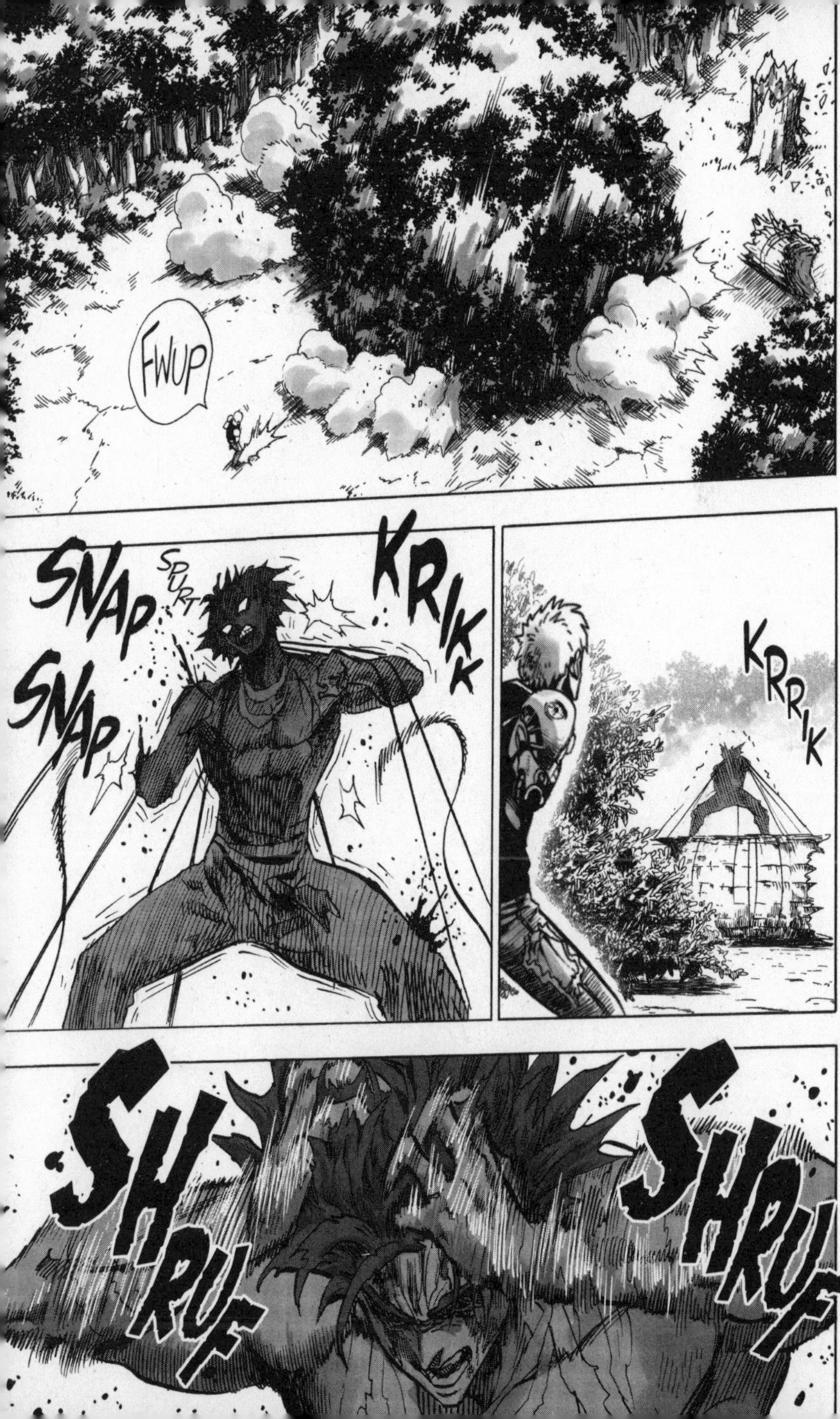
FWUP
KRRRIK
KRIKK
SPURT
SNAP
SNAP
SHRUF
SHRUF

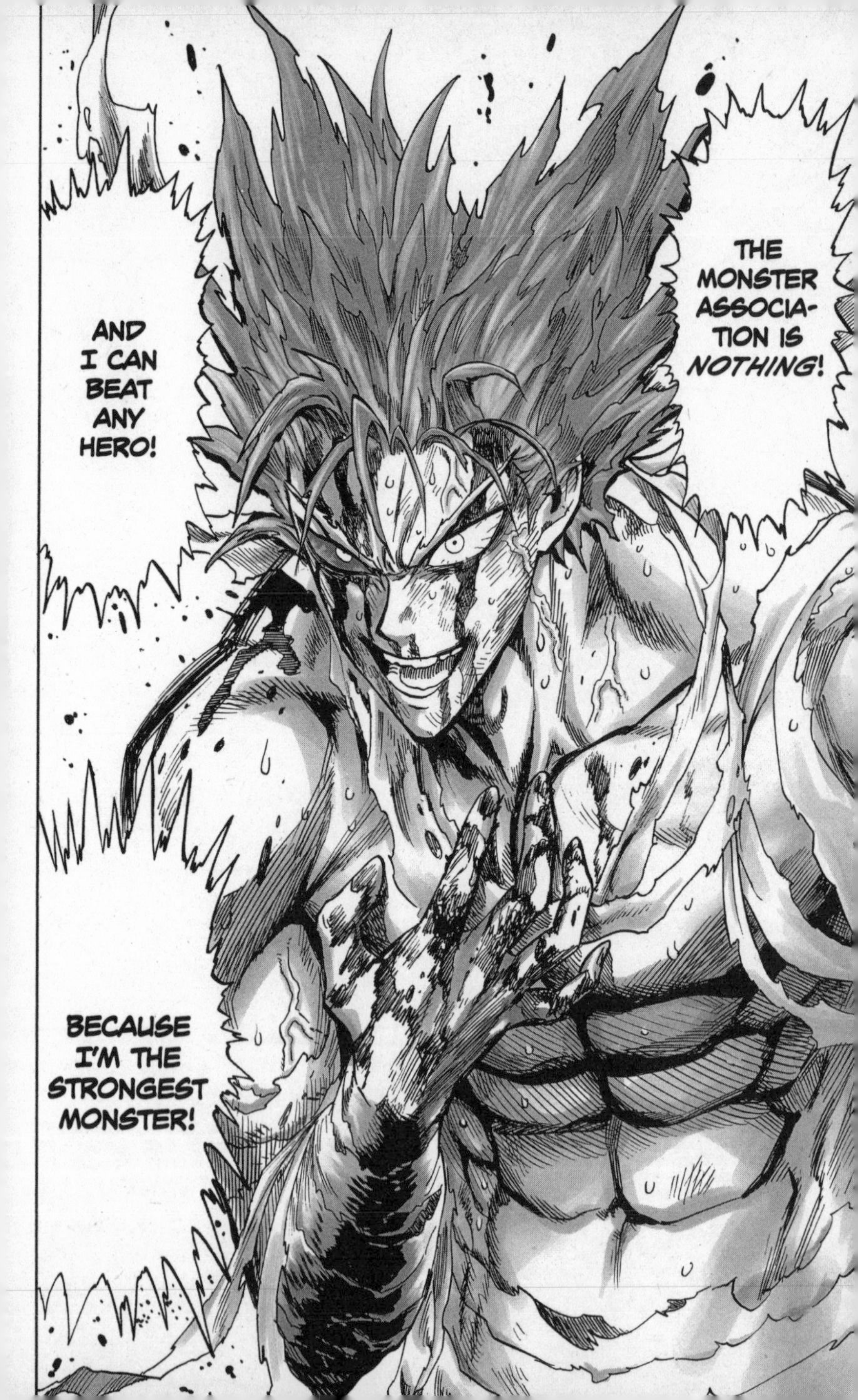
THE MONSTER ASSOCIA-TION IS *NOTHING!*
AND I CAN BEAT ANY HERO!
BECAUSE I'M THE STRONGEST MONSTER!

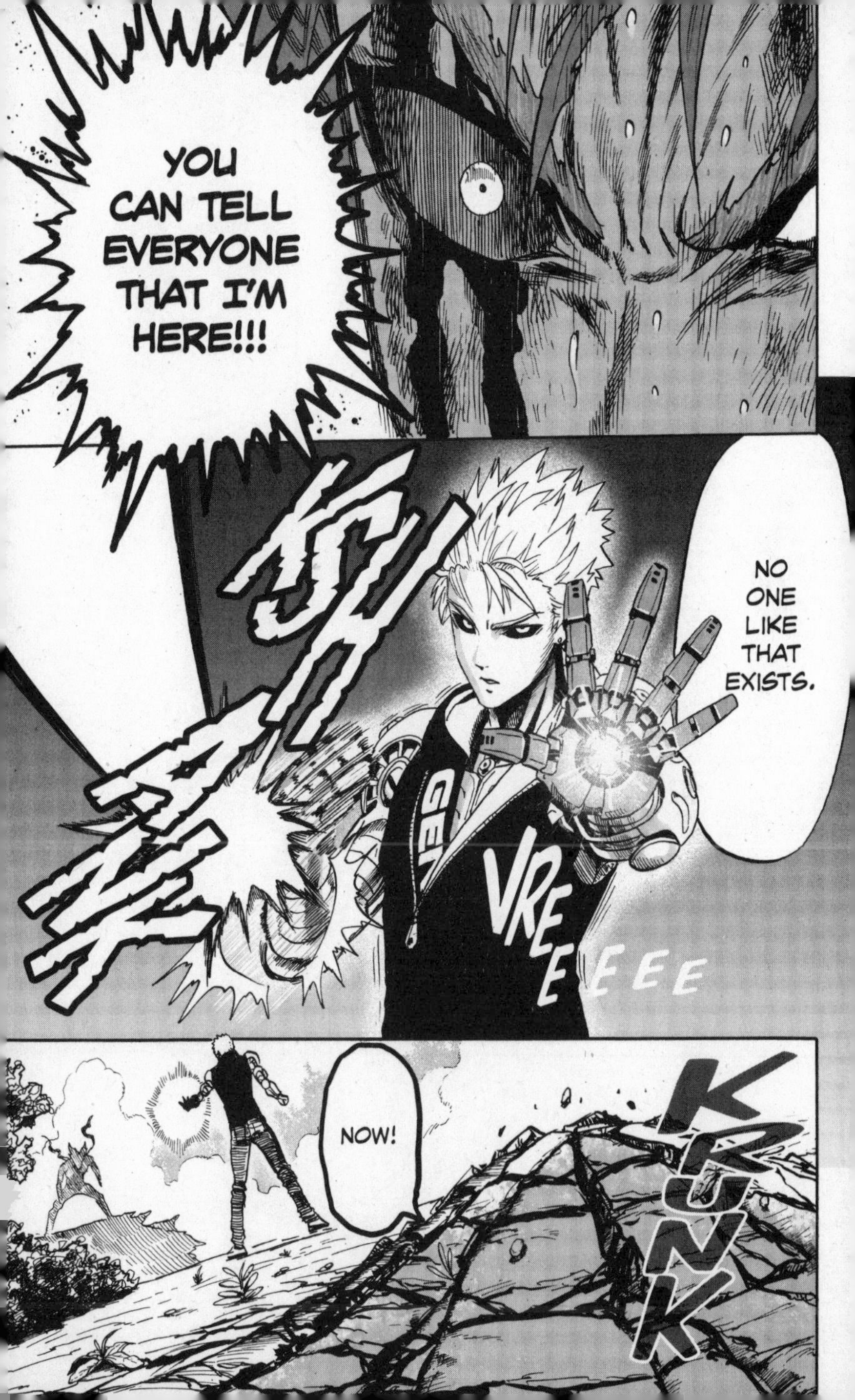
YOU CAN TELL EVERYONE THAT I'M HERE!!!
NO ONE LIKE THAT EXISTS.
VREEEEEE
NOW!

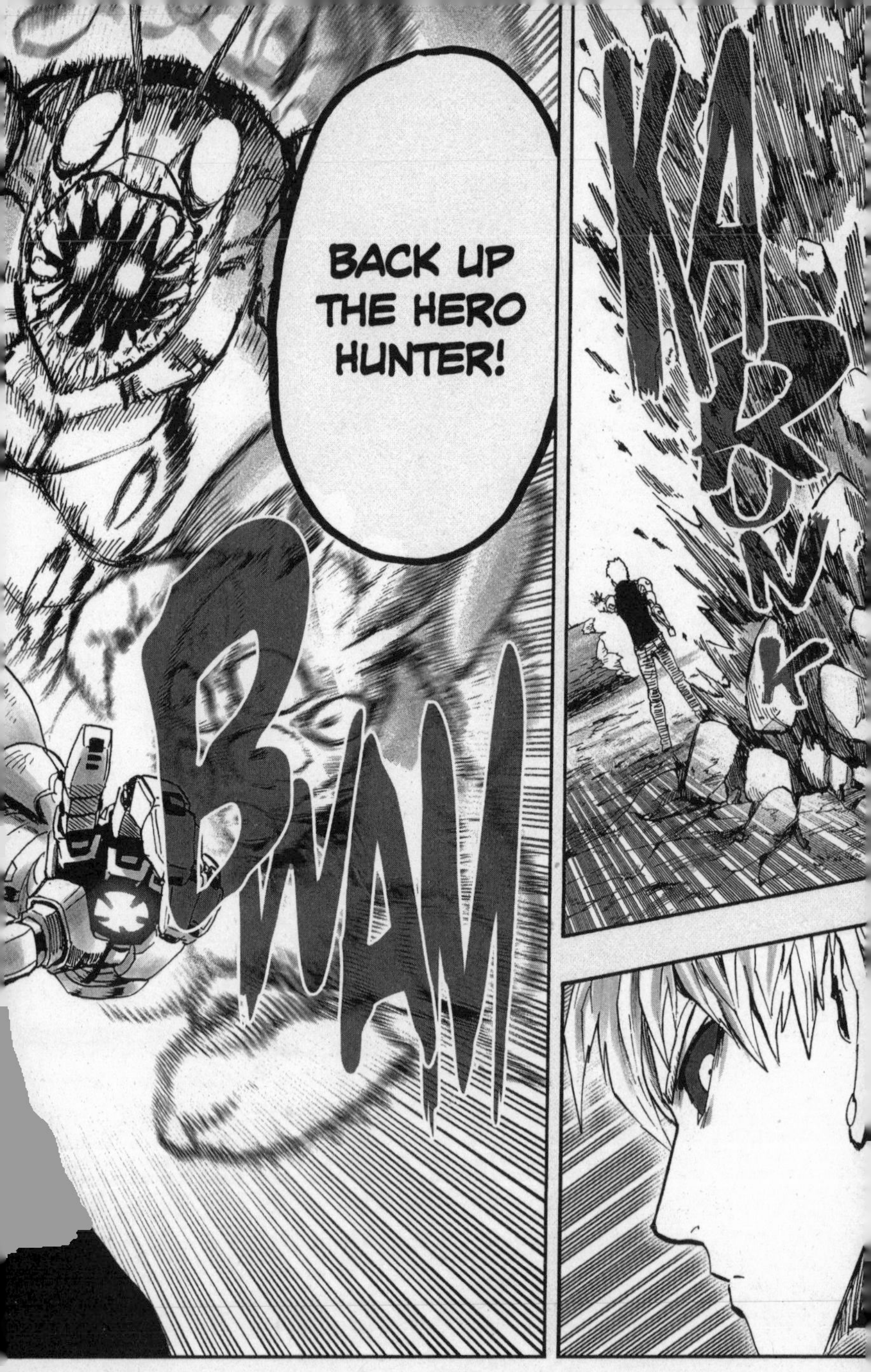
KARONK
BACK UP THE HERO HUNTER!
BWAM

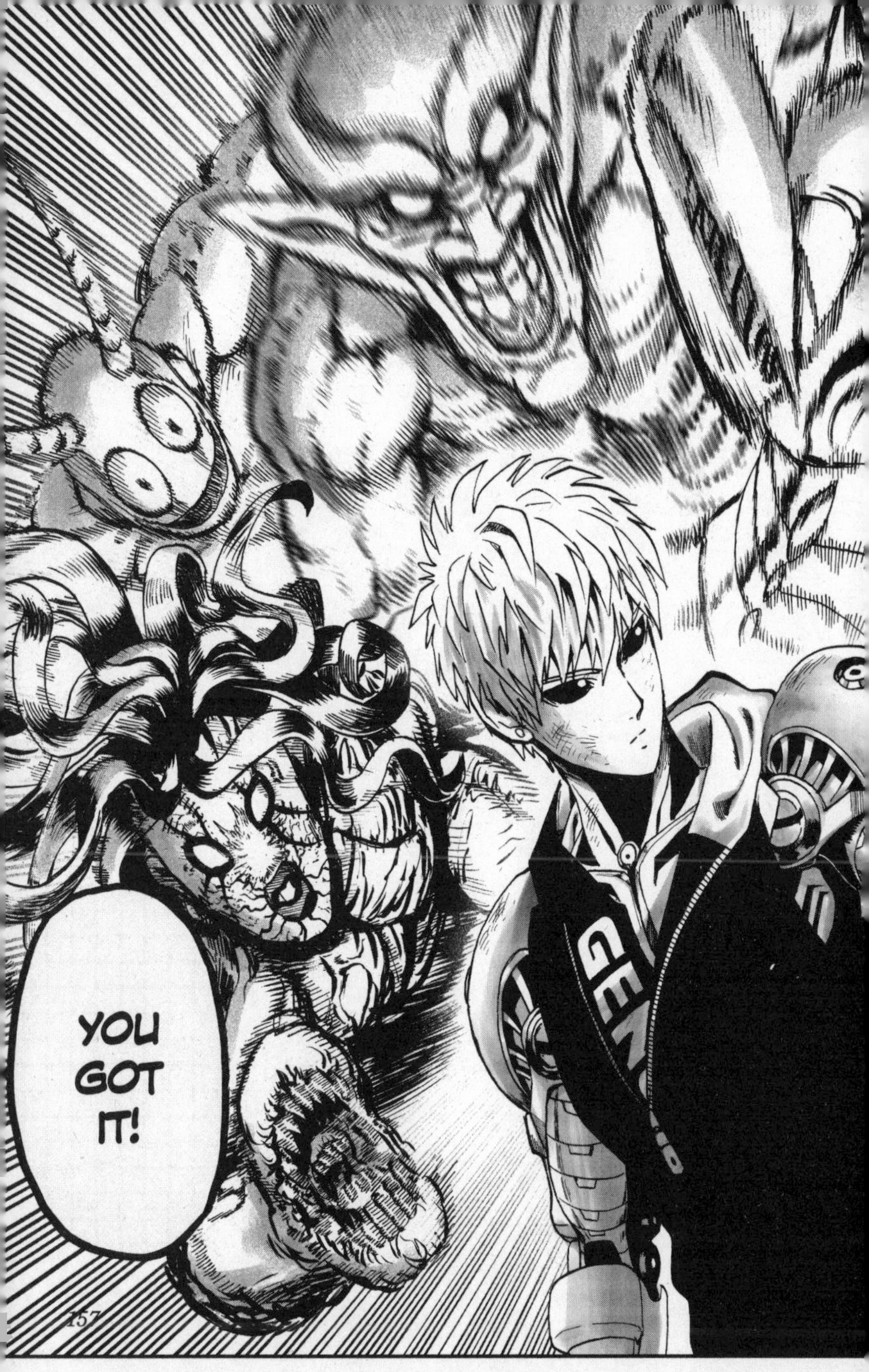
YOU GOT IT!

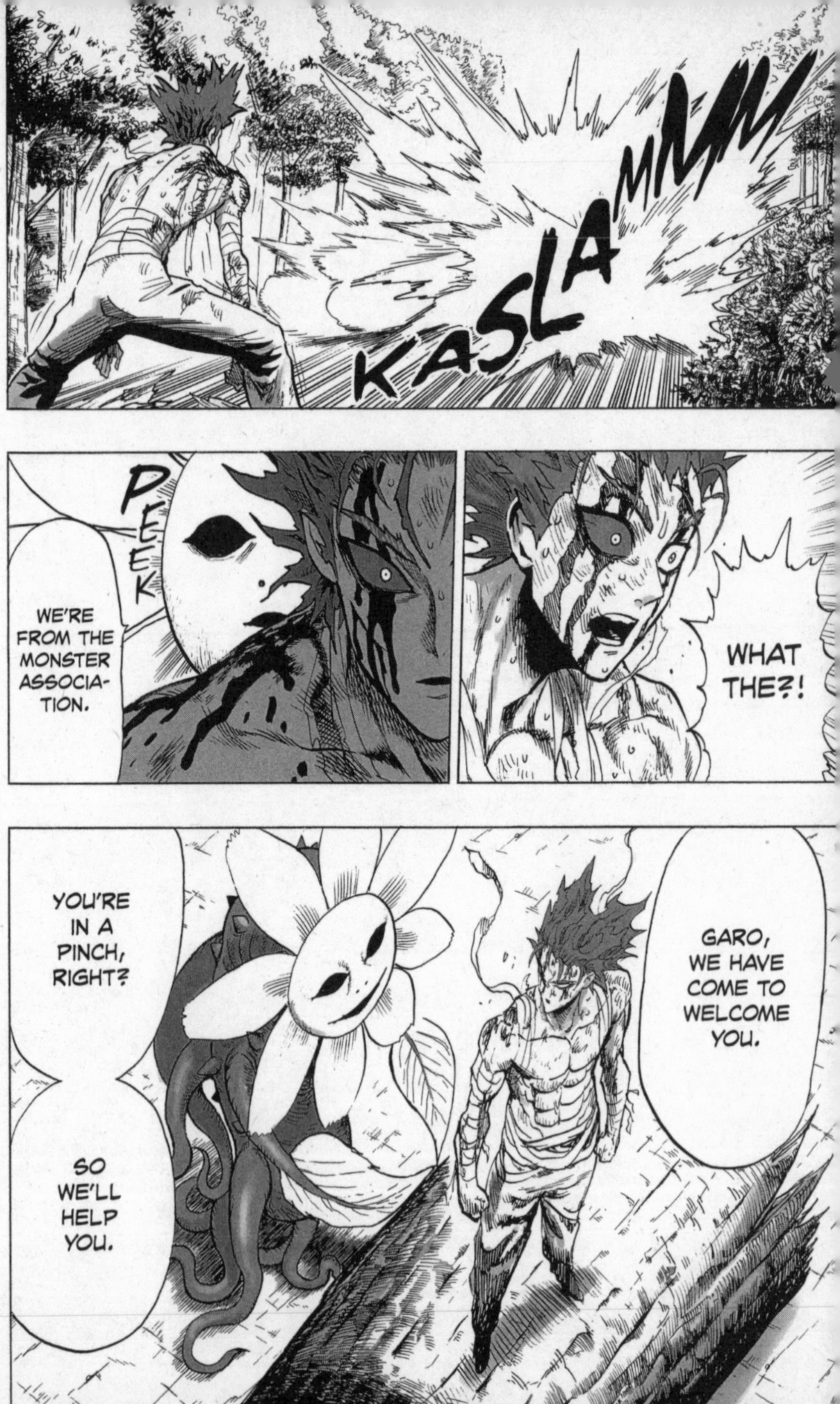
KASLAMMM
WHAT THE?!
PEEK
WE'RE FROM THE MONSTER ASSOCIA- TION.
GARO, WE HAVE COME TO WELCOME YOU.
YOU'RE IN A PINCH, RIGHT?
SO WE'LL HELP YOU.

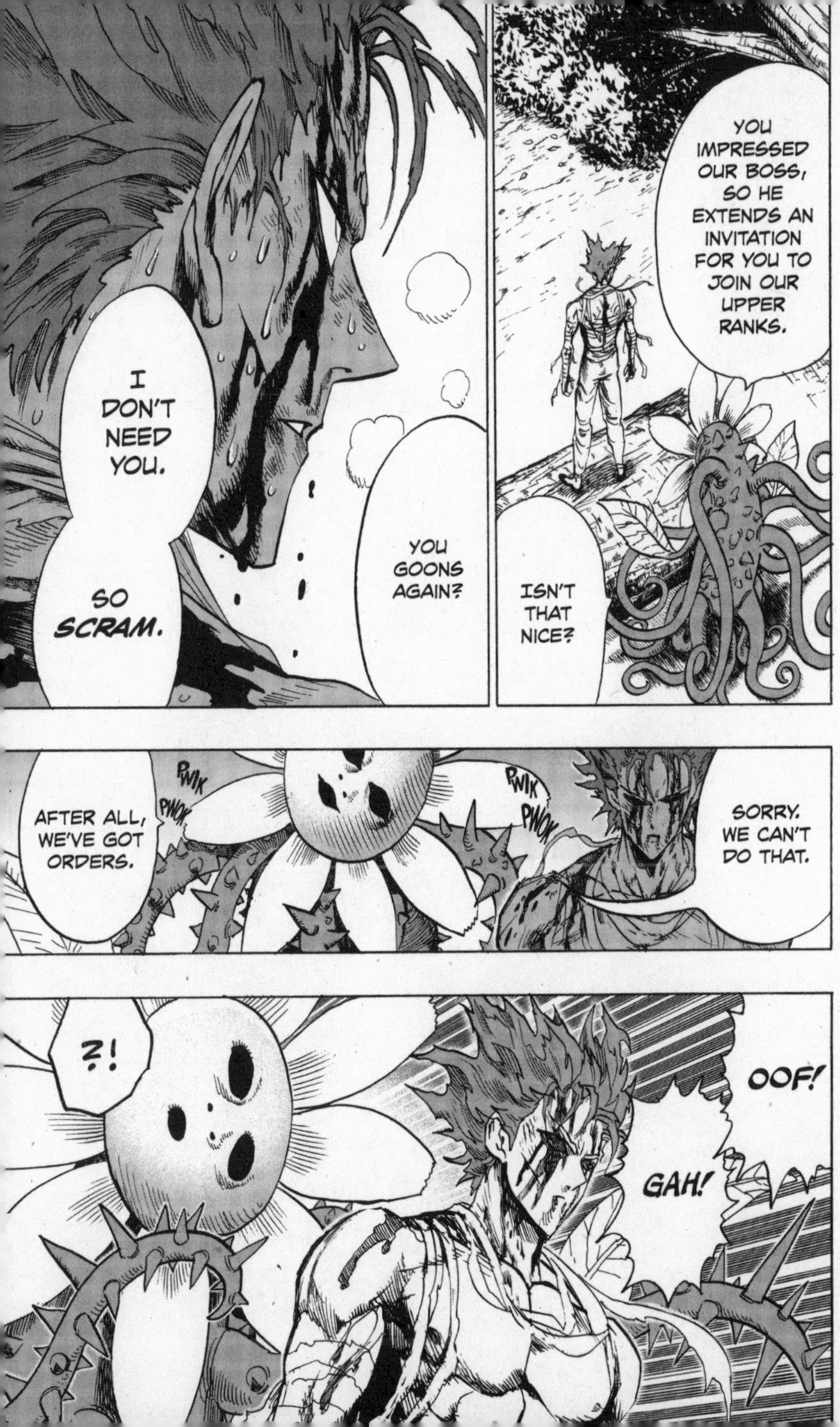
YOU IMPRESSED OUR BOSS, SO HE EXTENDS AN INVITATION FOR YOU TO JOIN OUR UPPER RANKS.
ISN'T THAT NICE?
YOU GOONS AGAIN?
I DON'T NEED YOU.
SO *SCRAM*.
SORRY. WE CAN'T DO THAT.
PWIK PWOK
PWIK PWOK
AFTER ALL, WE'VE GOT ORDERS.
OOF!
GAH!
?!

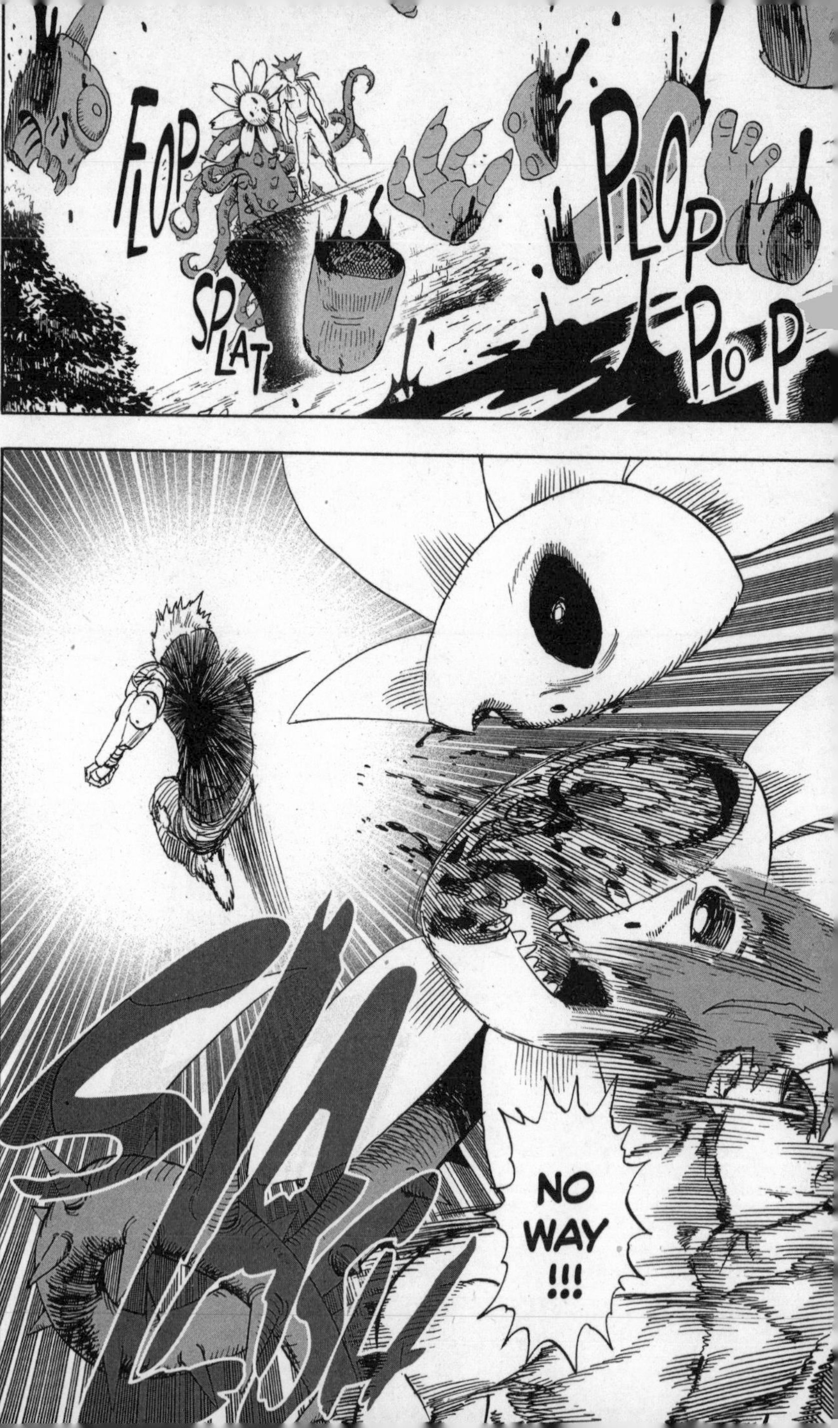
PLOP
PLOP
FLOP!
SPLAT
NO WAY !!!

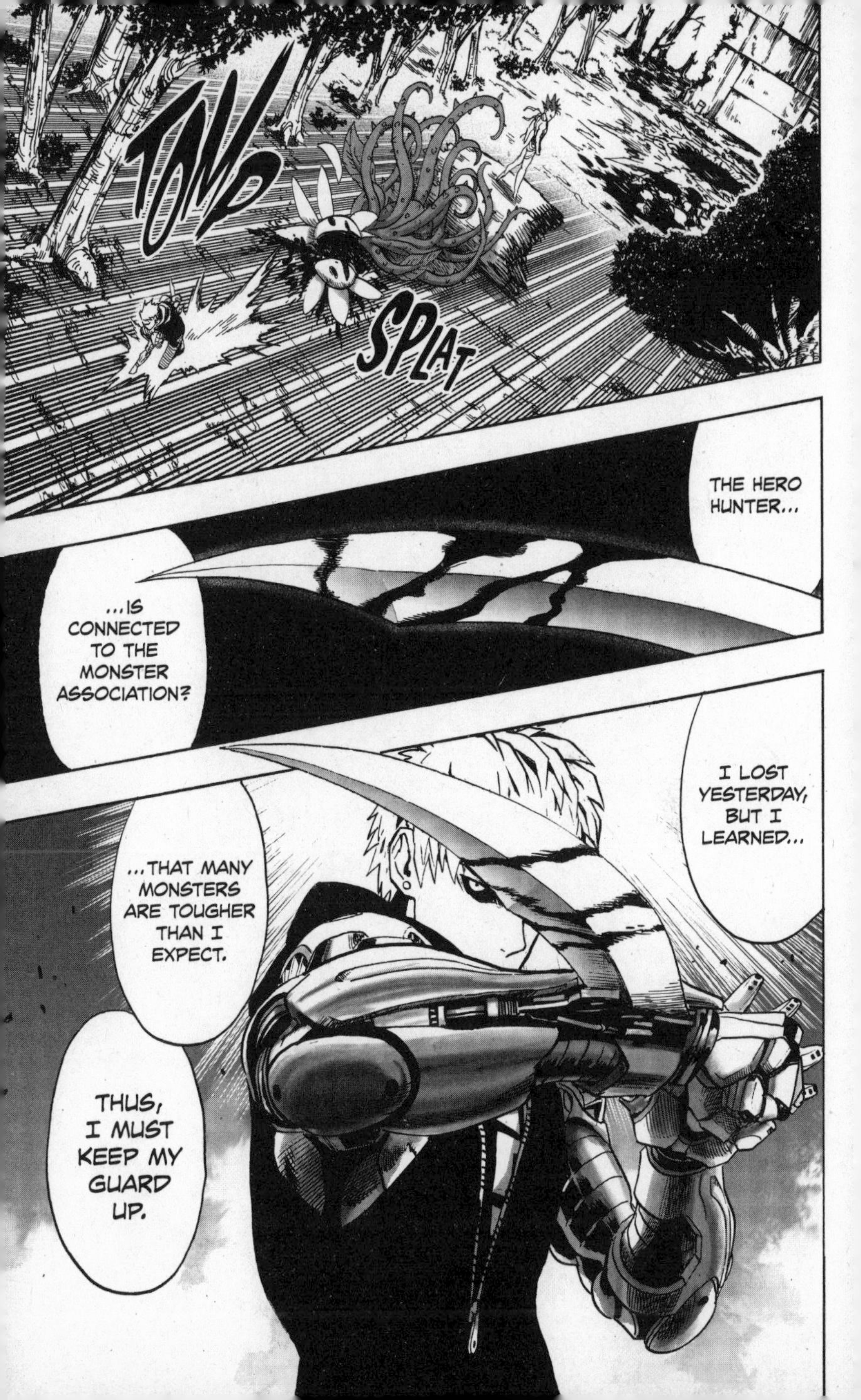
TOMP
SPLAT
THE HERO HUNTER...
...IS CONNECTED TO THE MONSTER ASSOCIATION?
I LOST YESTERDAY, BUT I LEARNED...
...THAT MANY MONSTERS ARE TOUGHER THAN I EXPECT.
THUS, I MUST KEEP MY GUARD UP.

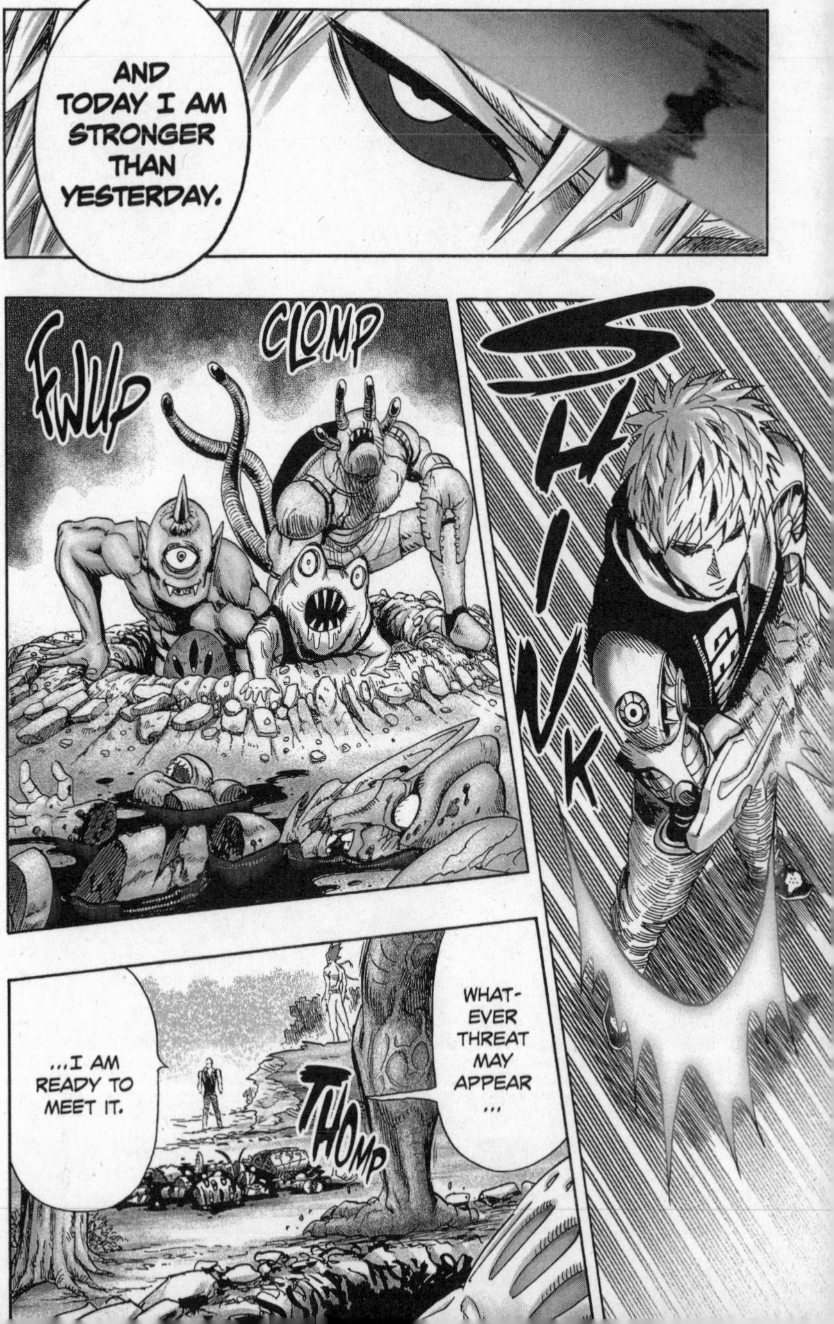
AND TODAY I AM STRONGER THAN YESTERDAY.
SHINK
CLOMP
FWUP
WHAT-EVER THREAT MAY APPEAR ...
THOMP
...I AM READY TO MEET IT.

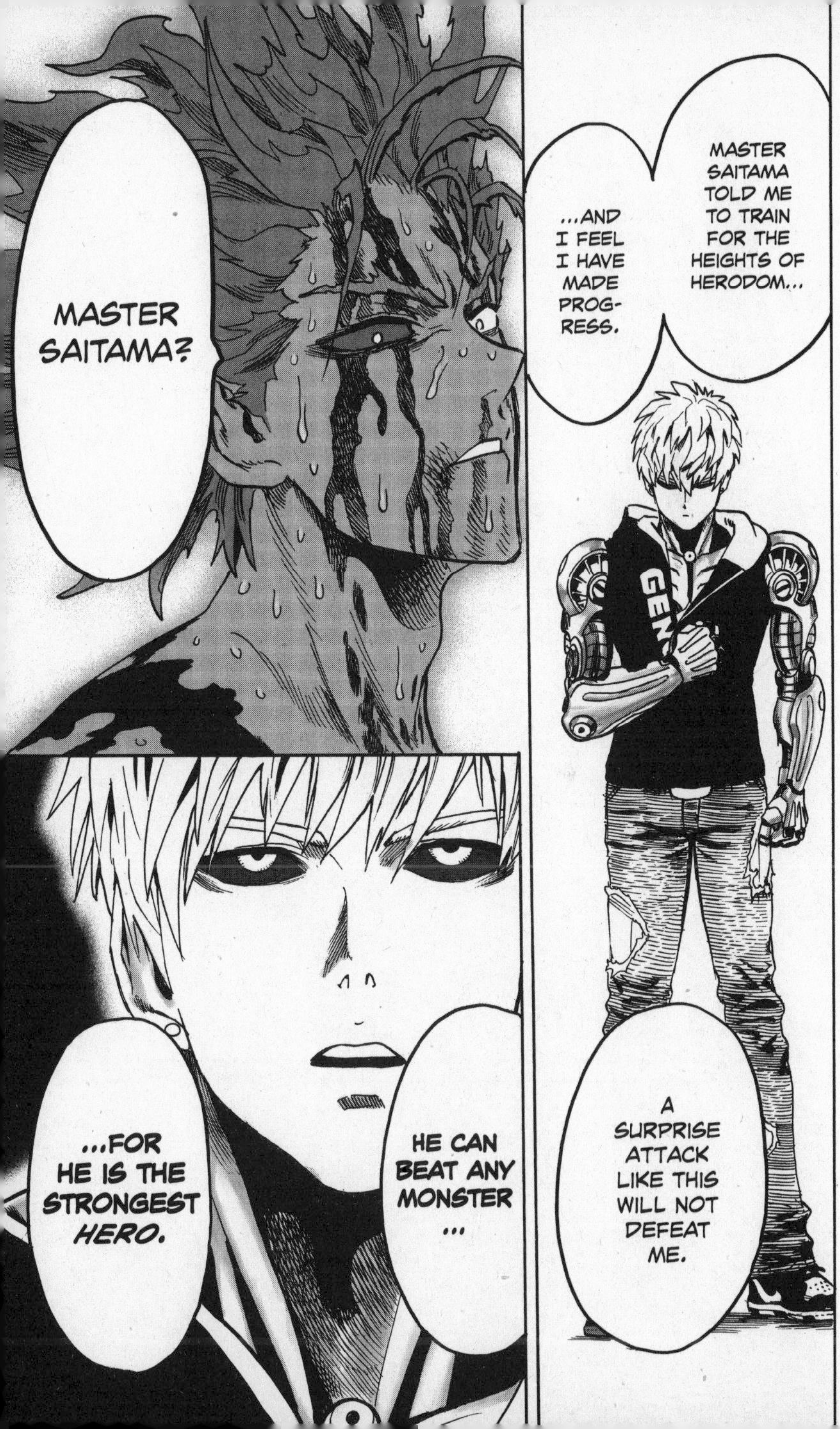
MASTER SAITAMA TOLD ME TO TRAIN FOR THE HEIGHTS OF HERODOM...
...AND I FEEL I HAVE MADE PROG-RESS.
A SURPRISE ATTACK LIKE THIS WILL NOT DEFEAT ME.
MASTER SAITAMA?
HE CAN BEAT ANY MONSTER ...
...FOR HE IS THE STRONGEST *HERO.*

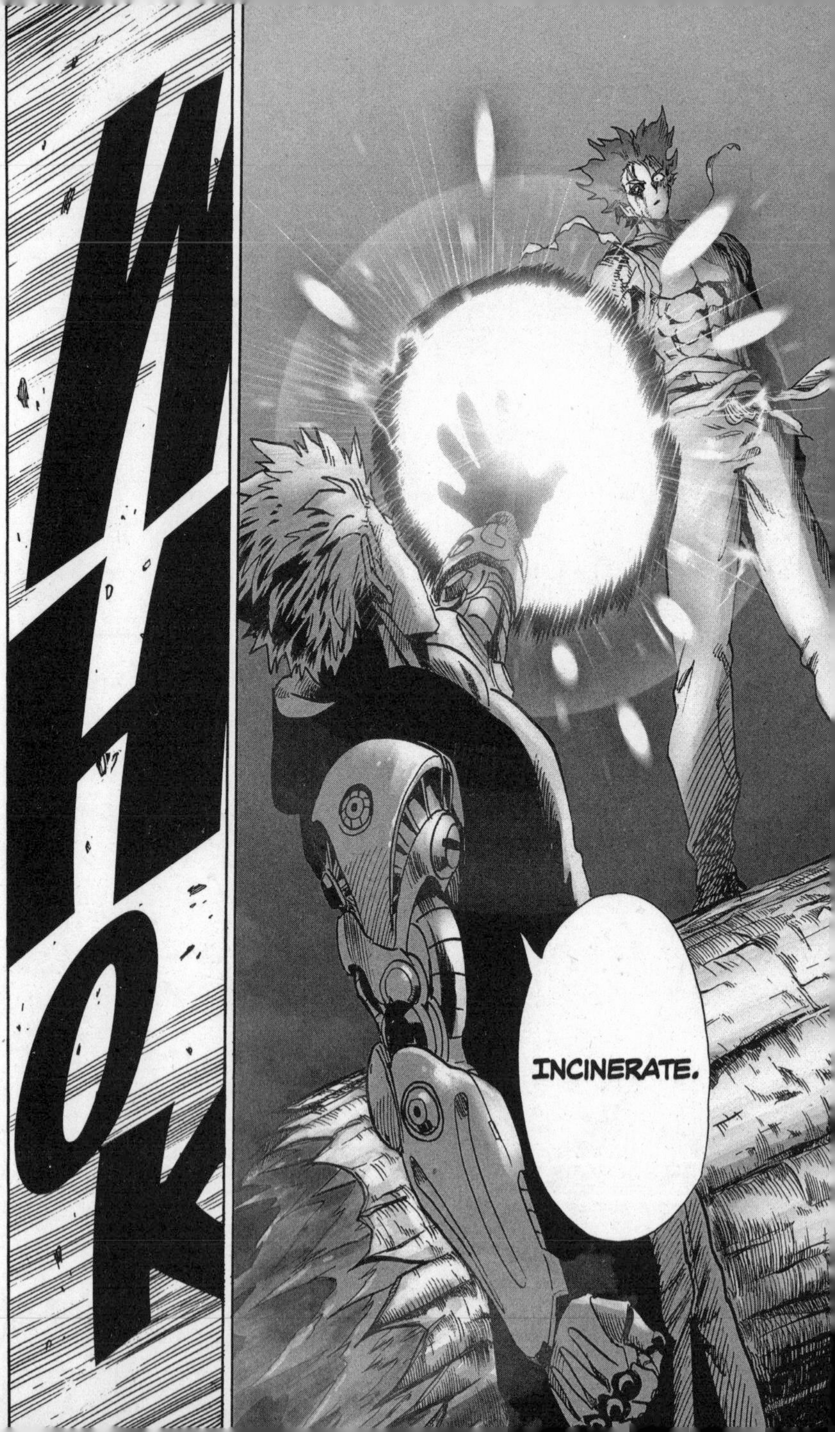
INCINERATE.

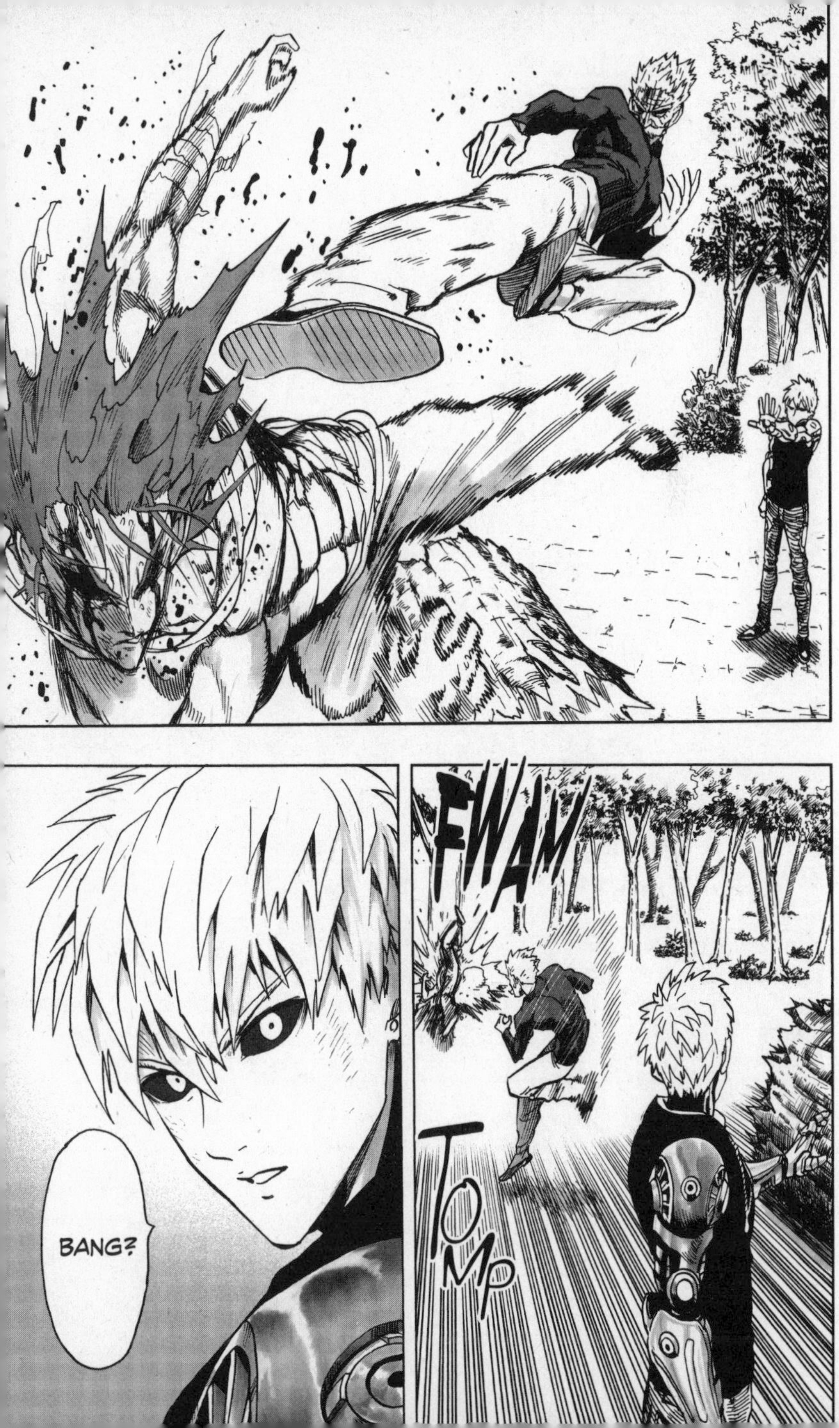
FWAM
TOMP
BANG?

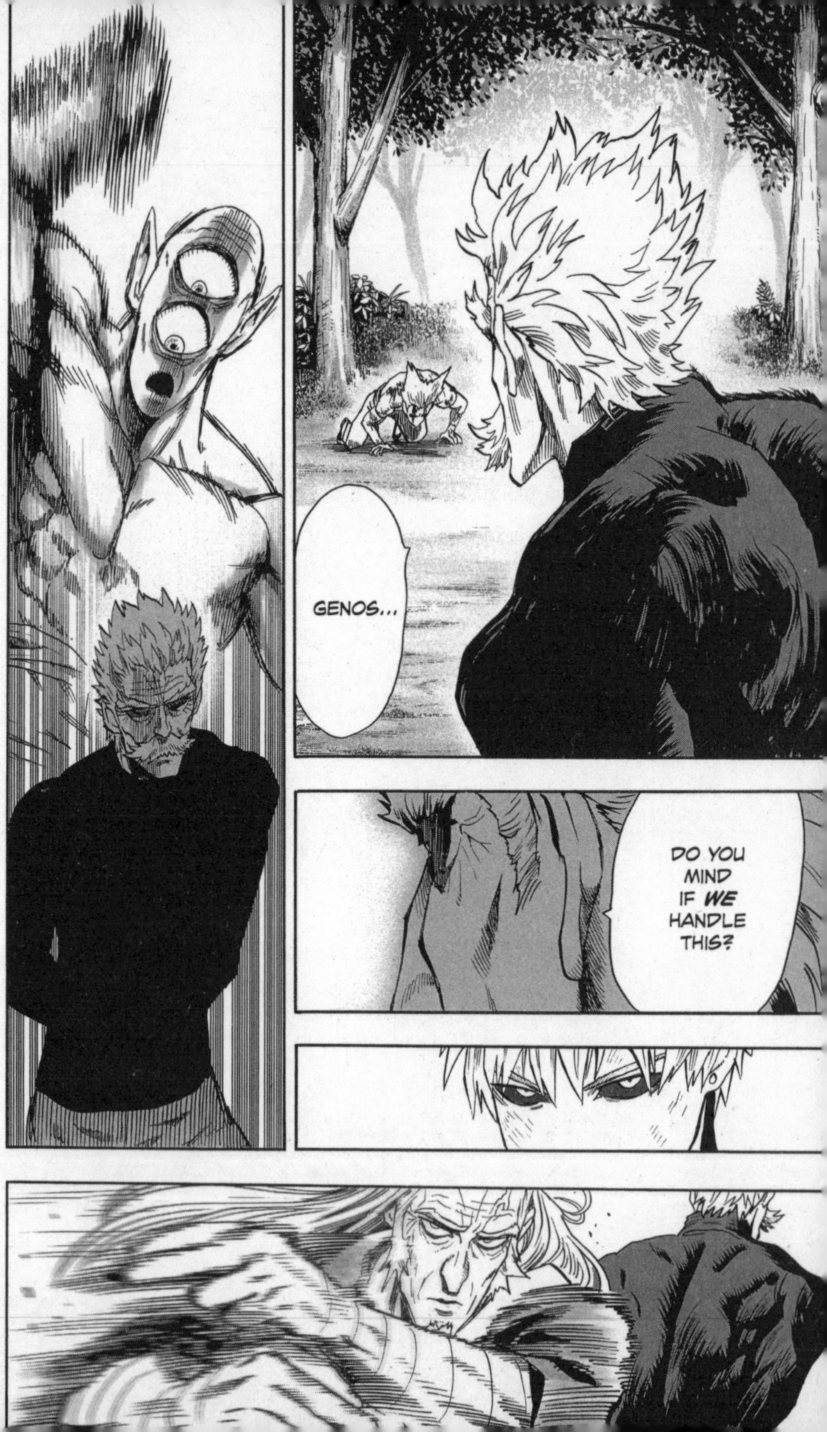
GENOS...
DO YOU MIND IF WE HANDLE THIS?

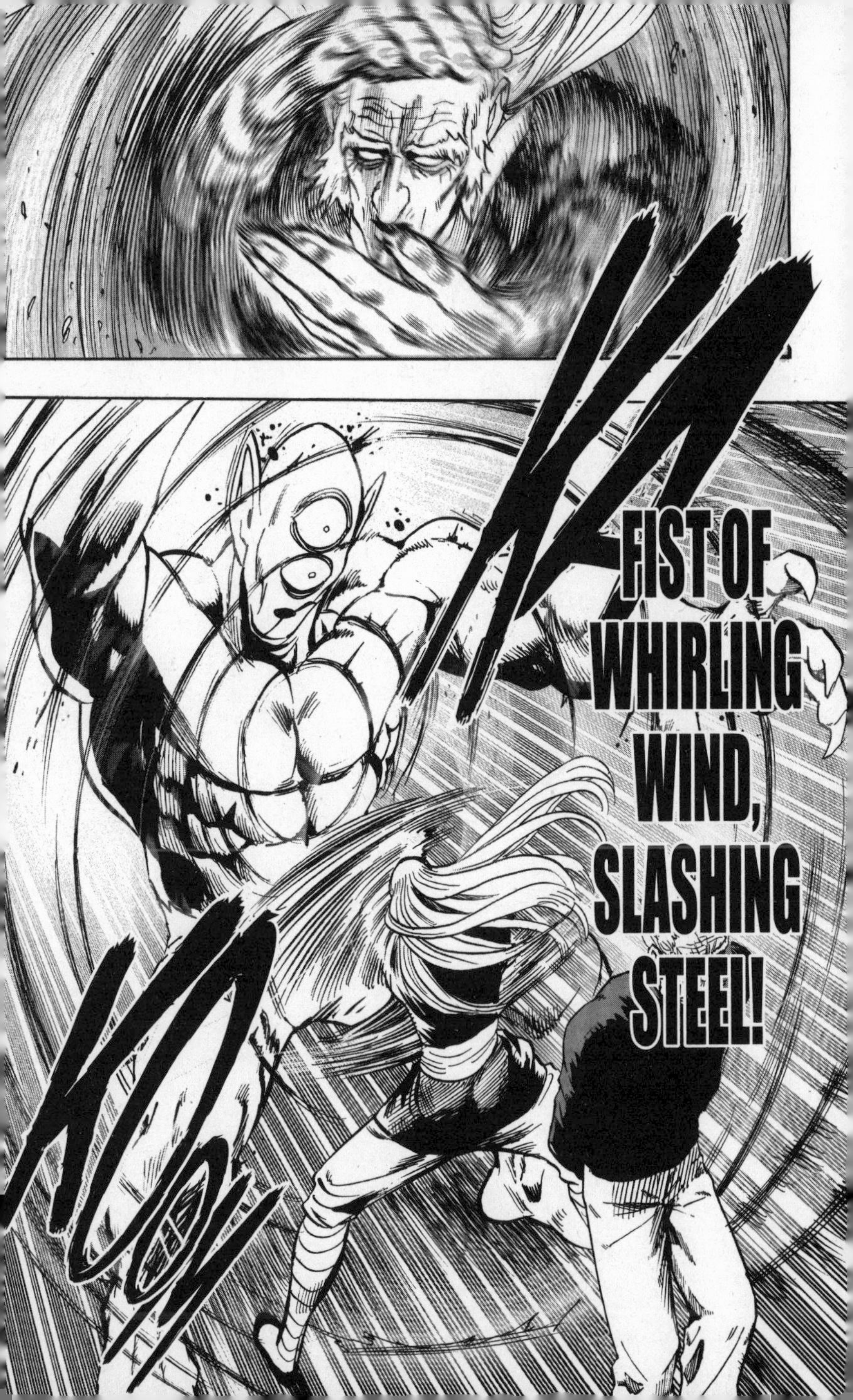
FIST OF WHIRLING WIND, SLASHING STEEL!

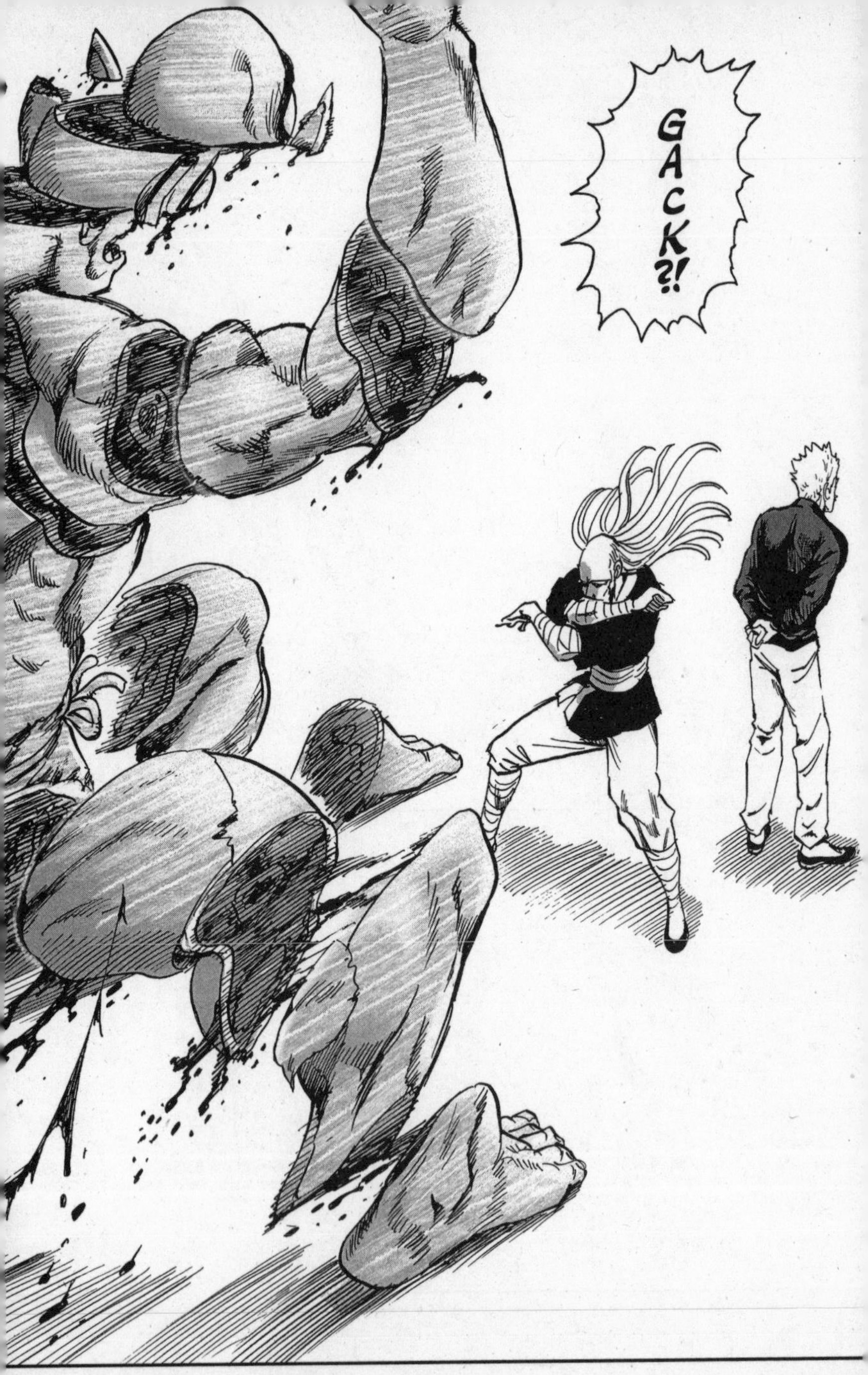
GACK?!

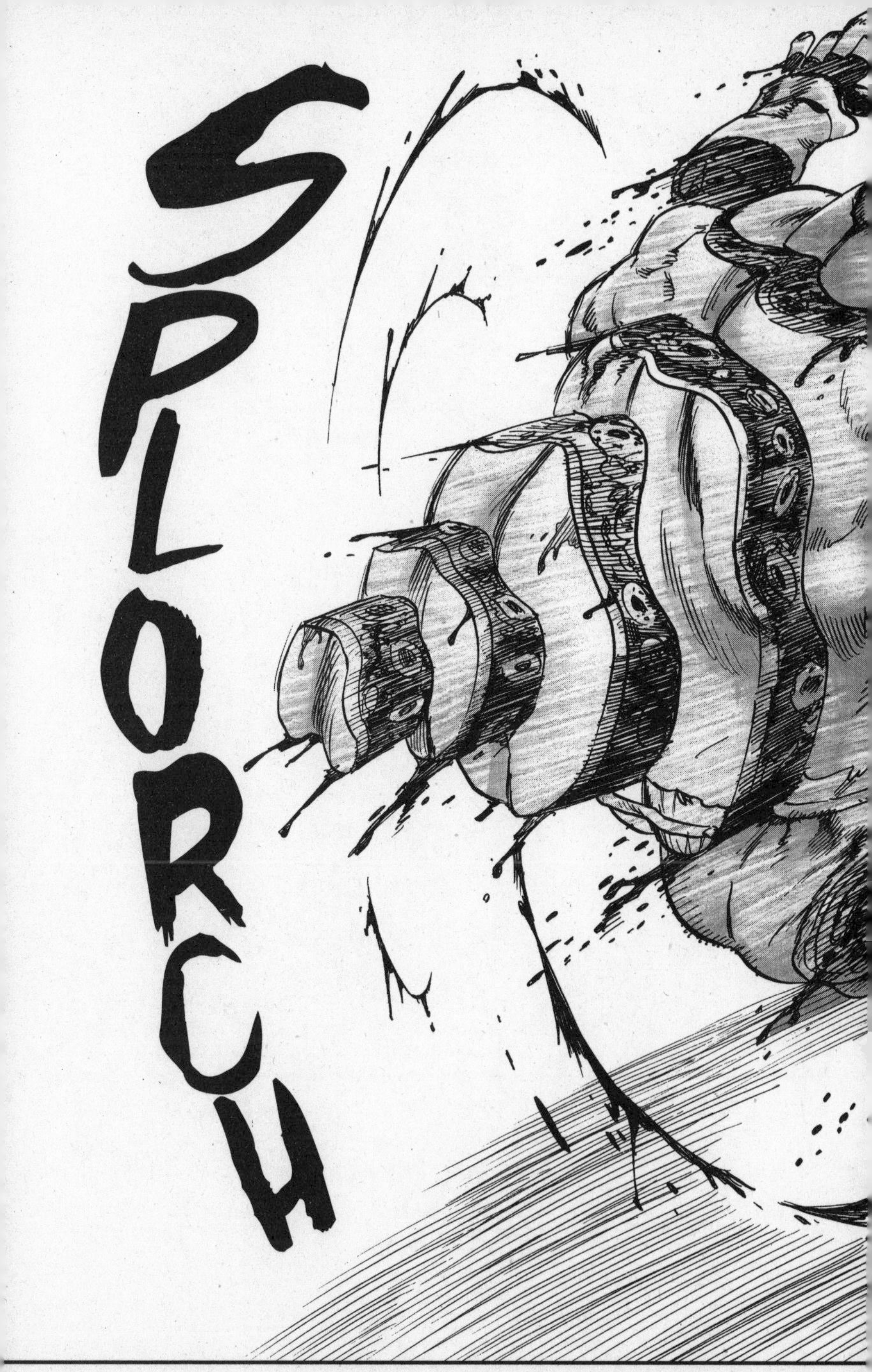
SPLORCH

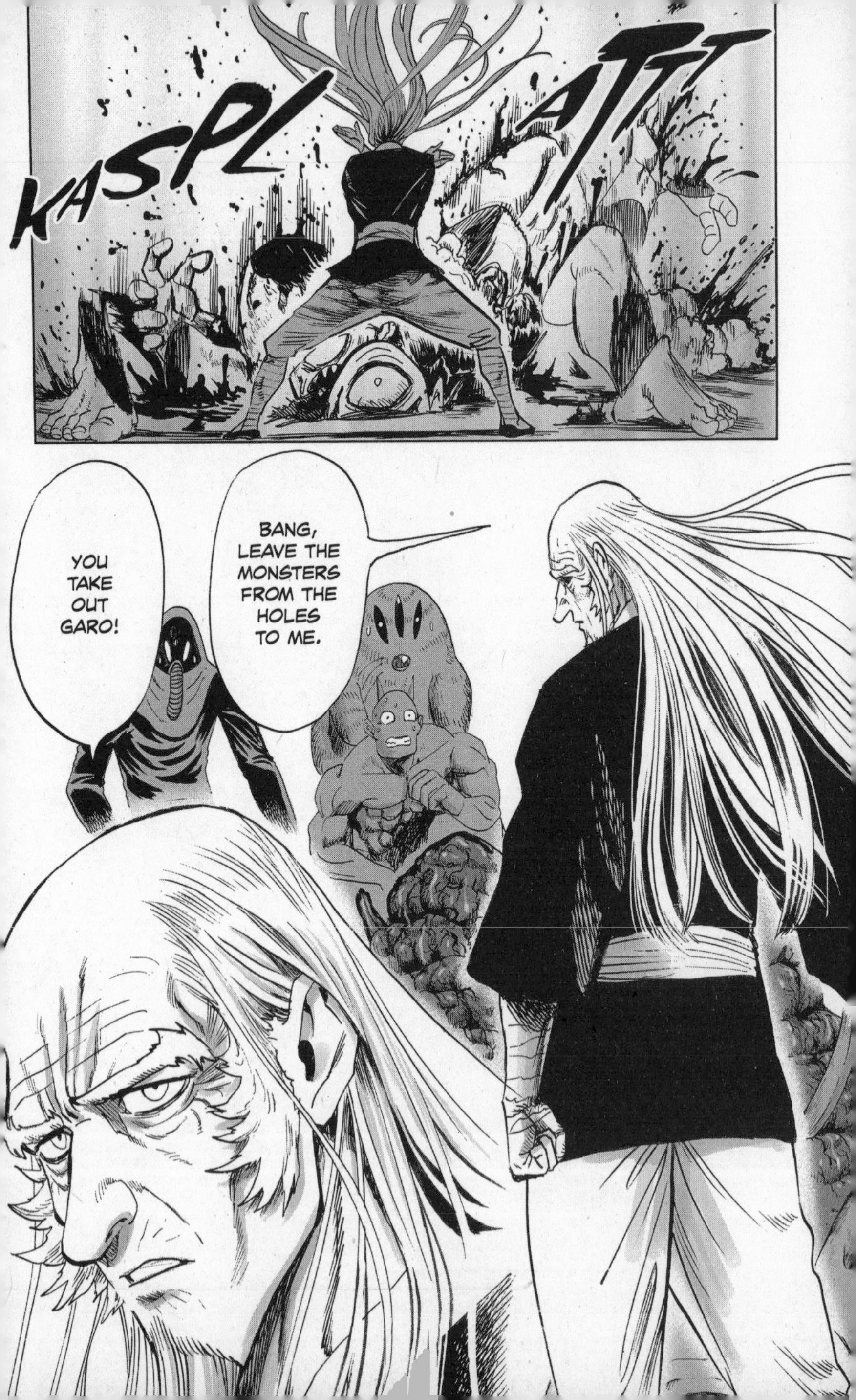
KASPLATT
BANG, LEAVE THE MONSTERS FROM THE HOLES TO ME.
YOU TAKE OUT GARO!

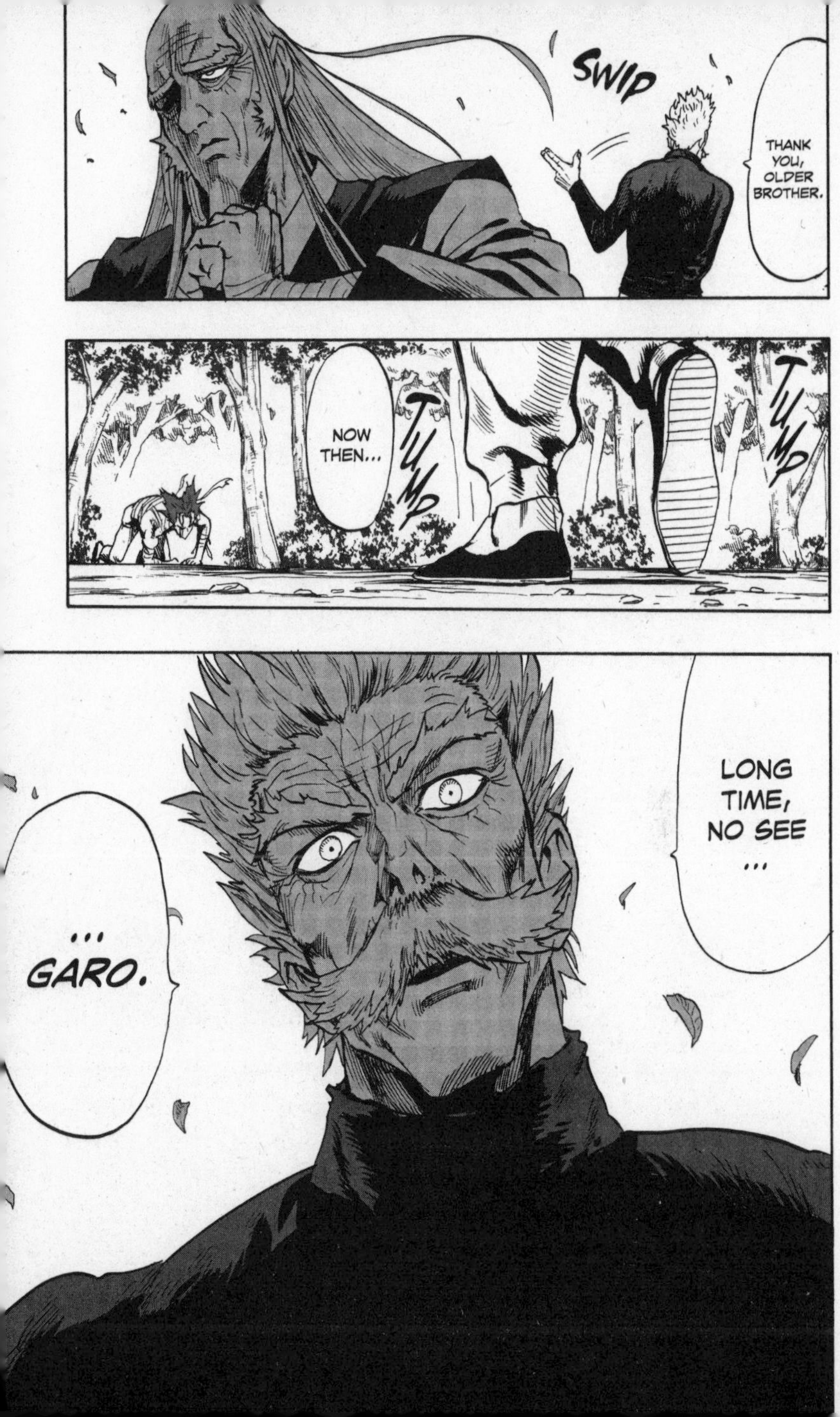
THANK YOU, OLDER BROTHER.
SWIP
TUMP
NOW THEN...
TUMP
LONG TIME, NO SEE ...
... GARO.

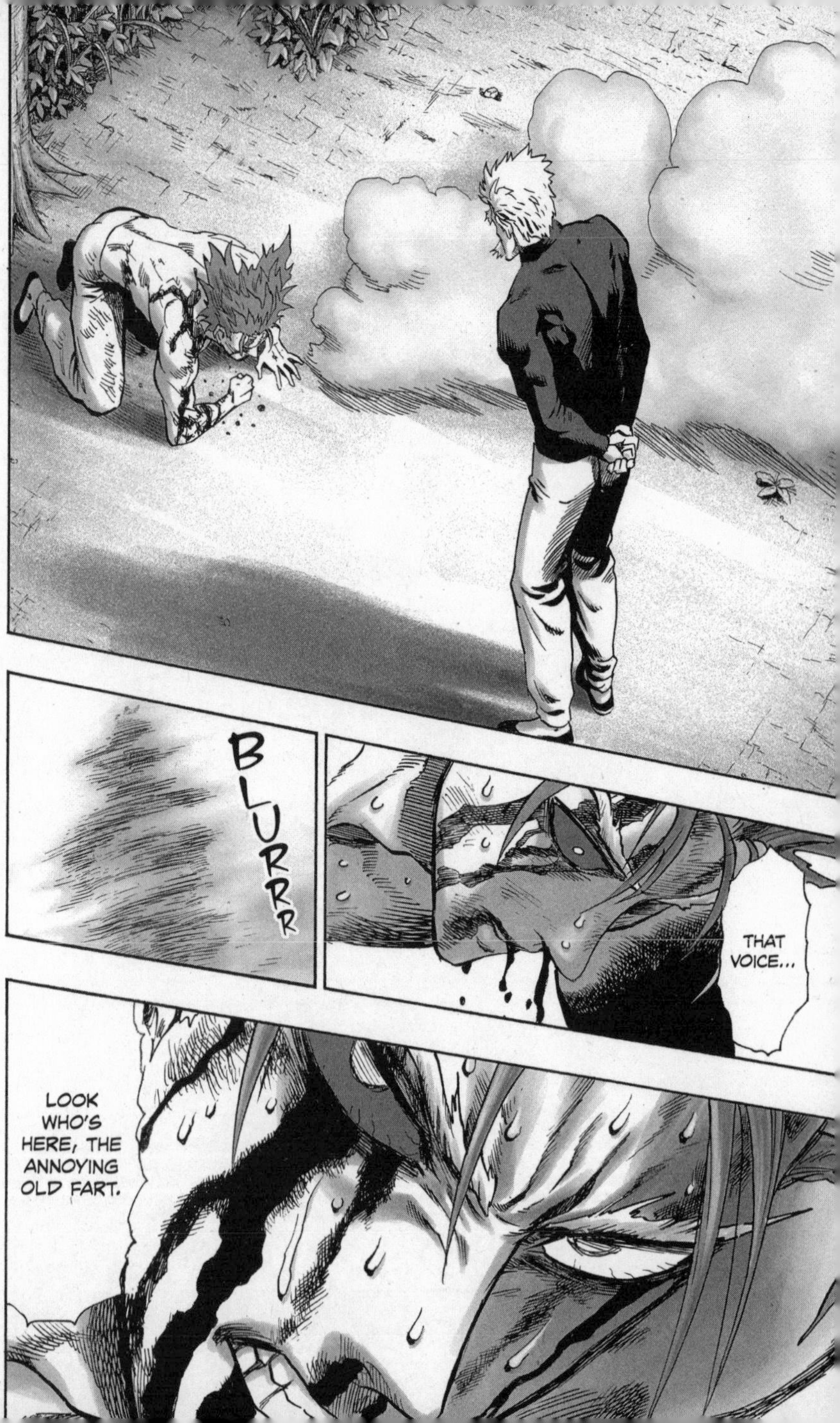
THAT VOICE...
BLURRR
LOOK WHO'S HERE, THE ANNOYING OLD FART.

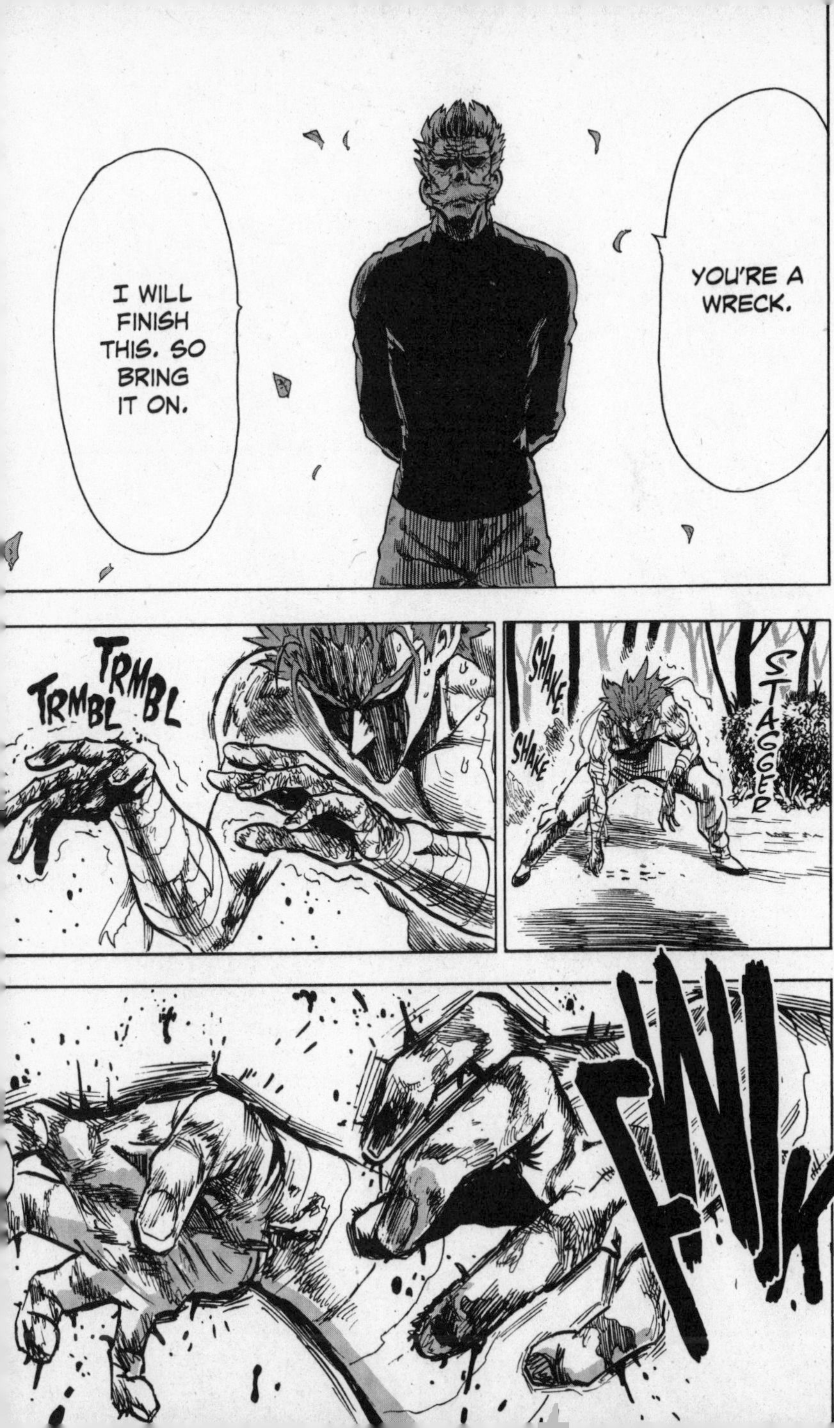
YOU'RE A WRECK.
I WILL FINISH THIS. SO BRING IT ON.
SHAKE
SHAKE
STAGGER
TRMBL
TRMBL

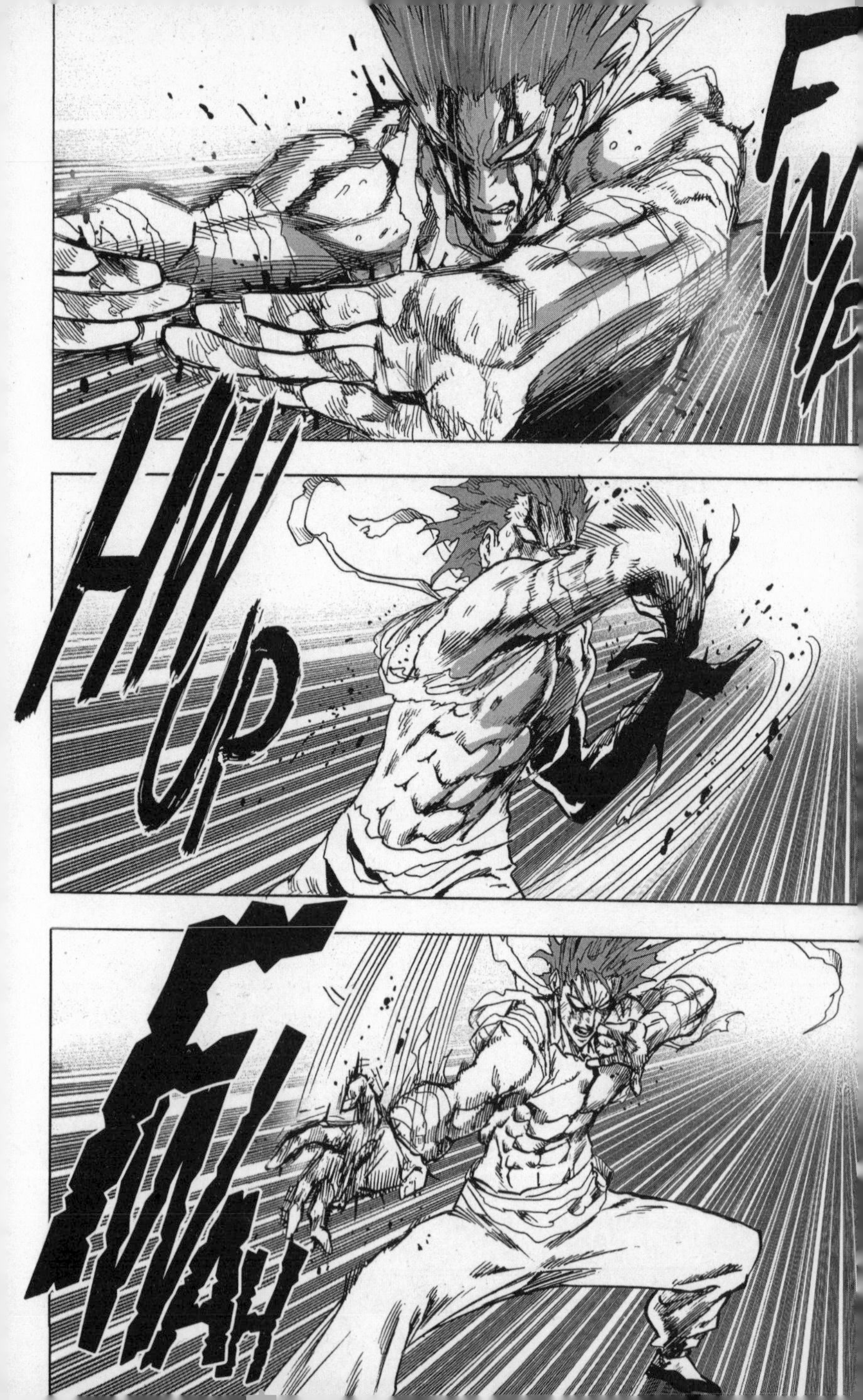
FWIP
HWUP
FWAH!

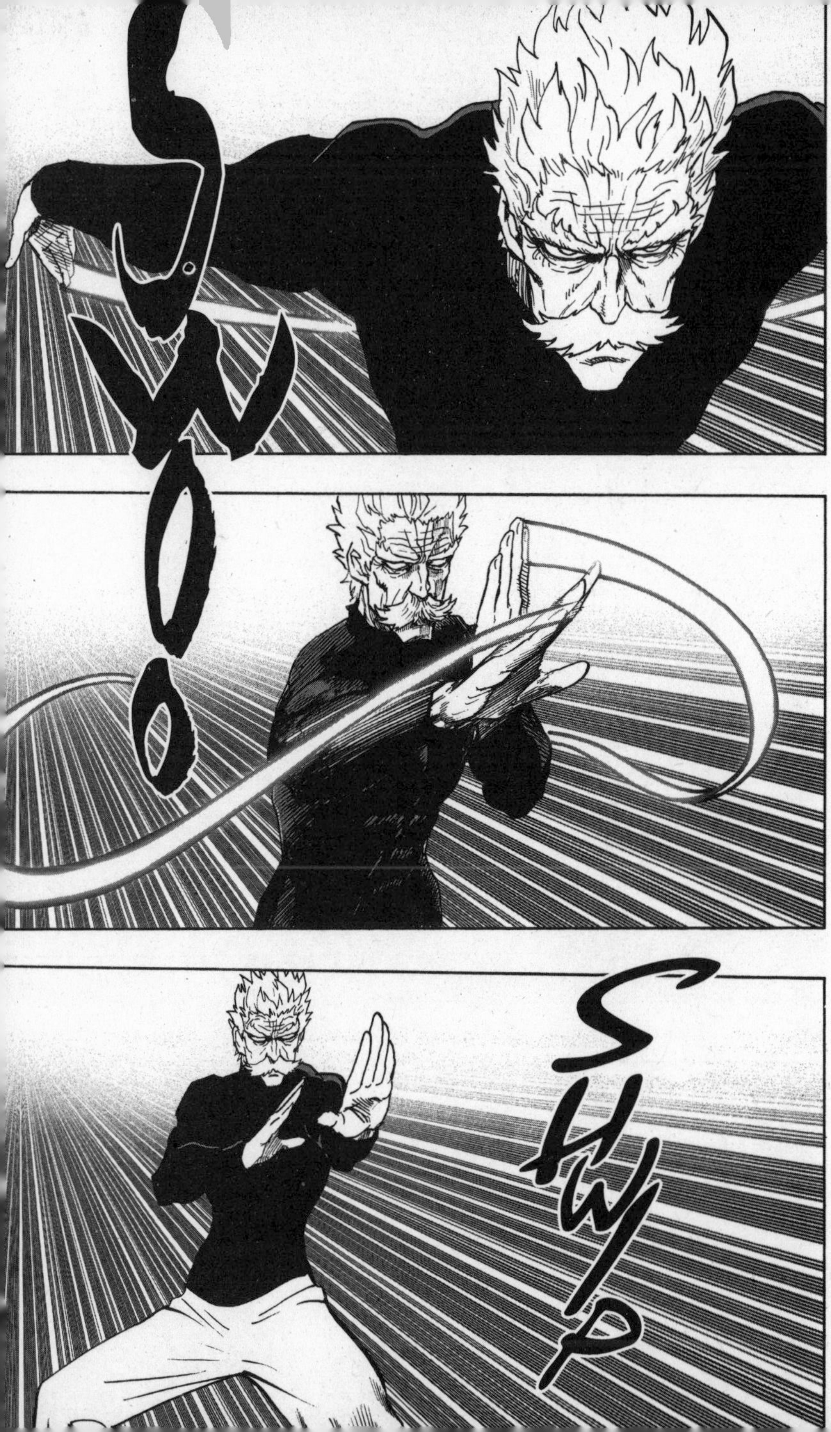
SHWOO
SHWIP

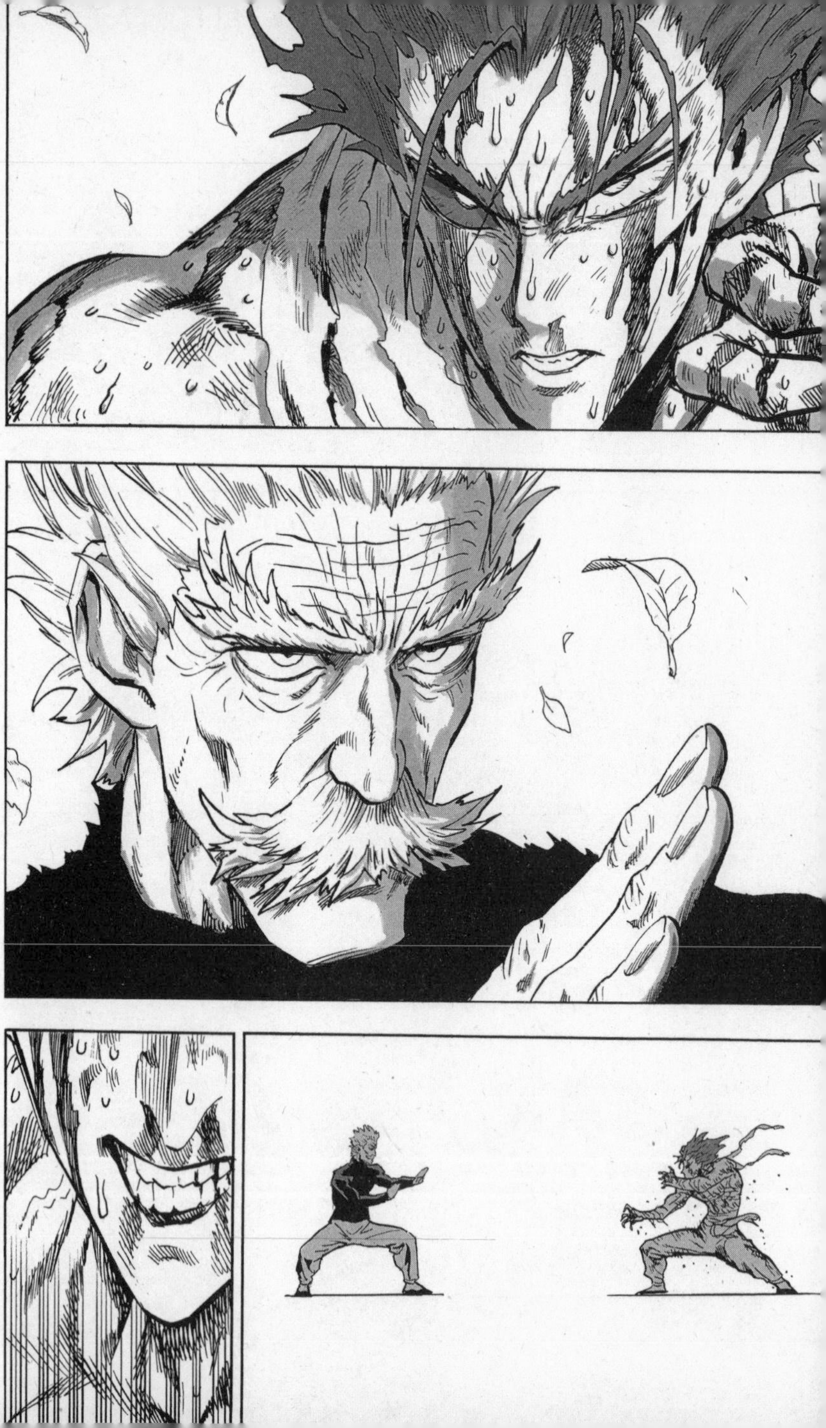

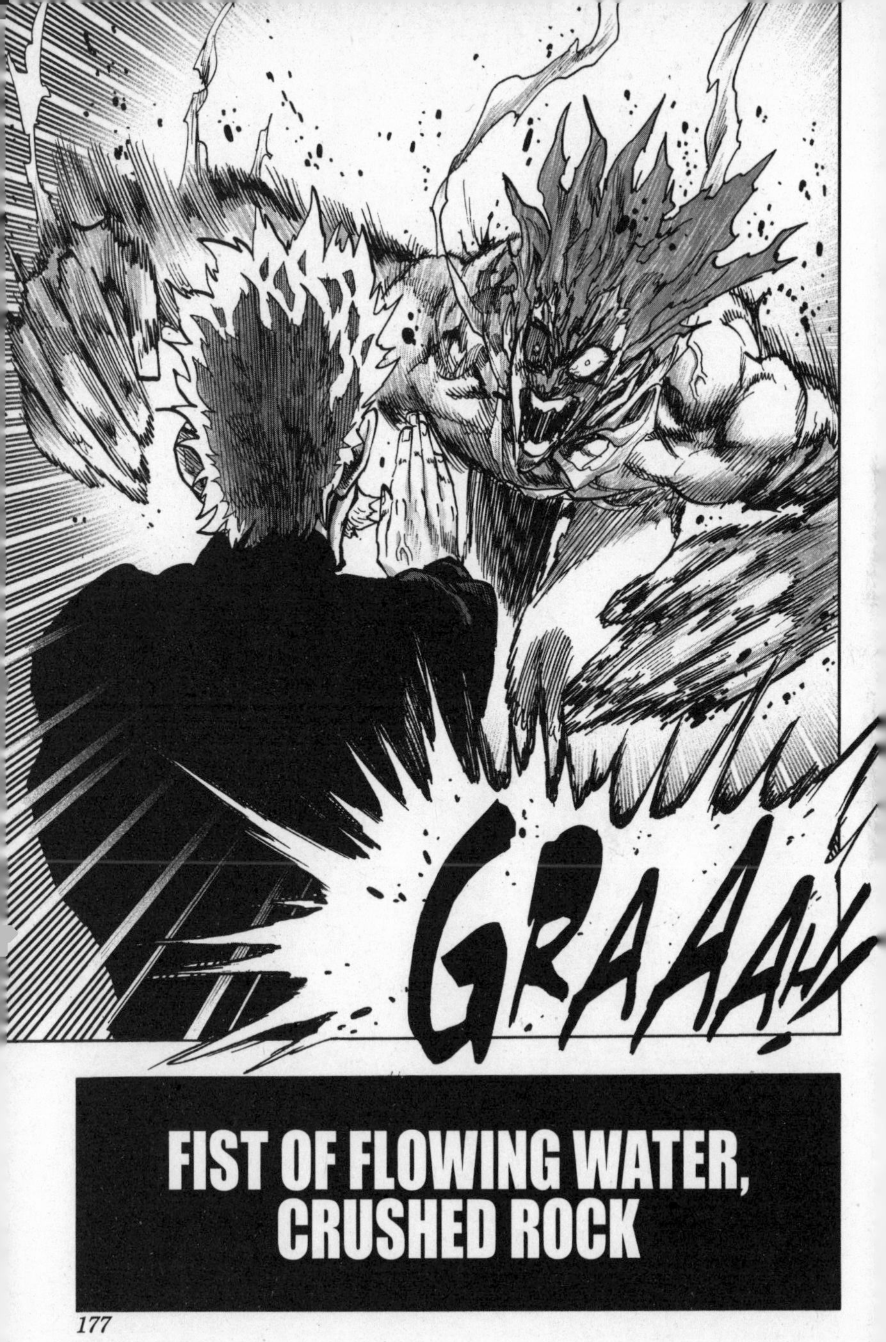
GRAAAH!

FIST OF FLOWING WATER, CRUSHED ROCK

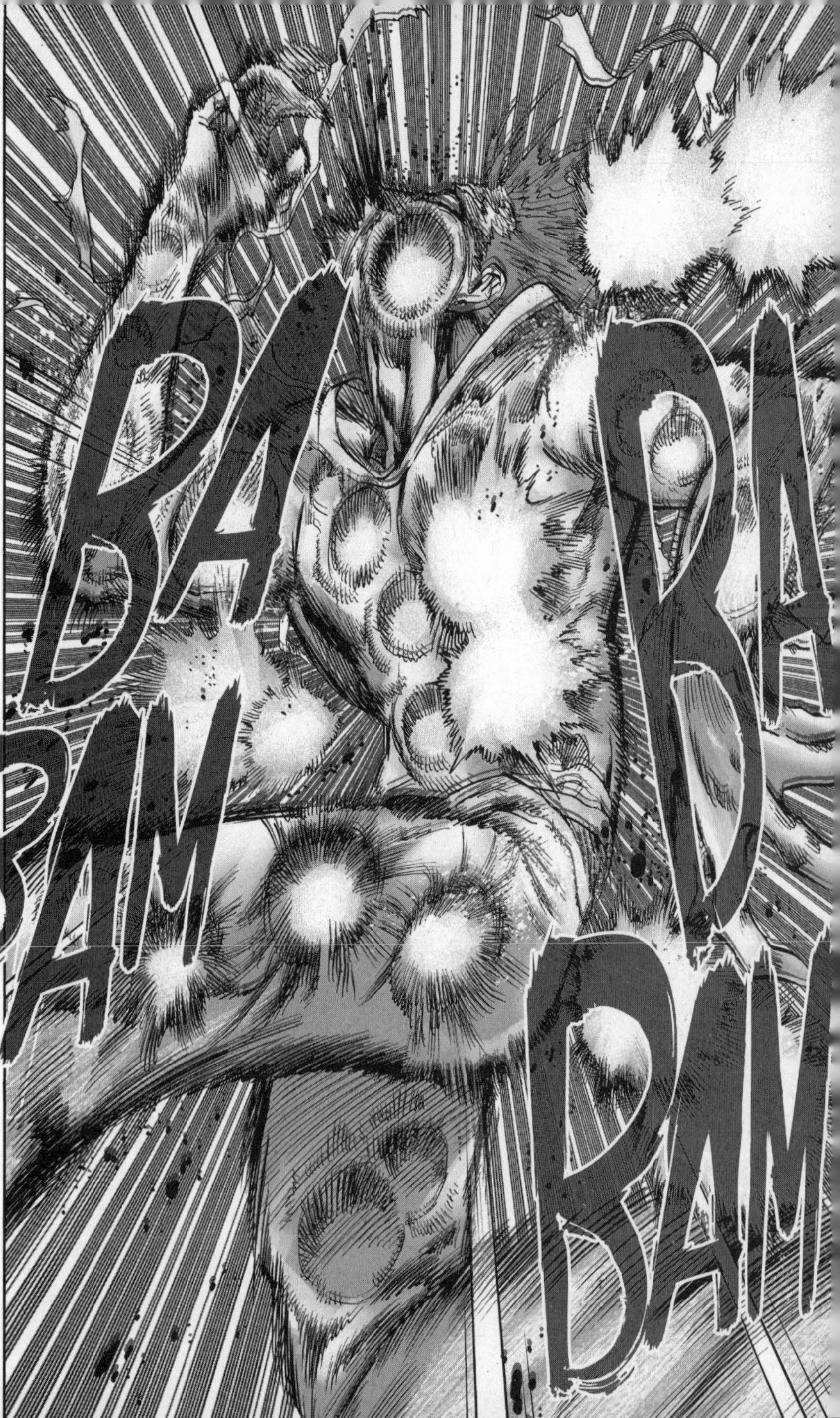
BAM
BAM
BAM
BAM

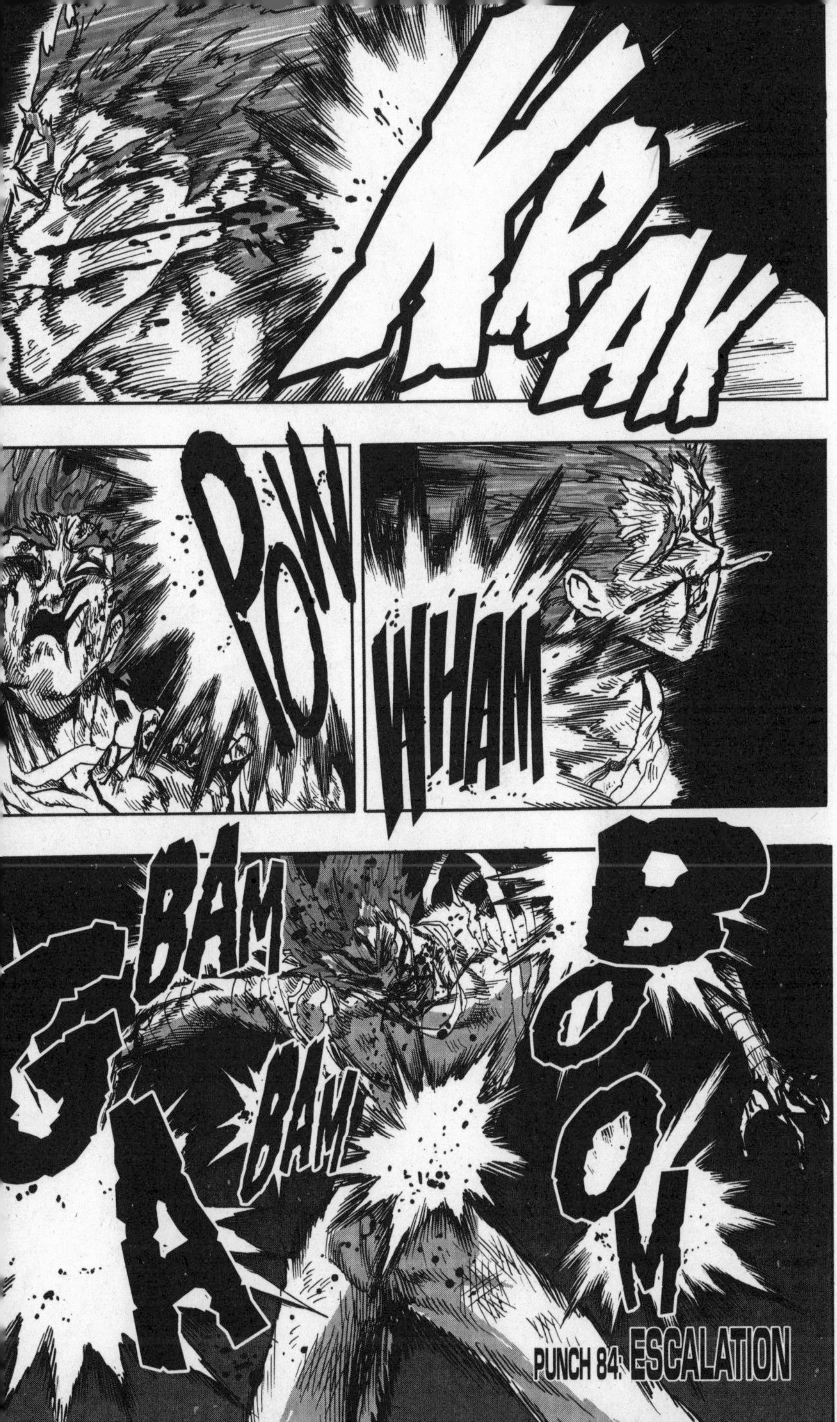
KRAK
WHAM
POW
BOOM
BAM
BAM
PUNCH 84: ESCALATION

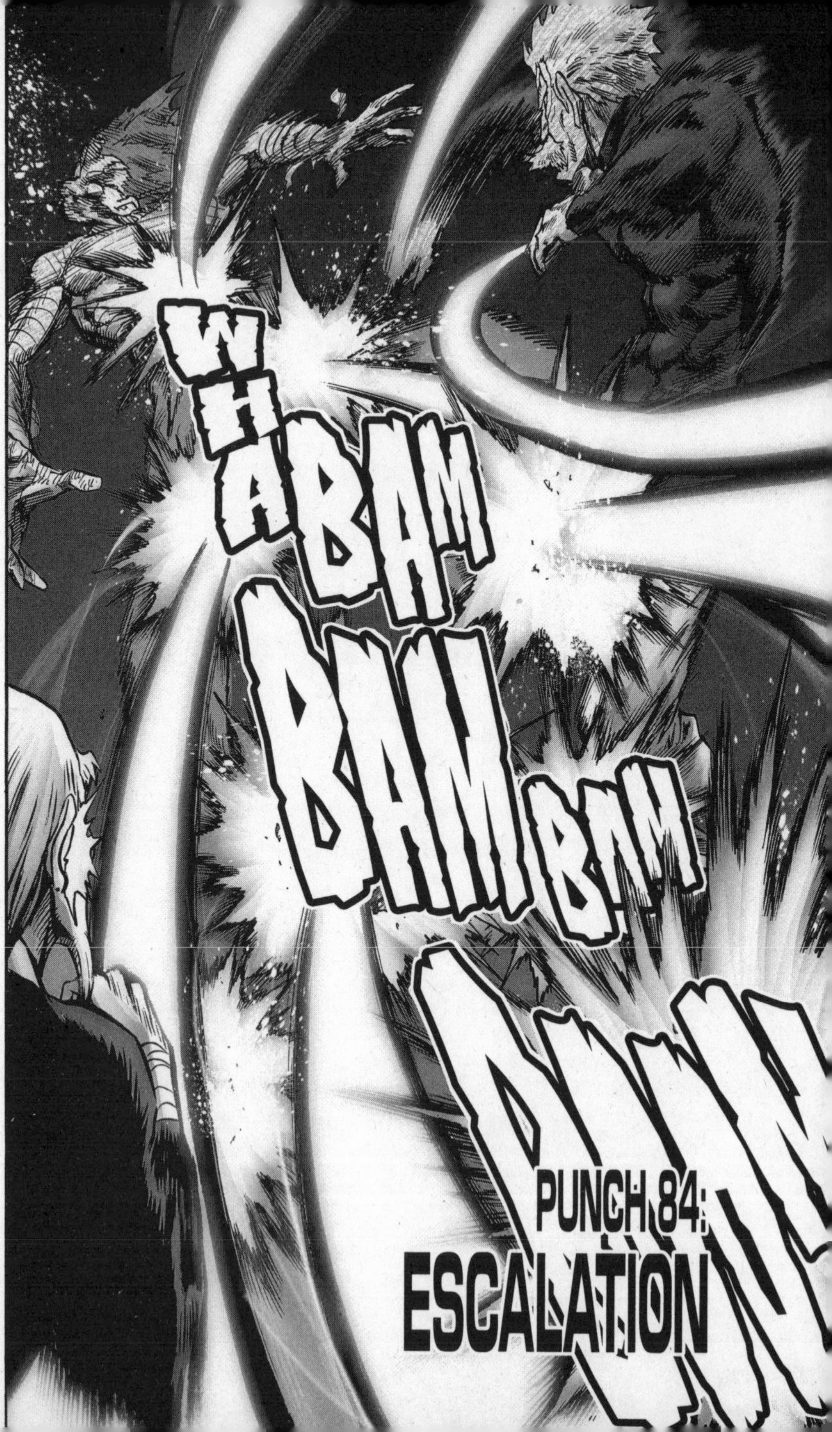
WHABAM
BAM
BAM
PUNCH 84:
ESCALATION

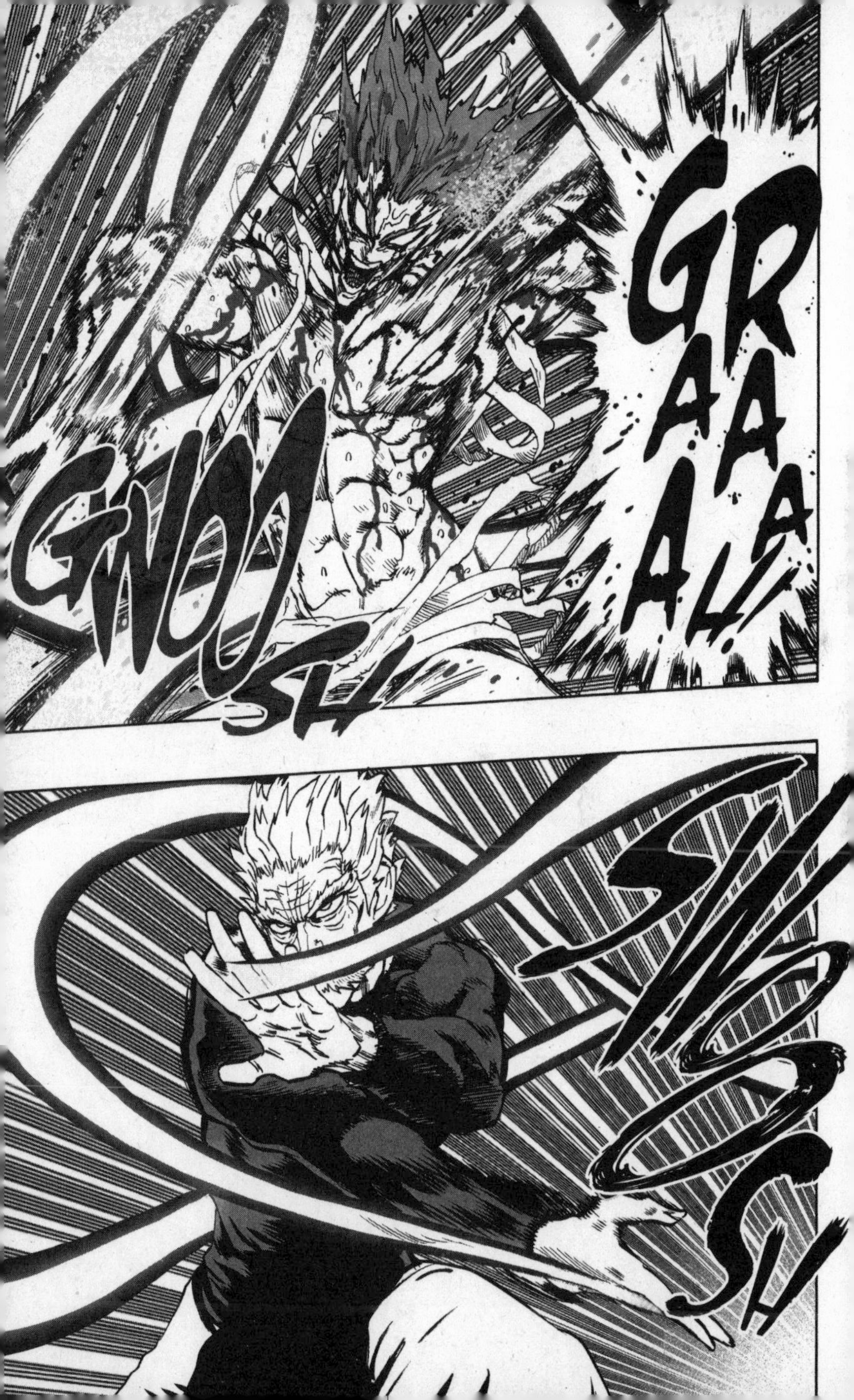
GRAAAAA!!
GNOOSH
SHSSS!

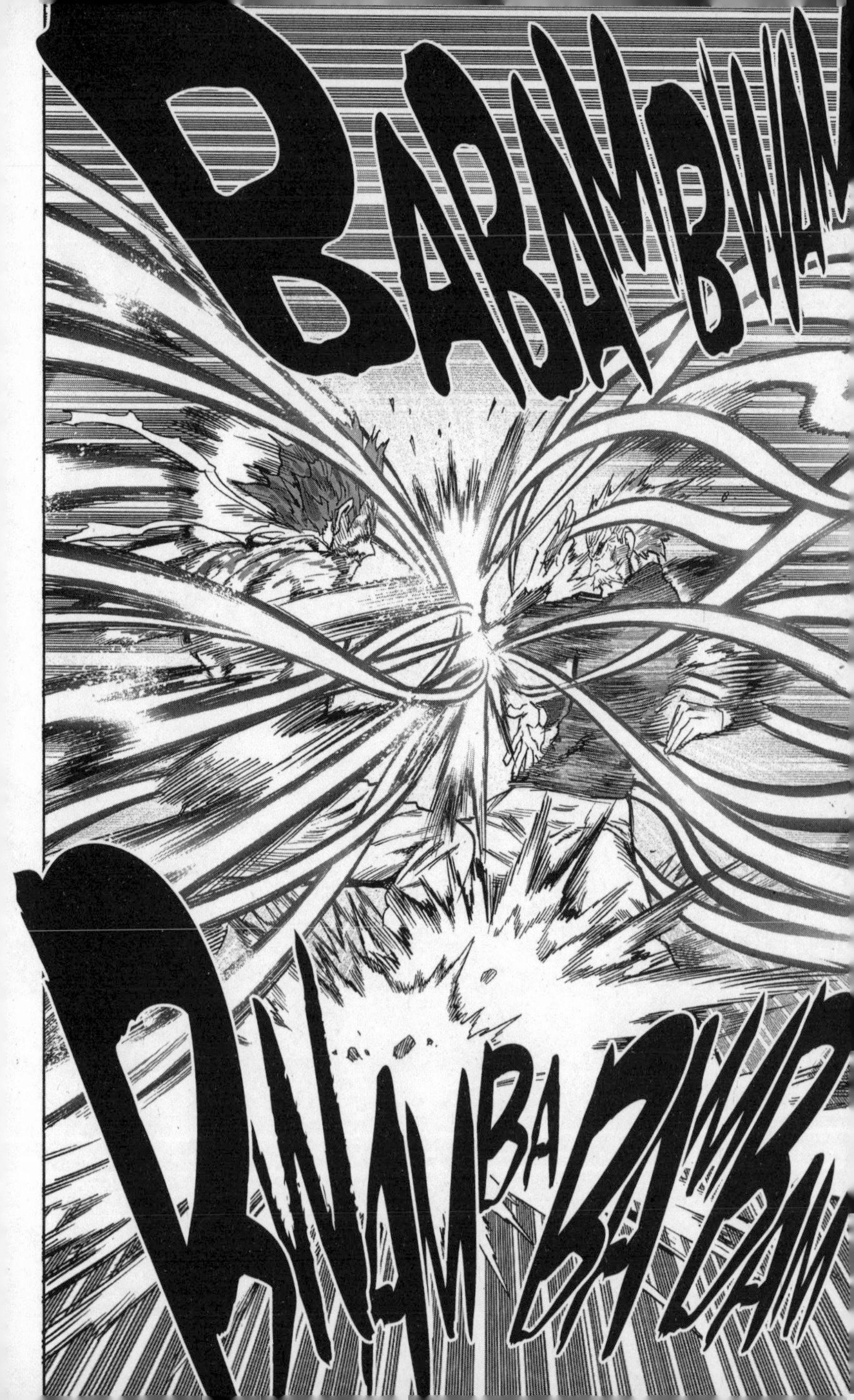
BABAMBWAM

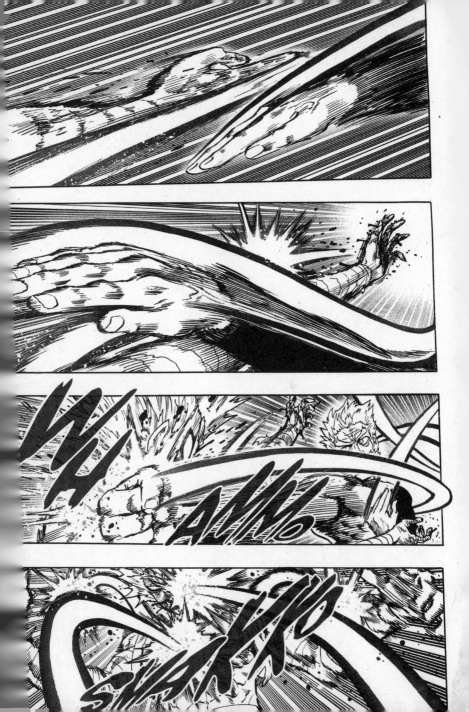

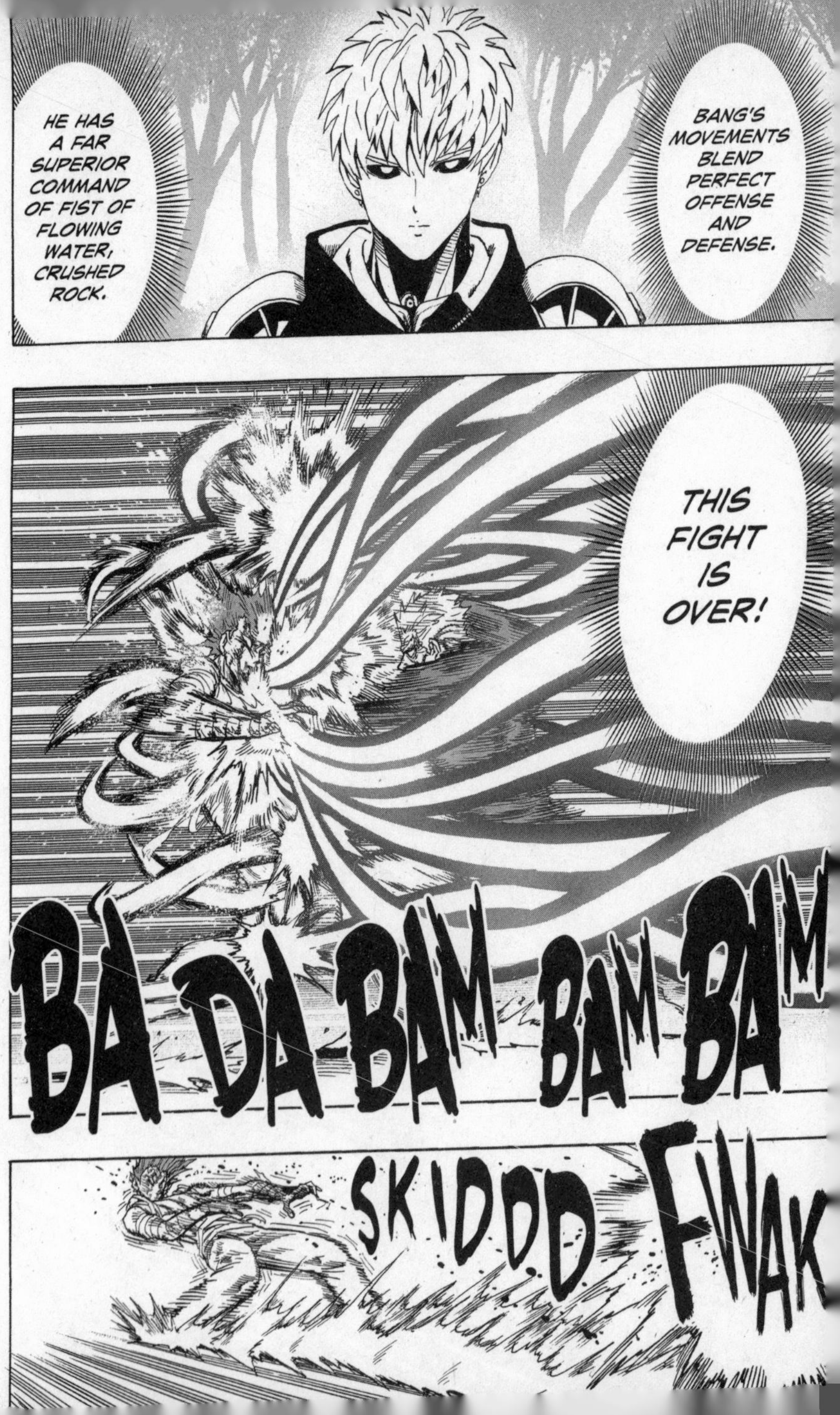
BANG'S MOVEMENTS BLEND PERFECT OFFENSE AND DEFENSE.
HE HAS A FAR SUPERIOR COMMAND OF FIST OF FLOWING WATER, CRUSHED ROCK.
THIS FIGHT IS OVER!
BA DA BAM BAM BAM
FWAK
SKIDDD

KCCH

GRAR!!!

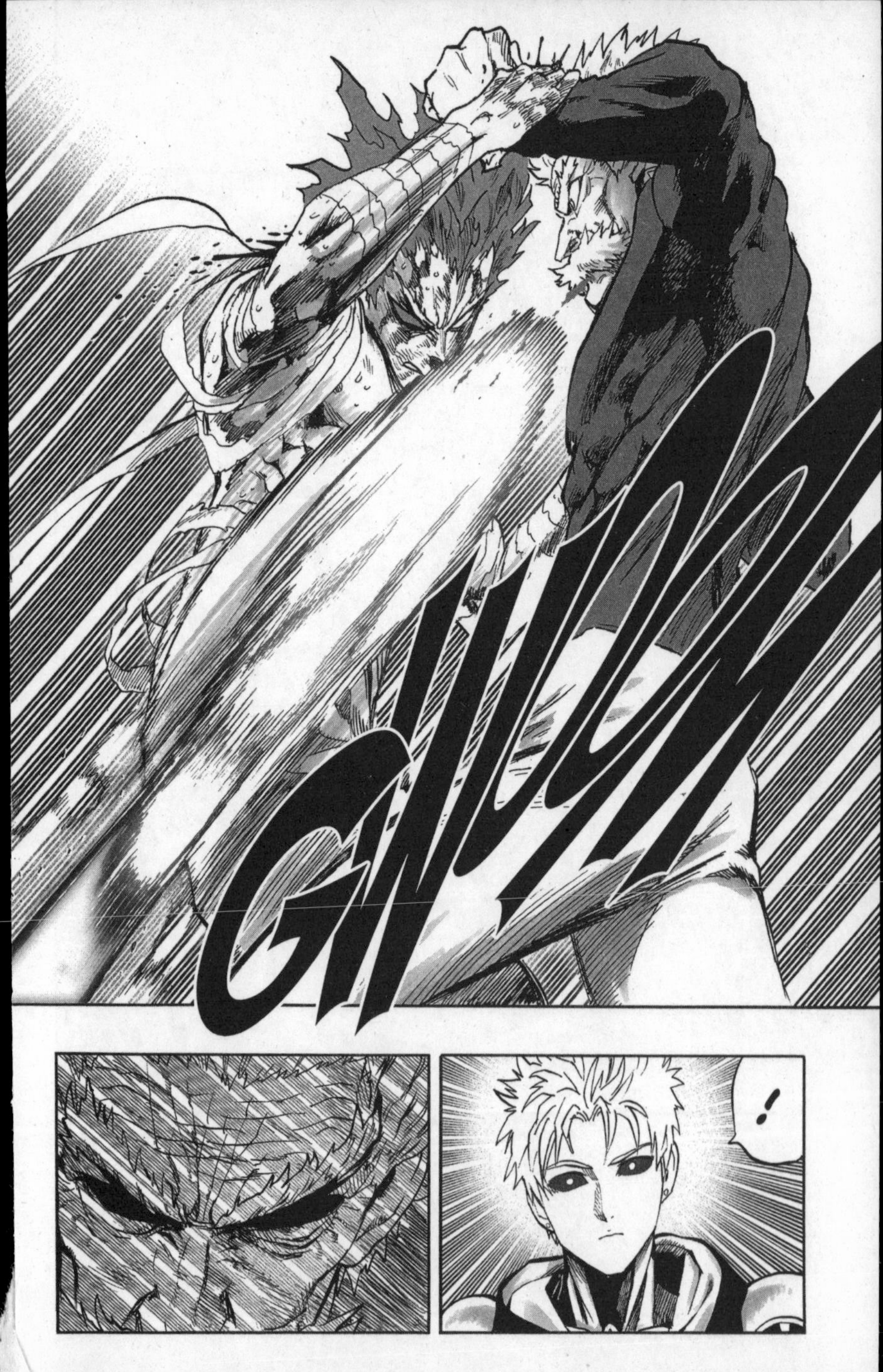
!

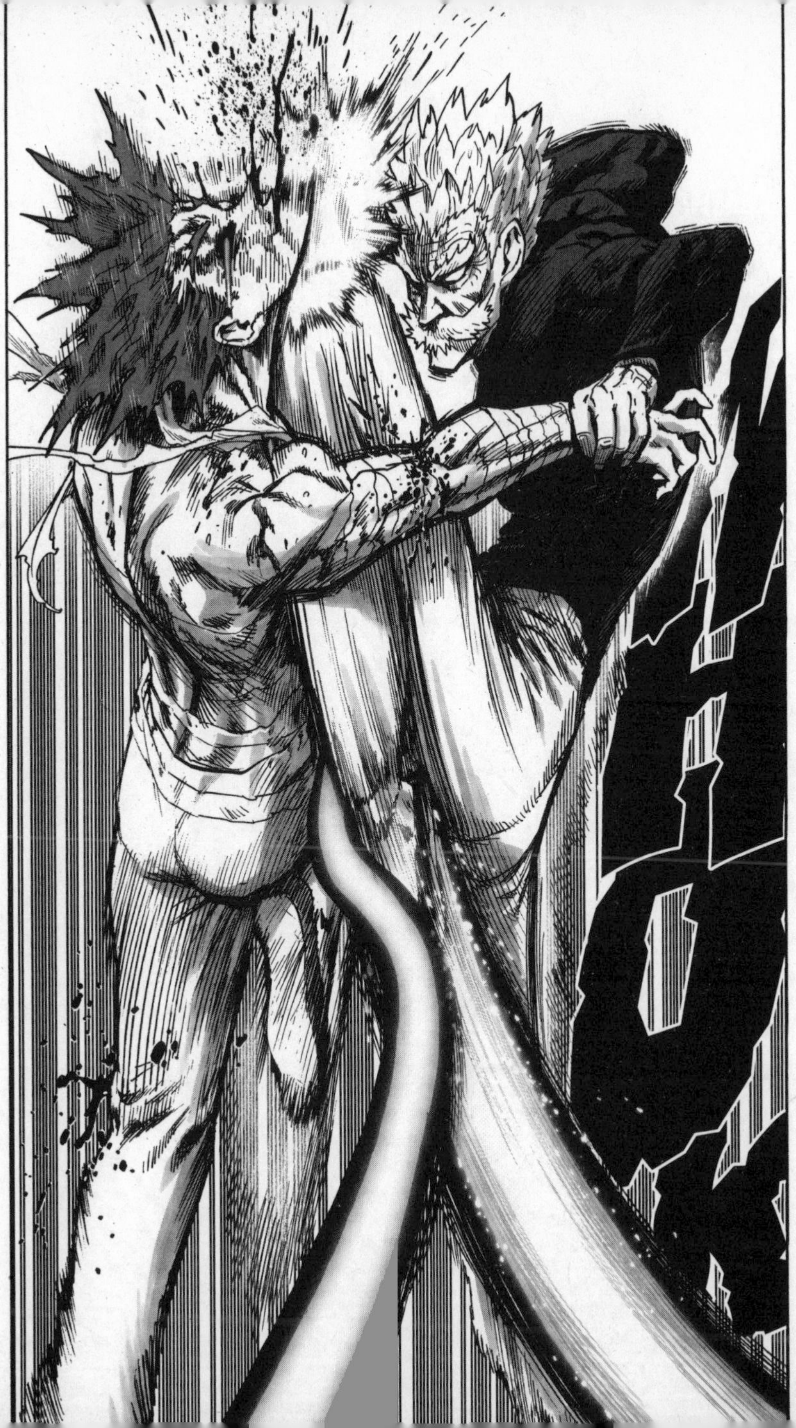

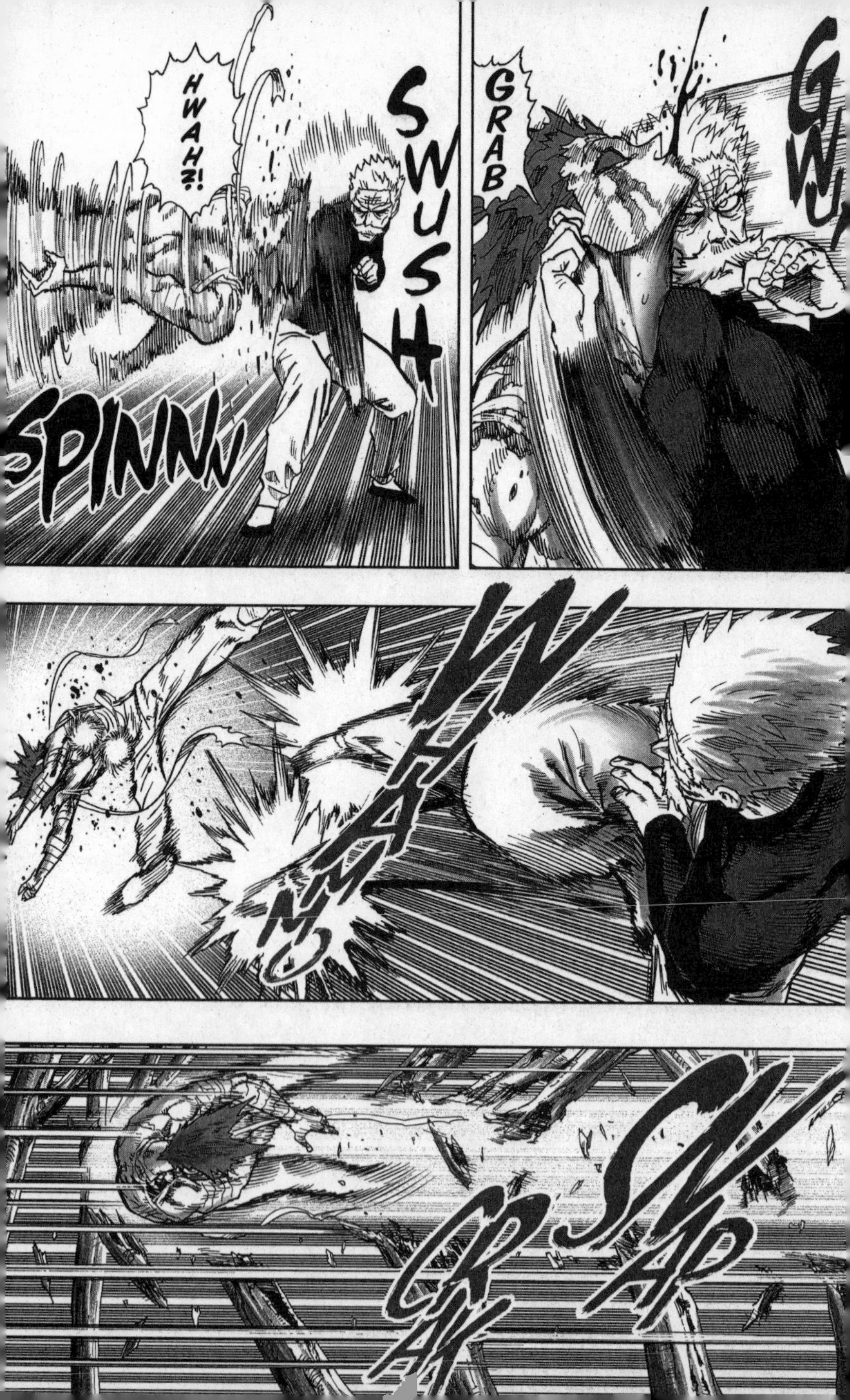
GWU
GRAB
SWUSH
HWAHZ!
SPINNN
WHAMMO
SNAP
CRACK

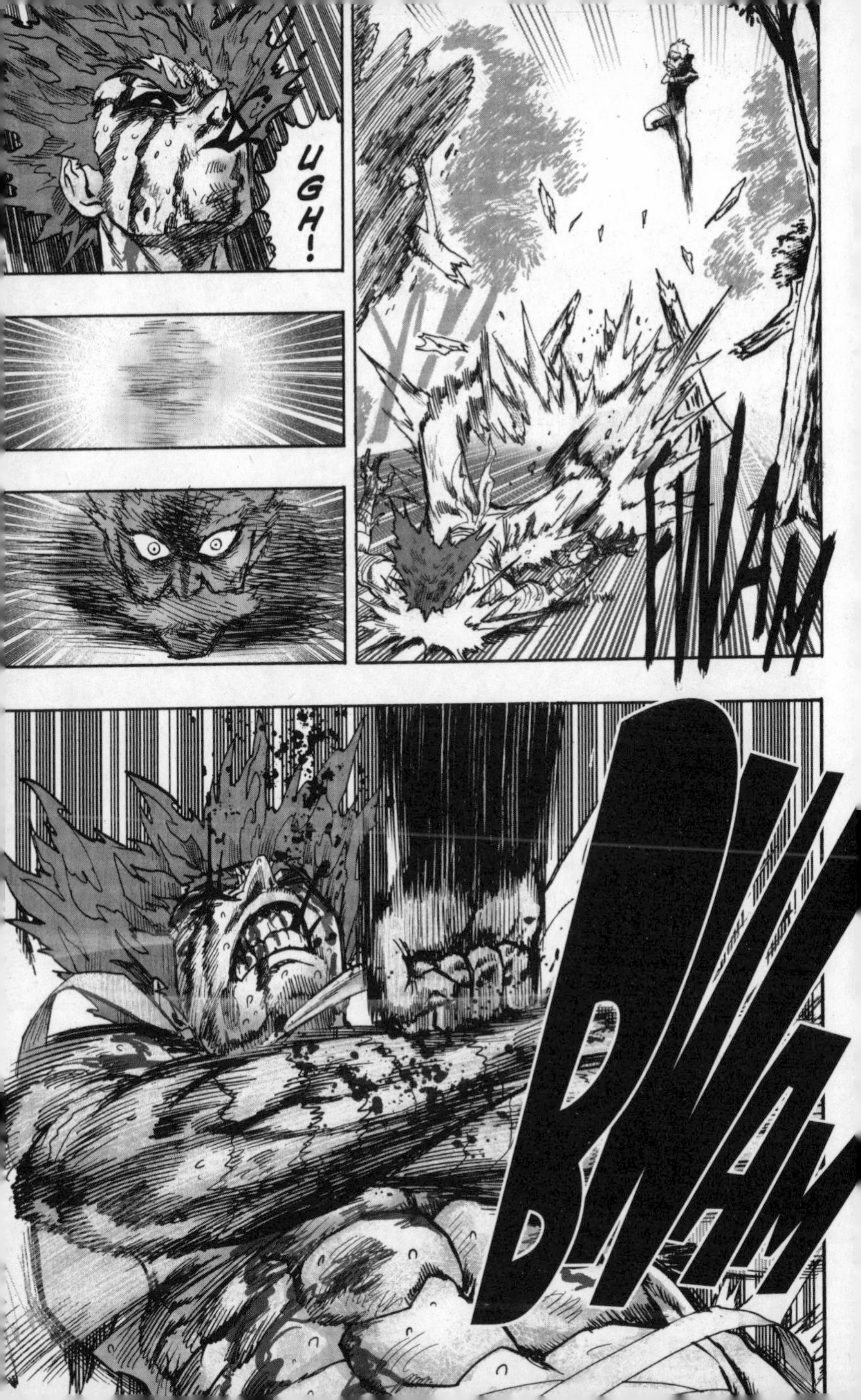
FWAM
UGH!
BWAM

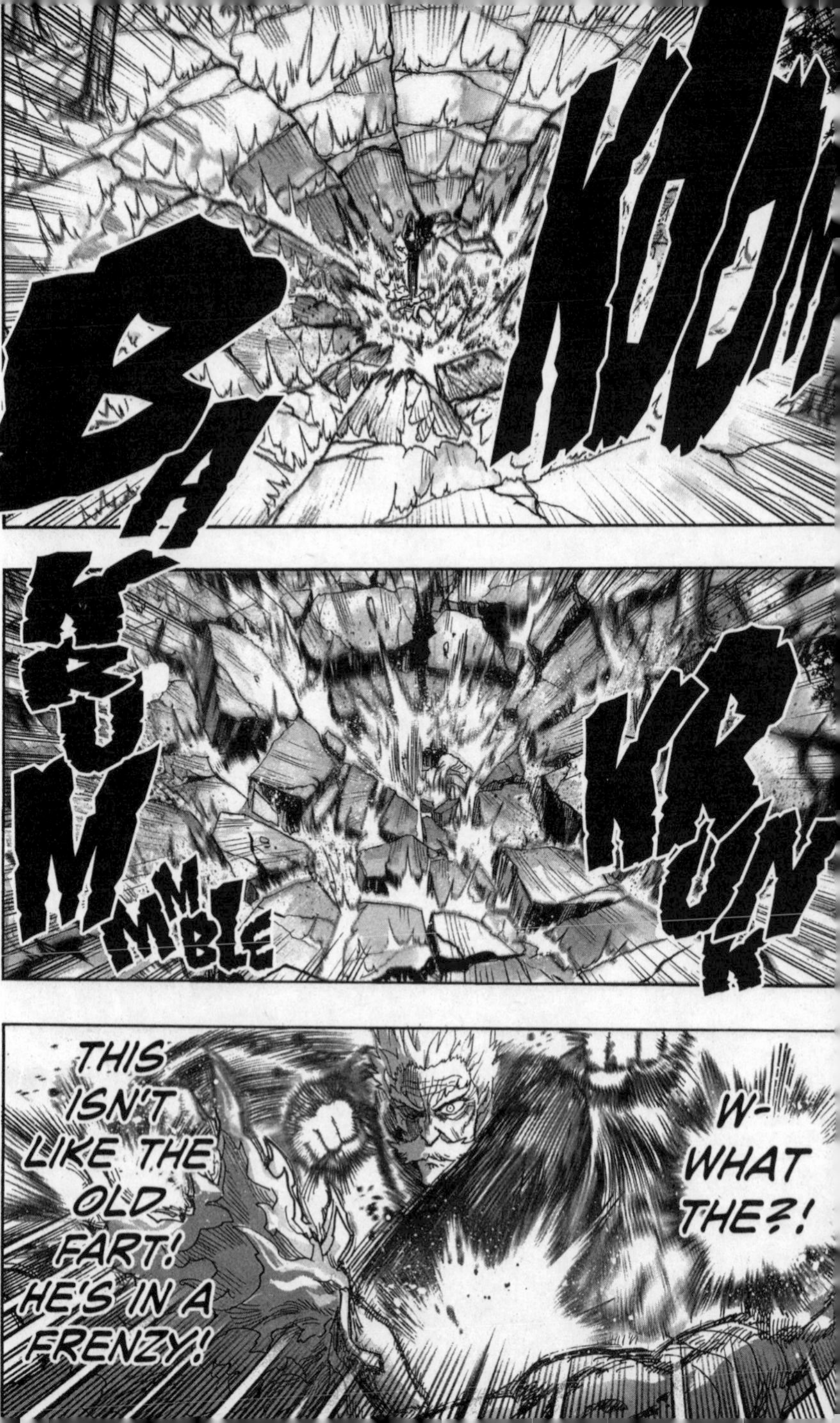
KRUNK
KRUMMMBLE
W-WHAT THE?!
THIS ISN'T LIKE THE OLD FART! HE'S IN A FRENZY!

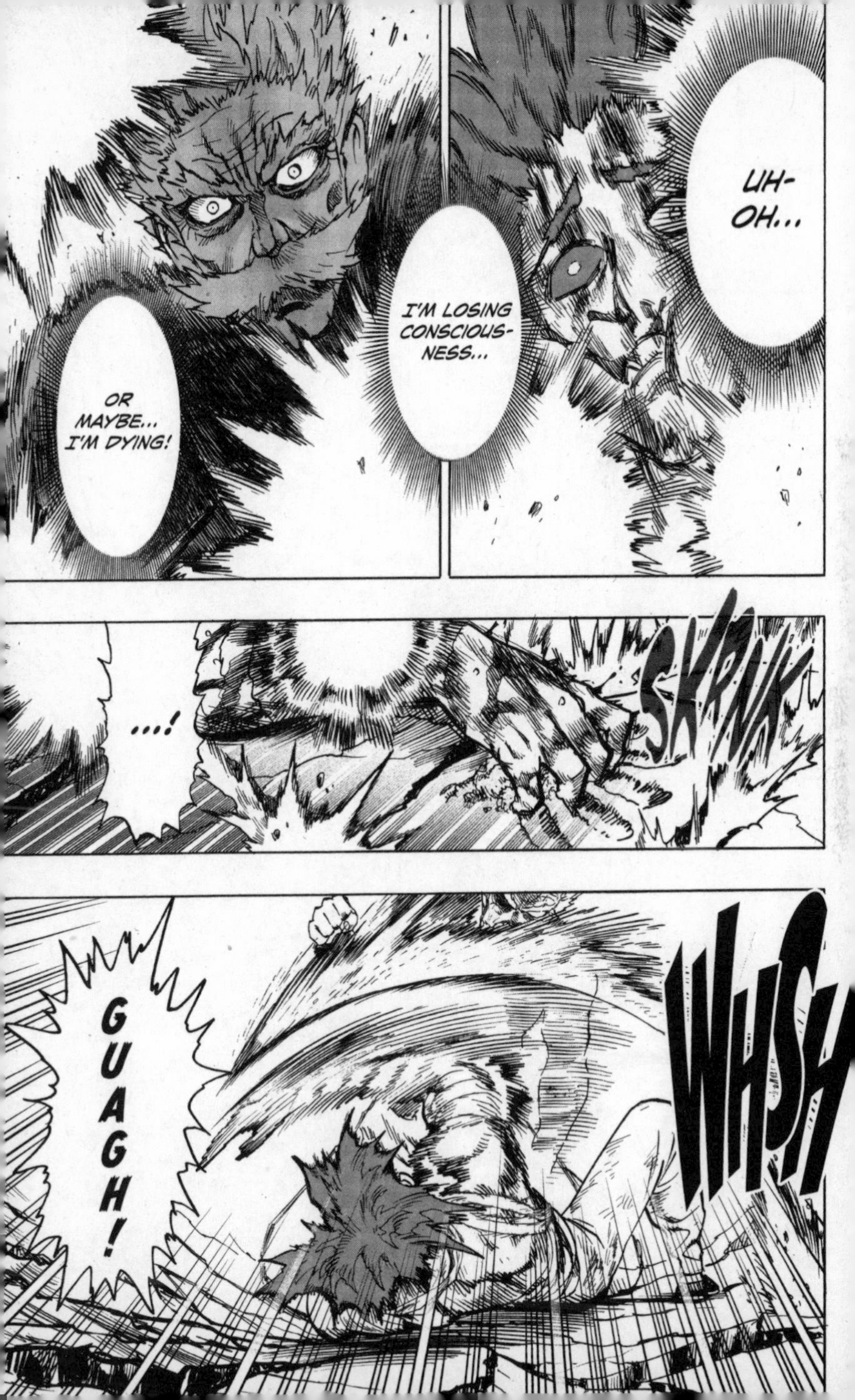
UH-OH...
I'M LOSING CONSCIOUS-NESS...
OR MAYBE... I'M DYING!
SKRNK
...!
WHSH
GUAGH!

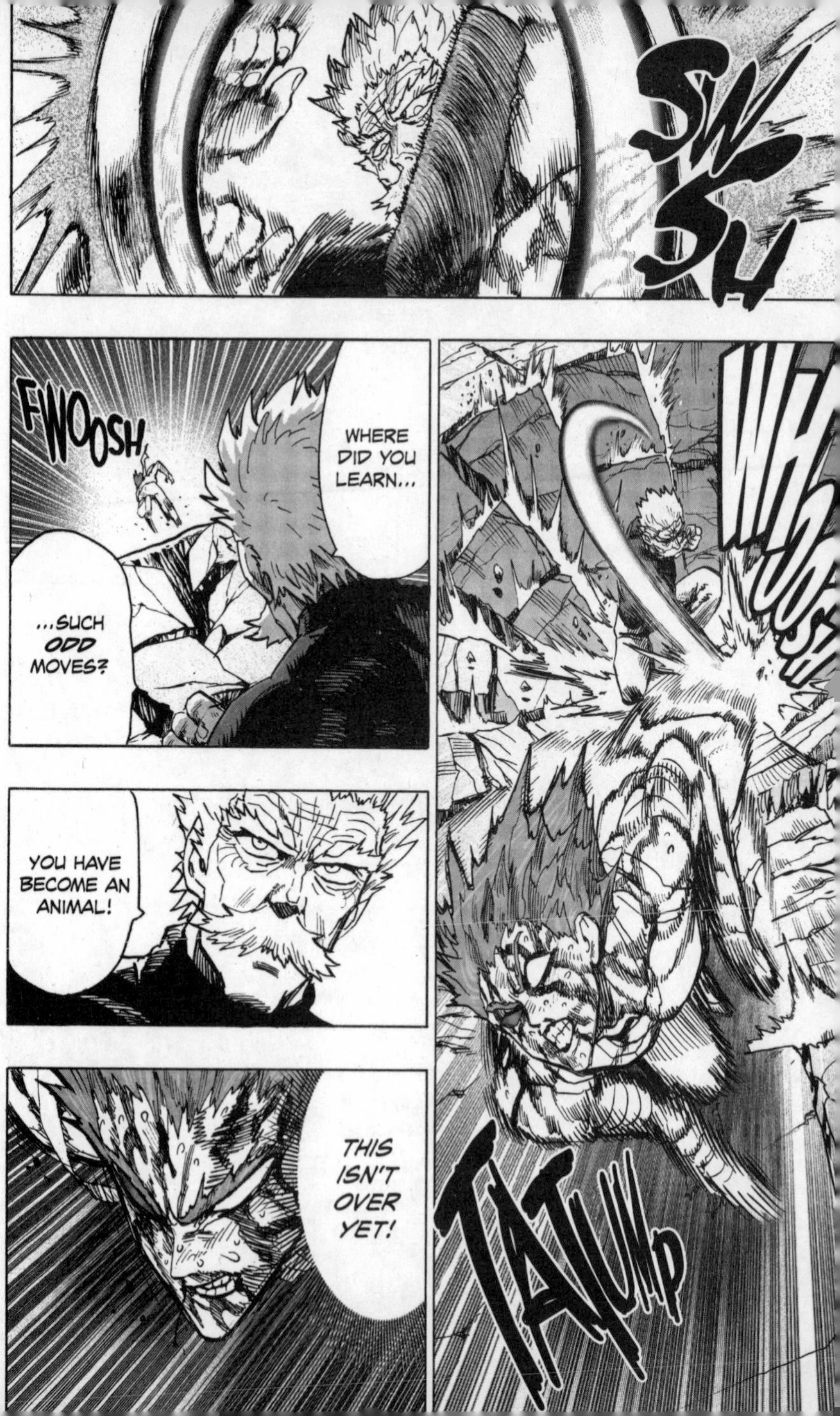
SWSH
WHOOSH
TATUMP
FWOOSH
WHERE DID YOU LEARN...
...SUCH *ODD* MOVES?
YOU HAVE BECOME AN ANIMAL!
THIS ISN'T OVER YET!

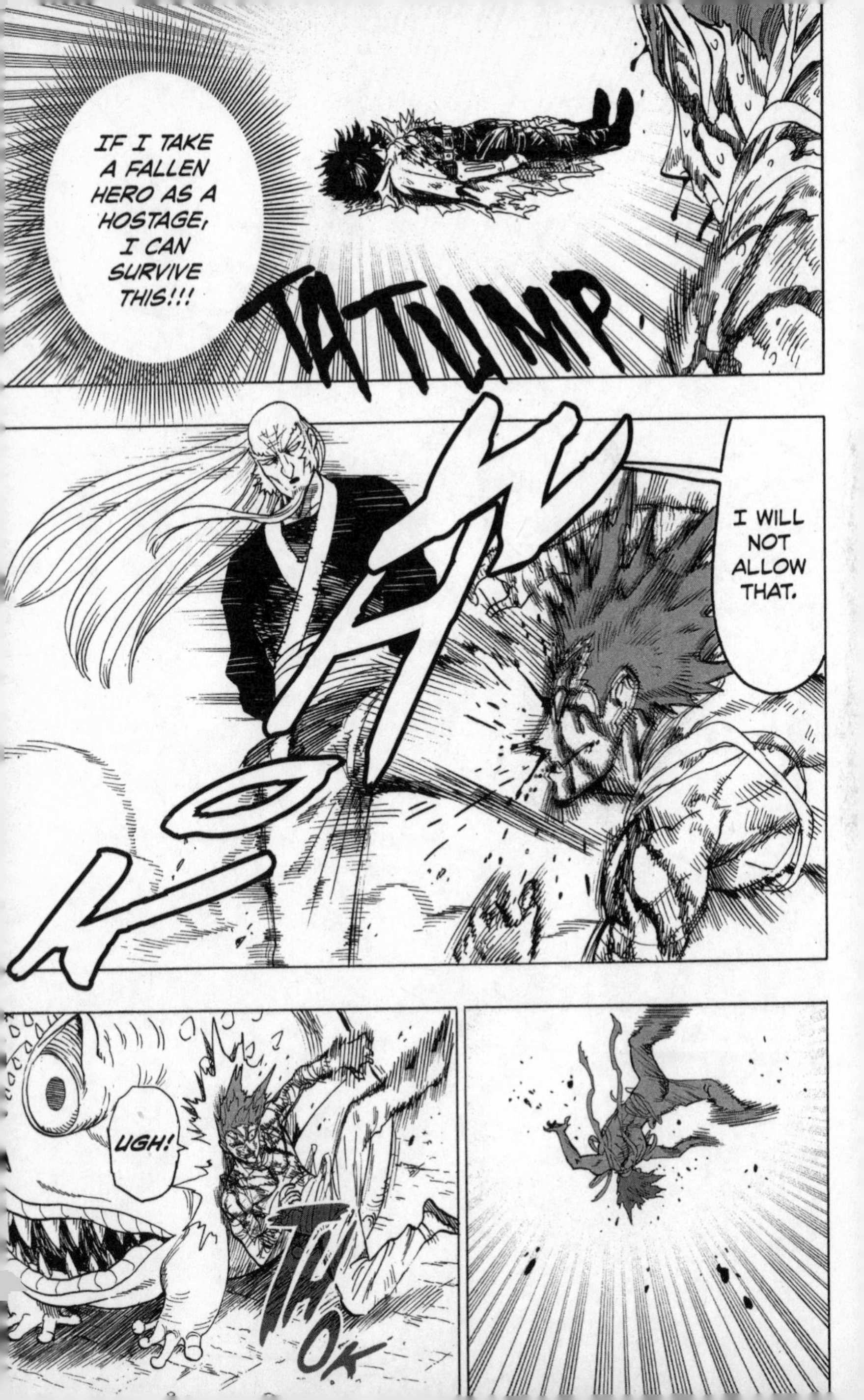
IF I TAKE A FALLEN HERO AS A HOSTAGE, I CAN SURVIVE THIS!!!
TATUMP
I WILL NOT ALLOW THAT.
UGH!

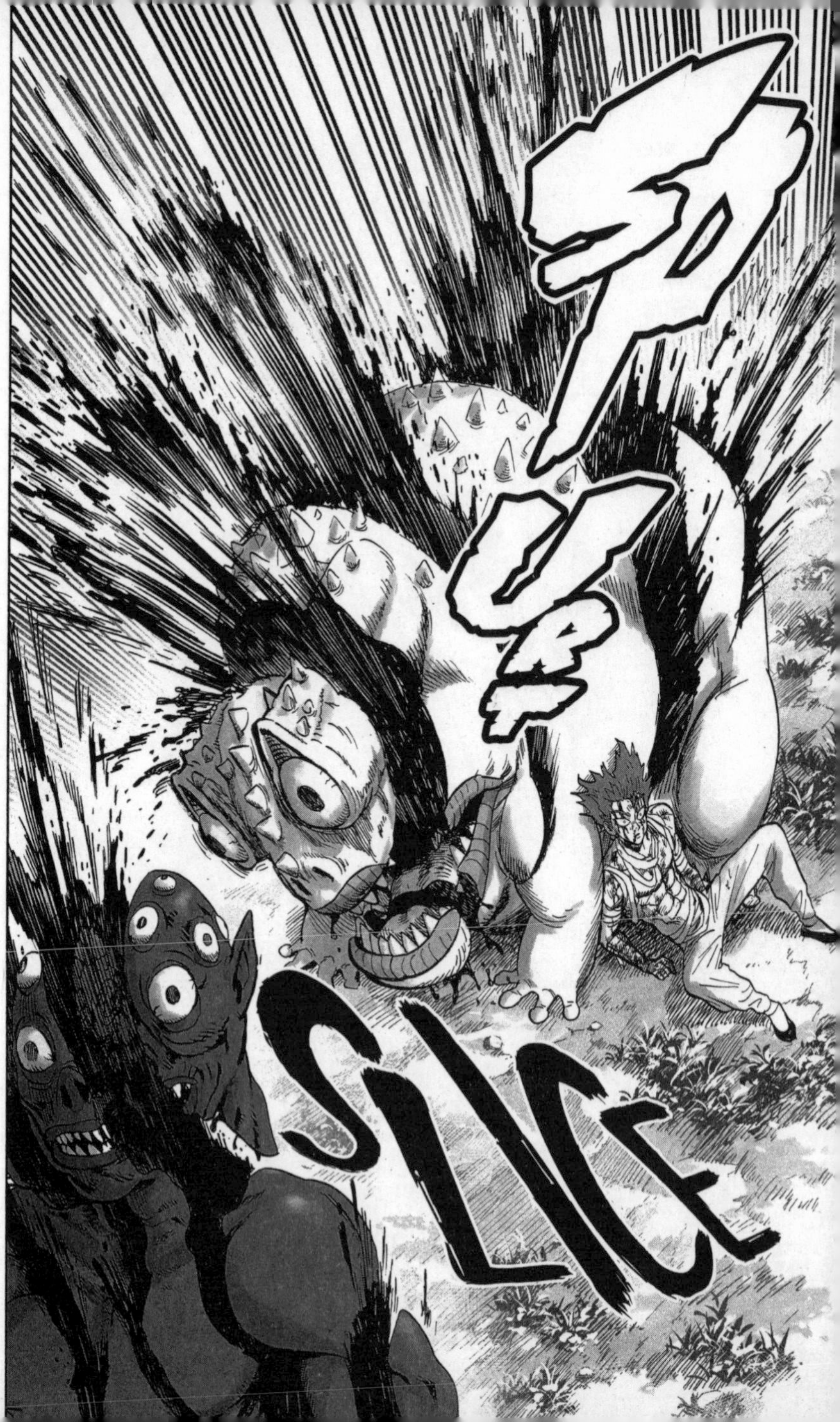
SLICE

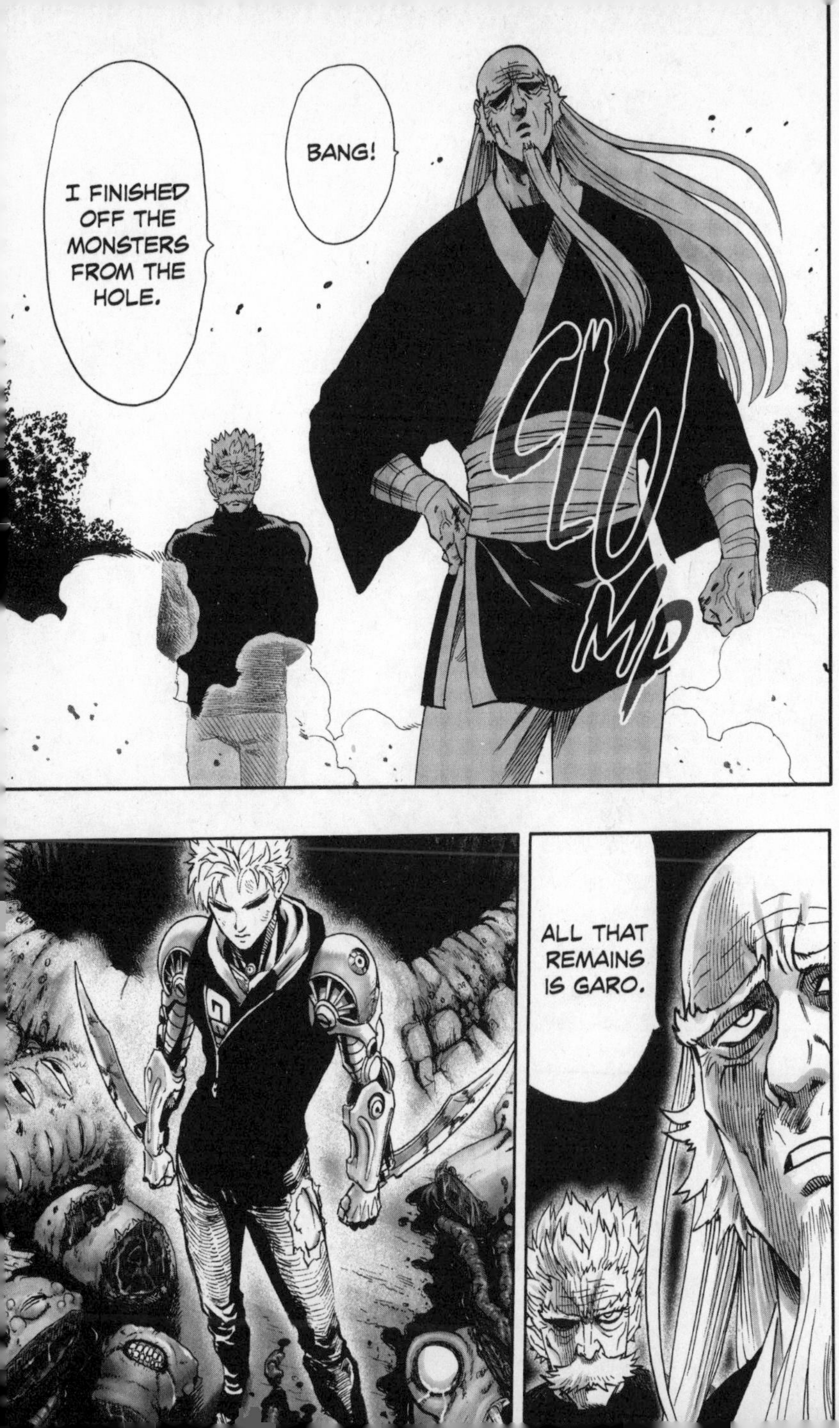
BANG!
I FINISHED OFF THE MONSTERS FROM THE HOLE.
CLOMP
ALL THAT REMAINS IS GARO.

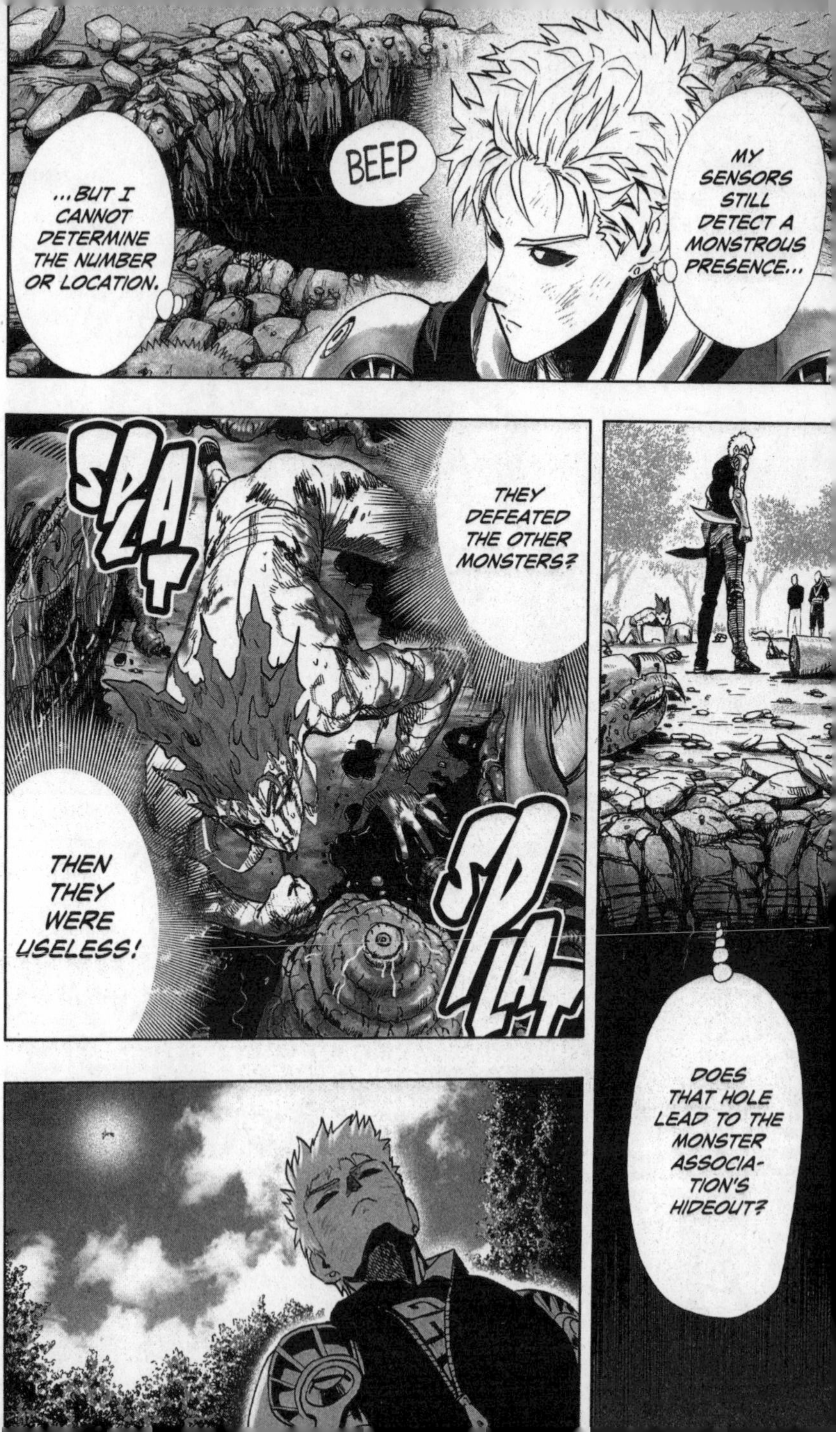
MY SENSORS STILL DETECT A MONSTROUS PRESENCE...
BEEP
...BUT I CANNOT DETERMINE THE NUMBER OR LOCATION.
DOES THAT HOLE LEAD TO THE MONSTER ASSOCIA-TION'S HIDEOUT?
THEY DEFEATED THE OTHER MONSTERS?
SPLAT
SPLAT
THEN THEY WERE USELESS!

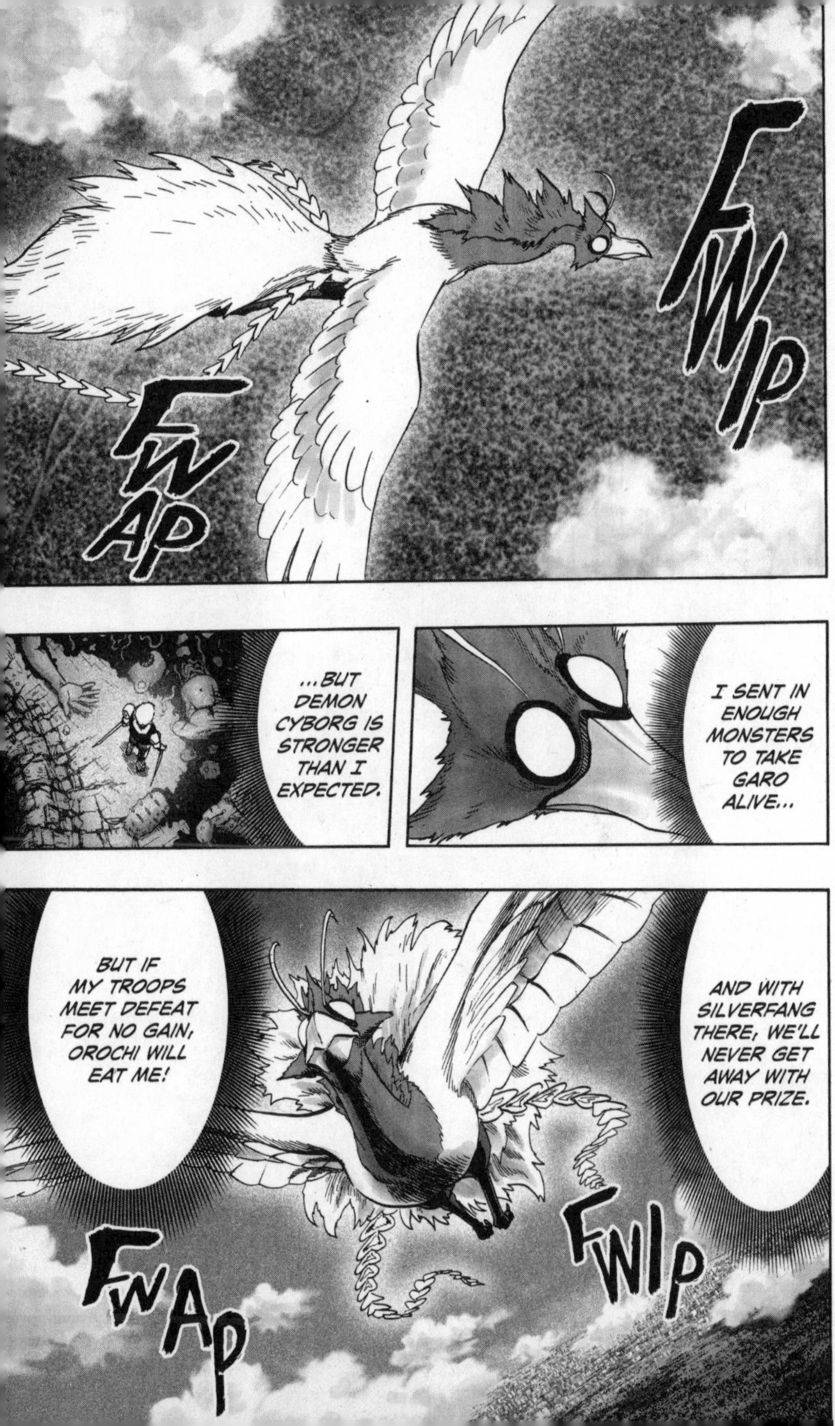
FWIP
FWAP
I SENT IN ENOUGH MONSTERS TO TAKE GARO ALIVE...
...BUT DEMON CYBORG IS STRONGER THAN I EXPECTED.
AND WITH SILVERFANG THERE, WE'LL NEVER GET AWAY WITH OUR PRIZE.
BUT IF MY TROOPS MEET DEFEAT FOR NO GAIN, OROCHI WILL EAT ME!
FWIP
FWAP

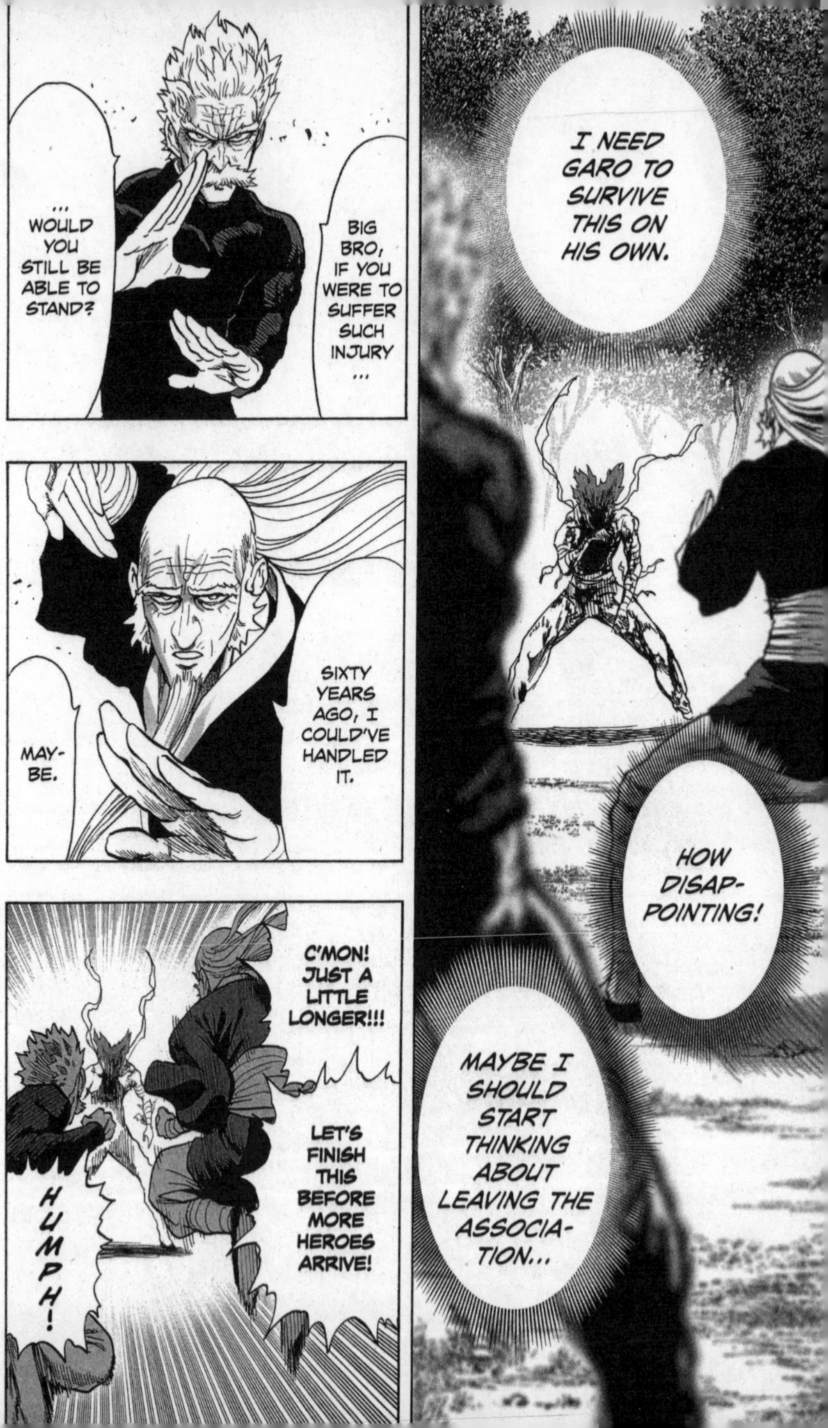
I NEED GARO TO SURVIVE THIS ON HIS OWN.
HOW DISAP-POINTING!
MAYBE I SHOULD START THINKING ABOUT LEAVING THE ASSOCIA-TION...
BIG BRO, IF YOU WERE TO SUFFER SUCH INJURY...
...WOULD YOU STILL BE ABLE TO STAND?
SIXTY YEARS AGO, I COULD'VE HANDLED IT.
MAY-BE.
C'MON! JUST A LITTLE LONGER!!!
LET'S FINISH THIS BEFORE MORE HEROES ARRIVE!
HUMPH!

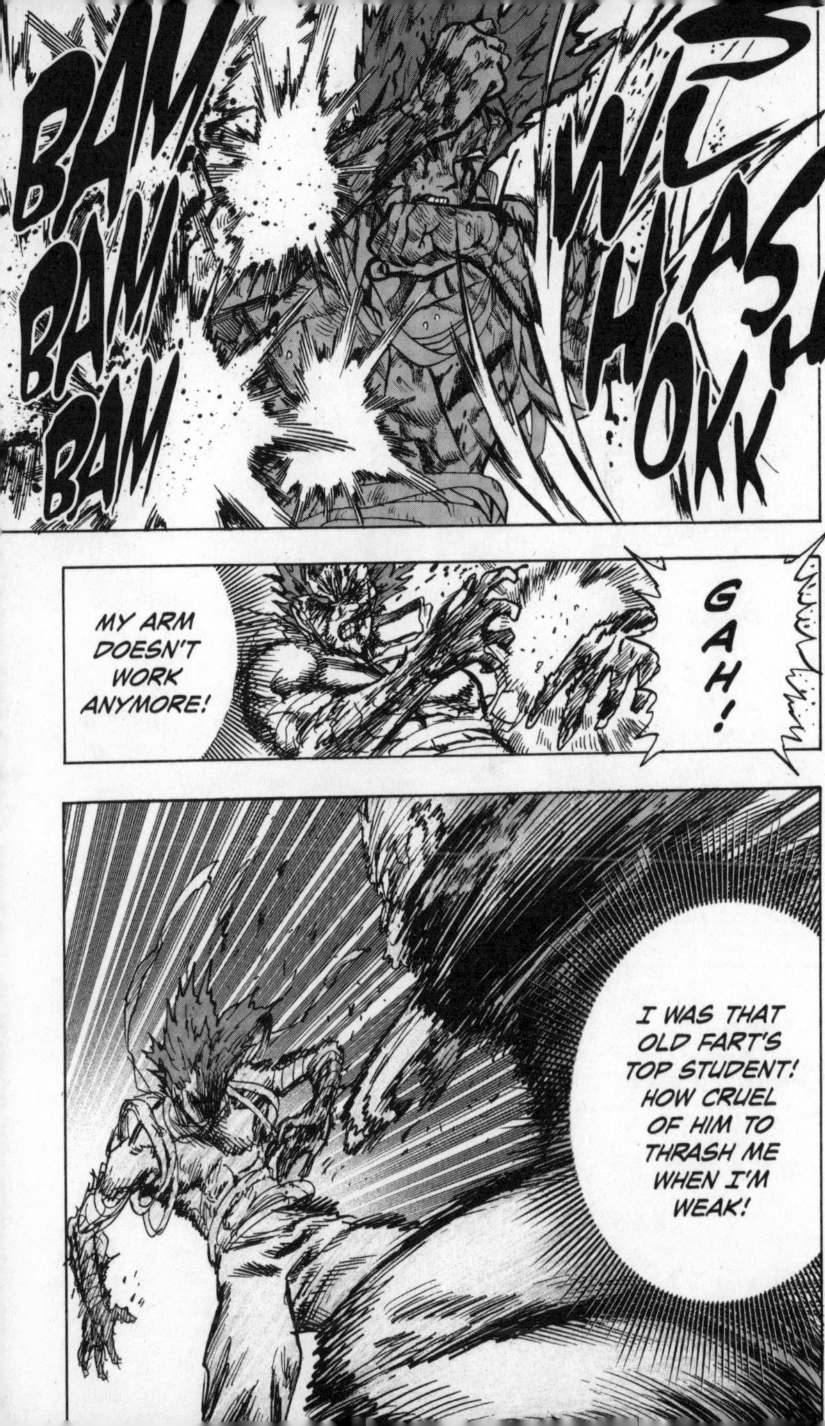
WHOKK
BAM BAM BAM BAM
GAH!
MY ARM DOESN'T WORK ANYMORE!
I WAS THAT OLD FART'S TOP STUDENT! HOW CRUEL OF HIM TO THRASH ME WHEN I'M WEAK!

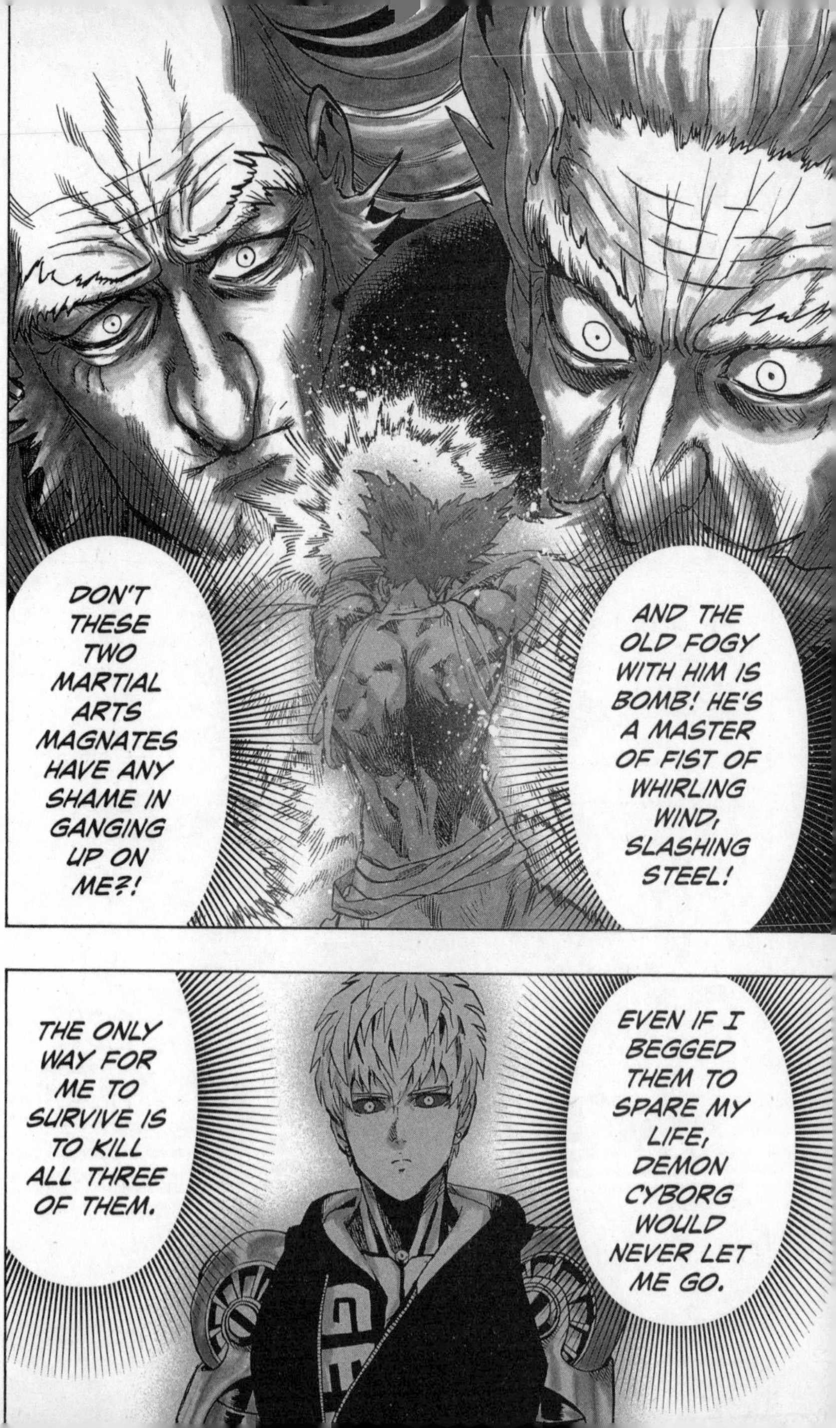
AND THE OLD FOGY WITH HIM IS BOMB! HE'S A MASTER OF FIST OF WHIRLING WIND, SLASHING STEEL!
DON'T THESE TWO MARTIAL ARTS MAGNATES HAVE ANY SHAME IN GANGING UP ON ME?!
EVEN IF I BEGGED THEM TO SPARE MY LIFE, DEMON CYBORG WOULD NEVER LET ME GO.
THE ONLY WAY FOR ME TO SURVIVE IS TO KILL ALL THREE OF THEM.

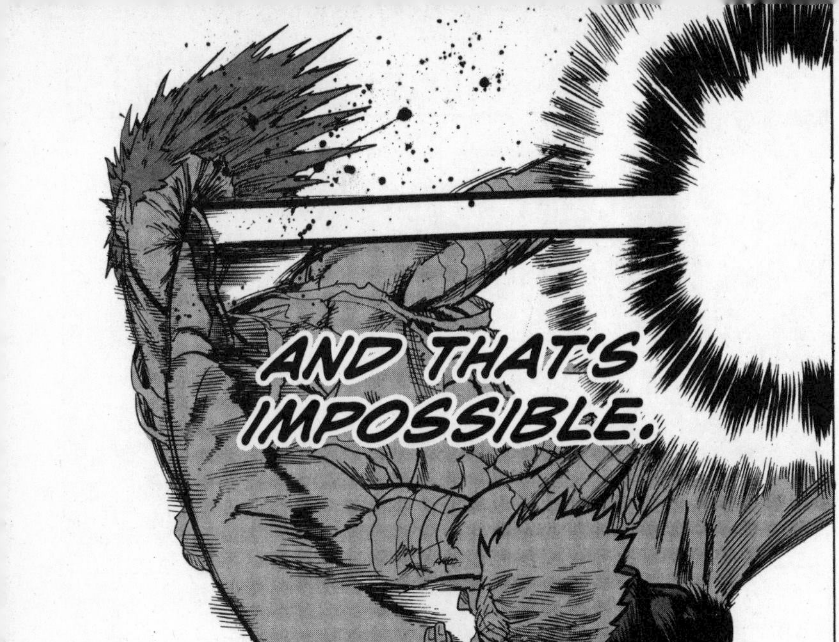
AND THAT'S IMPOSSIBLE.

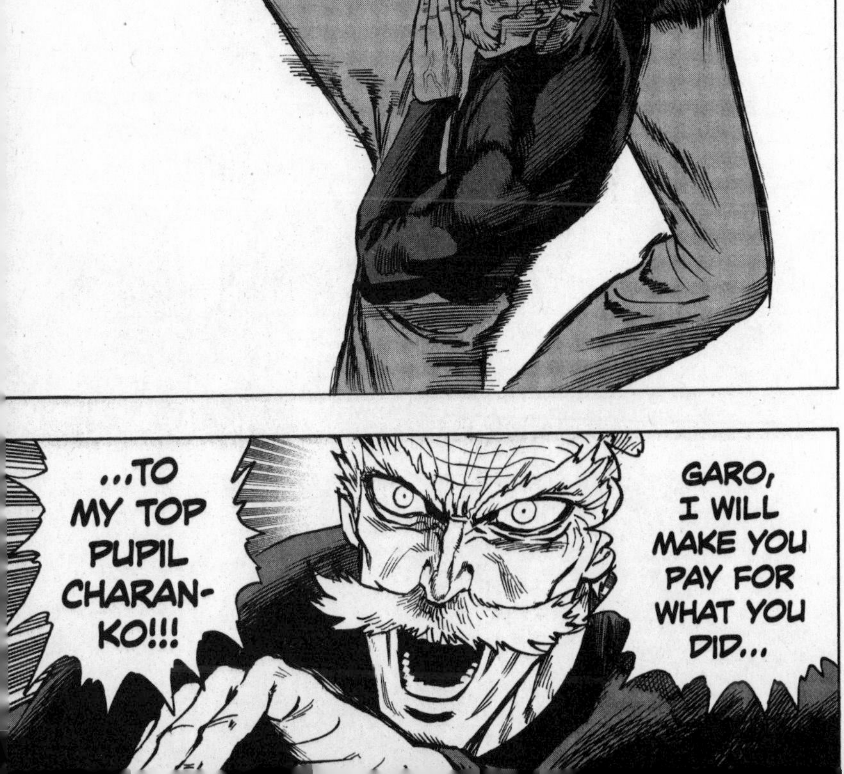
GARO, I WILL MAKE YOU PAY FOR WHAT YOU DID...
...TO MY TOP PUPIL CHARAN-KO!!!

BONUS MANGA: GROWTH PROCESS

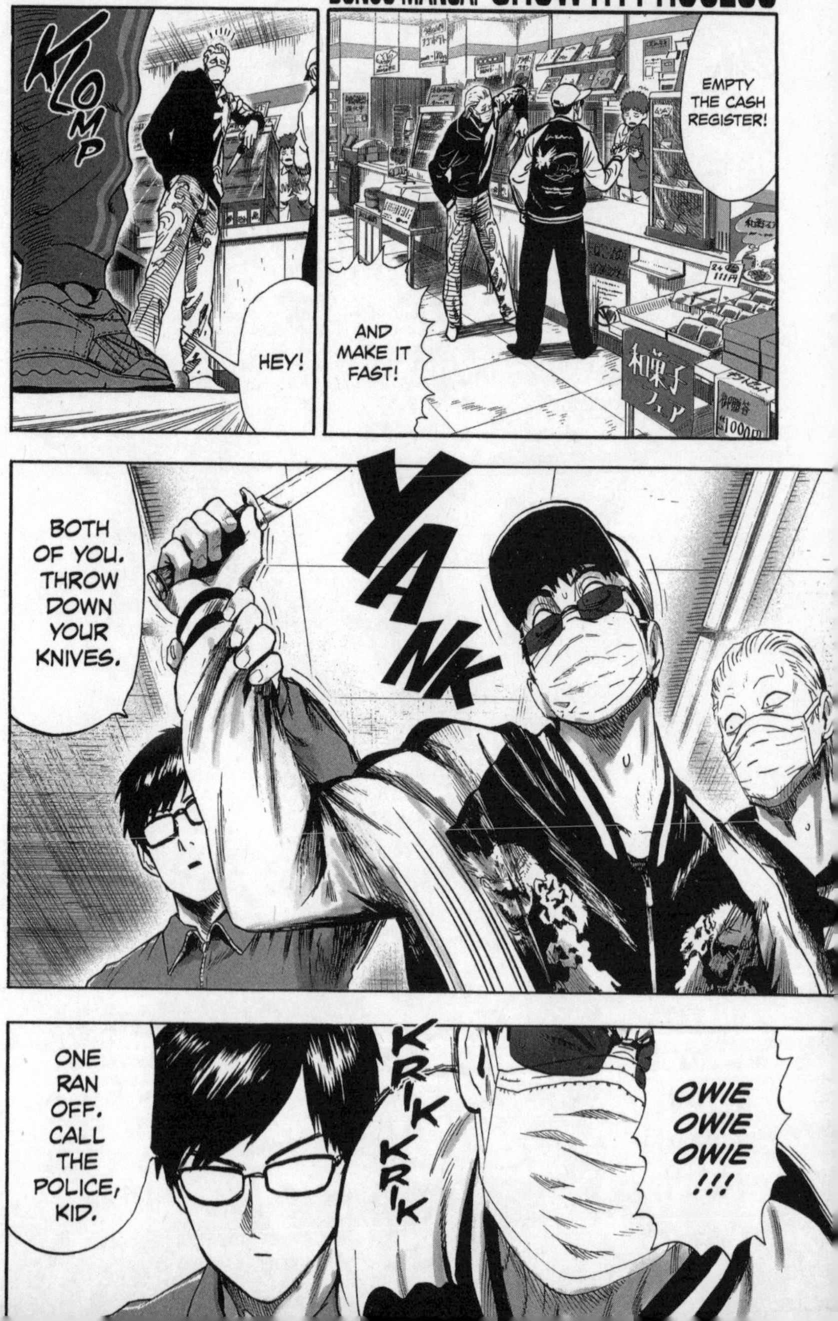
EMPTY THE CASH REGISTER!
AND MAKE IT FAST!
KLOMP
HEY!
YANK
BOTH OF YOU. THROW DOWN YOUR KNIVES.
OWIE OWIE OWIE !!!
KRIK KRIK
ONE RAN OFF. CALL THE POLICE, KID.

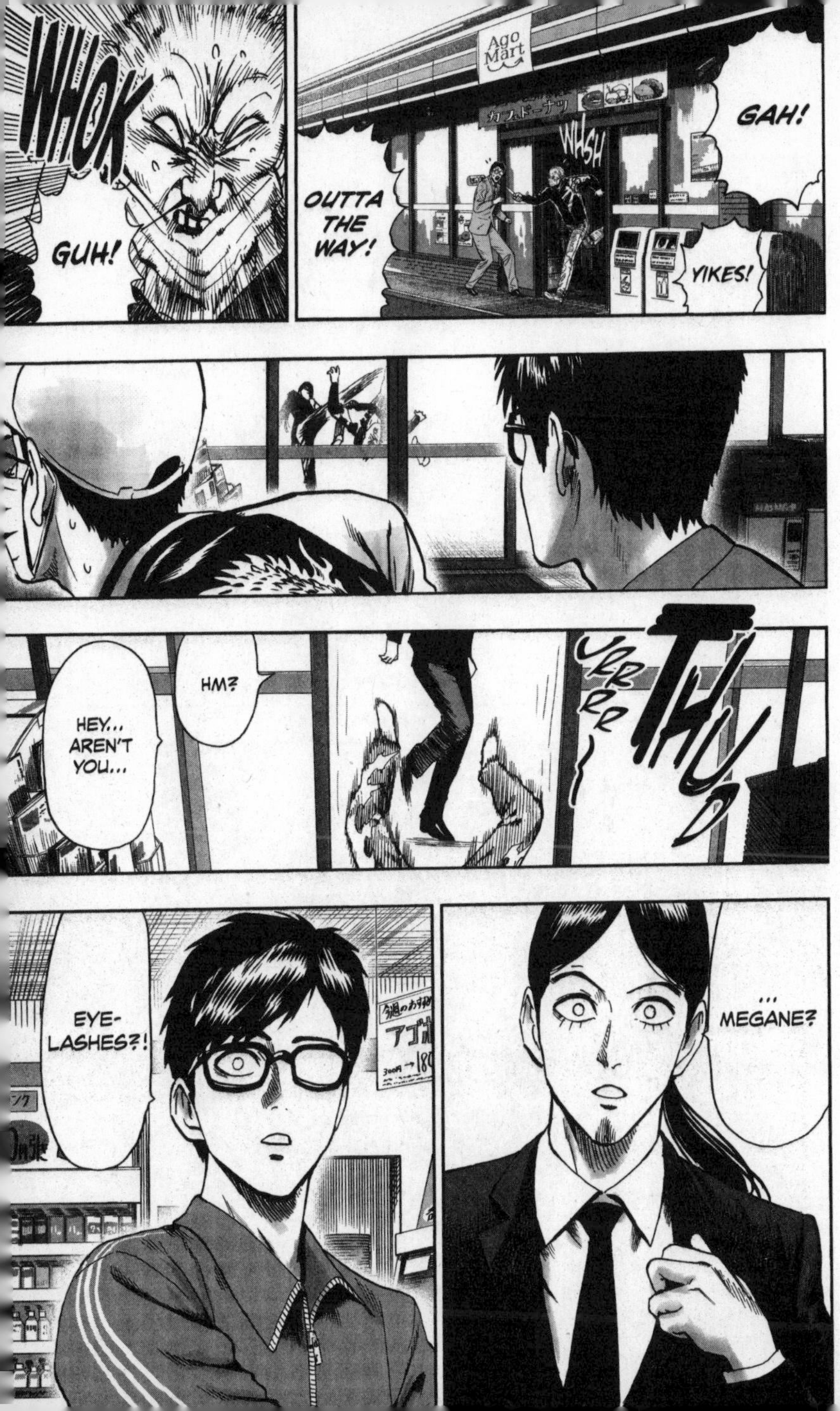
Ago Mart
GAH!
WHSH
OUTTA THE WAY!
YIKES!
WHOK
GUH!
THUD
URRRR~
HM?
HEY... AREN'T YOU...
... MEGANE?
EYE-LASHES?!

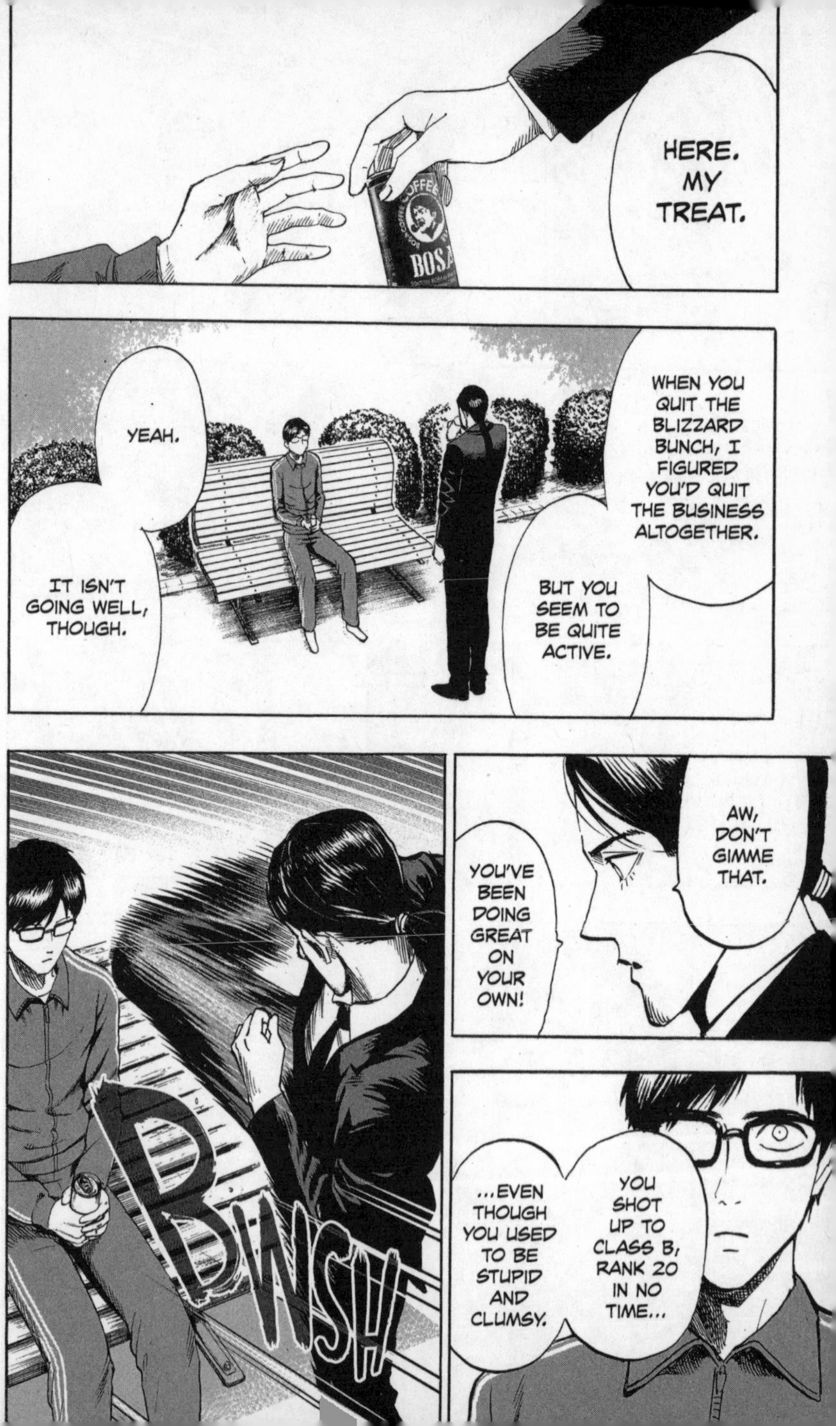
HERE. MY TREAT.
WHEN YOU QUIT THE BLIZZARD BUNCH, I FIGURED YOU'D QUIT THE BUSINESS ALTOGETHER.
BUT YOU SEEM TO BE QUITE ACTIVE.
YEAH.
IT ISN'T GOING WELL, THOUGH.
AW, DON'T GIMME THAT.
YOU'VE BEEN DOING GREAT ON YOUR OWN!
YOU SHOT UP TO CLASS B, RANK 20 IN NO TIME...
...EVEN THOUGH YOU USED TO BE STUPID AND CLUMSY.
BWSH!

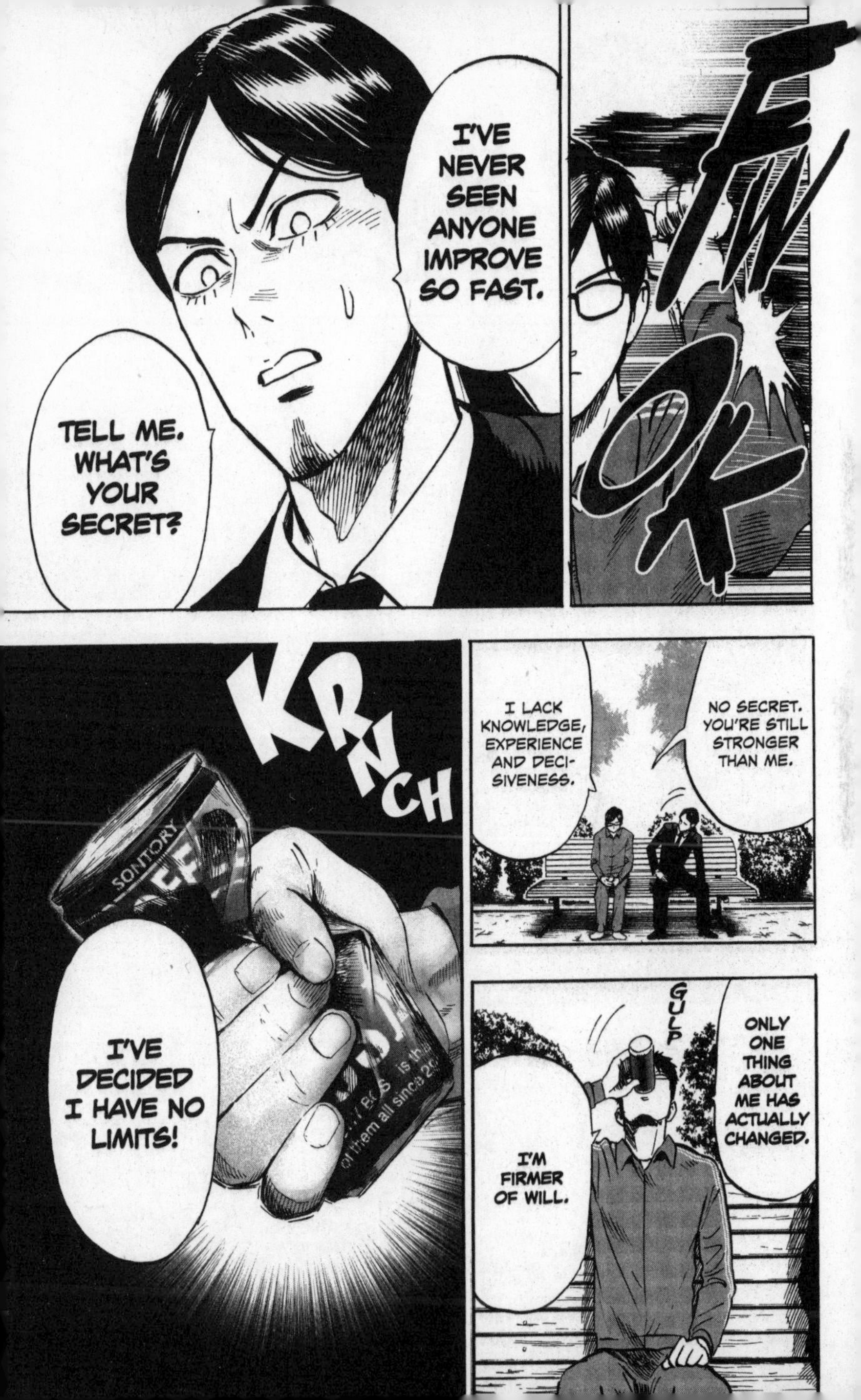
FWOK
I'VE NEVER SEEN ANYONE IMPROVE SO FAST.
TELL ME. WHAT'S YOUR SECRET?
NO SECRET. YOU'RE STILL STRONGER THAN ME.
I LACK KNOWLEDGE, EXPERIENCE AND DECI-SIVENESS.
GULP
ONLY ONE THING ABOUT ME HAS ACTUALLY CHANGED.
I'M FIRMER OF WILL.
KRNCH
SONTORY
I'VE DECIDED I HAVE NO LIMITS!

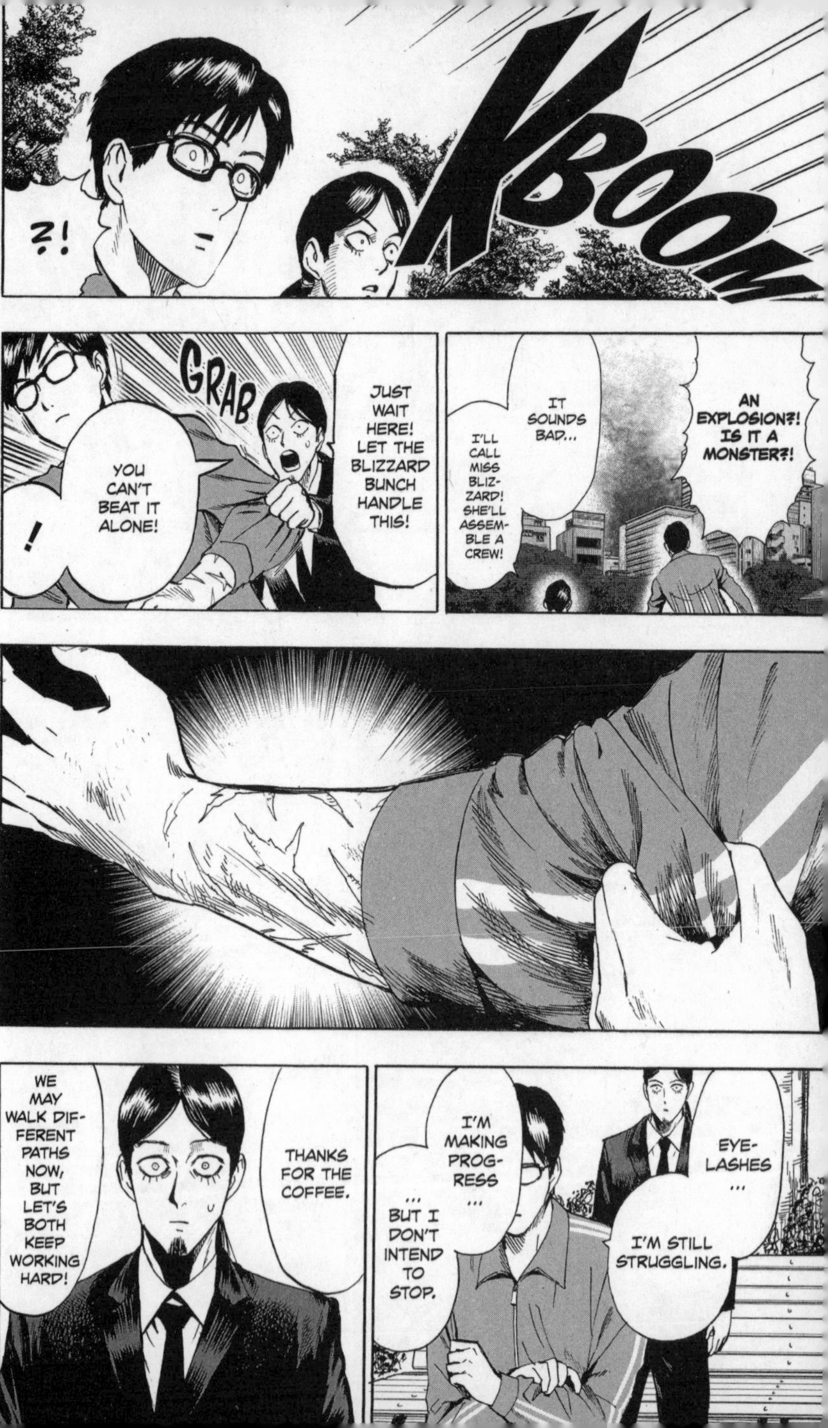
KBOOM
?!
AN EXPLOSION?! IS IT A MONSTER?!
IT SOUNDS BAD...
I'LL CALL MISS BLIZZARD! SHE'LL ASSEMBLE A CREW!
JUST WAIT HERE! LET THE BLIZZARD BUNCH HANDLE THIS!
GRAB
YOU CAN'T BEAT IT ALONE!
!
EYELASHES...
I'M STILL STRUGGLING.
I'M MAKING PROGRESS...
...BUT I DON'T INTEND TO STOP.
THANKS FOR THE COFFEE.
WE MAY WALK DIFFERENT PATHS NOW, BUT LET'S BOTH KEEP WORKING HARD!

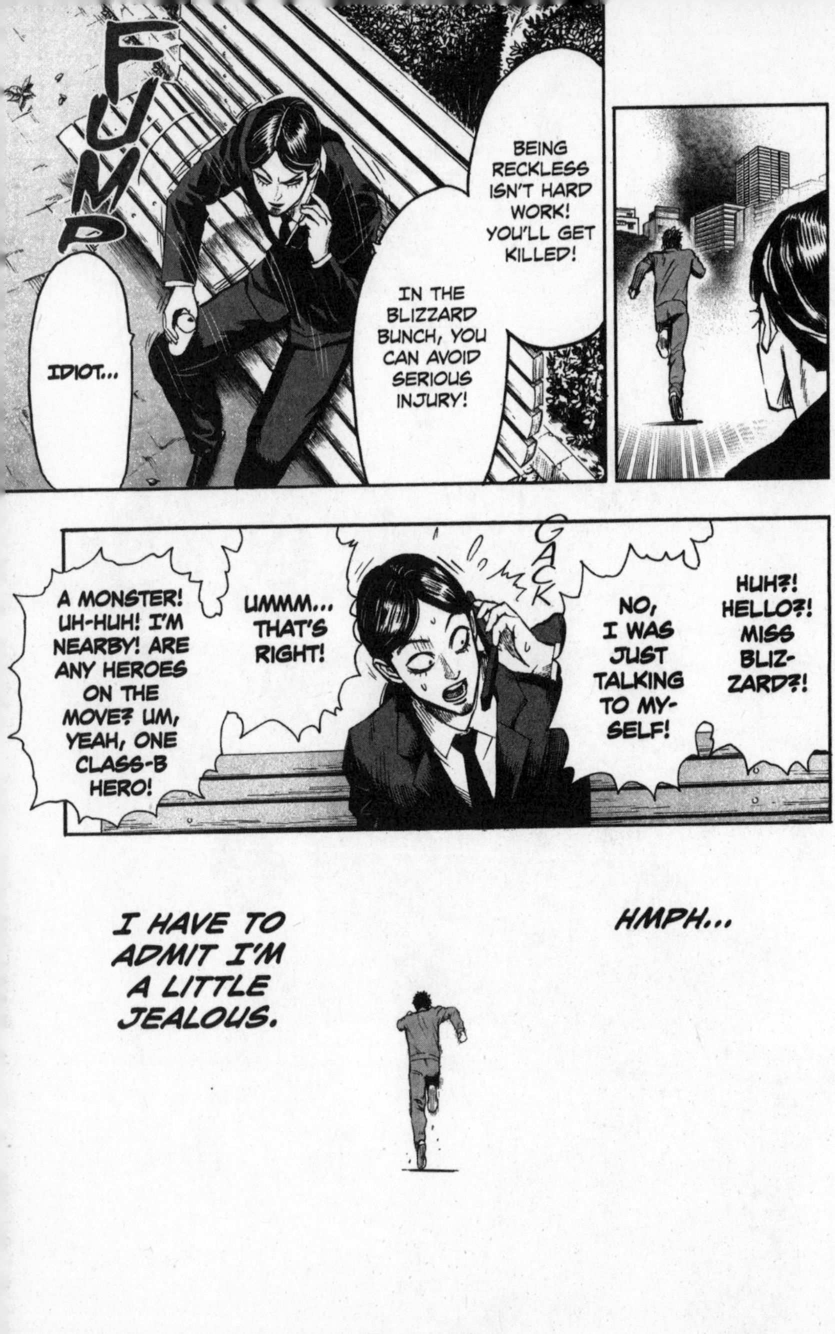
BEING RECKLESS ISN'T HARD WORK! YOU'LL GET KILLED!
IN THE BLIZZARD BUNCH, YOU CAN AVOID SERIOUS INJURY!
FUMP
IDIOT...
HUH?! HELLO?! MISS BLIZZARD?!
NO, I WAS JUST TALKING TO MYSELF!
GACK
UMMM... THAT'S RIGHT!
A MONSTER! UH-HUH! I'M NEARBY! ARE ANY HEROES ON THE MOVE? UM, YEAH, ONE CLASS-B HERO!
HMPH...
I HAVE TO ADMIT I'M A LITTLE JEALOUS.

16 Depleted (End)

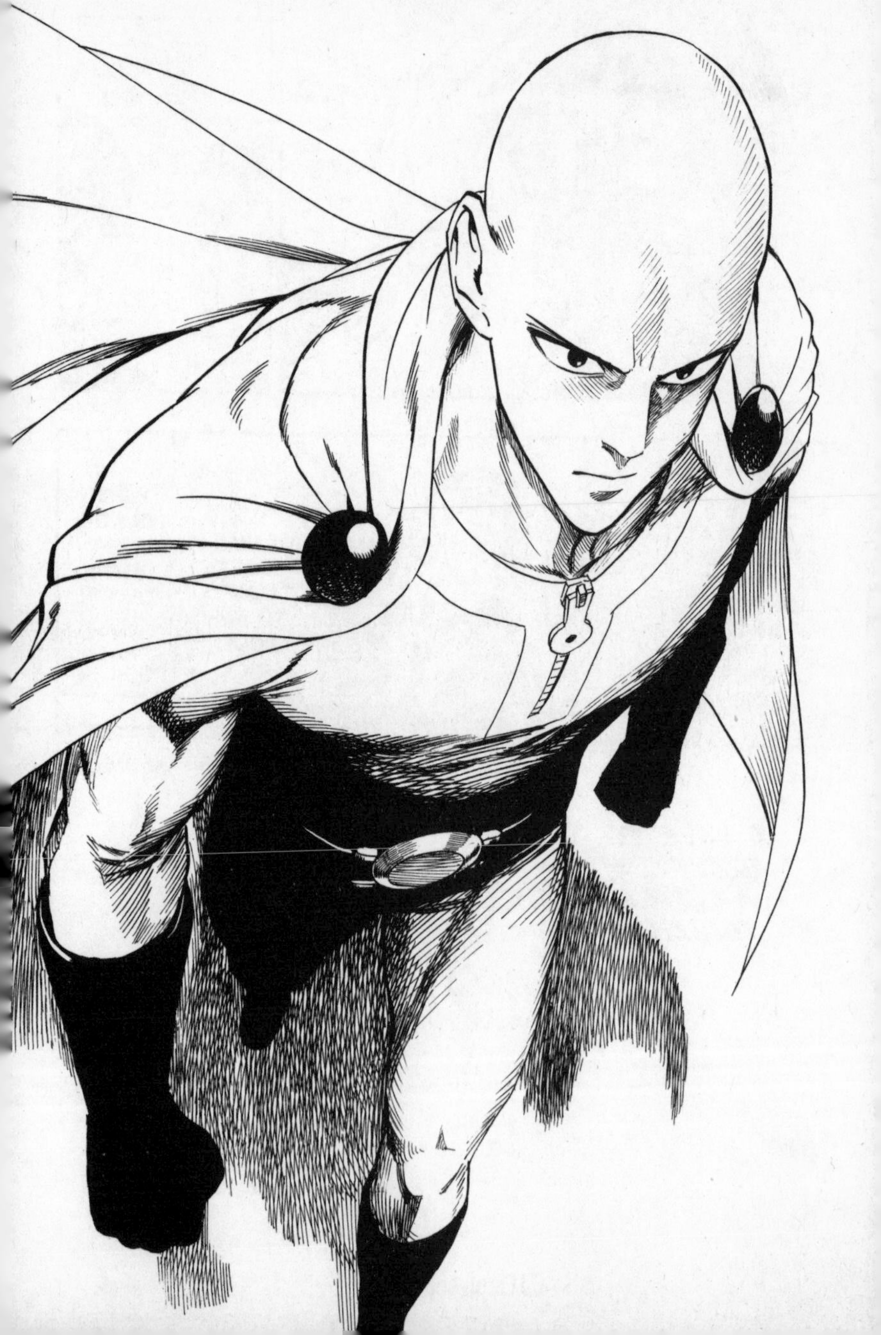

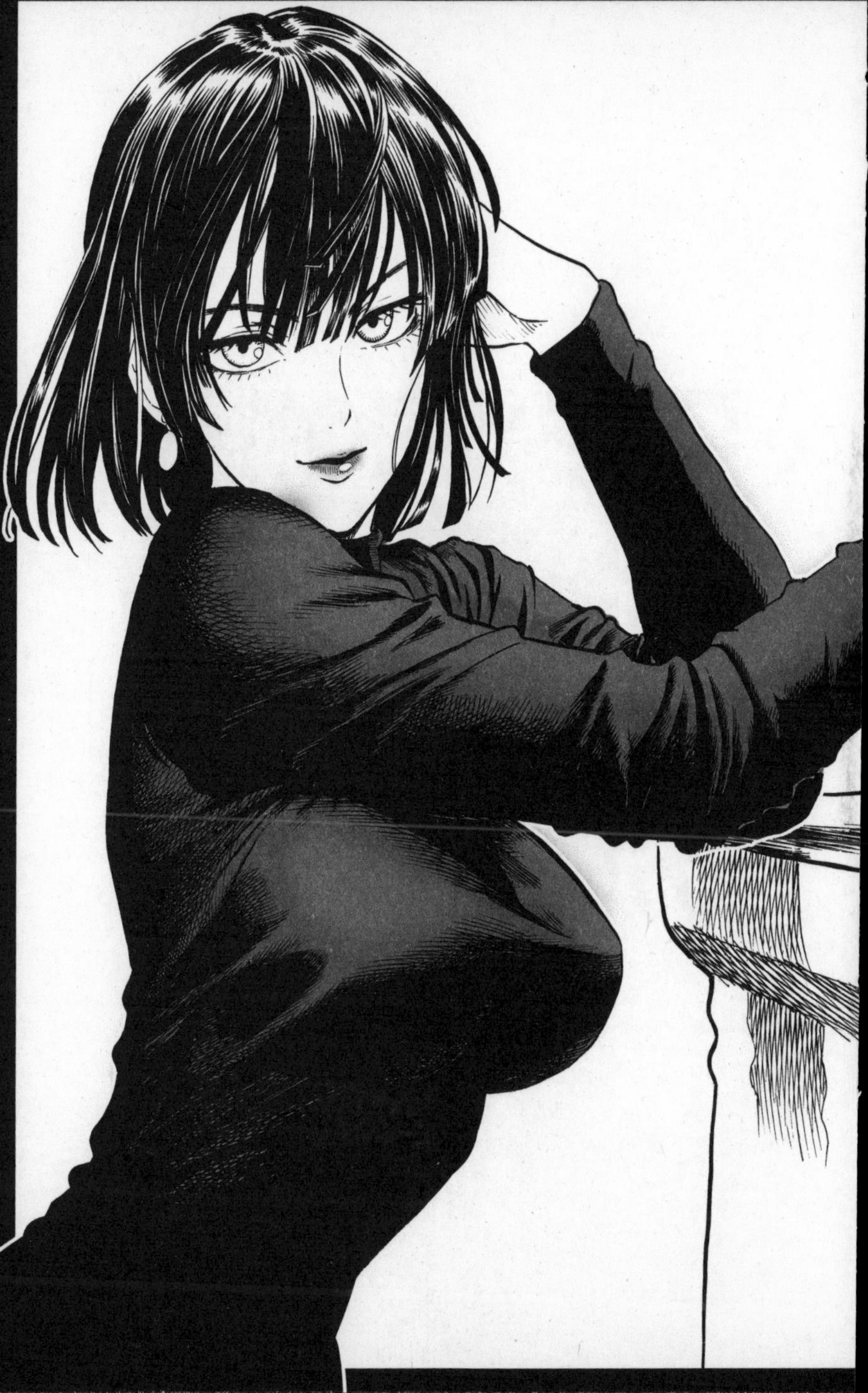

END NOTES

PAGE 139, PANEL 3:
The text on Saitama's shirt says *mentsuyu*, which means "noodle soup base."

ONE-PUNCH MAN

VOLUME 16

SHONEN JUMP MANGA EDITION

STORY BY | **ONE**
ART BY | **YUSUKE MURATA**

TRANSLATION | JOHN WERRY
TOUCH-UP ART AND LETTERING | JAMES GAUBATZ
DESIGN | SHAWN CARRICO
SHONEN JUMP SERIES EDITOR | JOHN BAE
GRAPHIC NOVEL EDITOR | JENNIFER LEBLANC

ONE-PUNCH MAN © 2012 by ONE, Yusuke Murata
All rights reserved.
First published in Japan in 2012 by SHUEISHA Inc., Tokyo.
English translation rights arranged by SHUEISHA Inc.

Printed in the U.S.A.

Published by VIZ Media, LLC
P.O. Box 77010
San Francisco, CA 94107

10 9 8 7 6 5 4 3 2 1
First printing, May 2019

VIZ MEDIA
viz.com

SHONEN JUMP
shonenjump.com

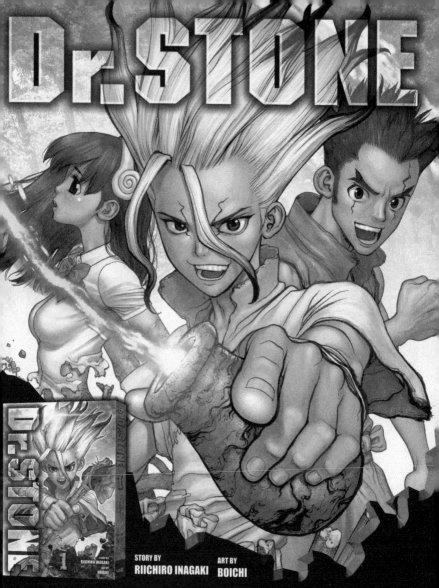

Dr.STONE

STORY BY
RIICHIRO INAGAKI

ART BY
BOICHI

One fateful day, all of humanity turned to stone. Many millennia later, Taiju frees himself from petrification and finds himself surrounded by statues. The situation looks grim—until he runs into his science-loving friend Senku! Together they plan to restart

DEMON SLAYER

KIMETSU NO YAIBA

Story and Art by

KOYOHARU GOTOUGE

In Taisho-era Japan, kindhearted Tanjiro Kamado makes a living selling charcoal. But his peaceful life is shattered when a demon slaughters his entire family. His little sister Nezuko is the only survivor, but she has been transformed into a demon herself! Tanjiro sets out on a dangerous journey to find a way to return his sister to normal and destroy the demon who ruined his life.

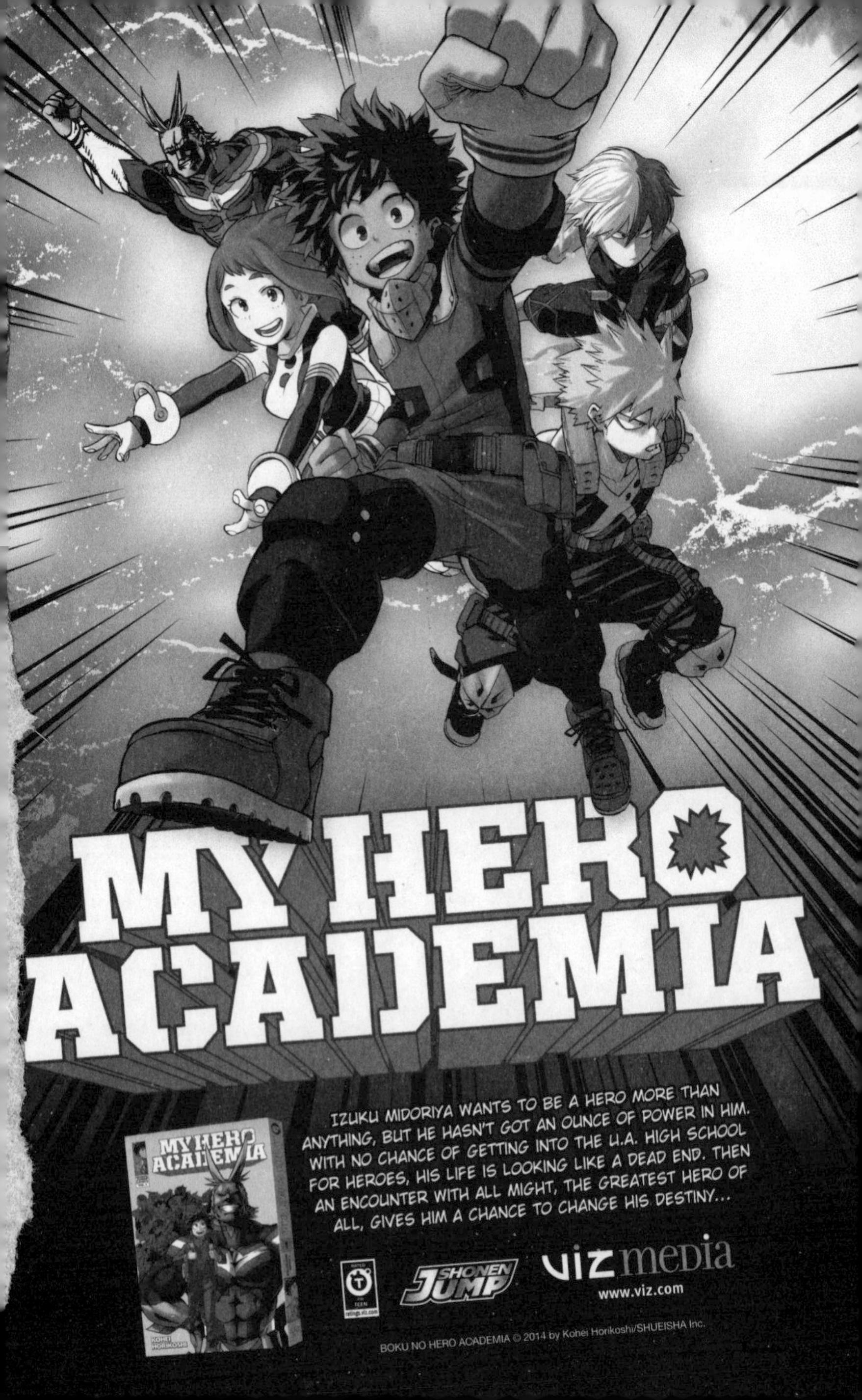
MY HERO ACADEMIA
IZUKU MIDORIYA WANTS TO BE A HERO MORE THAN ANYTHING, BUT HE HASN'T GOT AN OUNCE OF POWER IN HIM. WITH NO CHANCE OF GETTING INTO THE U.A. HIGH SCHOOL FOR HEROES, HIS LIFE IS LOOKING LIKE A DEAD END. THEN AN ENCOUNTER WITH ALL MIGHT, THE GREATEST HERO OF ALL, GIVES HIM A CHANCE TO CHANGE HIS DESTINY...
MY HERO ACADEMIA
KOHEI HORIKOSHI
RATED T TEEN
ratings.viz.com
SHONEN JUMP
viz media
www.viz.com
BOKU NO HERO ACADEMIA © 2014 by Kohei Horikoshi/SHUEISHA Inc.

STOP!

YOU'RE READING THE WRONG WAY!

★ ONE-PUNCH MAN READS FROM RIGHT TO LEFT, STARTING IN THE UPPER-RIGHT CORNER. JAPANESE IS READ FROM RIGHT TO LEFT, MEANING THAT ACTION, SOUND EFFECTS, AND WORD-BALLOON ORDER ARE COMPLETELY REVERSED FROM ENGLISH ORDER.

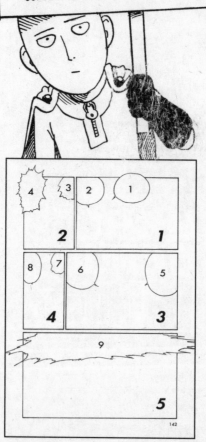